CHIP ZDARSKY RYAN NORTH

Jughead

VOLUME TWO

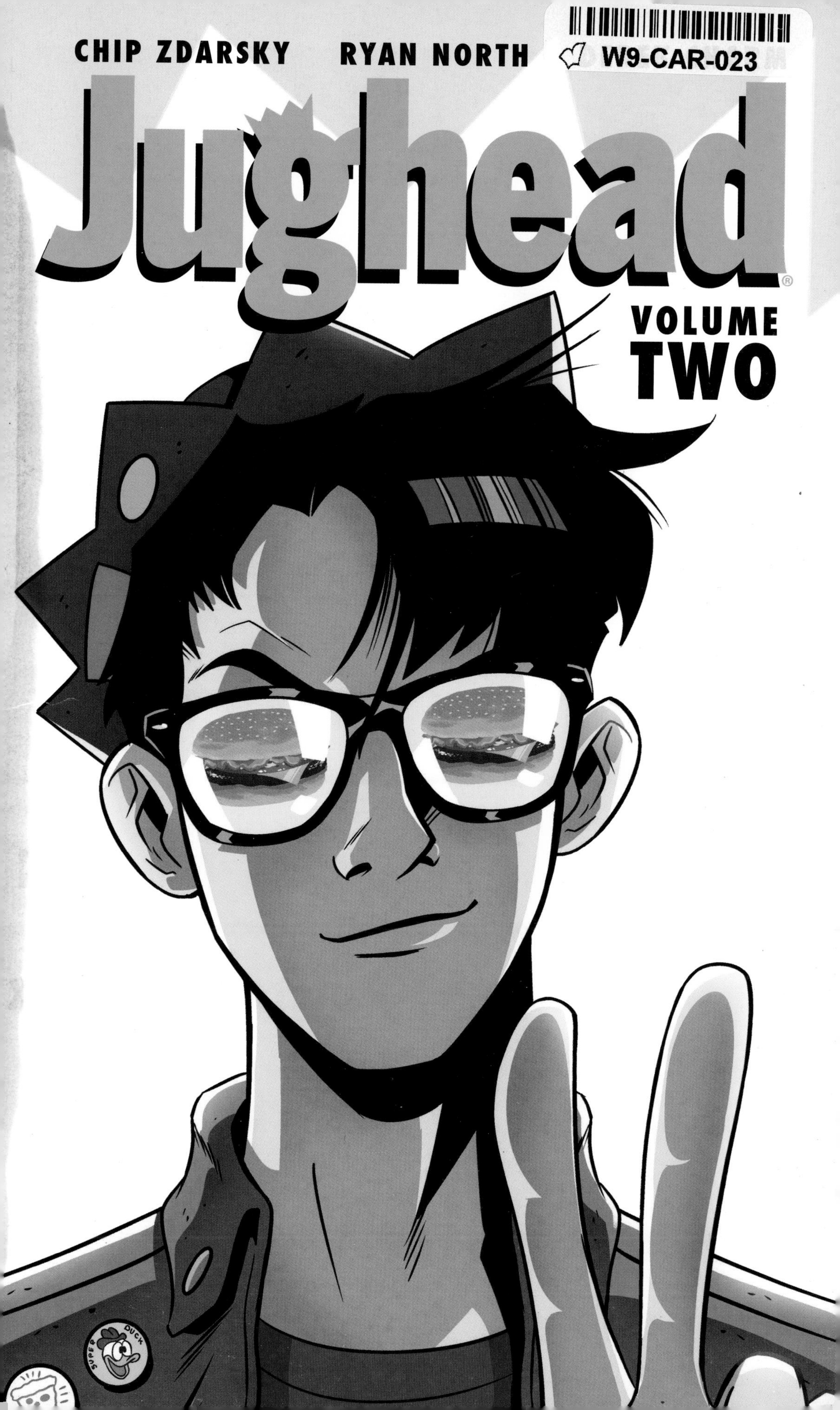
SUPER DUCK

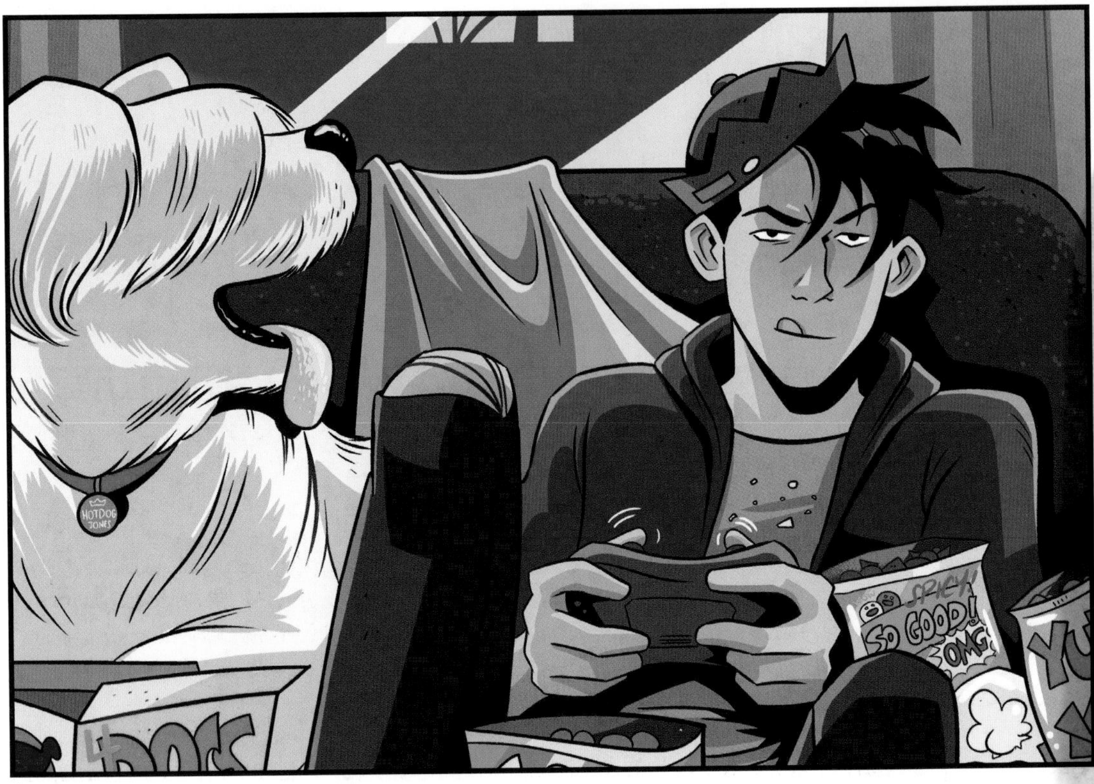
HOTDOG JONES
SPICY!
SO GOOD!
OMG

STORY BY:
CHIP ZDARSKY
(ISSUES 7-8)

RYAN NORTH
(ISSUES 9-11)

ART BY:
DEREK CHARM

LETTERING BY:
JACK MORELLI

EDITOR:
MIKE PELLERITO

ASSOCIATE EDITOR:
STEPHEN OSWALD

ASSISTANT EDITOR:
JAMIE LEE ROTANTE

EDITOR-IN-CHIEF:
VICTOR GORELICK

GRAPHIC DESIGN:
KARI McLACHLAN

PUBLISHER:
JON GOLDWATER

AN INTRODUCTION TO

Jughead®

by Chris Cummins

Burgers are delicious.

If there is one worldview driving Forsythe P. Jones III (Jughead to his friends), that is it. The pursuit of hamburgers is everything to Jughead. And can you blame him? As foodstuffs go they are among the tastiest! In Riverdale there are some universal truths: Archie will always be torn between Betty and Veronica, Mr. Lodge will be forever in the midst of a business deal, and, most notably, Jughead will eternally be hungry.

Attempting to figure out the root cause of ol' Jug's insatiable appetite is a fool's errand, best left to the cultural anthropologists and comics-loving, thesis-writing grad students to ponder. For you could no easier stop our whoopee cap-wearing hero from desiring burgers than you could tap dance on the sun. This is a ketchup-drenched fact that has been endearing the character to audiences for over 75 years now.

Since the world of Riverdale was rebooted in the comics in 2015, Archie and his pals and gals have experienced a creative revitalization that has introduced them to a new generation of readers. Collecting issues 7 through 11 of *Jughead*, this book you hold in your hands includes some of the funniest adventures ever featured on the printed page. From a wilderness misadventure in which Archie and Jughead must contend with a Mantle family reunion, an angry bear and Mr. Weatherbee to Jughead's first crush (on a woman in a burger suit who turns out to be, spoiler alert, Sabrina the Teenage Witch), the stories you are about to read will leave you feeling as happy and nourished as a meal at Pop Tate's Choklit Shoppe.

Before we get into the burger-fueled fun (man, this intro says the word "burger" a lot, eh?), we must acknowledge the considerable talents of *Jughead*'s fantastic creative team. Writers Chip Zdarsky (on issues 7 and 8) and Ryan North (on issues 9 through 11) have teamed with artist Derek Charm to fully immerse you in Jughead's offbeat world. We know you'll enjoy time there, but you should probably bring along a hamburger or two, just in case.

ISSUE SEVEN

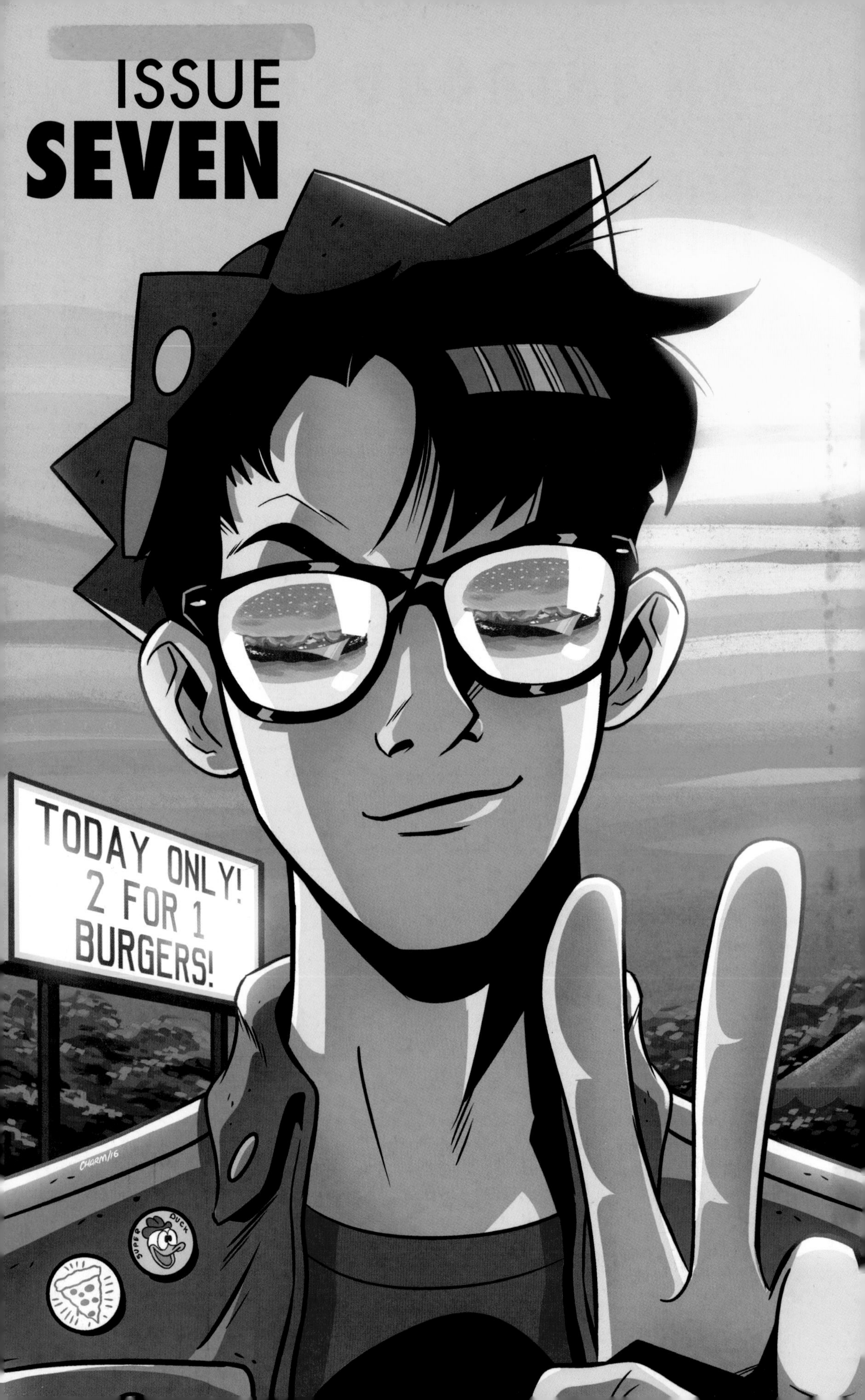
TODAY ONLY!
2 FOR 1
BURGERS!
CHARM/16
SUPER DUCK

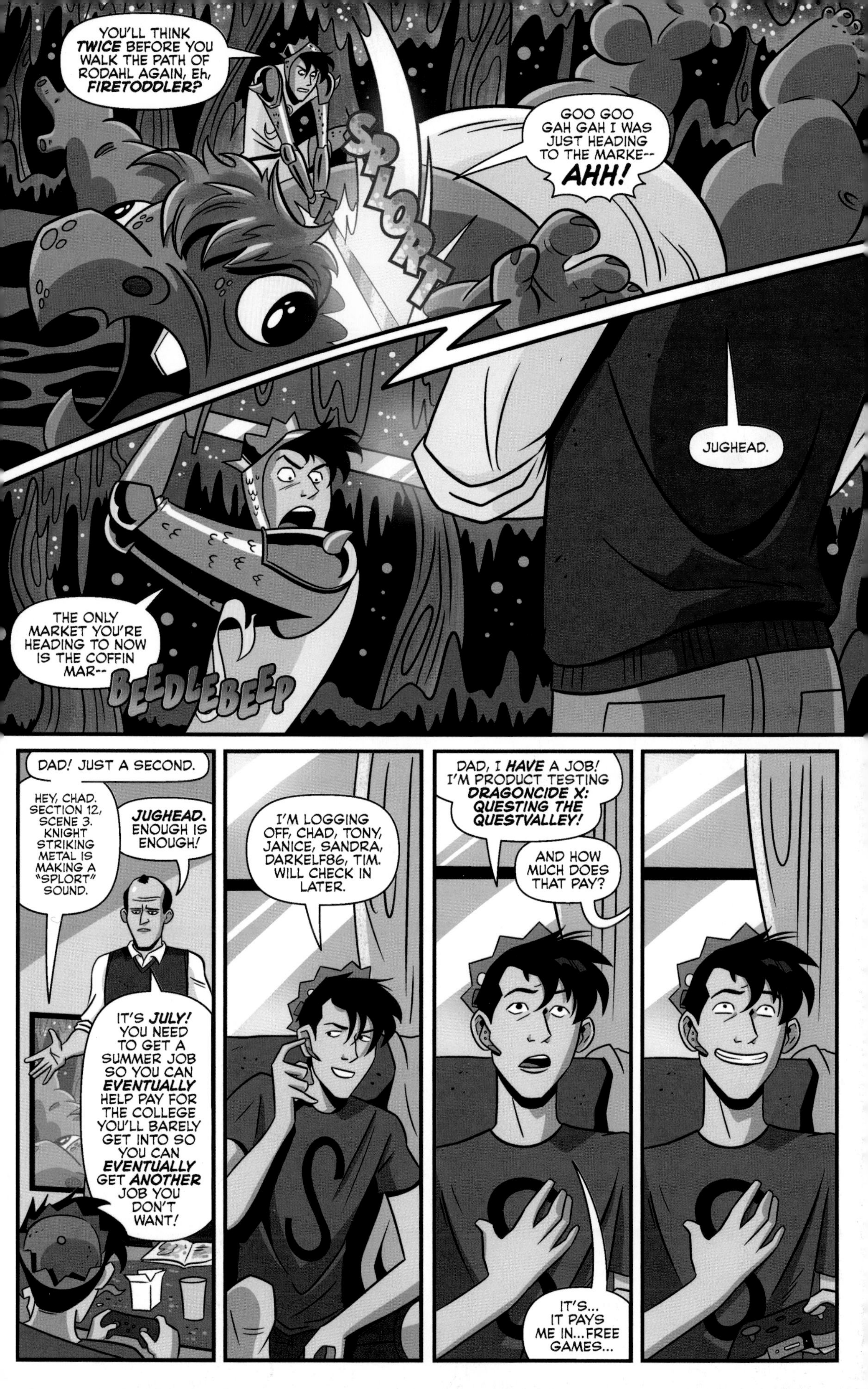
YOU'LL THINK TWICE BEFORE YOU WALK THE PATH OF RODAHL AGAIN, Eh, FIRETODDLER?
SPLORT
GOO GOO GAH GAH I WAS JUST HEADING TO THE MARKE-- AHH!
JUGHEAD.
THE ONLY MARKET YOU'RE HEADING TO NOW IS THE COFFIN MAR--
BEEDLEBEEP
DAD! JUST A SECOND.
HEY, CHAD. SECTION 12, SCENE 3. KNIGHT STRIKING METAL IS MAKING A "SPLORT" SOUND.
JUGHEAD. ENOUGH IS ENOUGH!
IT'S JULY! YOU NEED TO GET A SUMMER JOB SO YOU CAN EVENTUALLY HELP PAY FOR THE COLLEGE YOU'LL BARELY GET INTO SO YOU CAN EVENTUALLY GET ANOTHER JOB YOU DON'T WANT!
I'M LOGGING OFF, CHAD, TONY, JANICE, SANDRA, DARKELF86, TIM. WILL CHECK IN LATER.
DAD, I HAVE A JOB! I'M PRODUCT TESTING DRAGONCIDE X: QUESTING THE QUESTVALLEY!
AND HOW MUCH DOES THAT PAY?
IT'S... IT PAYS ME IN...FREE GAMES...

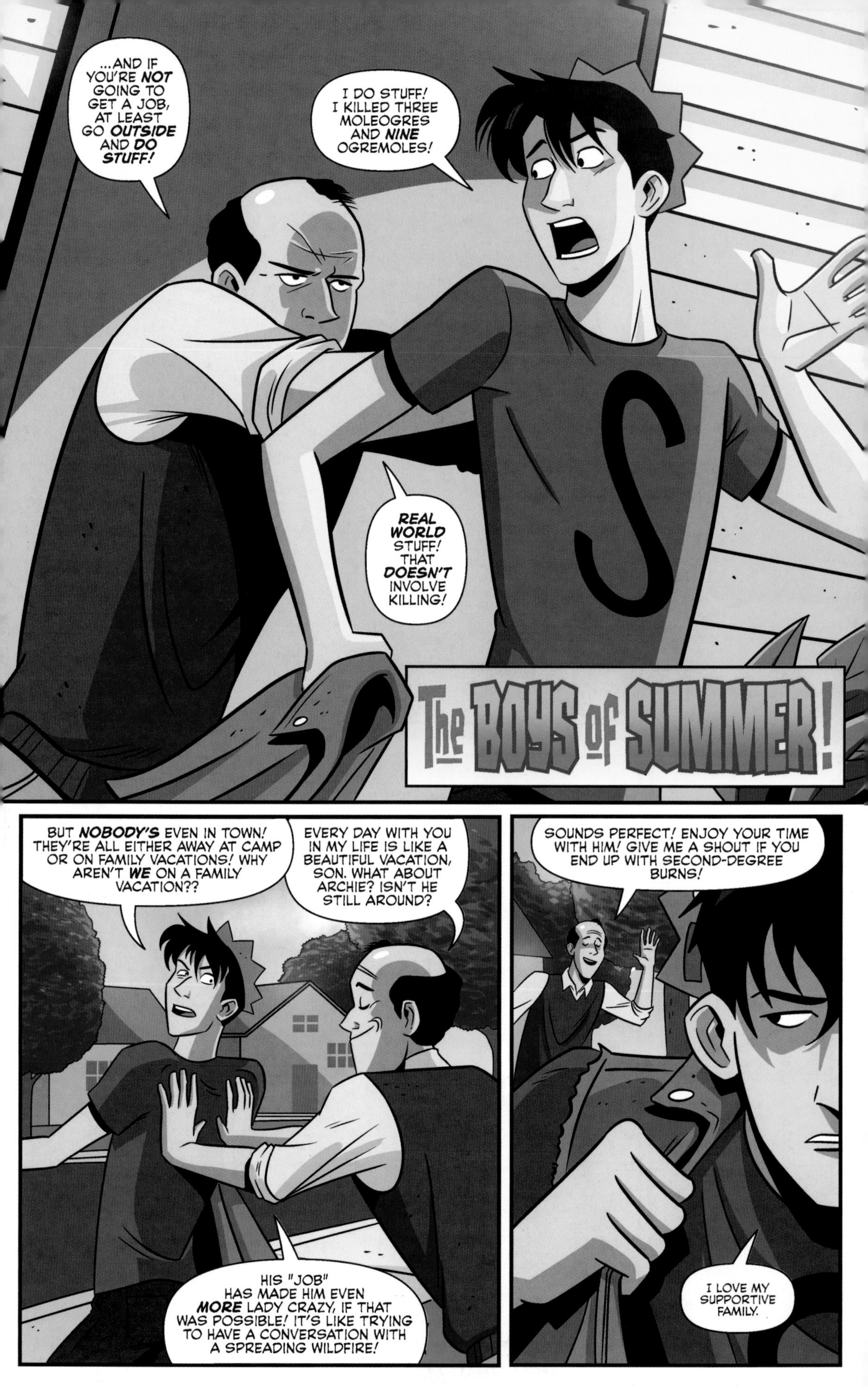
...AND IF YOU'RE NOT GOING TO GET A JOB, AT LEAST GO OUTSIDE AND DO STUFF!
I DO STUFF! I KILLED THREE MOLEOGRES AND NINE OGREMOLES!
REAL WORLD STUFF! THAT DOESN'T INVOLVE KILLING!
The BOYS of SUMMER!
BUT NOBODY'S EVEN IN TOWN! THEY'RE ALL EITHER AWAY AT CAMP OR ON FAMILY VACATIONS! WHY AREN'T WE ON A FAMILY VACATION??
EVERY DAY WITH YOU IN MY LIFE IS LIKE A BEAUTIFUL VACATION, SON. WHAT ABOUT ARCHIE? ISN'T HE STILL AROUND?
HIS "JOB" HAS MADE HIM EVEN MORE LADY CRAZY, IF THAT WAS POSSIBLE! IT'S LIKE TRYING TO HAVE A CONVERSATION WITH A SPREADING WILDFIRE!
SOUNDS PERFECT! ENJOY YOUR TIME WITH HIM! GIVE ME A SHOUT IF YOU END UP WITH SECOND-DEGREE BURNS!
I LOVE MY SUPPORTIVE FAMILY.

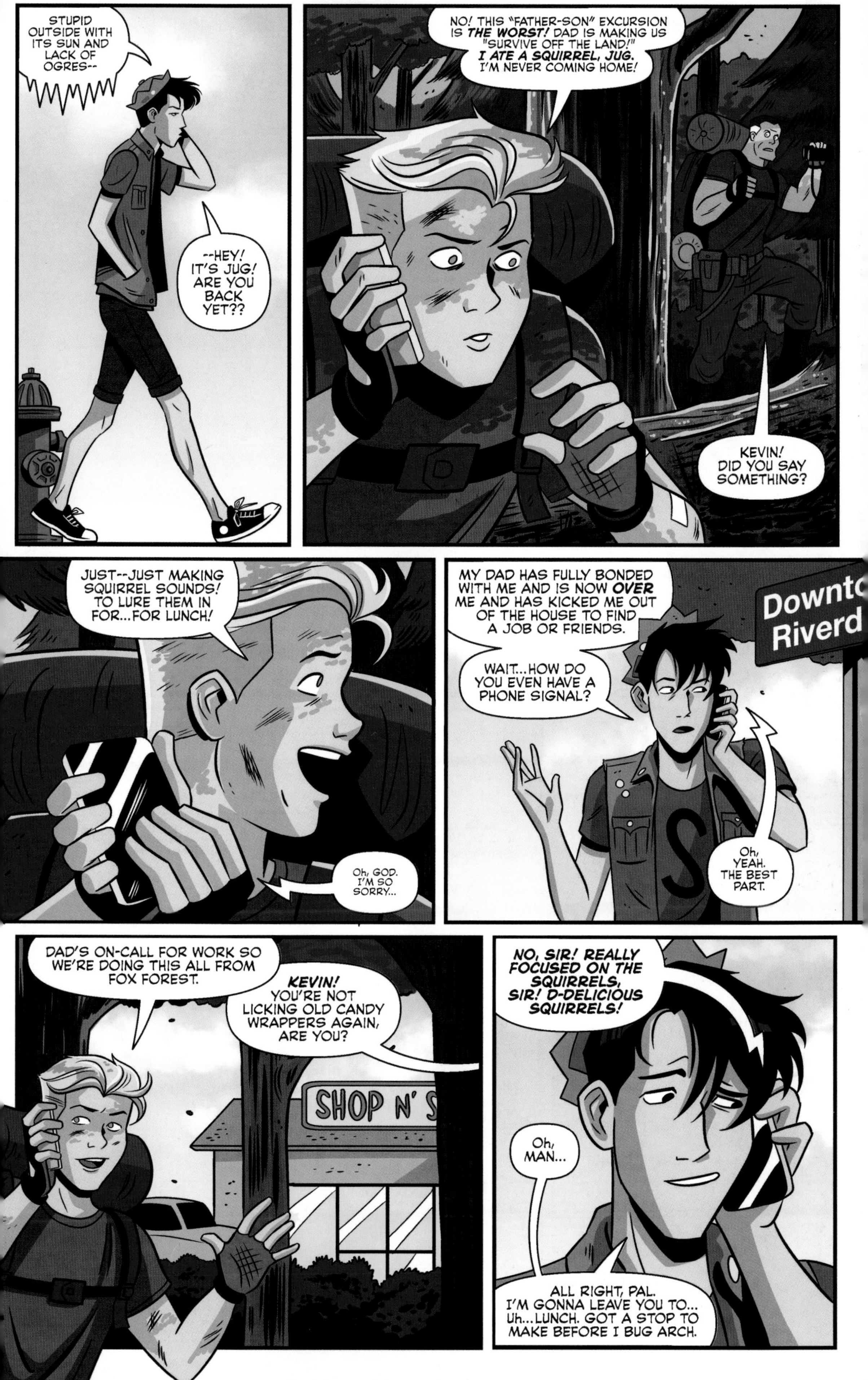
STUPID OUTSIDE WITH ITS SUN AND LACK OF OGRES--
--HEY! IT'S JUG! ARE YOU BACK YET??
NO! THIS "FATHER-SON" EXCURSION IS THE WORST! DAD IS MAKING US "SURVIVE OFF THE LAND!" I ATE A SQUIRREL, JUG. I'M NEVER COMING HOME!
KEVIN! DID YOU SAY SOMETHING?
JUST--JUST MAKING SQUIRREL SOUNDS! TO LURE THEM IN FOR...FOR LUNCH!
Oh, GOD. I'M SO SORRY...
MY DAD HAS FULLY BONDED WITH ME AND IS NOW OVER ME AND HAS KICKED ME OUT OF THE HOUSE TO FIND A JOB OR FRIENDS.
WAIT...HOW DO YOU EVEN HAVE A PHONE SIGNAL?
Oh, YEAH. THE BEST PART.
DAD'S ON-CALL FOR WORK SO WE'RE DOING THIS ALL FROM FOX FOREST.
KEVIN! YOU'RE NOT LICKING OLD CANDY WRAPPERS AGAIN, ARE YOU?
NO, SIR! REALLY FOCUSED ON THE SQUIRRELS, SIR! D-DELICIOUS SQUIRRELS!
Oh, MAN...
ALL RIGHT, PAL. I'M GONNA LEAVE YOU TO... Uh...LUNCH. GOT A STOP TO MAKE BEFORE I BUG ARCH.

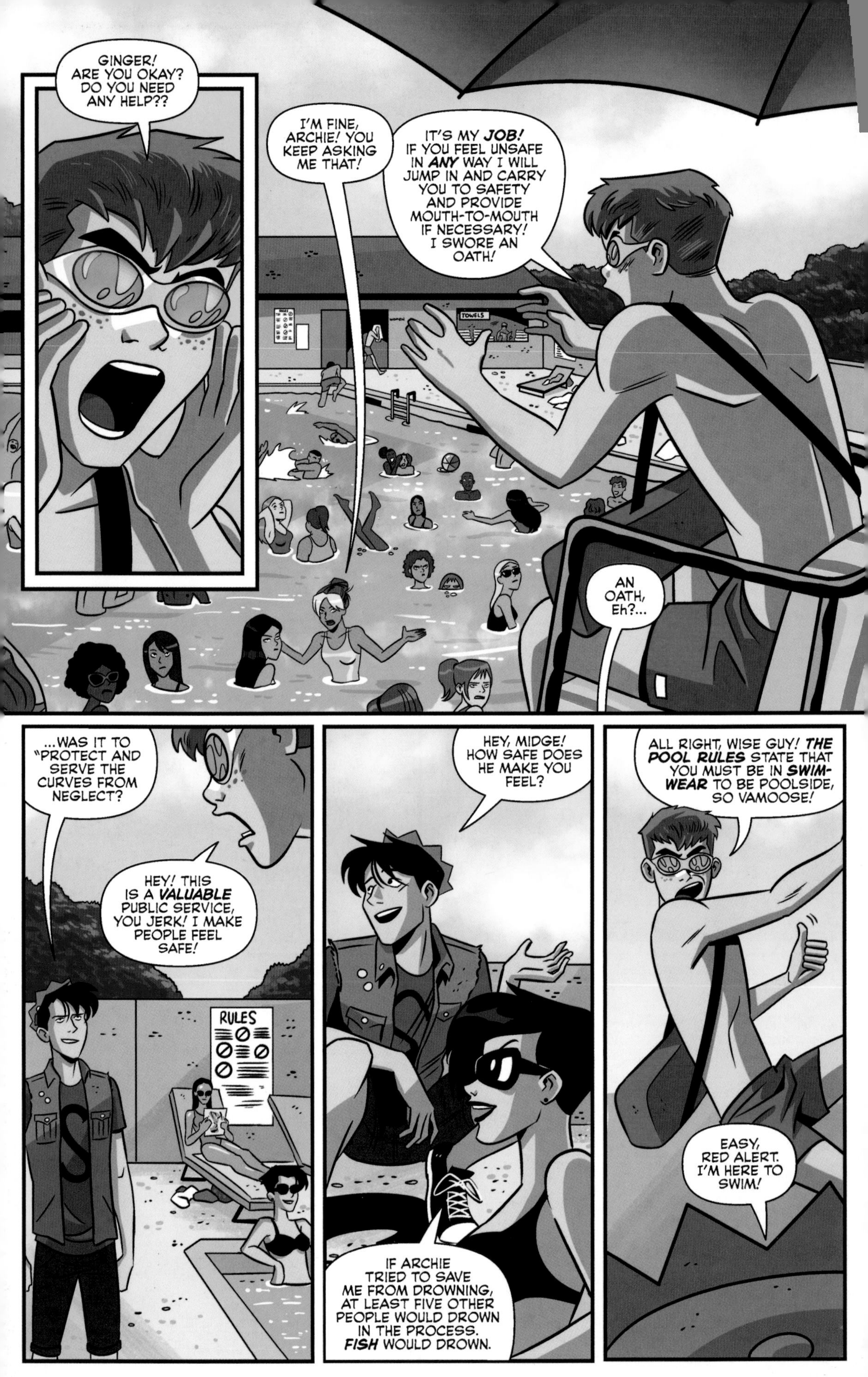
GINGER! ARE YOU OKAY? DO YOU NEED ANY HELP??
I'M FINE, ARCHIE! YOU KEEP ASKING ME THAT!
IT'S MY *JOB!* IF YOU FEEL UNSAFE IN *ANY* WAY I WILL JUMP IN AND CARRY YOU TO SAFETY AND PROVIDE MOUTH-TO-MOUTH IF NECESSARY! I SWORE AN OATH!
TOWELS
AN OATH, Eh?...
...WAS IT TO "PROTECT AND SERVE THE CURVES FROM NEGLECT?
HEY! THIS IS A *VALUABLE* PUBLIC SERVICE, YOU JERK! I MAKE PEOPLE FEEL SAFE!
RULES
HEY, MIDGE! HOW SAFE DOES HE MAKE YOU FEEL?
IF ARCHIE TRIED TO SAVE ME FROM DROWNING, AT LEAST FIVE OTHER PEOPLE WOULD DROWN IN THE PROCESS. *FISH* WOULD DROWN.
ALL RIGHT, WISE GUY! *THE POOL RULES* STATE THAT YOU MUST BE IN *SWIM-WEAR* TO BE POOLSIDE, SO VAMOOSE!
EASY, RED ALERT. I'M HERE TO SWIM!

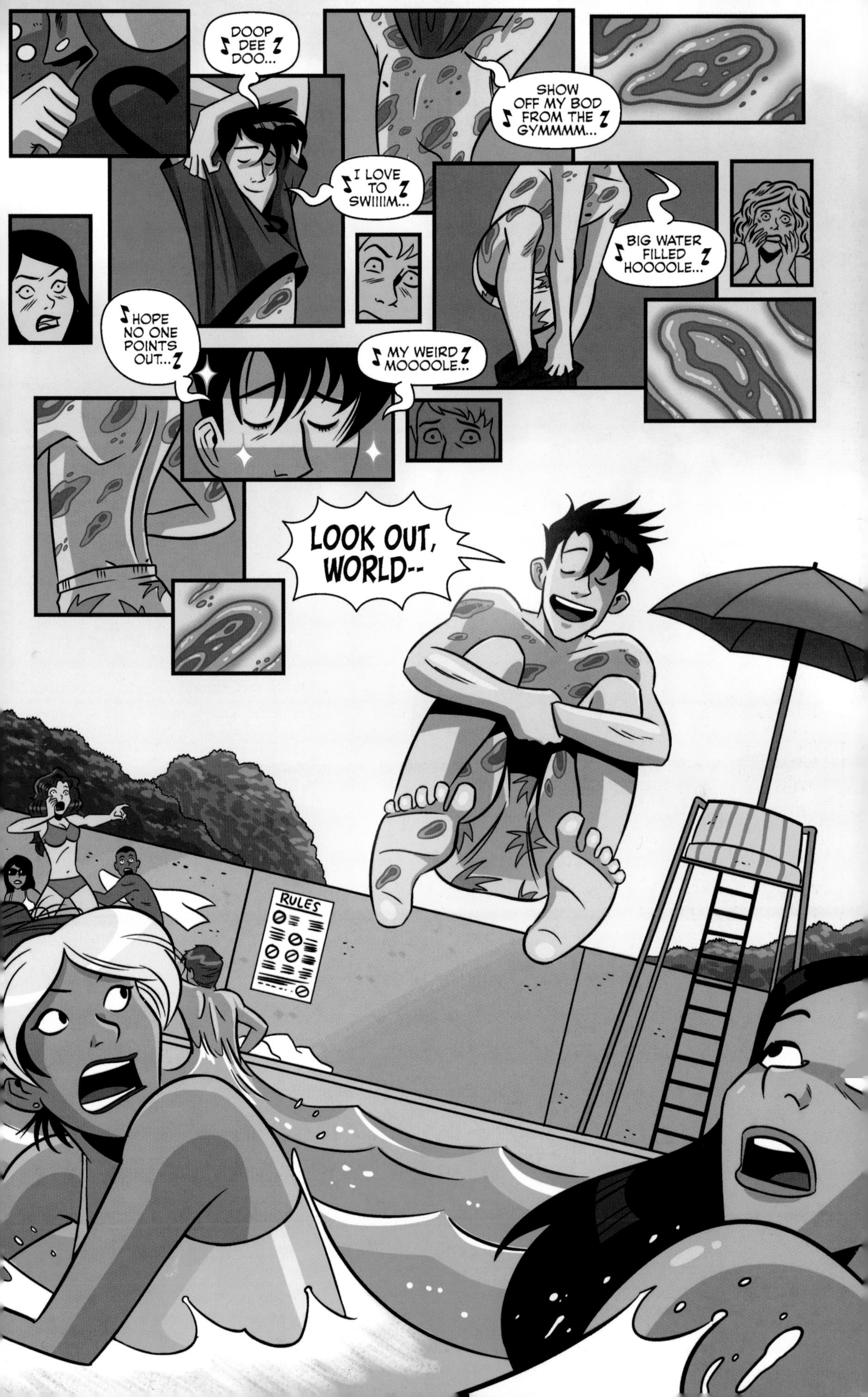
DOOP DEE DOO...
I LOVE TO SWIIIIM...
SHOW OFF MY BOD FROM THE GYMMMM...
BIG WATER FILLED HOOOOLE...
HOPE NO ONE POINTS OUT...
MY WEIRD MOOOOLE...
LOOK OUT, WORLD--
RULES

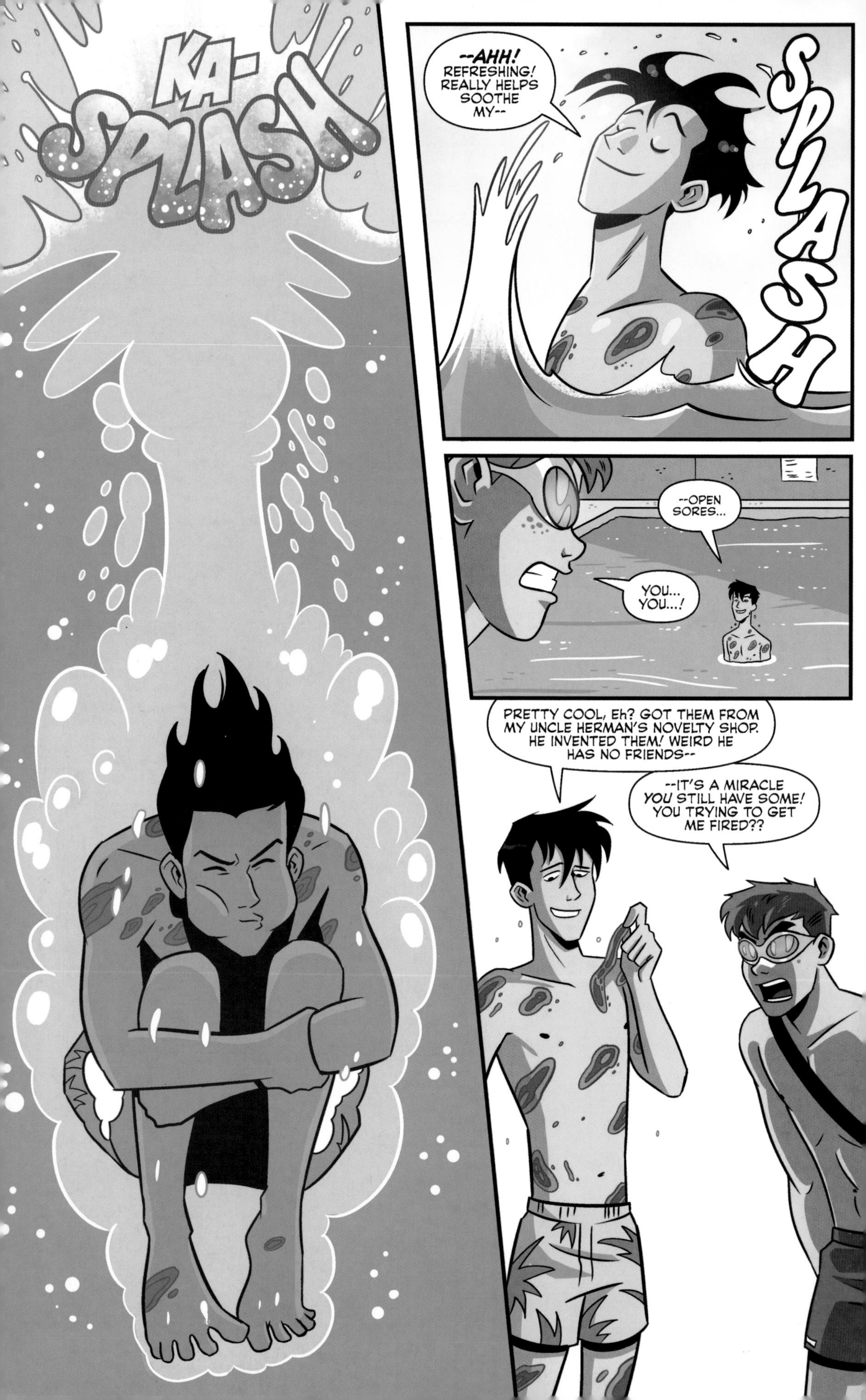
KA-SPLASH
--AHH! REFRESHING! REALLY HELPS SOOTHE MY--
SPLASH
--OPEN SORES...
YOU... YOU...!
PRETTY COOL, Eh? GOT THEM FROM MY UNCLE HERMAN'S NOVELTY SHOP. HE INVENTED THEM! WEIRD HE HAS NO FRIENDS--
--IT'S A MIRACLE YOU STILL HAVE SOME! YOU TRYING TO GET ME FIRED??

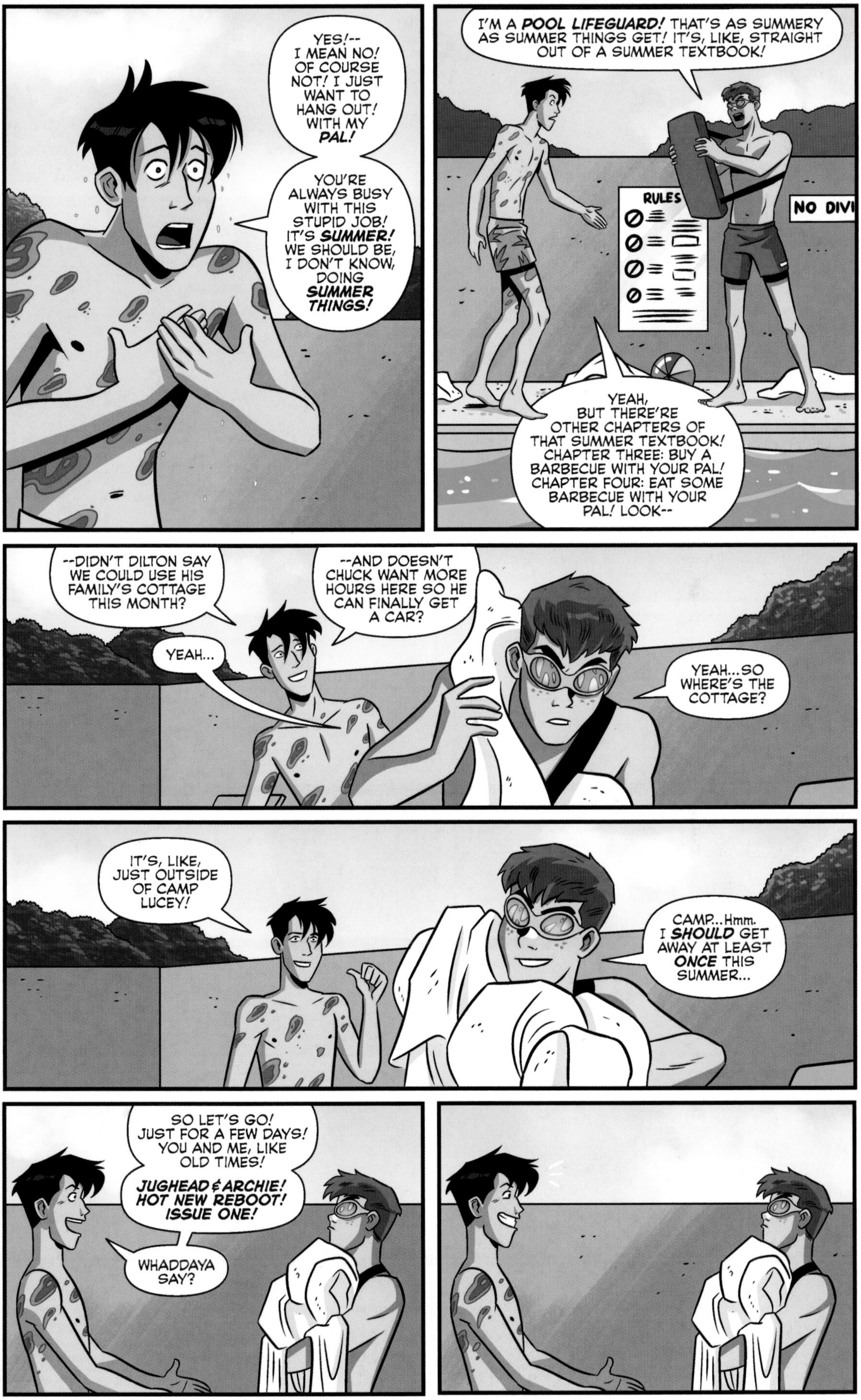

YES!-- I MEAN NO! OF COURSE NOT! I JUST WANT TO HANG OUT! WITH MY PAL!
YOU'RE ALWAYS BUSY WITH THIS STUPID JOB! IT'S SUMMER! WE SHOULD BE, I DON'T KNOW, DOING SUMMER THINGS!
I'M A POOL LIFEGUARD! THAT'S AS SUMMERY AS SUMMER THINGS GET! IT'S, LIKE, STRAIGHT OUT OF A SUMMER TEXTBOOK!
RULES
NO DIVI
YEAH, BUT THERE'RE OTHER CHAPTERS OF THAT SUMMER TEXTBOOK! CHAPTER THREE: BUY A BARBECUE WITH YOUR PAL! CHAPTER FOUR: EAT SOME BARBECUE WITH YOUR PAL! LOOK--
--DIDN'T DILTON SAY WE COULD USE HIS FAMILY'S COTTAGE THIS MONTH?
--AND DOESN'T CHUCK WANT MORE HOURS HERE SO HE CAN FINALLY GET A CAR?
YEAH...
YEAH...SO WHERE'S THE COTTAGE?
IT'S, LIKE, JUST OUTSIDE OF CAMP LUCEY!
CAMP...Hmm. I SHOULD GET AWAY AT LEAST ONCE THIS SUMMER...
SO LET'S GO! JUST FOR A FEW DAYS! YOU AND ME, LIKE OLD TIMES!
JUGHEAD & ARCHIE! HOT NEW REBOOT! ISSUE ONE!
WHADDAYA SAY?

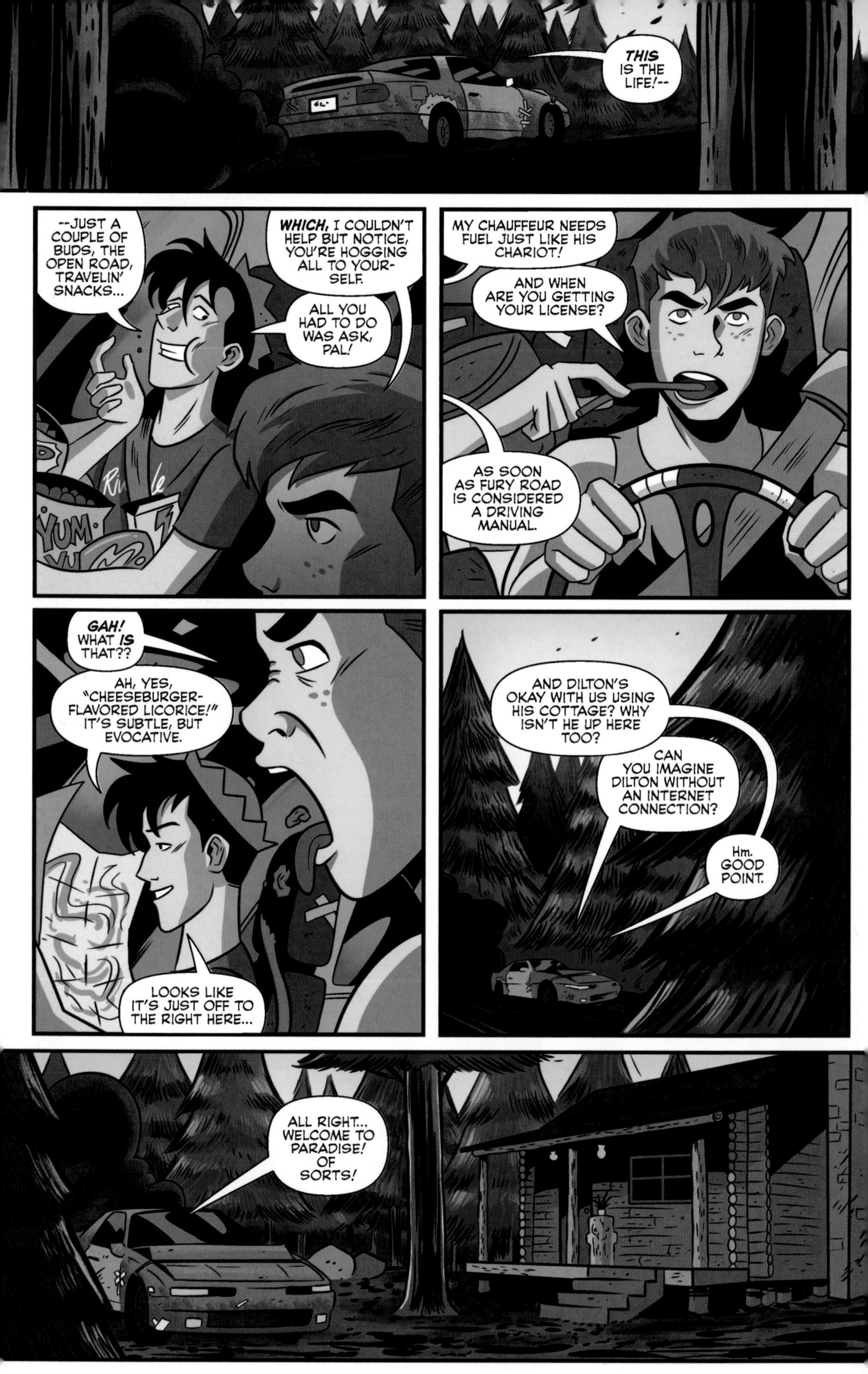
THIS IS THE LIFE!--
--JUST A COUPLE OF BUDS, THE OPEN ROAD, TRAVELIN' SNACKS...
WHICH, I COULDN'T HELP BUT NOTICE, YOU'RE HOGGING ALL TO YOURSELF.
ALL YOU HAD TO DO WAS ASK, PAL!
MY CHAUFFEUR NEEDS FUEL JUST LIKE HIS CHARIOT!
AND WHEN ARE YOU GETTING YOUR LICENSE?
AS SOON AS FURY ROAD IS CONSIDERED A DRIVING MANUAL.
GAH! WHAT IS THAT??
AH, YES, "CHEESEBURGER-FLAVORED LICORICE!" IT'S SUBTLE, BUT EVOCATIVE.
LOOKS LIKE IT'S JUST OFF TO THE RIGHT HERE...
AND DILTON'S OKAY WITH US USING HIS COTTAGE? WHY ISN'T HE UP HERE TOO?
CAN YOU IMAGINE DILTON WITHOUT AN INTERNET CONNECTION?
Hm. GOOD POINT.
ALL RIGHT... WELCOME TO PARADISE! OF SORTS!

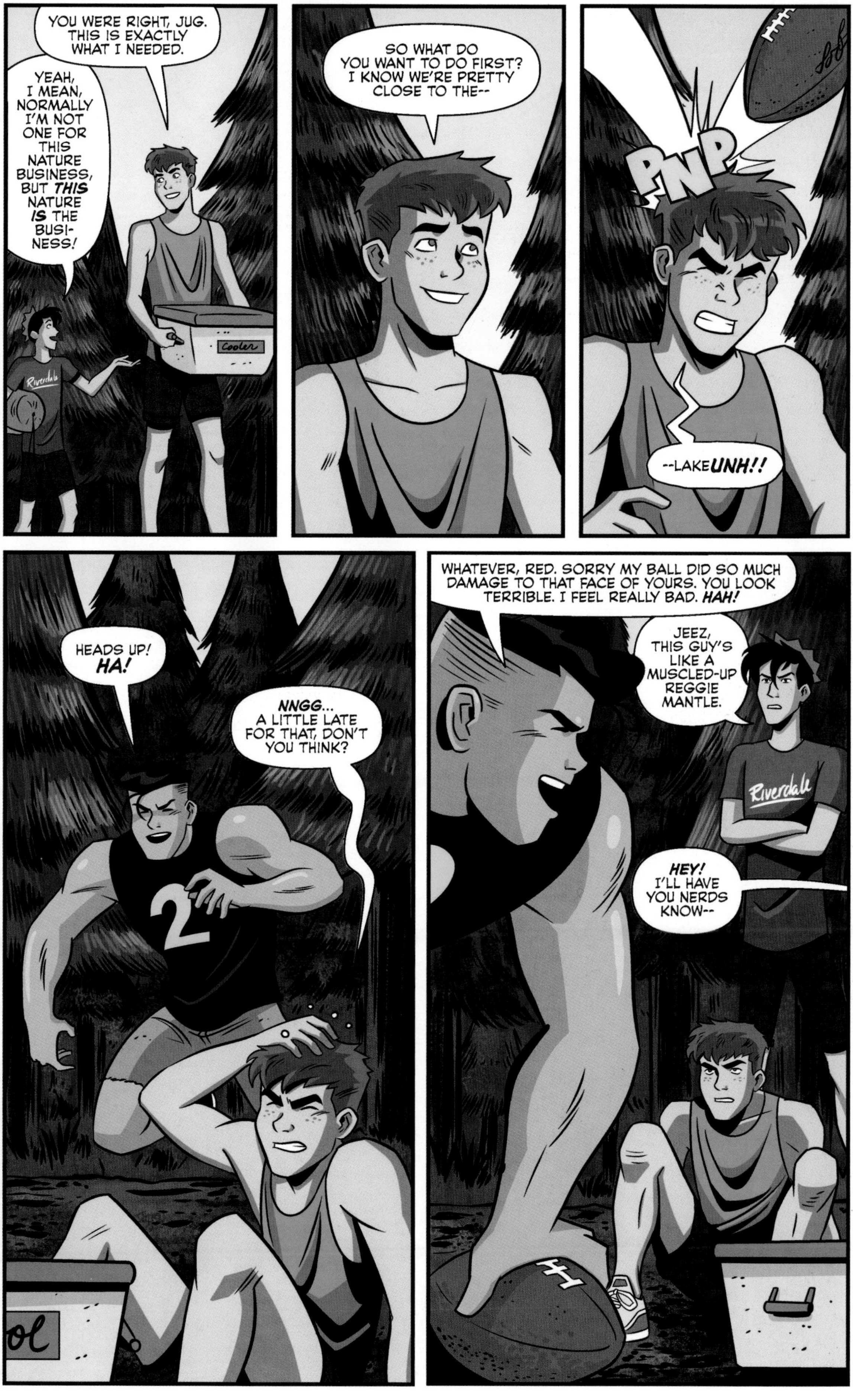
YOU WERE RIGHT, JUG. THIS IS EXACTLY WHAT I NEEDED.
YEAH, I MEAN, NORMALLY I'M NOT ONE FOR THIS NATURE BUSINESS, BUT *THIS* NATURE *IS* THE BUSI-NESS!
Riverdale
Cooler
SO WHAT DO YOU WANT TO DO FIRST? I KNOW WE'RE PRETTY CLOSE TO THE--
PNP
--LAKE*UNH!!*
HEADS UP! *HA!*
NNGG... A LITTLE LATE FOR THAT, DON'T YOU THINK?
2
WHATEVER, RED. SORRY MY BALL DID SO MUCH DAMAGE TO THAT FACE OF YOURS. YOU LOOK TERRIBLE. I FEEL REALLY BAD. *HAH!*
JEEZ, THIS GUY'S LIKE A MUSCLED-UP REGGIE MANTLE.
Riverdale
HEY! I'LL HAVE YOU NERDS KNOW--

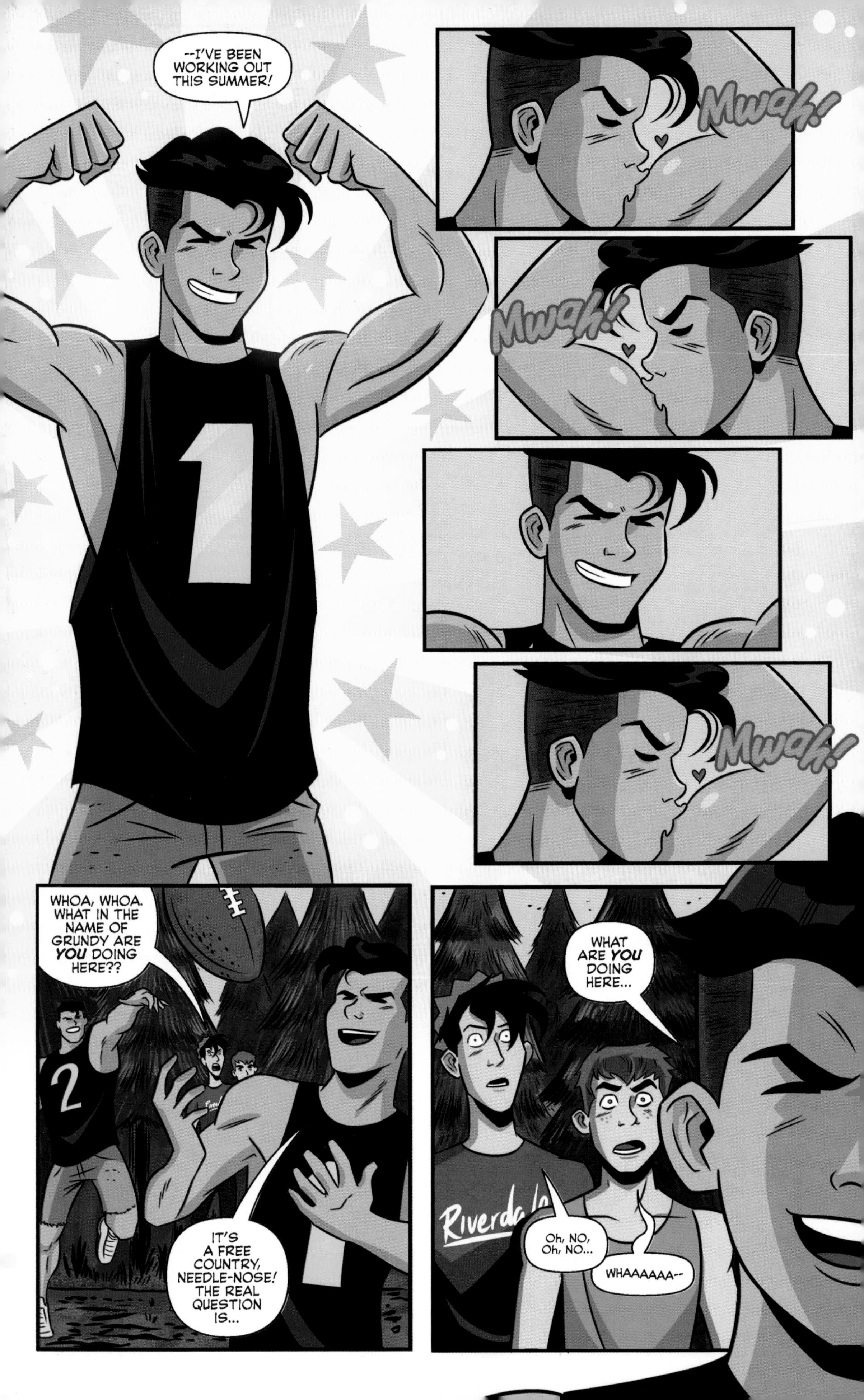
--I'VE BEEN WORKING OUT THIS SUMMER!
Mwah!
Mwah!
Mwah!
WHOA, WHOA. WHAT IN THE NAME OF GRUNDY ARE YOU DOING HERE??
IT'S A FREE COUNTRY, NEEDLE-NOSE! THE REAL QUESTION IS...
WHAT ARE YOU DOING HERE...
Oh, NO, Oh, NO...
WHAAAAAA--

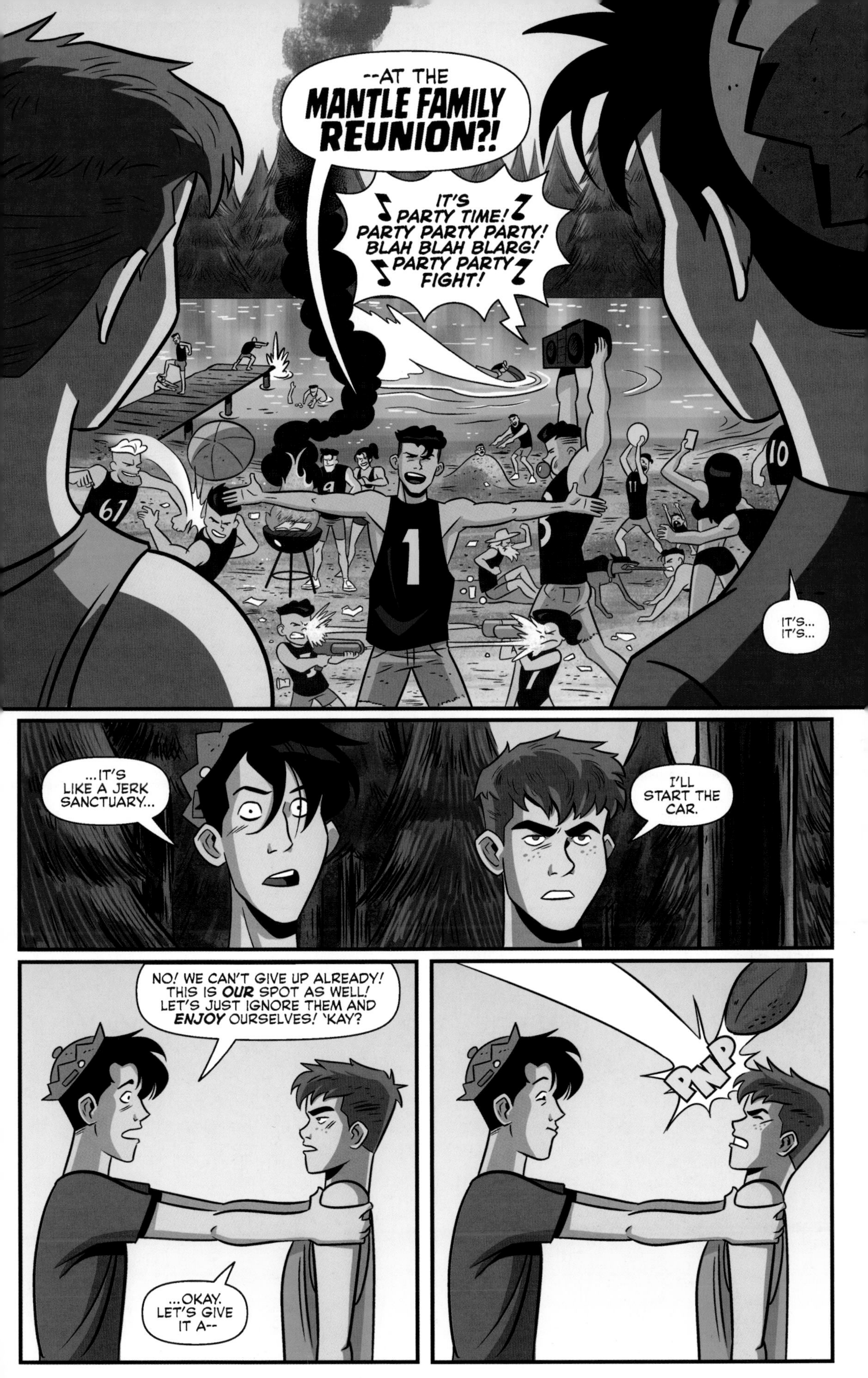
--AT THE MANTLE FAMILY REUNION?!
IT'S PARTY TIME! PARTY PARTY PARTY! BLAH BLAH BLARG! PARTY PARTY FIGHT!
IT'S... IT'S...
...IT'S LIKE A JERK SANCTUARY...
I'LL START THE CAR.
NO! WE CAN'T GIVE UP ALREADY! THIS IS OUR SPOT AS WELL! LET'S JUST IGNORE THEM AND ENJOY OURSELVES! 'KAY?
...OKAY. LET'S GIVE IT A--
PNP

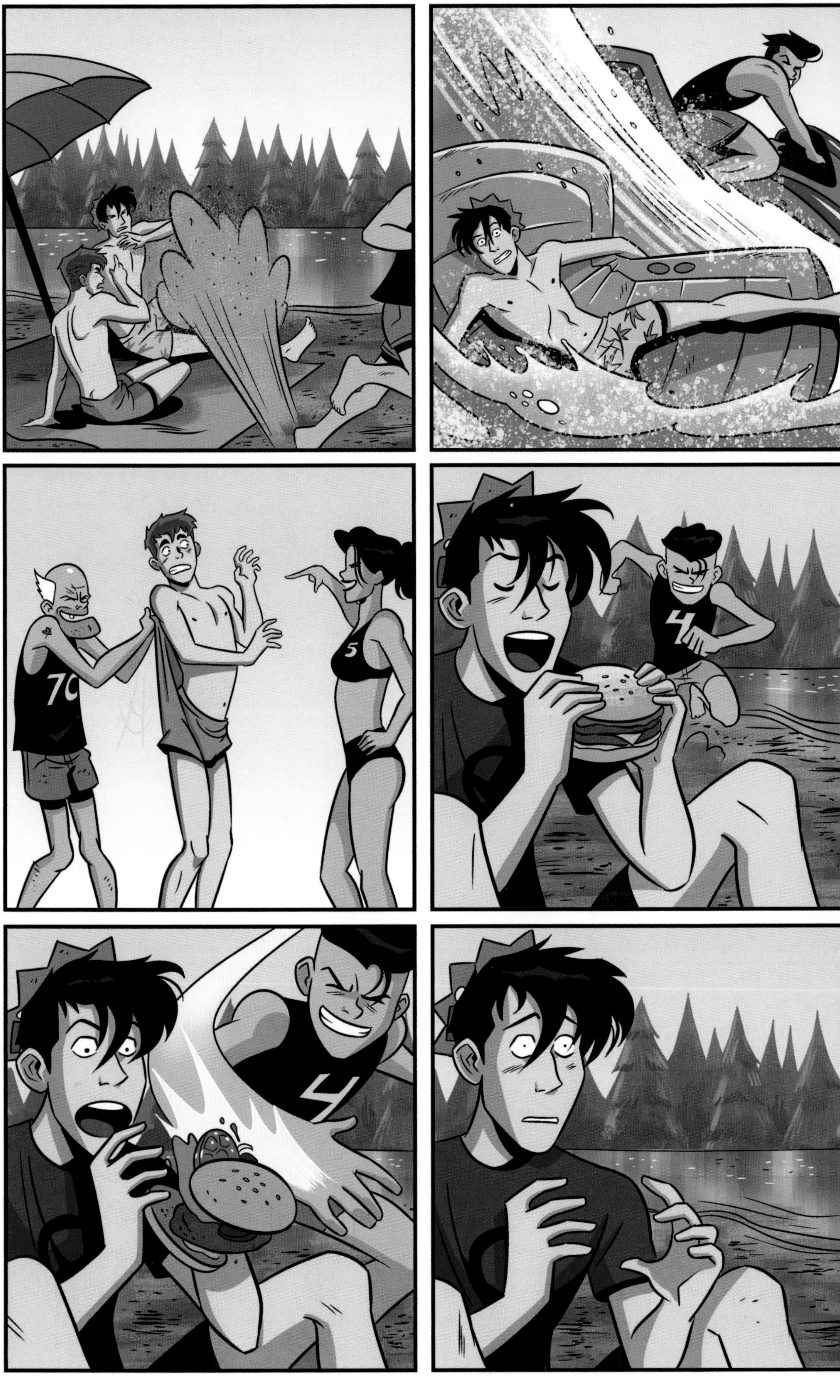
70
5
4
4

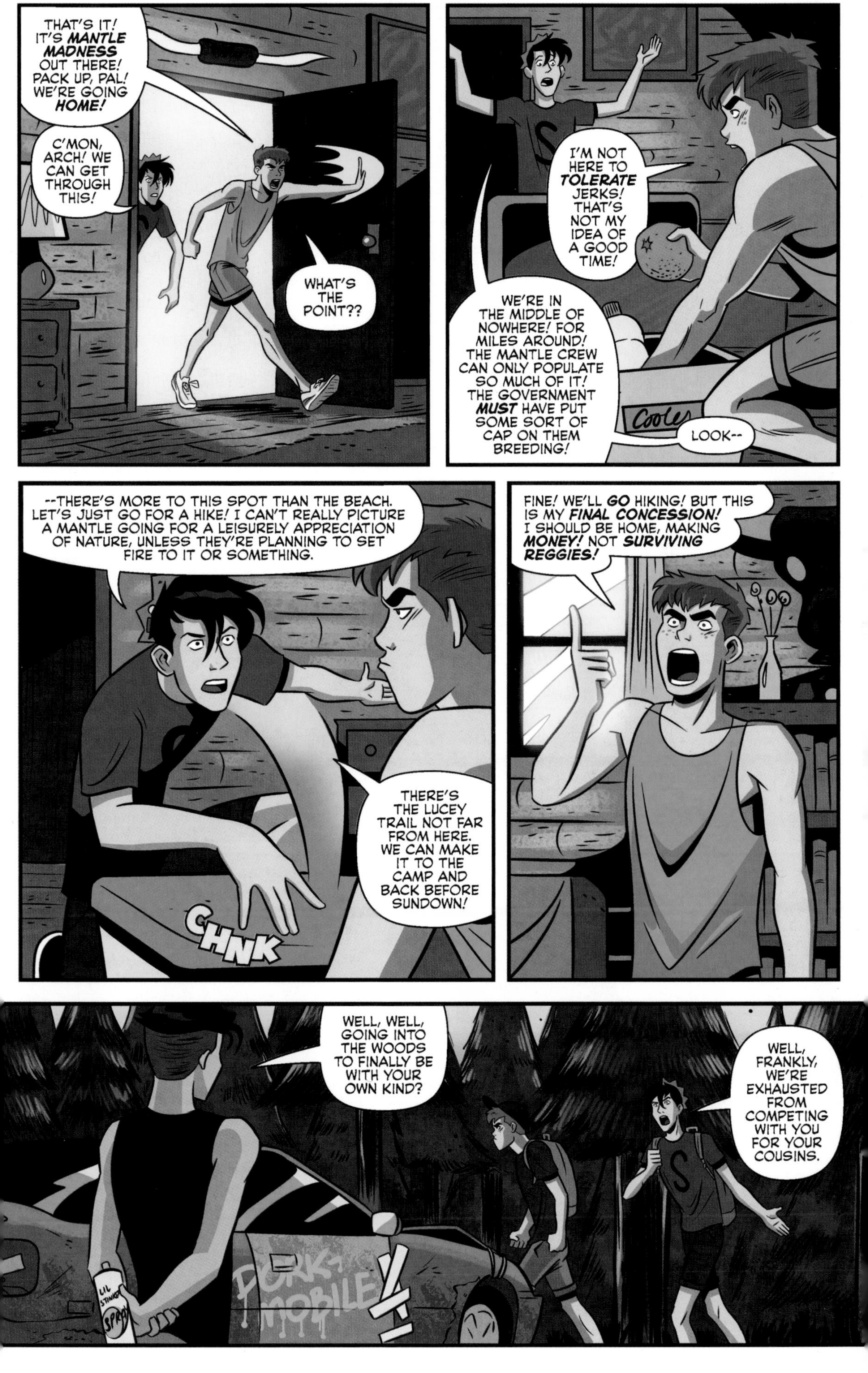
THAT'S IT! IT'S MANTLE MADNESS OUT THERE! PACK UP, PAL! WE'RE GOING HOME!
C'MON, ARCH! WE CAN GET THROUGH THIS!
WHAT'S THE POINT??
I'M NOT HERE TO TOLERATE JERKS! THAT'S NOT MY IDEA OF A GOOD TIME!
WE'RE IN THE MIDDLE OF NOWHERE! FOR MILES AROUND! THE MANTLE CREW CAN ONLY POPULATE SO MUCH OF IT! THE GOVERNMENT MUST HAVE PUT SOME SORT OF CAP ON THEM BREEDING!
LOOK--
--THERE'S MORE TO THIS SPOT THAN THE BEACH. LET'S JUST GO FOR A HIKE! I CAN'T REALLY PICTURE A MANTLE GOING FOR A LEISURELY APPRECIATION OF NATURE, UNLESS THEY'RE PLANNING TO SET FIRE TO IT OR SOMETHING.
THERE'S THE LUCEY TRAIL NOT FAR FROM HERE. WE CAN MAKE IT TO THE CAMP AND BACK BEFORE SUNDOWN!
CHNK
FINE! WE'LL GO HIKING! BUT THIS IS MY FINAL CONCESSION! I SHOULD BE HOME, MAKING MONEY! NOT SURVIVING REGGIES!
WELL, WELL, GOING INTO THE WOODS TO FINALLY BE WITH YOUR OWN KIND?
WELL, FRANKLY, WE'RE EXHAUSTED FROM COMPETING WITH YOU FOR YOUR COUSINS.
LIL STINKER SPRAY
DORK-MOBILE

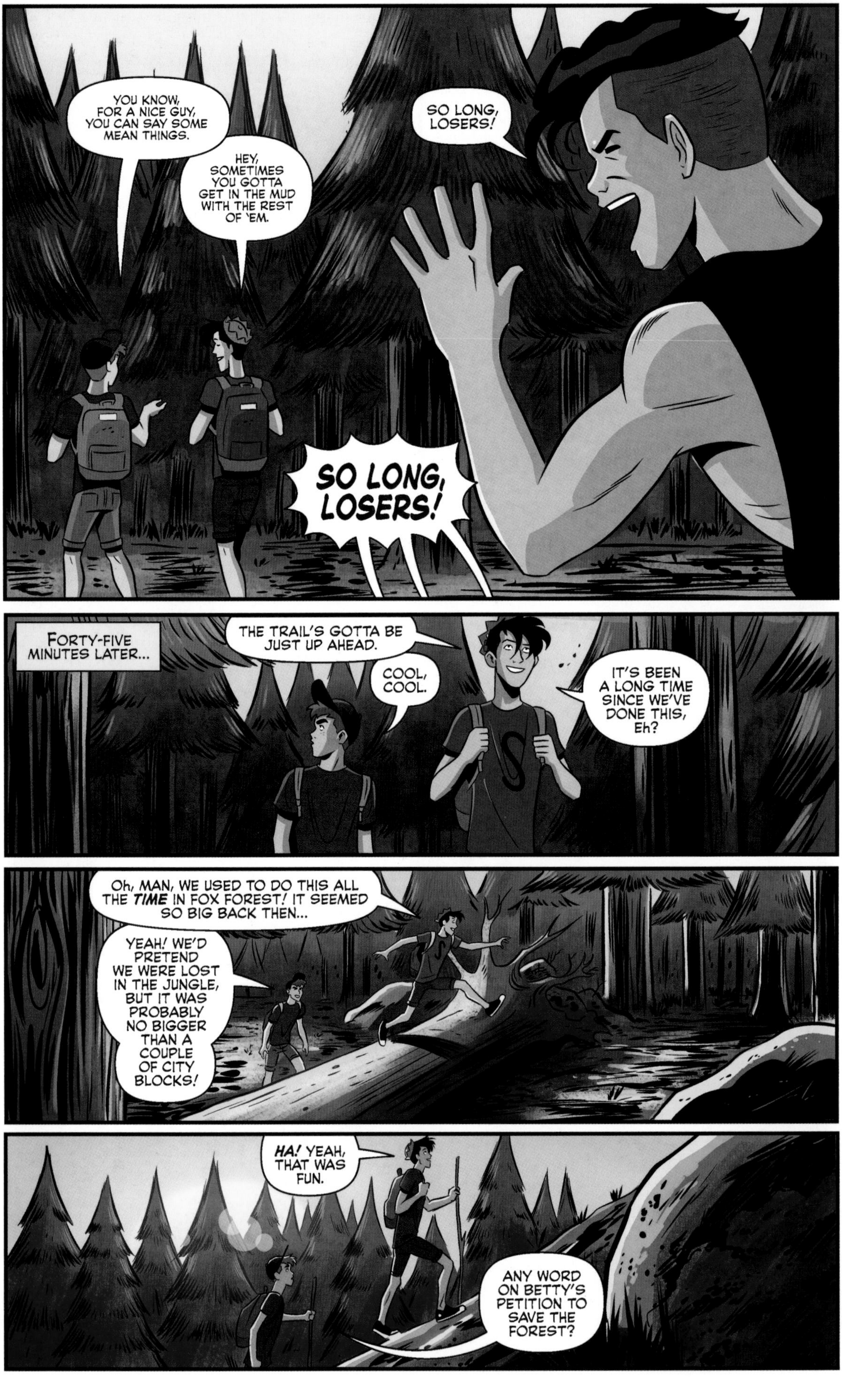
YOU KNOW, FOR A NICE GUY, YOU CAN SAY SOME MEAN THINGS.
HEY, SOMETIMES YOU GOTTA GET IN THE MUD WITH THE REST OF 'EM.
SO LONG, LOSERS!
SO LONG, LOSERS!
FORTY-FIVE MINUTES LATER...
THE TRAIL'S GOTTA BE JUST UP AHEAD.
COOL, COOL.
IT'S BEEN A LONG TIME SINCE WE'VE DONE THIS, EH?
OH, MAN, WE USED TO DO THIS ALL THE TIME IN FOX FOREST! IT SEEMED SO BIG BACK THEN...
YEAH! WE'D PRETEND WE WERE LOST IN THE JUNGLE, BUT IT WAS PROBABLY NO BIGGER THAN A COUPLE OF CITY BLOCKS!
HA! YEAH, THAT WAS FUN.
ANY WORD ON BETTY'S PETITION TO SAVE THE FOREST?

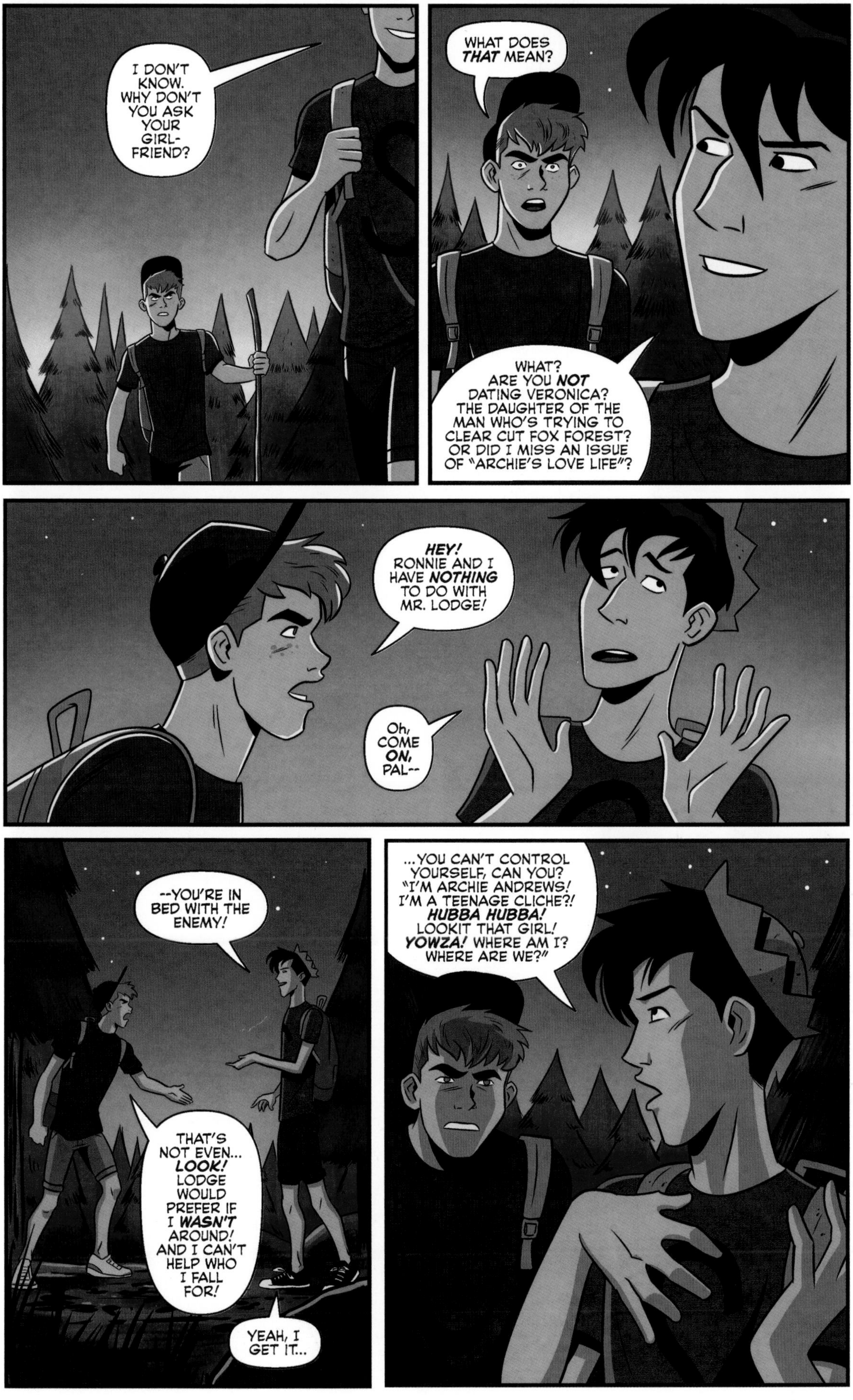
I DON'T KNOW. WHY DON'T YOU ASK YOUR GIRL-FRIEND?
WHAT DOES *THAT* MEAN?
WHAT? ARE YOU *NOT* DATING VERONICA? THE DAUGHTER OF THE MAN WHO'S TRYING TO CLEAR CUT FOX FOREST? OR DID I MISS AN ISSUE OF "ARCHIE'S LOVE LIFE"?
HEY! RONNIE AND I HAVE *NOTHING* TO DO WITH MR. LODGE!
Oh, COME *ON,* PAL--
--YOU'RE IN BED WITH THE ENEMY!
THAT'S NOT EVEN... *LOOK!* LODGE WOULD PREFER IF I *WASN'T* AROUND! AND I CAN'T HELP WHO I FALL FOR!
YEAH, I GET IT...
...YOU CAN'T CONTROL YOURSELF, CAN YOU? "I'M ARCHIE ANDREWS! I'M A TEENAGE CLICHE?! *HUBBA HUBBA!* LOOKIT THAT GIRL! *YOWZA!* WHERE AM I? WHERE ARE WE?"

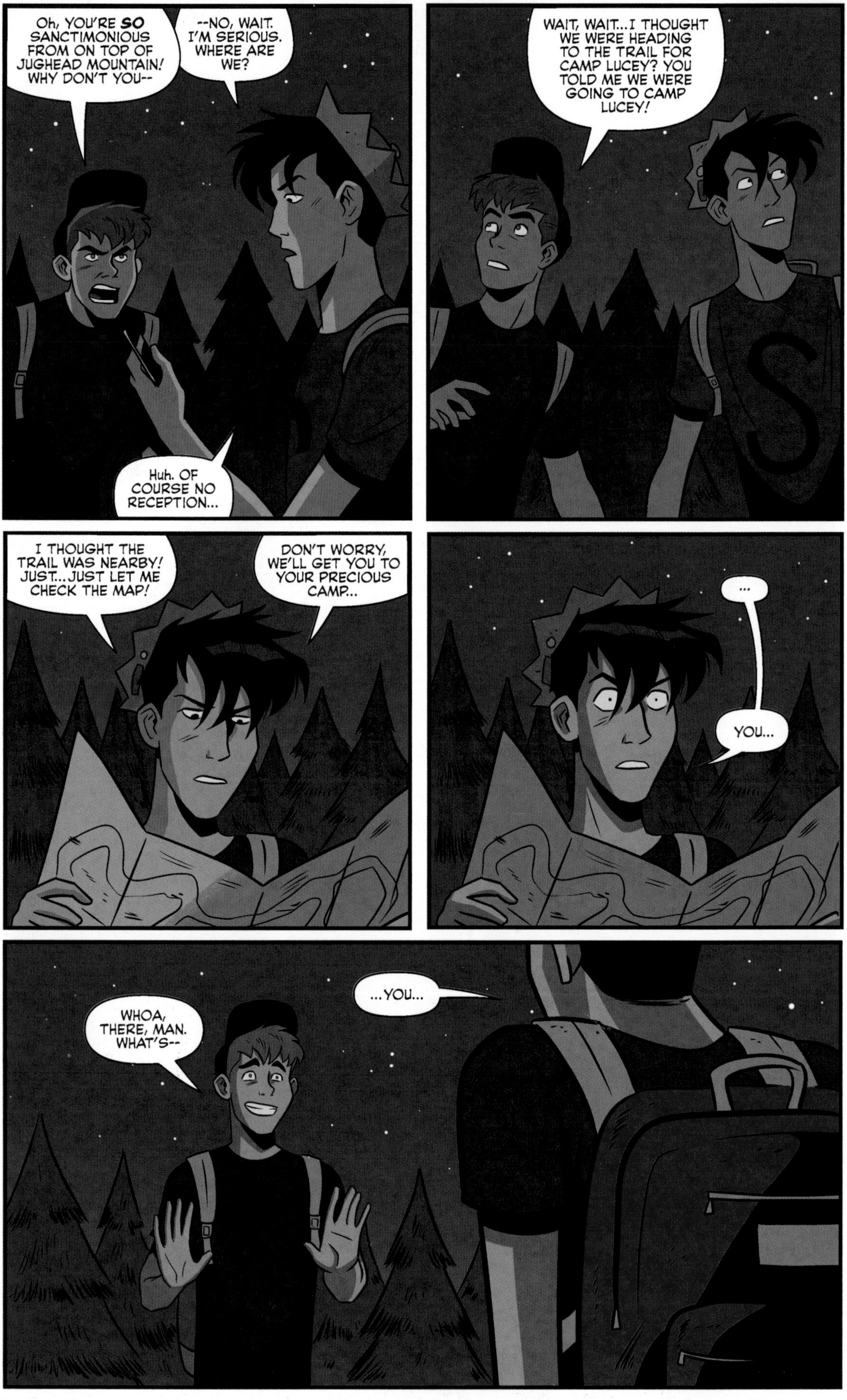
Oh, YOU'RE **SO** SANCTIMONIOUS FROM ON TOP OF JUGHEAD MOUNTAIN! WHY DON'T YOU--
--NO, WAIT. I'M SERIOUS. WHERE ARE WE?
Huh. OF COURSE NO RECEPTION...
WAIT, WAIT...I THOUGHT WE WERE HEADING TO THE TRAIL FOR CAMP LUCEY? YOU TOLD ME WE WERE GOING TO CAMP LUCEY!
I THOUGHT THE TRAIL WAS NEARBY! JUST...JUST LET ME CHECK THE MAP!
DON'T WORRY, WE'LL GET YOU TO YOUR PRECIOUS CAMP...
...
YOU...
...YOU...
WHOA, THERE, MAN. WHAT'S--

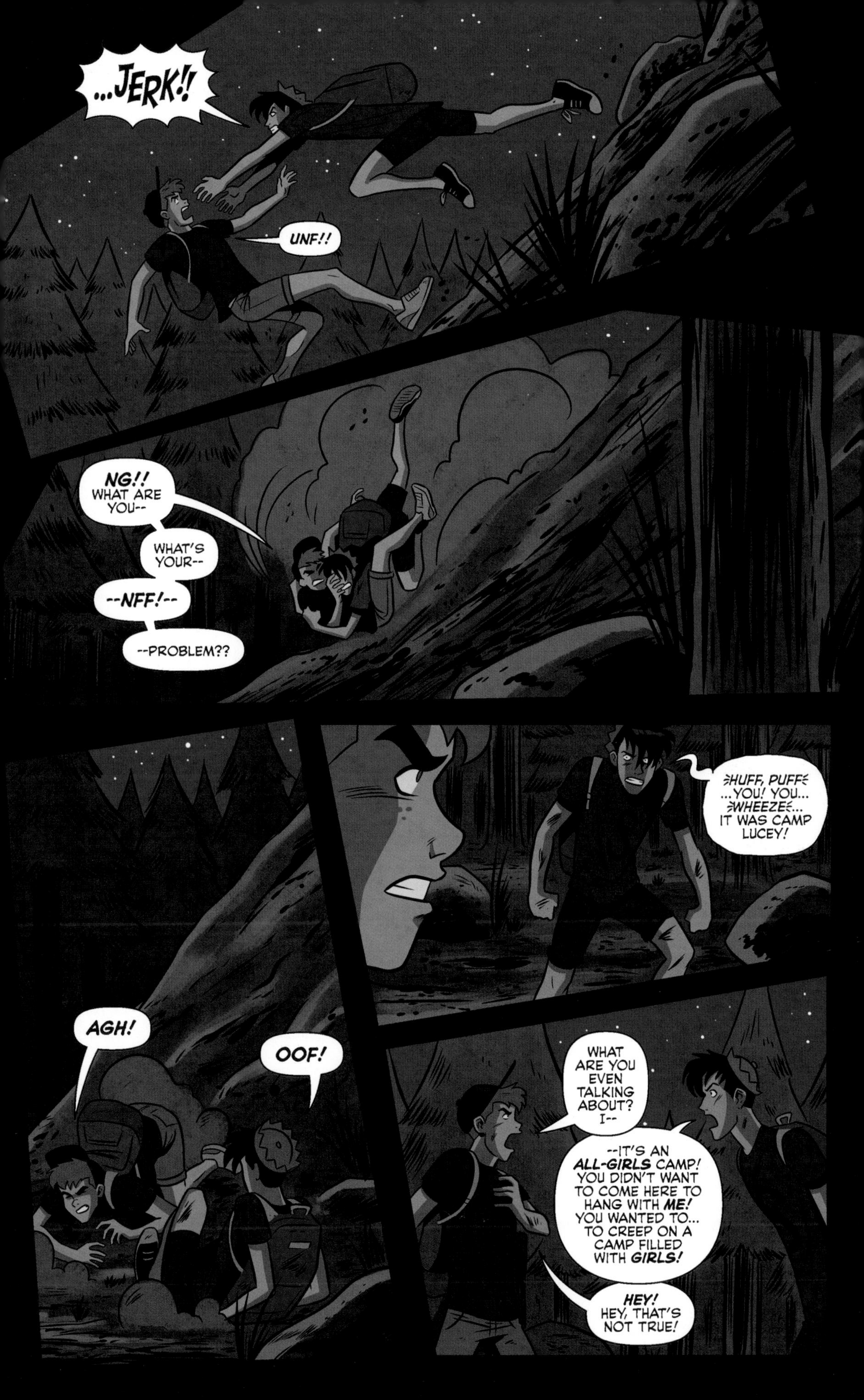
...JERK!!
UNF!!
NG!! WHAT ARE YOU--
WHAT'S YOUR--
--NFF!--
--PROBLEM??
AGH!
OOF!
HUFF, PUFF ...YOU! YOU... WHEEZE... IT WAS CAMP LUCEY!
WHAT ARE YOU EVEN TALKING ABOUT? I--
--IT'S AN ALL-GIRLS CAMP! YOU DIDN'T WANT TO COME HERE TO HANG WITH ME! YOU WANTED TO... TO CREEP ON A CAMP FILLED WITH GIRLS!
HEY! HEY, THAT'S NOT TRUE!

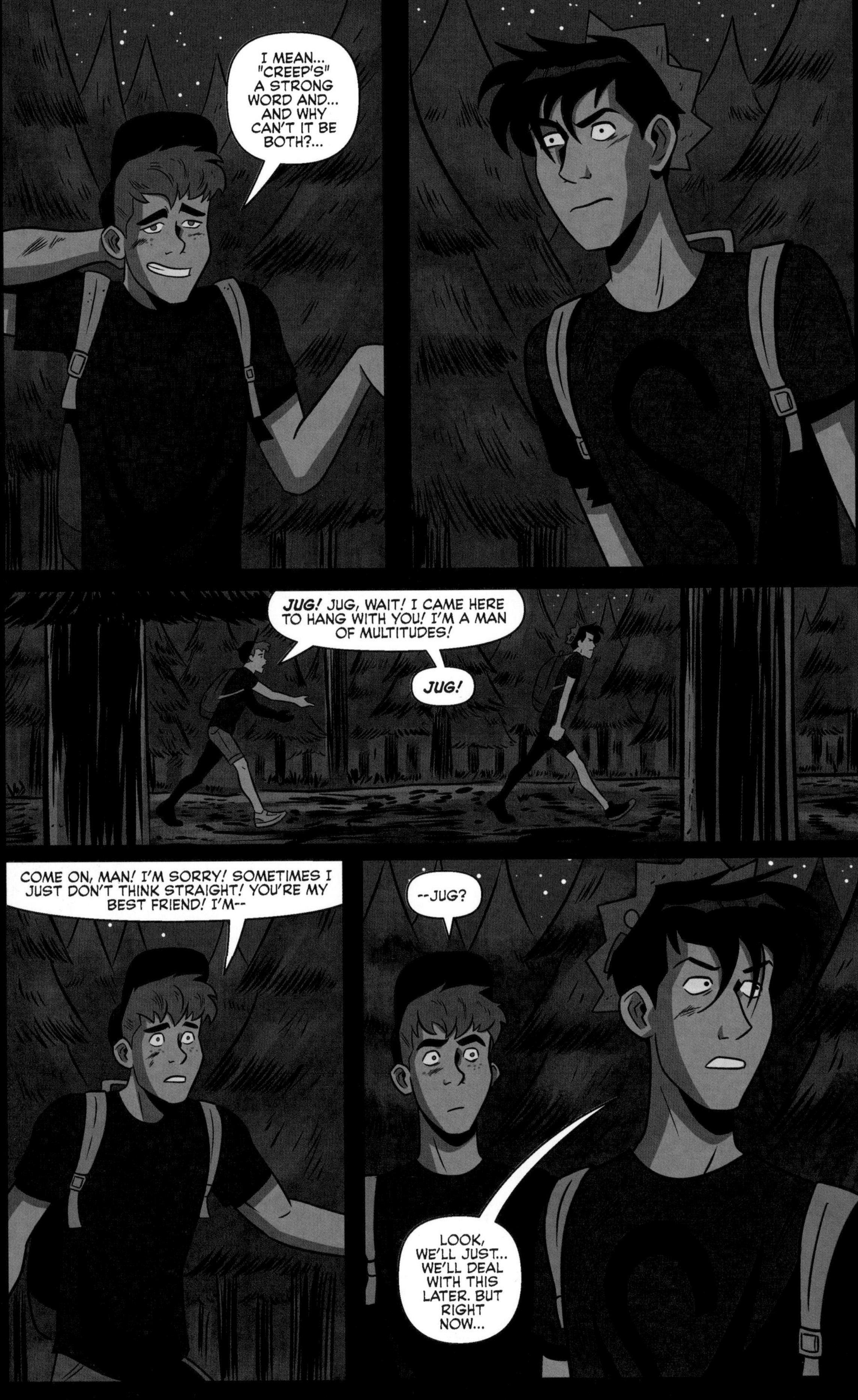
I MEAN... "CREEP'S" A STRONG WORD AND... AND WHY CAN'T IT BE BOTH?...
JUG! JUG, WAIT! I CAME HERE TO HANG WITH YOU! I'M A MAN OF MULTITUDES!
JUG!
COME ON, MAN! I'M SORRY! SOMETIMES I JUST DON'T THINK STRAIGHT! YOU'RE MY BEST FRIEND! I'M--
--JUG?
LOOK, WE'LL JUST... WE'LL DEAL WITH THIS LATER. BUT RIGHT NOW...

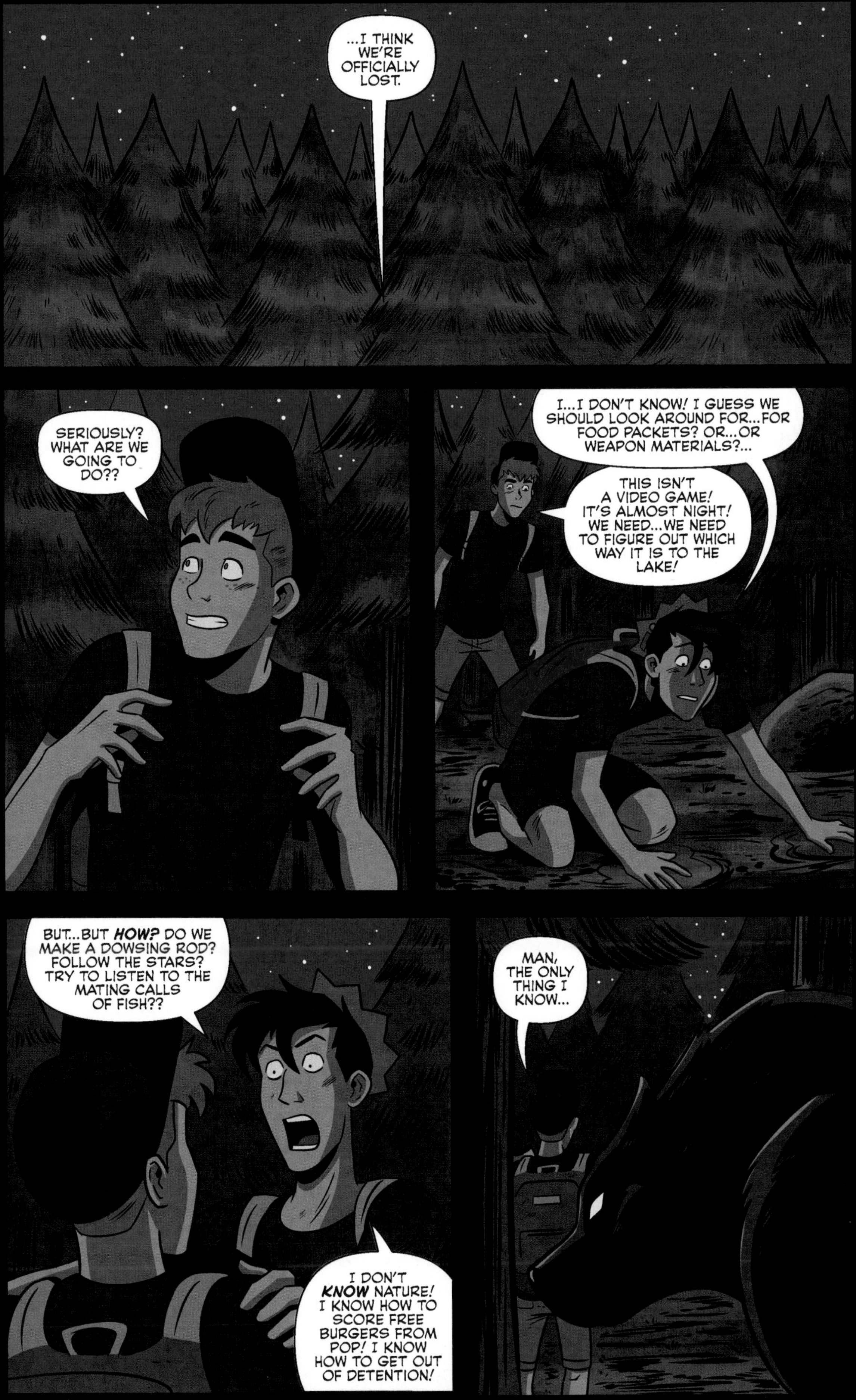
...I THINK WE'RE OFFICIALLY LOST.
SERIOUSLY? WHAT ARE WE GOING TO DO??
I...I DON'T KNOW! I GUESS WE SHOULD LOOK AROUND FOR...FOR FOOD PACKETS? OR...OR WEAPON MATERIALS?...
THIS ISN'T A VIDEO GAME! IT'S ALMOST NIGHT! WE NEED...WE NEED TO FIGURE OUT WHICH WAY IT IS TO THE LAKE!
BUT...BUT *HOW?* DO WE MAKE A DOWSING ROD? FOLLOW THE STARS? TRY TO LISTEN TO THE MATING CALLS OF FISH??
I DON'T *KNOW* NATURE! I KNOW HOW TO SCORE FREE BURGERS FROM POP! I KNOW HOW TO GET OUT OF DETENTION!
MAN, THE ONLY THING I KNOW...

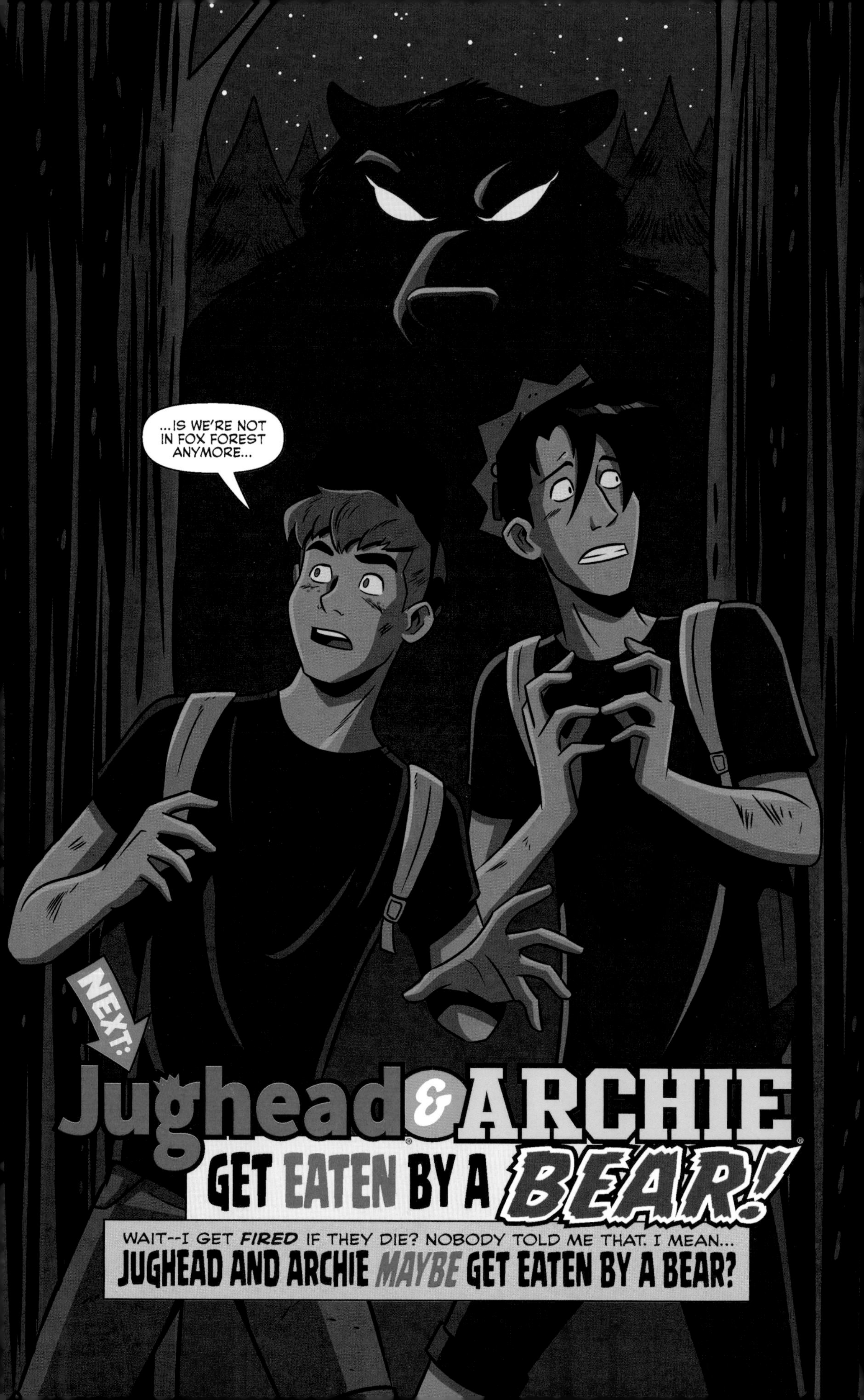
...IS WE'RE NOT IN FOX FOREST ANYMORE...
NEXT:
Jughead & ARCHIE
GET EATEN BY A BEAR!
WAIT--I GET FIRED IF THEY DIE? NOBODY TOLD ME THAT. I MEAN...
JUGHEAD AND ARCHIE MAYBE GET EATEN BY A BEAR?

TO BE
CONTINUED...

ISSUE **EIGHT**

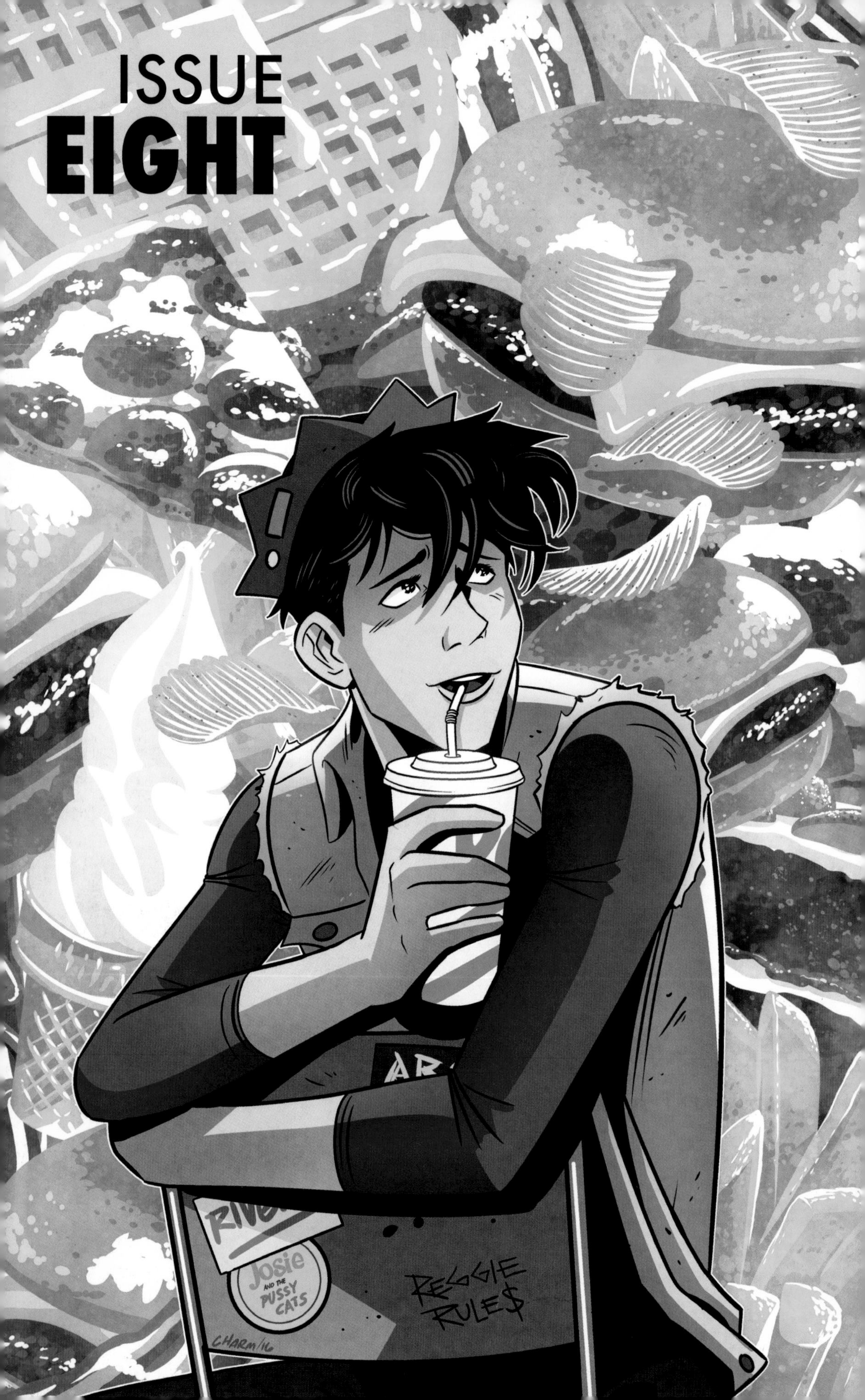

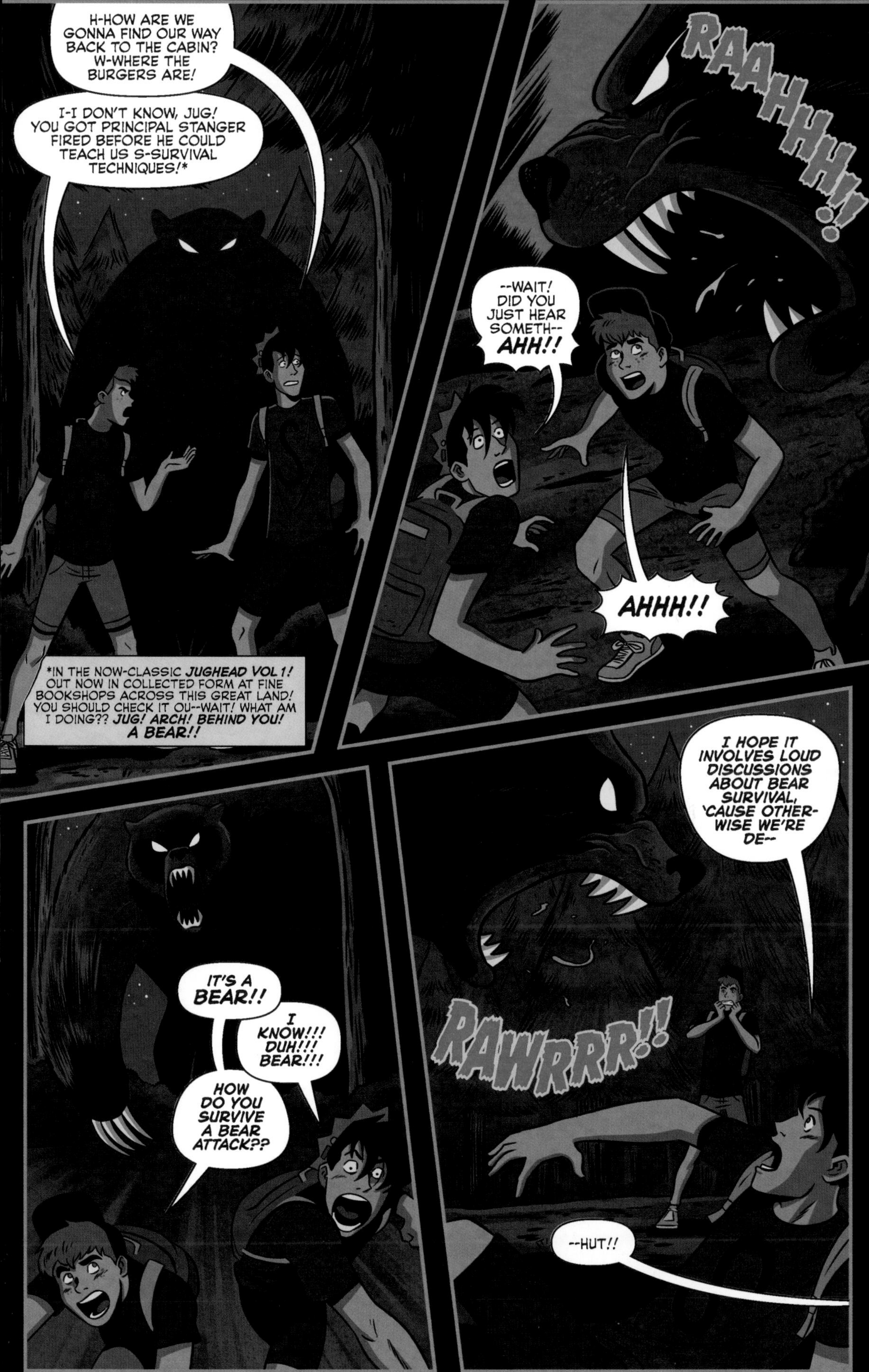
H-HOW ARE WE GONNA FIND OUR WAY BACK TO THE CABIN? W-WHERE THE BURGERS ARE!
I-I DON'T KNOW, JUG! YOU GOT PRINCIPAL STANGER FIRED BEFORE HE COULD TEACH US S-SURVIVAL TECHNIQUES!*
*IN THE NOW-CLASSIC JUGHEAD VOL 1! OUT NOW IN COLLECTED FORM AT FINE BOOKSHOPS ACROSS THIS GREAT LAND! YOU SHOULD CHECK IT OU--WAIT! WHAT AM I DOING?? JUG! ARCH! BEHIND YOU! A BEAR!!
RAAHHHH!!
--WAIT! DID YOU JUST HEAR SOMETH-- AHH!!
AHHH!!
IT'S A BEAR!!
I KNOW!!! DUH!!! BEAR!!!
HOW DO YOU SURVIVE A BEAR ATTACK??
I HOPE IT INVOLVES LOUD DISCUSSIONS ABOUT BEAR SURVIVAL, 'CAUSE OTHER-WISE WE'RE DE--
RAWRRR!!
--HUT!!

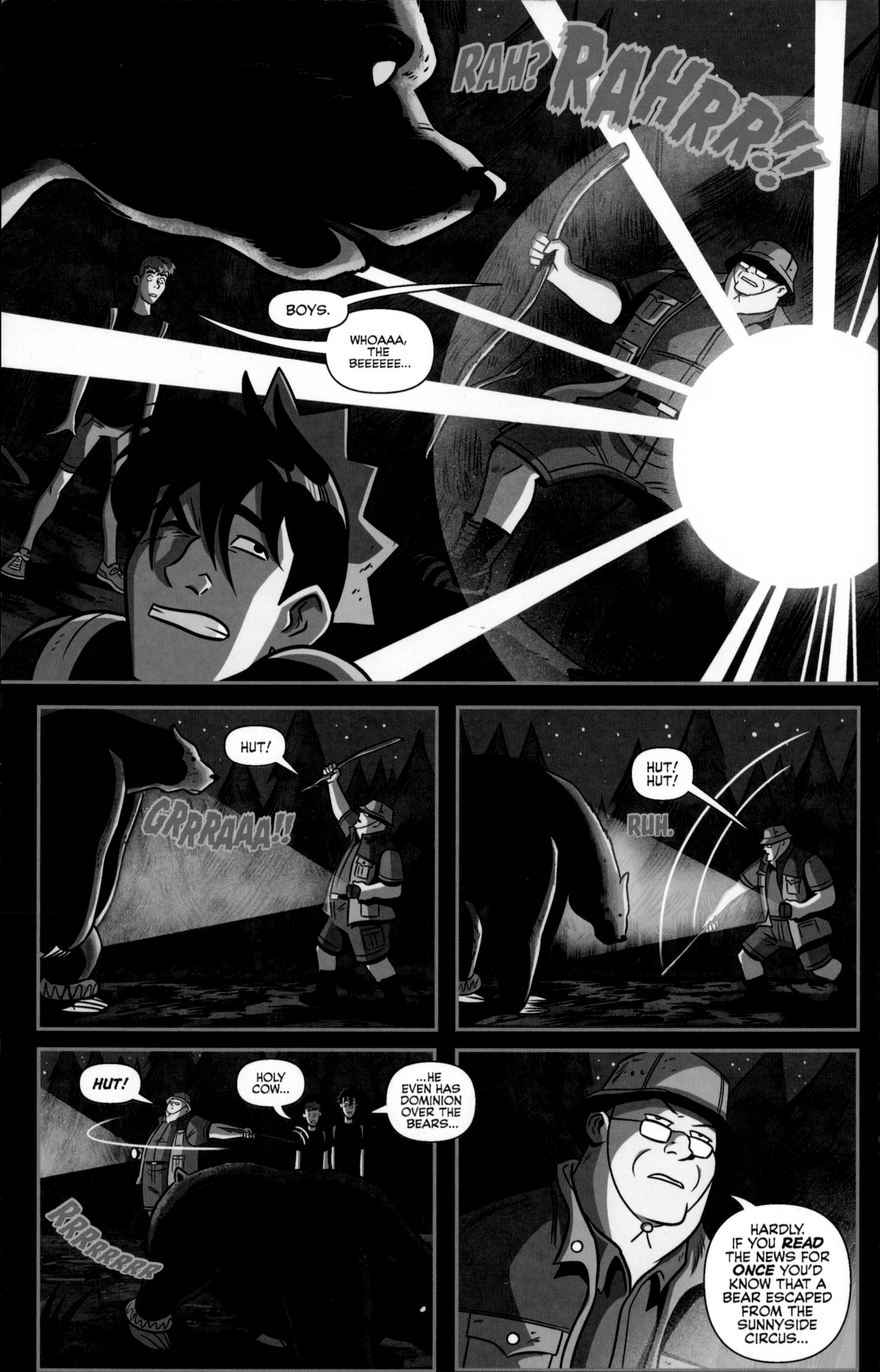
RAH? RAHRR!!
BOYS.
WHOAAA, THE BEEEEEE...
HUT!
GRRRAAA!!
HUT! HUT!
RUH.
HUT!
HOLY COW...
...HE EVEN HAS DOMINION OVER THE BEARS...
RRRRRRRR
HARDLY. IF YOU READ THE NEWS FOR ONCE YOU'D KNOW THAT A BEAR ESCAPED FROM THE SUNNYSIDE CIRCUS...

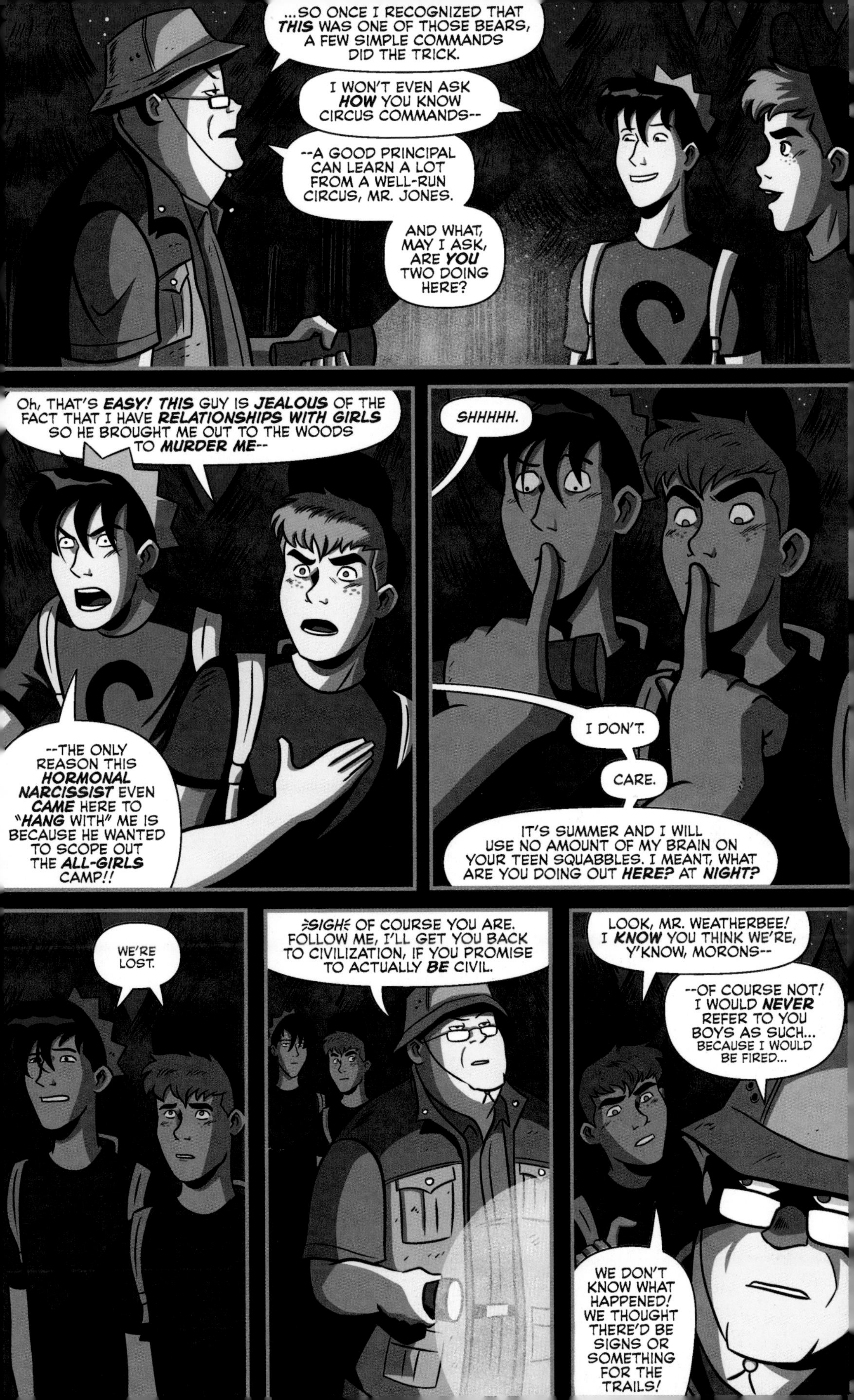
...SO ONCE I RECOGNIZED THAT THIS WAS ONE OF THOSE BEARS, A FEW SIMPLE COMMANDS DID THE TRICK.
I WON'T EVEN ASK HOW YOU KNOW CIRCUS COMMANDS--
--A GOOD PRINCIPAL CAN LEARN A LOT FROM A WELL-RUN CIRCUS, MR. JONES.
AND WHAT, MAY I ASK, ARE YOU TWO DOING HERE?
Oh, THAT'S EASY! THIS GUY IS JEALOUS OF THE FACT THAT I HAVE RELATIONSHIPS WITH GIRLS SO HE BROUGHT ME OUT TO THE WOODS TO MURDER ME--
--THE ONLY REASON THIS HORMONAL NARCISSIST EVEN CAME HERE TO "HANG WITH" ME IS BECAUSE HE WANTED TO SCOPE OUT THE ALL-GIRLS CAMP!!
SHHHHH.
I DON'T.
CARE.
IT'S SUMMER AND I WILL USE NO AMOUNT OF MY BRAIN ON YOUR TEEN SQUABBLES. I MEANT, WHAT ARE YOU DOING OUT HERE? AT NIGHT?
WE'RE LOST.
SIGH OF COURSE YOU ARE. FOLLOW ME, I'LL GET YOU BACK TO CIVILIZATION, IF YOU PROMISE TO ACTUALLY BE CIVIL.
LOOK, MR. WEATHERBEE! I KNOW YOU THINK WE'RE, Y'KNOW, MORONS--
--OF COURSE NOT! I WOULD NEVER REFER TO YOU BOYS AS SUCH... BECAUSE I WOULD BE FIRED...
WE DON'T KNOW WHAT HAPPENED! WE THOUGHT THERE'D BE SIGNS OR SOMETHING FOR THE TRAILS!

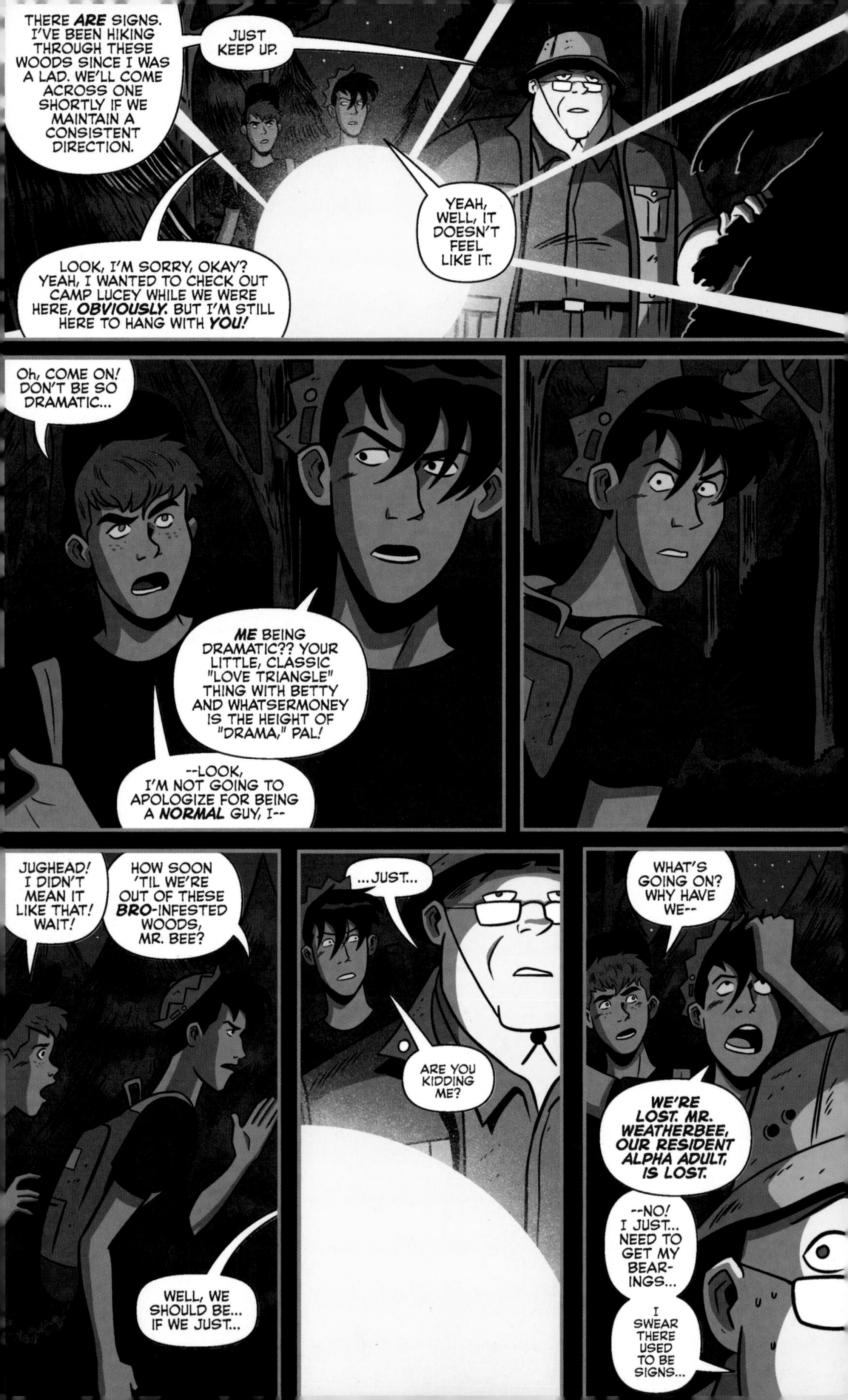
THERE ARE SIGNS. I'VE BEEN HIKING THROUGH THESE WOODS SINCE I WAS A LAD. WE'LL COME ACROSS ONE SHORTLY IF WE MAINTAIN A CONSISTENT DIRECTION.
JUST KEEP UP.
YEAH, WELL, IT DOESN'T FEEL LIKE IT.
LOOK, I'M SORRY, OKAY? YEAH, I WANTED TO CHECK OUT CAMP LUCEY WHILE WE WERE HERE, OBVIOUSLY. BUT I'M STILL HERE TO HANG WITH YOU!
Oh, COME ON! DON'T BE SO DRAMATIC...
ME BEING DRAMATIC?? YOUR LITTLE, CLASSIC "LOVE TRIANGLE" THING WITH BETTY AND WHATSERMONEY IS THE HEIGHT OF "DRAMA," PAL!
--LOOK, I'M NOT GOING TO APOLOGIZE FOR BEING A NORMAL GUY, I--
JUGHEAD! I DIDN'T MEAN IT LIKE THAT! WAIT!
HOW SOON 'TIL WE'RE OUT OF THESE BRO-INFESTED WOODS, MR. BEE?
WELL, WE SHOULD BE... IF WE JUST...
...JUST...
ARE YOU KIDDING ME?
WHAT'S GOING ON? WHY HAVE WE--
WE'RE LOST. MR. WEATHERBEE, OUR RESIDENT ALPHA ADULT, IS LOST.
--NO! I JUST... NEED TO GET MY BEAR-INGS...
I SWEAR THERE USED TO BE SIGNS...

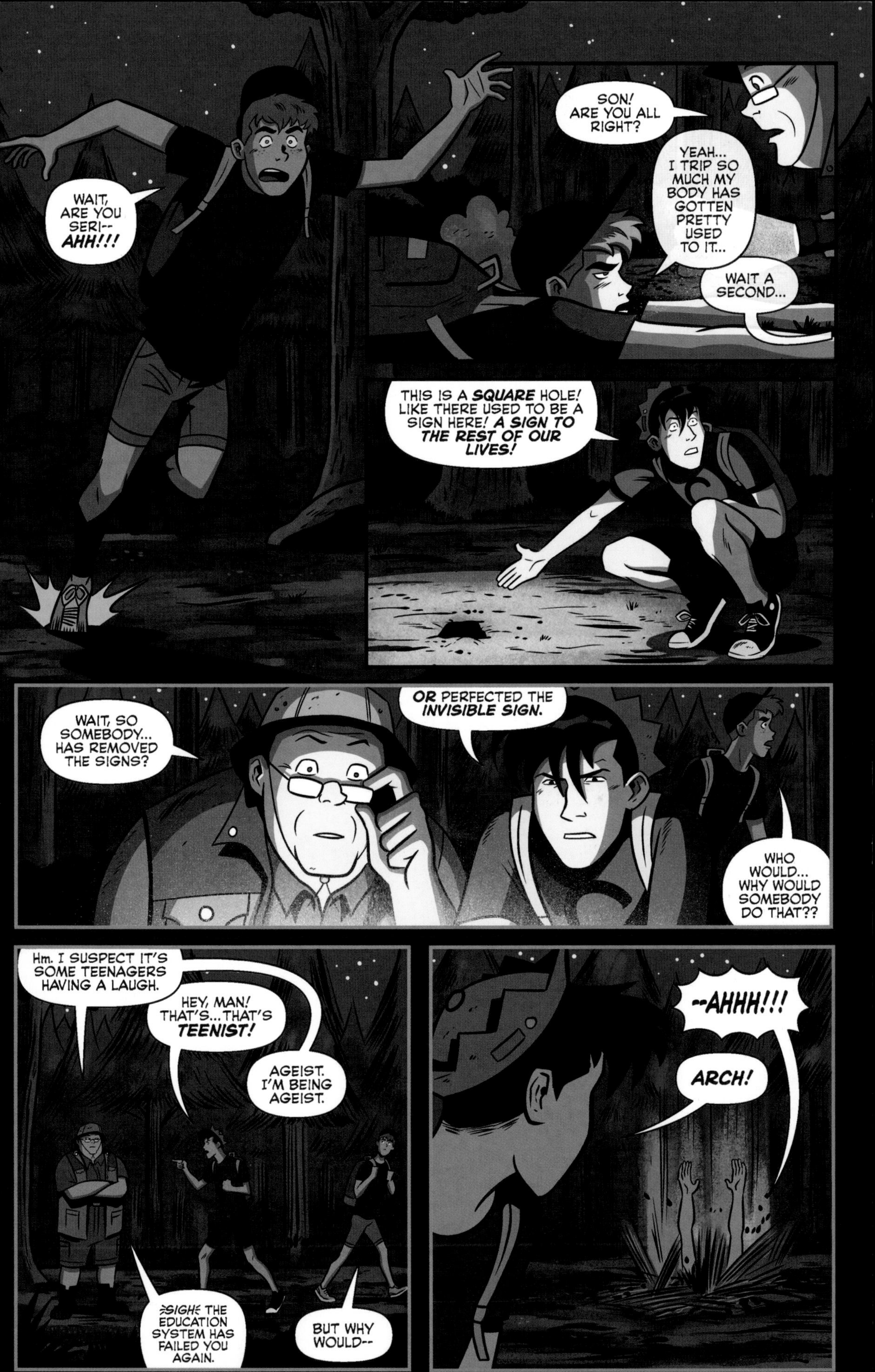
WAIT, ARE YOU SERI-- AHH!!!
SON! ARE YOU ALL RIGHT?
YEAH... I TRIP SO MUCH MY BODY HAS GOTTEN PRETTY USED TO IT...
WAIT A SECOND...
THIS IS A SQUARE HOLE! LIKE THERE USED TO BE A SIGN HERE! A SIGN TO THE REST OF OUR LIVES!
WAIT, SO SOMEBODY... HAS REMOVED THE SIGNS?
OR PERFECTED THE INVISIBLE SIGN.
WHO WOULD... WHY WOULD SOMEBODY DO THAT??
Hm. I SUSPECT IT'S SOME TEENAGERS HAVING A LAUGH.
HEY, MAN! THAT'S...THAT'S TEENIST!
AGEIST. I'M BEING AGEIST.
SIGH THE EDUCATION SYSTEM HAS FAILED YOU AGAIN.
BUT WHY WOULD--
--AHHH!!!
ARCH!

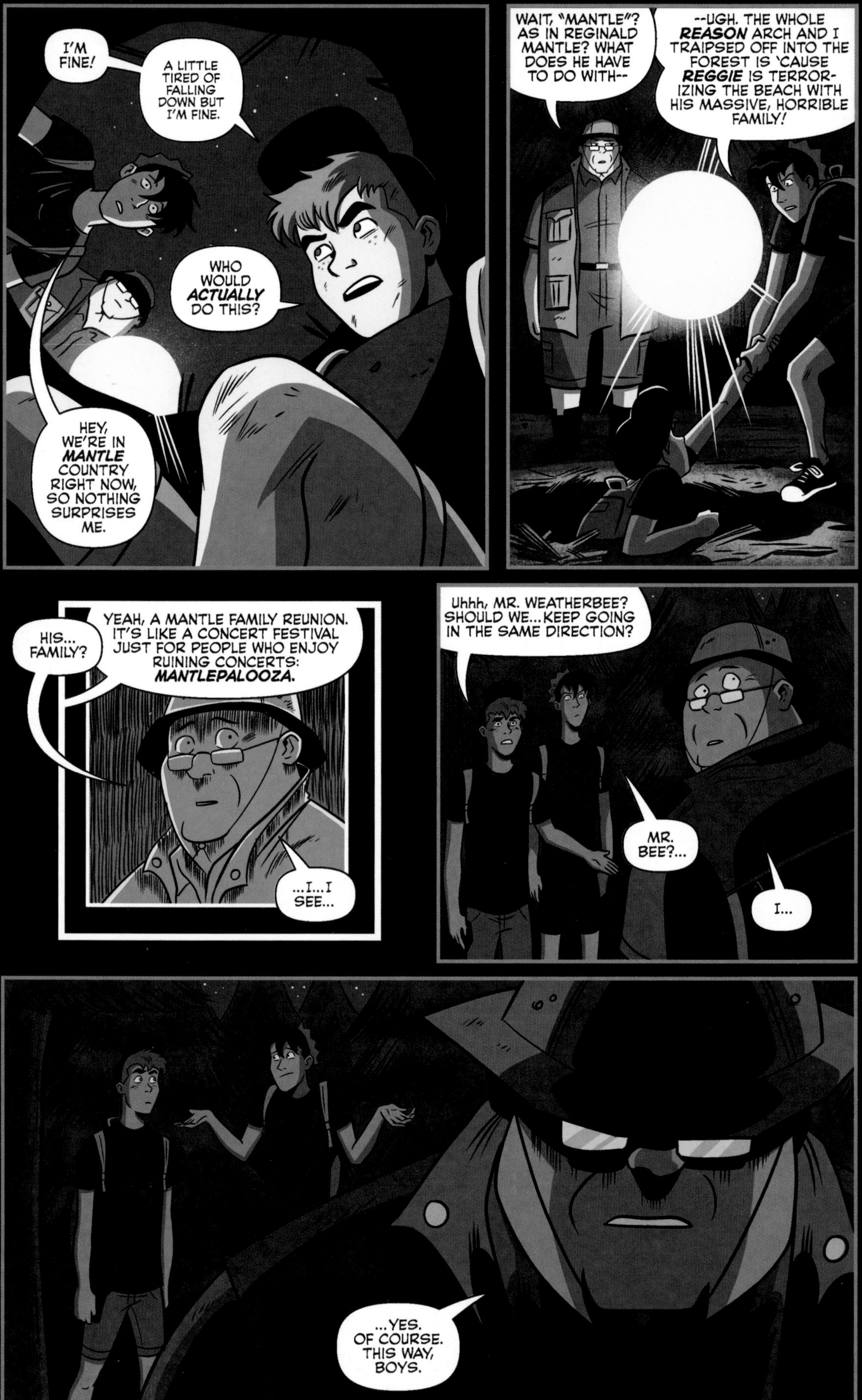
I'M FINE!
A LITTLE TIRED OF FALLING DOWN BUT I'M FINE.
WHO WOULD **ACTUALLY** DO THIS?
HEY, WE'RE IN **MANTLE** COUNTRY RIGHT NOW, SO NOTHING SURPRISES ME.
WAIT, "MANTLE"? AS IN REGINALD MANTLE? WHAT DOES HE HAVE TO DO WITH--
--UGH. THE WHOLE **REASON** ARCH AND I TRAIPSED OFF INTO THE FOREST IS 'CAUSE **REGGIE** IS TERROR-IZING THE BEACH WITH HIS MASSIVE, HORRIBLE FAMILY!
HIS... FAMILY?
YEAH, A MANTLE FAMILY REUNION. IT'S LIKE A CONCERT FESTIVAL JUST FOR PEOPLE WHO ENJOY RUINING CONCERTS: **MANTLEPALOOZA.**
...I...I SEE...
Uhhh, MR. WEATHERBEE? SHOULD WE...KEEP GOING IN THE SAME DIRECTION?
MR. BEE?...
I...
...YES. OF COURSE. THIS WAY, BOYS.

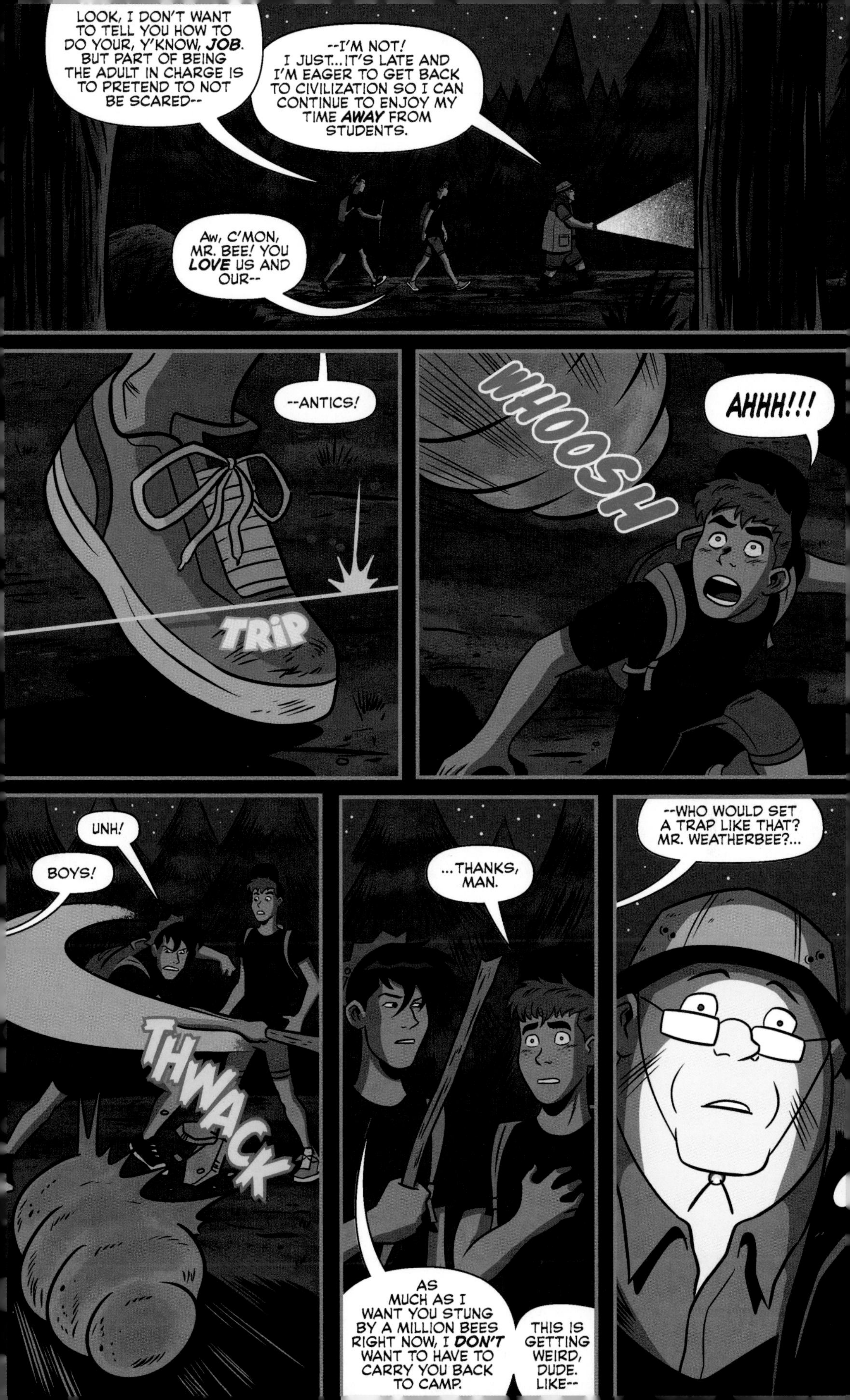
LOOK, I DON'T WANT TO TELL YOU HOW TO DO YOUR, Y'KNOW, JOB. BUT PART OF BEING THE ADULT IN CHARGE IS TO PRETEND TO NOT BE SCARED--
--I'M NOT! I JUST...IT'S LATE AND I'M EAGER TO GET BACK TO CIVILIZATION SO I CAN CONTINUE TO ENJOY MY TIME AWAY FROM STUDENTS.
AW, C'MON, MR. BEE! YOU LOVE US AND OUR--
--ANTICS!
TRIP
WHOOSH
AHHH!!!
UNH!
BOYS!
THWACK
...THANKS, MAN.
AS MUCH AS I WANT YOU STUNG BY A MILLION BEES RIGHT NOW, I DON'T WANT TO HAVE TO CARRY YOU BACK TO CAMP.
--WHO WOULD SET A TRAP LIKE THAT? MR. WEATHERBEE?...
THIS IS GETTING WEIRD, DUDE. LIKE--

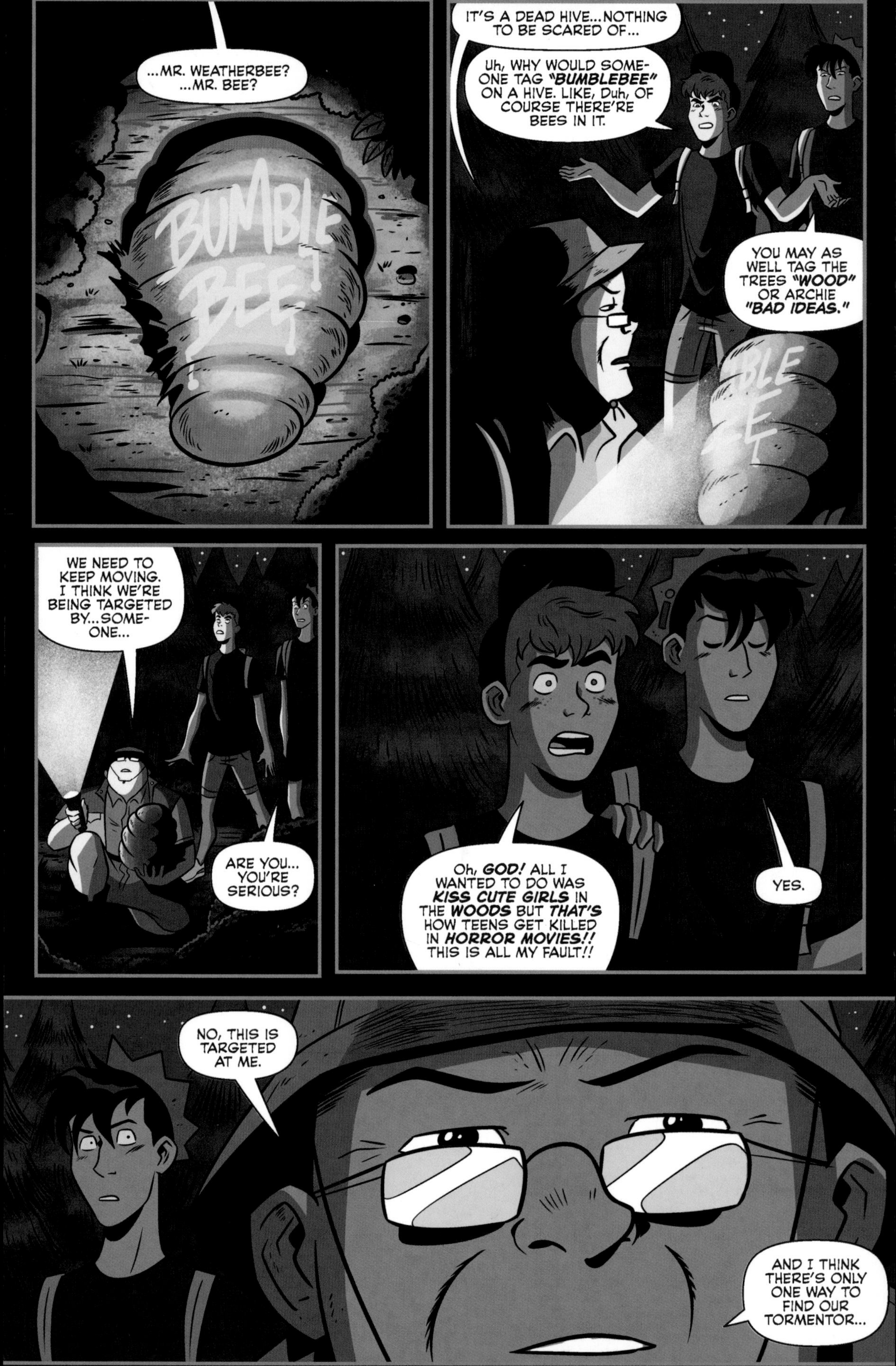
...MR. WEATHERBEE?
...MR. BEE?
BUMBLE BEE!
IT'S A DEAD HIVE...NOTHING TO BE SCARED OF...
Uh, WHY WOULD SOME-ONE TAG "BUMBLEBEE" ON A HIVE. LIKE, Duh, OF COURSE THERE'RE BEES IN IT.
YOU MAY AS WELL TAG THE TREES "WOOD" OR ARCHIE "BAD IDEAS."
WE NEED TO KEEP MOVING. I THINK WE'RE BEING TARGETED BY...SOME-ONE...
ARE YOU... YOU'RE SERIOUS?
Oh, GOD! ALL I WANTED TO DO WAS KISS CUTE GIRLS IN THE WOODS BUT THAT'S HOW TEENS GET KILLED IN HORROR MOVIES!! THIS IS ALL MY FAULT!!
YES.
NO, THIS IS TARGETED AT ME.
AND I THINK THERE'S ONLY ONE WAY TO FIND OUR TORMENTOR...

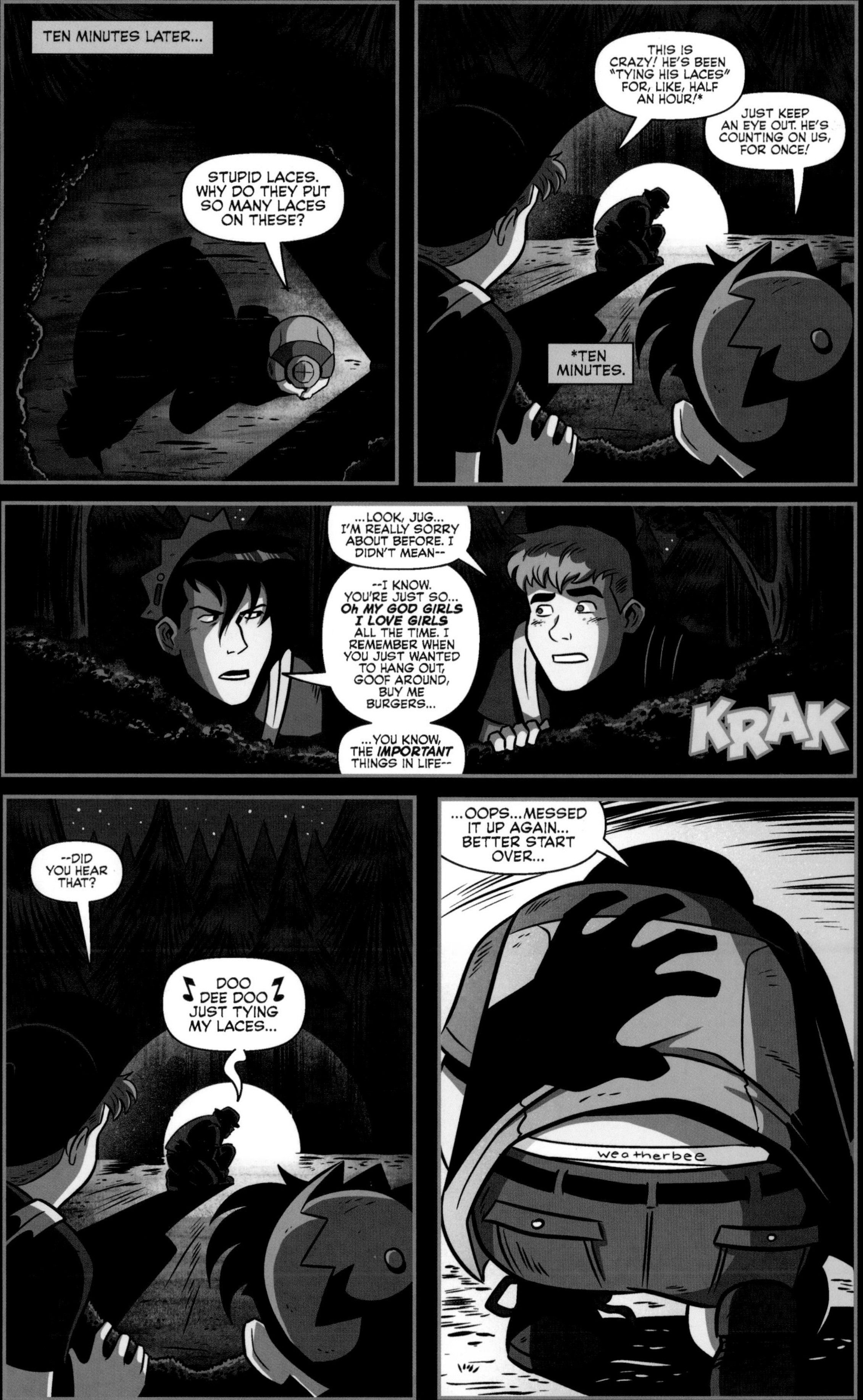
TEN MINUTES LATER...
STUPID LACES. WHY DO THEY PUT SO MANY LACES ON THESE?
THIS IS CRAZY! HE'S BEEN "TYING HIS LACES" FOR, LIKE, HALF AN HOUR!*
JUST KEEP AN EYE OUT. HE'S COUNTING ON US, FOR ONCE!
*TEN MINUTES.
...LOOK, JUG... I'M REALLY SORRY ABOUT BEFORE. I DIDN'T MEAN--
--I KNOW. YOU'RE JUST SO... ***Oh MY GOD GIRLS I LOVE GIRLS*** ALL THE TIME. I REMEMBER WHEN YOU JUST WANTED TO HANG OUT, GOOF AROUND, BUY ME BURGERS...
...YOU KNOW, THE ***IMPORTANT*** THINGS IN LIFE--
KRAK
--DID YOU HEAR THAT?
DOO DEE DOO JUST TYING MY LACES...
...OOPS...MESSED IT UP AGAIN... BETTER START OVER...
weatherbee

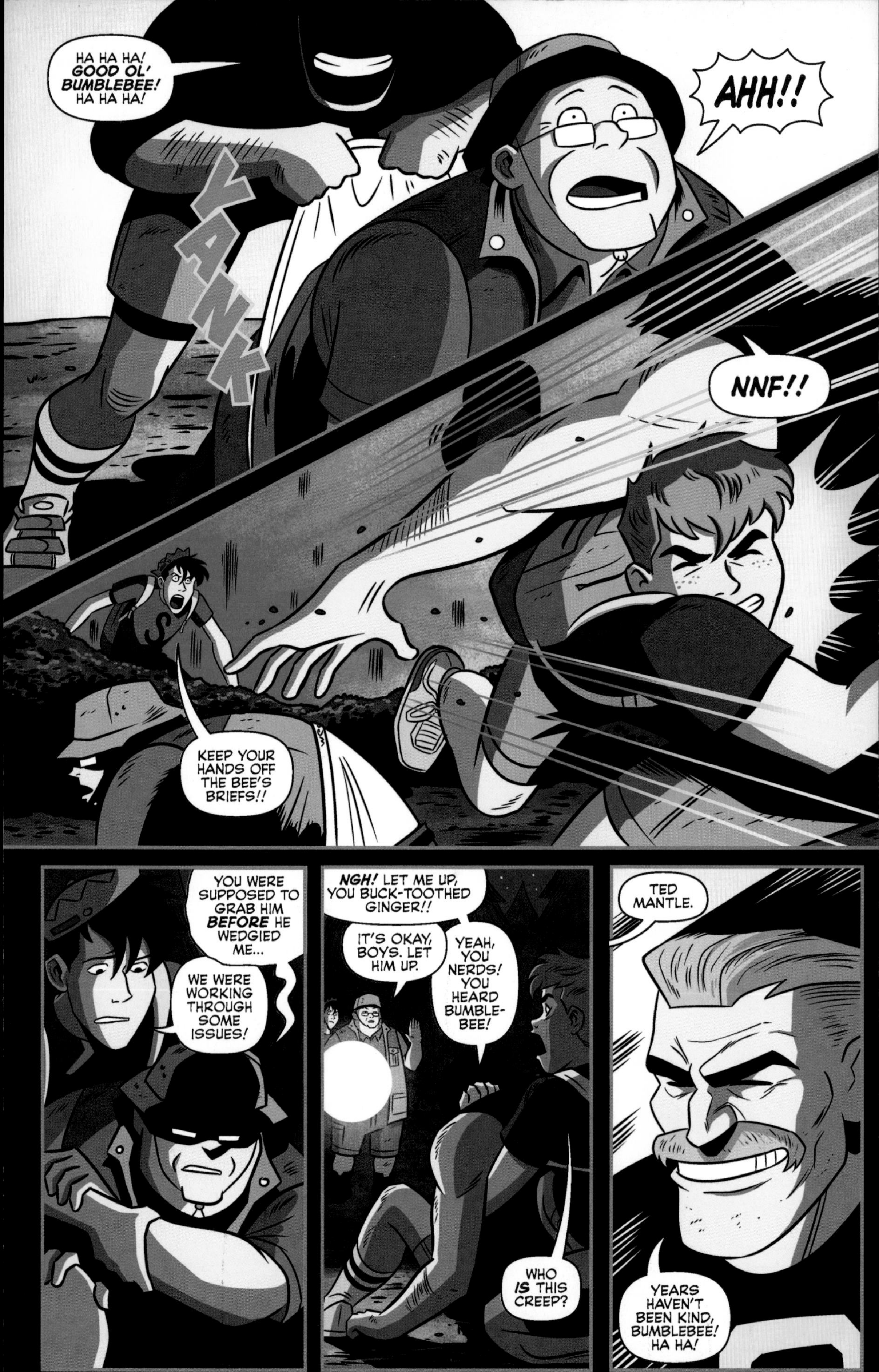
HA HA HA! ***GOOD OL'*** ***BUMBLEBEE!*** HA HA HA!
YANK
AHH!!
NNF!!
KEEP YOUR HANDS OFF THE BEE'S BRIEFS!!
YOU WERE SUPPOSED TO GRAB HIM ***BEFORE*** HE WEDGIED ME...
WE WERE WORKING THROUGH SOME ISSUES!
NGH! LET ME UP, YOU BUCK-TOOTHED GINGER!!
IT'S OKAY, BOYS. LET HIM UP.
YEAH, YOU NERDS! YOU HEARD BUMBLE-BEE!
WHO ***IS*** THIS CREEP?
TED MANTLE.
YEARS HAVEN'T BEEN KIND, BUMBLEBEE! HA HA!

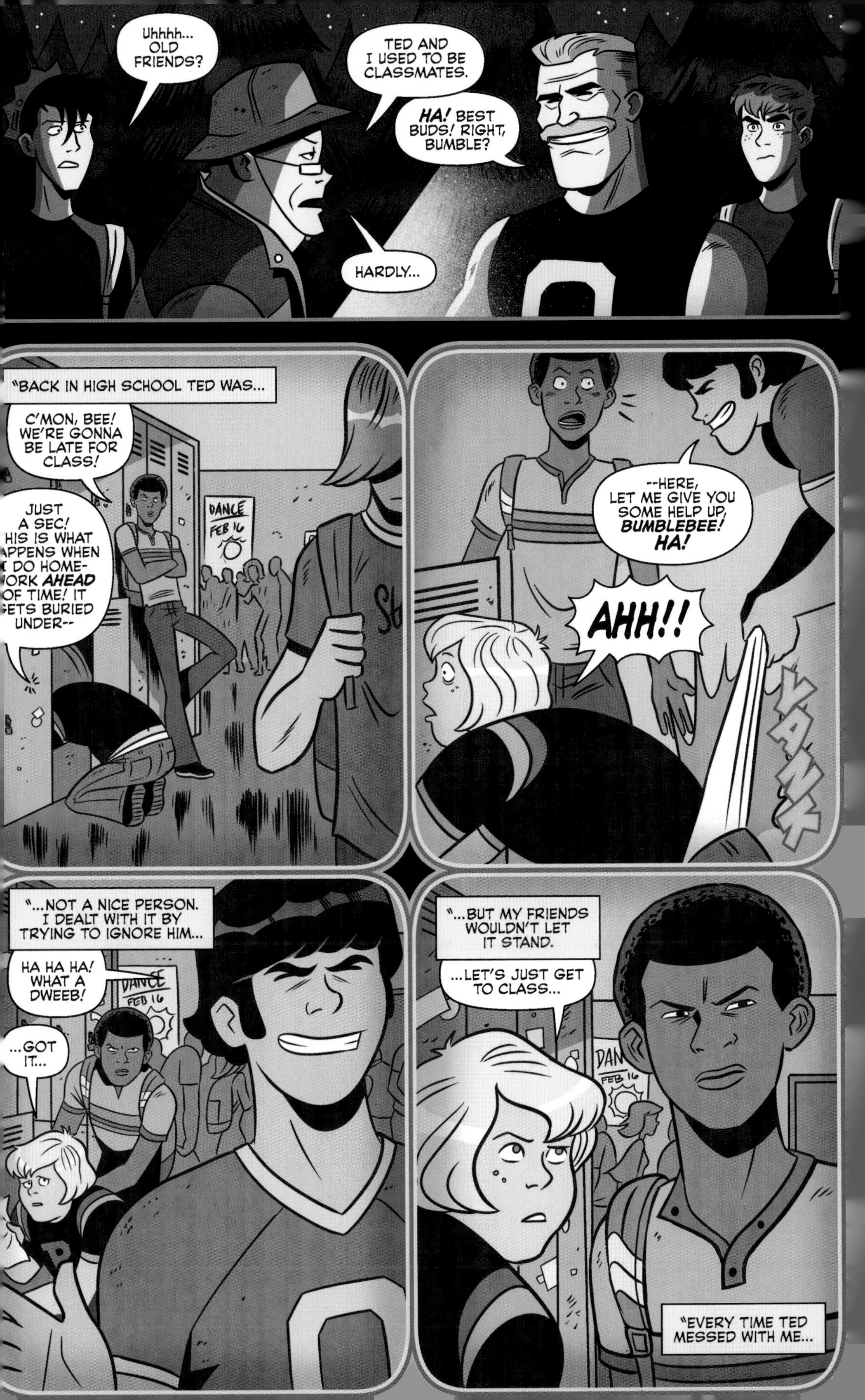
Uhhhh... OLD FRIENDS?
TED AND I USED TO BE CLASSMATES.
HA! BEST BUDS! RIGHT, BUMBLE?
HARDLY...
"BACK IN HIGH SCHOOL TED WAS...
C'MON, BEE! WE'RE GONNA BE LATE FOR CLASS!
JUST A SEC! HIS IS WHAT APPENS WHEN DO HOME-ORK AHEAD OF TIME! IT ETS BURIED UNDER--
DANCE FEB 16
--HERE, LET ME GIVE YOU SOME HELP UP, BUMBLEBEE! HA!
AHH!!
YANK
"...NOT A NICE PERSON. I DEALT WITH IT BY TRYING TO IGNORE HIM...
HA HA HA! WHAT A DWEEB!
...GOT IT...
"...BUT MY FRIENDS WOULDN'T LET IT STAND.
...LET'S JUST GET TO CLASS...
"EVERY TIME TED MESSED WITH ME...

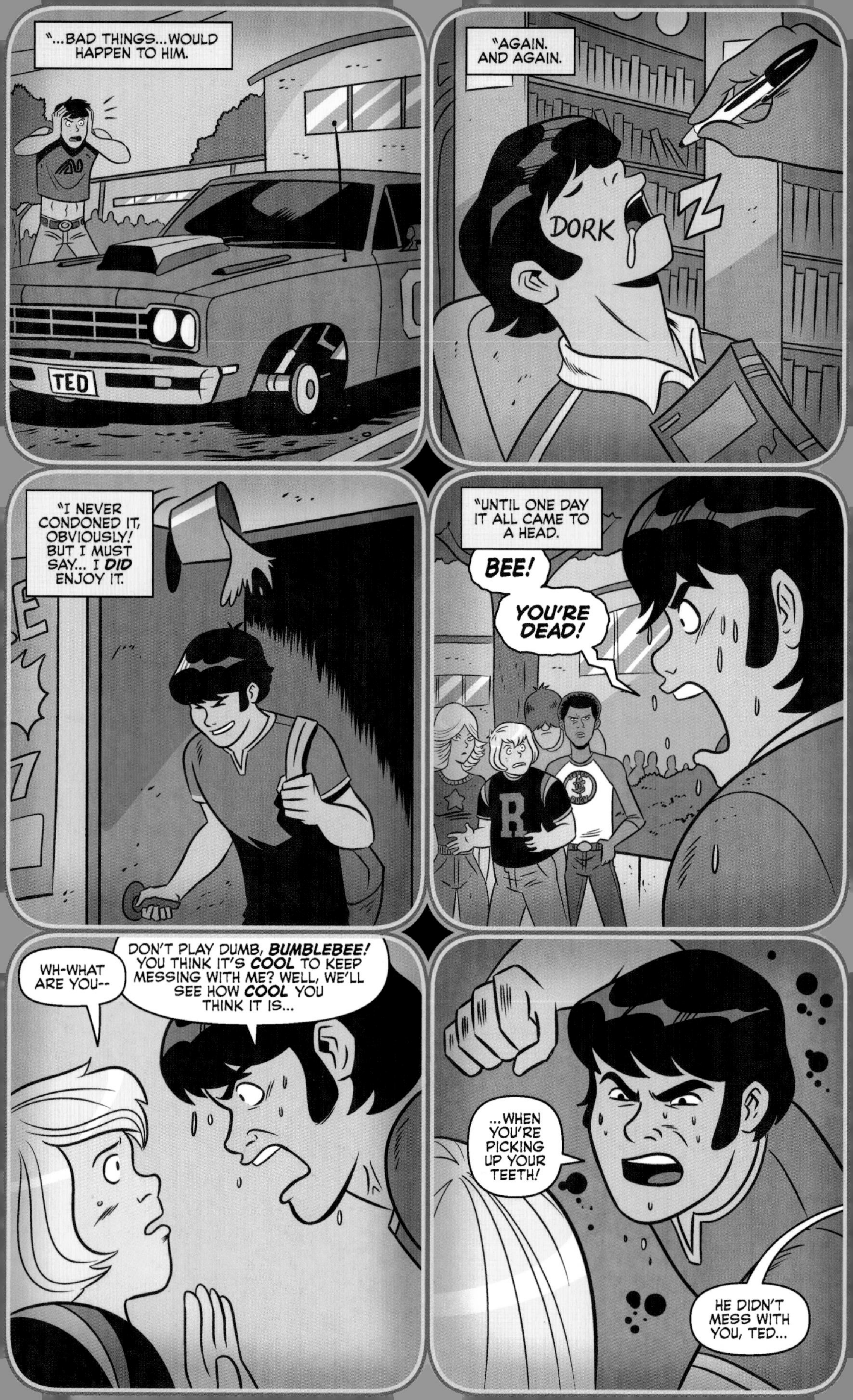
"...BAD THINGS...WOULD HAPPEN TO HIM.
TED
"AGAIN. AND AGAIN.
DORK
Z
"I NEVER CONDONED IT, OBVIOUSLY! BUT I MUST SAY... I *DID* ENJOY IT.
"UNTIL ONE DAY IT ALL CAME TO A HEAD.
BEE!
YOU'RE DEAD!
WH-WHAT ARE YOU--
DON'T PLAY DUMB, *BUMBLEBEE!* YOU THINK IT'S *COOL* TO KEEP MESSING WITH ME? WELL, WE'LL SEE HOW *COOL* YOU THINK IT IS...
...WHEN YOU'RE PICKING UP YOUR TEETH!
HE DIDN'T MESS WITH YOU, TED...

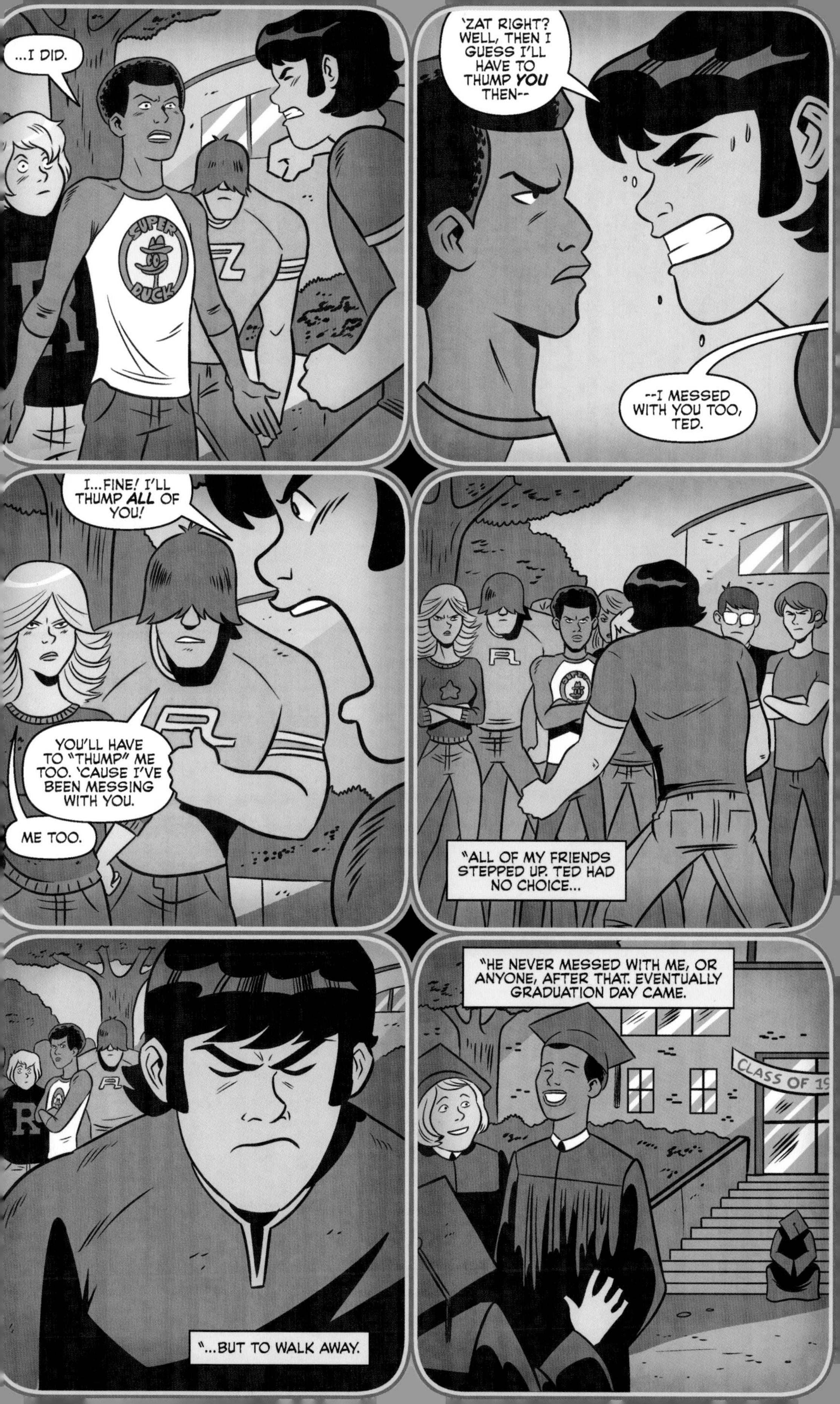
...I DID.
SUPER DUCK
'ZAT RIGHT? WELL, THEN I GUESS I'LL HAVE TO THUMP *YOU* THEN--
--I MESSED WITH YOU TOO, TED.
I...FINE! I'LL THUMP *ALL* OF YOU!
YOU'LL HAVE TO "THUMP" ME TOO. 'CAUSE I'VE BEEN MESSING WITH YOU.
ME TOO.
"ALL OF MY FRIENDS STEPPED UP. TED HAD NO CHOICE...
"...BUT TO WALK AWAY.
"HE NEVER MESSED WITH ME, OR ANYONE, AFTER THAT. EVENTUALLY GRADUATION DAY CAME.
CLASS OF 19

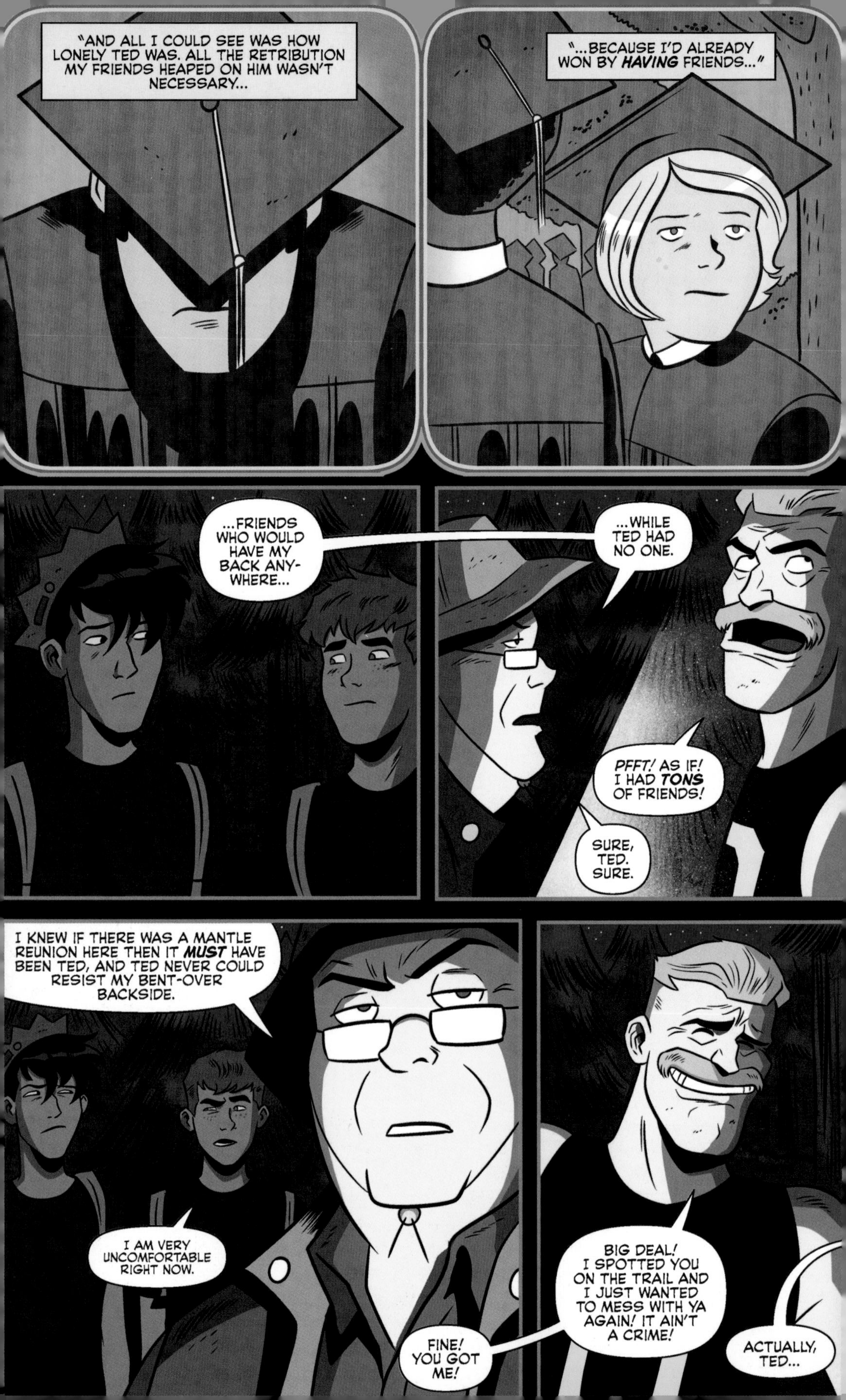
"AND ALL I COULD SEE WAS HOW LONELY TED WAS. ALL THE RETRIBUTION MY FRIENDS HEAPED ON HIM WASN'T NECESSARY...
"...BECAUSE I'D ALREADY WON BY *HAVING* FRIENDS..."
...FRIENDS WHO WOULD HAVE MY BACK ANY-WHERE...
...WHILE TED HAD NO ONE.
PFFT! AS IF! I HAD *TONS* OF FRIENDS!
SURE, TED. SURE.
I KNEW IF THERE WAS A MANTLE REUNION HERE THEN IT *MUST* HAVE BEEN TED, AND TED NEVER COULD RESIST MY BENT-OVER BACKSIDE.
I AM VERY UNCOMFORTABLE RIGHT NOW.
BIG DEAL! I SPOTTED YOU ON THE TRAIL AND I JUST WANTED TO MESS WITH YA AGAIN! IT AIN'T A CRIME!
FINE! YOU GOT ME!
ACTUALLY, TED...

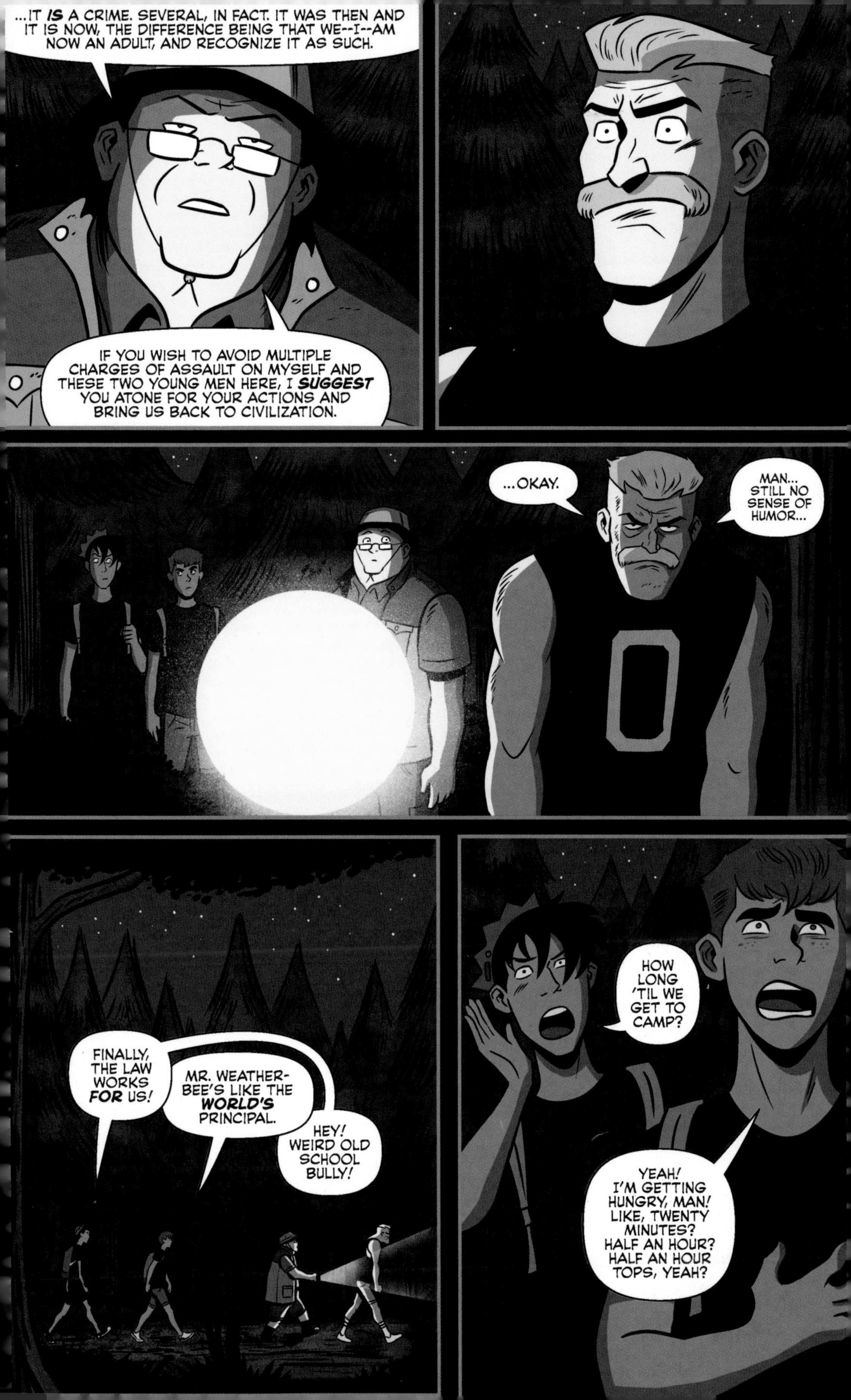

...IT *IS* A CRIME. SEVERAL, IN FACT. IT WAS THEN AND IT IS NOW, THE DIFFERENCE BEING THAT WE--I--AM NOW AN ADULT, AND RECOGNIZE IT AS SUCH.
IF YOU WISH TO AVOID MULTIPLE CHARGES OF ASSAULT ON MYSELF AND THESE TWO YOUNG MEN HERE, I ***SUGGEST*** YOU ATONE FOR YOUR ACTIONS AND BRING US BACK TO CIVILIZATION.
...OKAY.
MAN... STILL NO SENSE OF HUMOR...
FINALLY, THE LAW WORKS ***FOR*** US!
MR. WEATHERBEE'S LIKE THE ***WORLD'S*** PRINCIPAL.
HEY! WEIRD OLD SCHOOL BULLY!
HOW LONG 'TIL WE GET TO CAMP?
YEAH! I'M GETTING HUNGRY, MAN! LIKE, TWENTY MINUTES? HALF AN HOUR? HALF AN HOUR TOPS, YEAH?

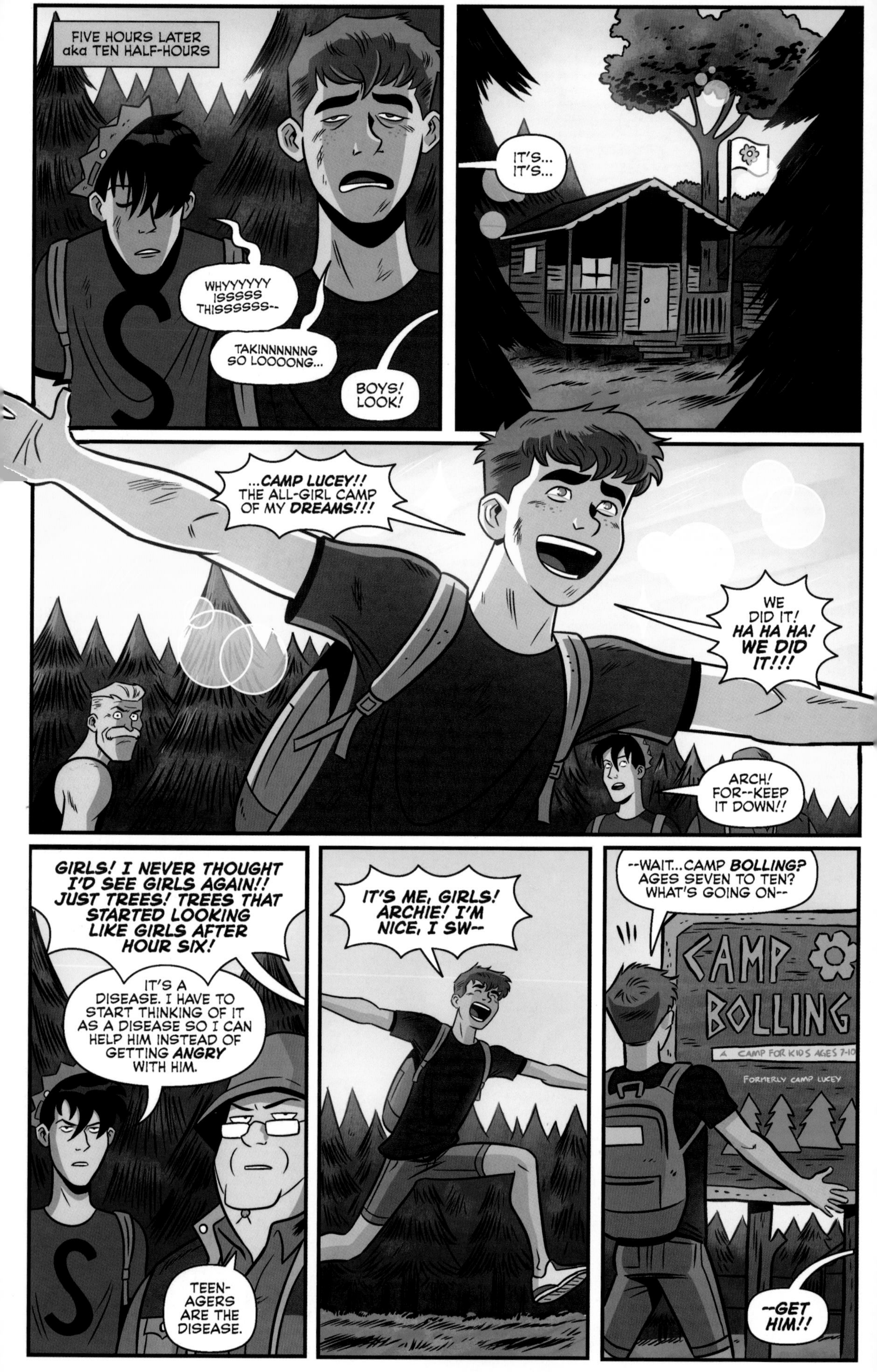
FIVE HOURS LATER aka TEN HALF-HOURS
WHYYYYYY ISSSSS THISSSSSS--
TAKINNNNNNG SO LOOOONG...
BOYS! LOOK!
IT'S... IT'S...
...CAMP LUCEY!! THE ALL-GIRL CAMP OF MY DREAMS!!!
WE DID IT! HA HA HA! WE DID IT!!!
ARCH! FOR--KEEP IT DOWN!!
GIRLS! I NEVER THOUGHT I'D SEE GIRLS AGAIN!! JUST TREES! TREES THAT STARTED LOOKING LIKE GIRLS AFTER HOUR SIX!
IT'S A DISEASE. I HAVE TO START THINKING OF IT AS A DISEASE SO I CAN HELP HIM INSTEAD OF GETTING ANGRY WITH HIM.
TEEN-AGERS ARE THE DISEASE.
IT'S ME, GIRLS! ARCHIE! I'M NICE, I SW--
--WAIT...CAMP BOLLING? AGES SEVEN TO TEN? WHAT'S GOING ON--
CAMP BOLLING
A CAMP FOR KIDS AGES 7-10
FORMERLY CAMP LUCEY
--GET HIM!!

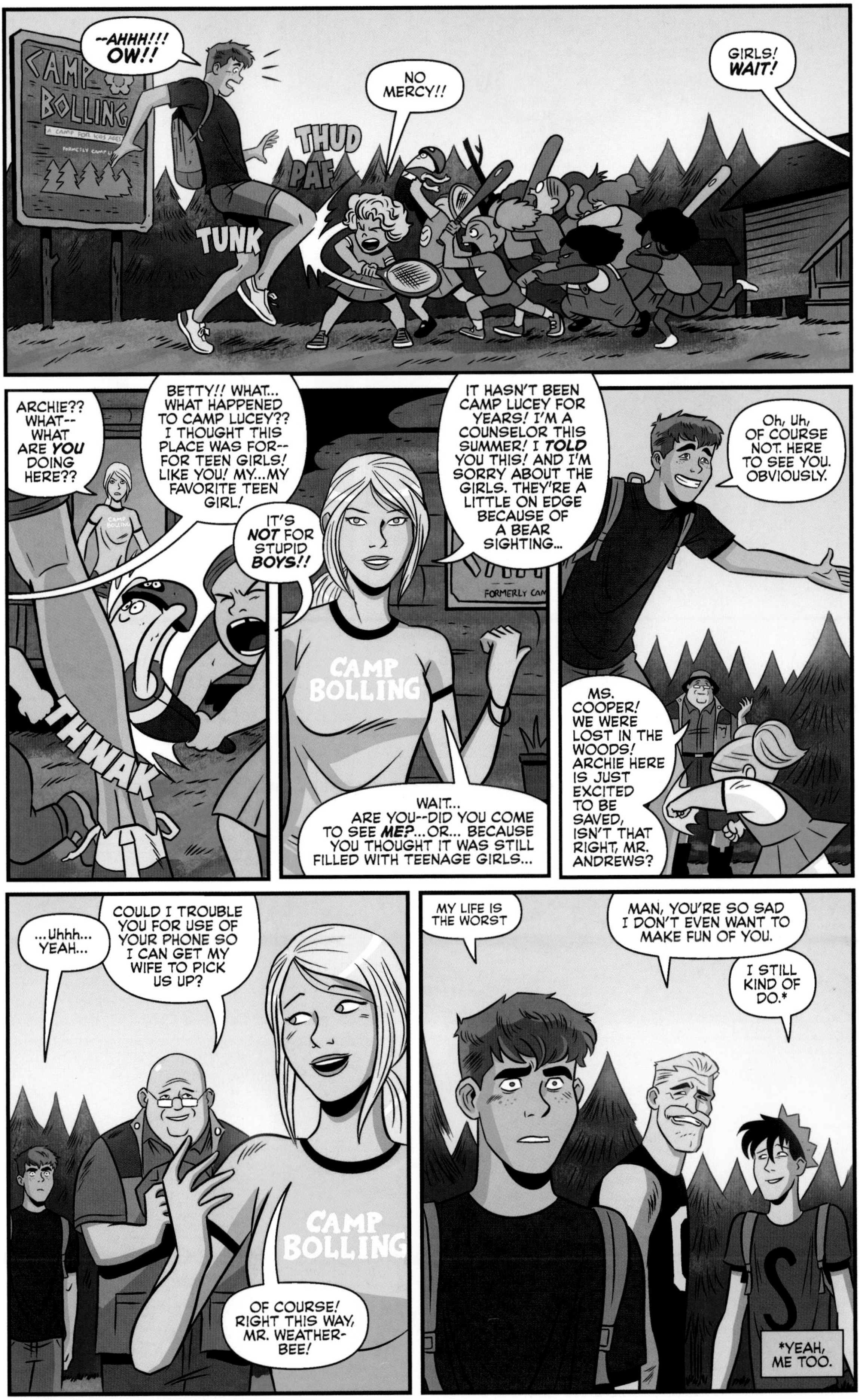
--AHHH!!! OW!!
CAMP BOLLING
A CAMP FOR KIDS AGES
FORMERLY CAMP LUCEY
THUD
PAF
TUNK
NO MERCY!!
GIRLS! WAIT!
ARCHIE?? WHAT--WHAT ARE YOU DOING HERE??
BETTY!! WHAT... WHAT HAPPENED TO CAMP LUCEY?? I THOUGHT THIS PLACE WAS FOR--FOR TEEN GIRLS! LIKE YOU! MY...MY FAVORITE TEEN GIRL!
IT'S NOT FOR STUPID BOYS!!
THWAK
IT HASN'T BEEN CAMP LUCEY FOR YEARS! I'M A COUNSELOR THIS SUMMER! I TOLD YOU THIS! AND I'M SORRY ABOUT THE GIRLS. THEY'RE A LITTLE ON EDGE BECAUSE OF A BEAR SIGHTING...
CAMP BOLLING
WAIT... ARE YOU--DID YOU COME TO SEE ME?...OR... BECAUSE YOU THOUGHT IT WAS STILL FILLED WITH TEENAGE GIRLS...
Oh, Uh, OF COURSE NOT. HERE TO SEE YOU. OBVIOUSLY.
MS. COOPER! WE WERE LOST IN THE WOODS! ARCHIE HERE IS JUST EXCITED TO BE SAVED, ISN'T THAT RIGHT, MR. ANDREWS?
...Uhhh... YEAH...
COULD I TROUBLE YOU FOR USE OF YOUR PHONE SO I CAN GET MY WIFE TO PICK US UP?
CAMP BOLLING
OF COURSE! RIGHT THIS WAY, MR. WEATHERBEE!
MY LIFE IS THE WORST
MAN, YOU'RE SO SAD I DON'T EVEN WANT TO MAKE FUN OF YOU.
I STILL KIND OF DO.*
*YEAH, ME TOO.

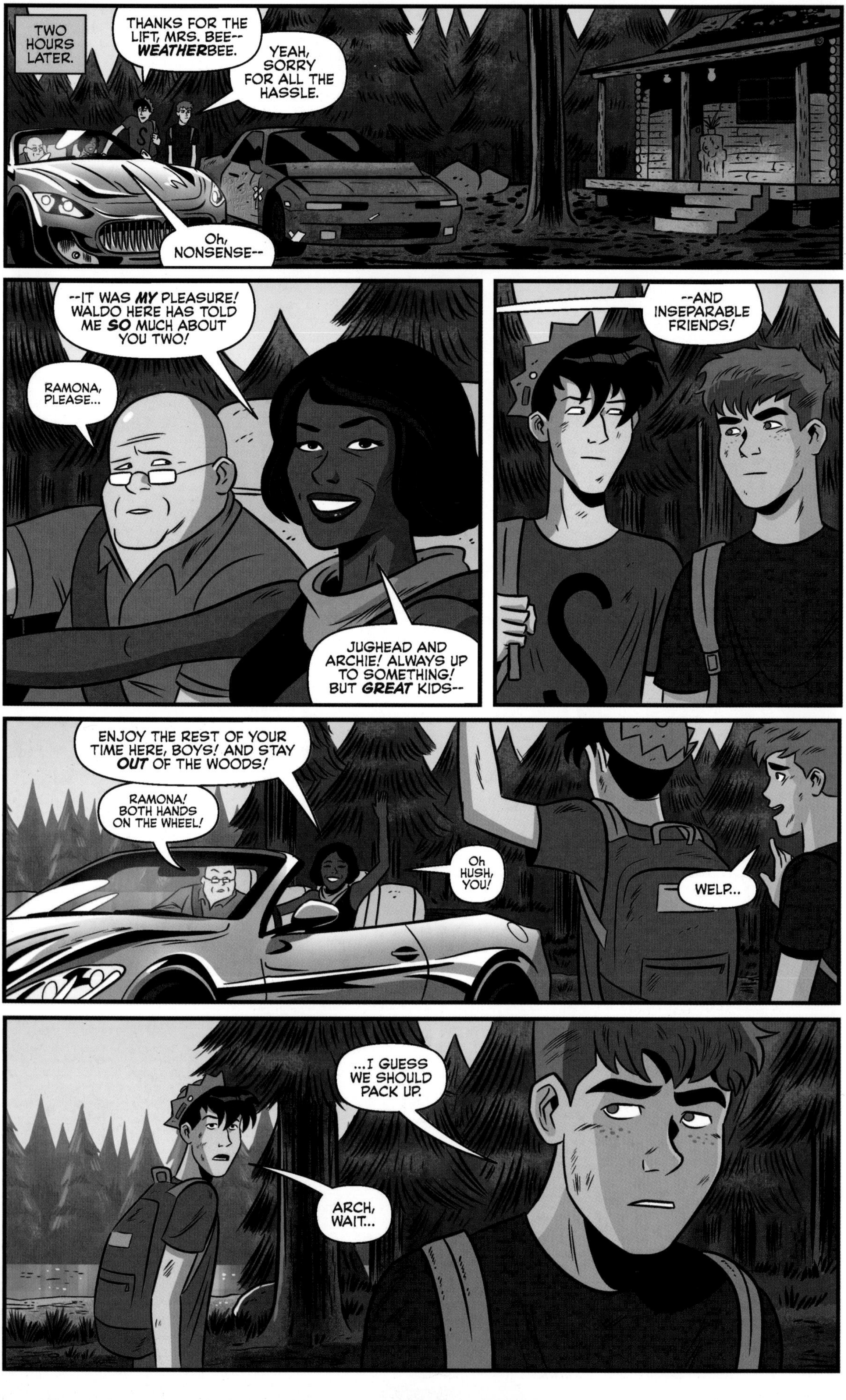
TWO HOURS LATER.
THANKS FOR THE LIFT, MRS. BEE-- WEATHERBEE.
YEAH, SORRY FOR ALL THE HASSLE.
Oh, NONSENSE--
--IT WAS MY PLEASURE! WALDO HERE HAS TOLD ME SO MUCH ABOUT YOU TWO!
RAMONA, PLEASE...
JUGHEAD AND ARCHIE! ALWAYS UP TO SOMETHING! BUT GREAT KIDS--
--AND INSEPARABLE FRIENDS!
ENJOY THE REST OF YOUR TIME HERE, BOYS! AND STAY OUT OF THE WOODS!
RAMONA! BOTH HANDS ON THE WHEEL!
Oh HUSH, YOU!
WELP...
...I GUESS WE SHOULD PACK UP.
ARCH, WAIT...

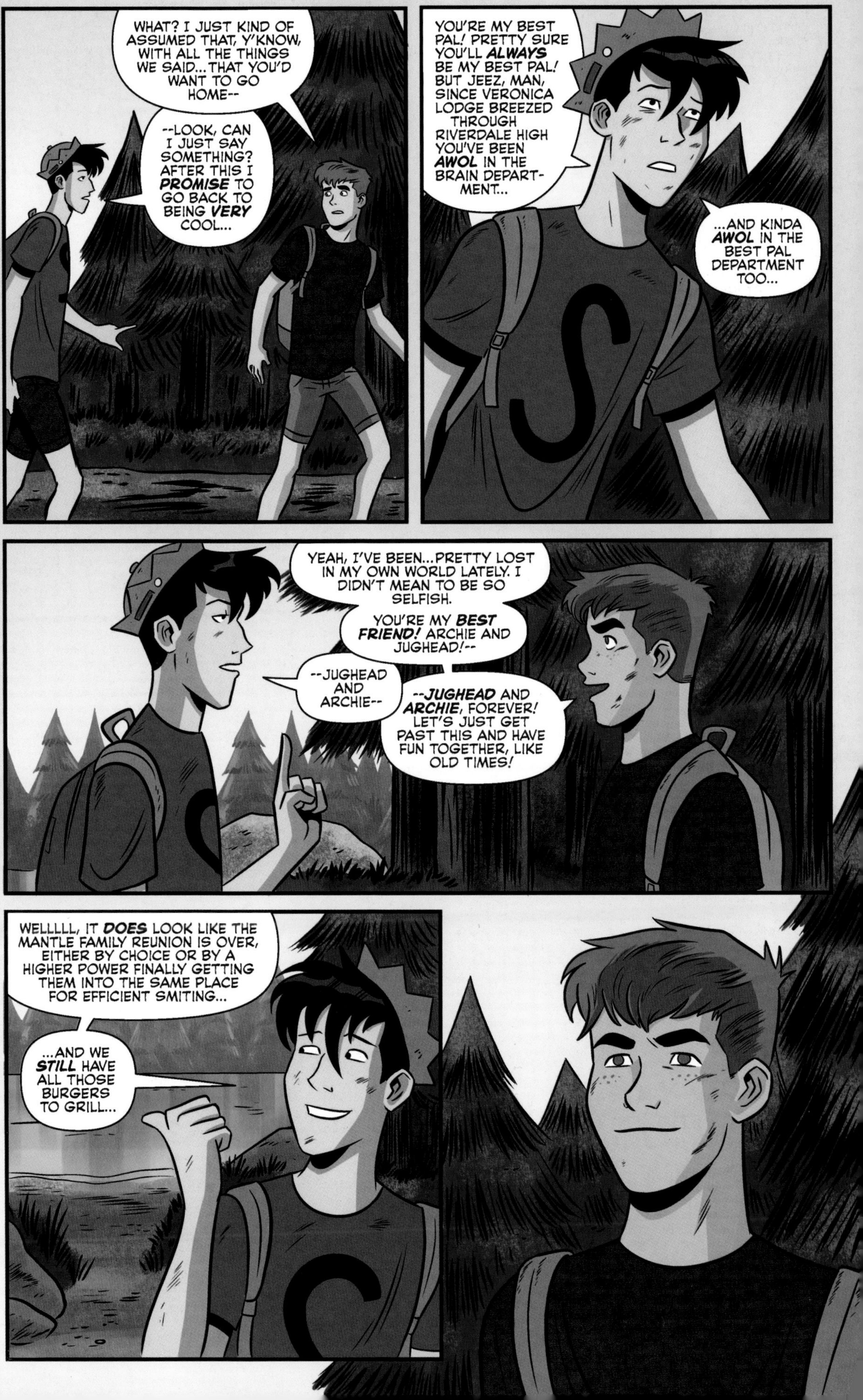
WHAT? I JUST KIND OF ASSUMED THAT, Y'KNOW, WITH ALL THE THINGS WE SAID...THAT YOU'D WANT TO GO HOME--
--LOOK, CAN I JUST SAY SOMETHING? AFTER THIS I PROMISE TO GO BACK TO BEING VERY COOL...
YOU'RE MY BEST PAL! PRETTY SURE YOU'LL ALWAYS BE MY BEST PAL! BUT JEEZ, MAN, SINCE VERONICA LODGE BREEZED THROUGH RIVERDALE HIGH YOU'VE BEEN AWOL IN THE BRAIN DEPARTMENT...
...AND KINDA AWOL IN THE BEST PAL DEPARTMENT TOO...
YEAH, I'VE BEEN...PRETTY LOST IN MY OWN WORLD LATELY. I DIDN'T MEAN TO BE SO SELFISH.
YOU'RE MY BEST FRIEND! ARCHIE AND JUGHEAD!--
--JUGHEAD AND ARCHIE--
--JUGHEAD AND ARCHIE, FOREVER! LET'S JUST GET PAST THIS AND HAVE FUN TOGETHER, LIKE OLD TIMES!
WELLLLL, IT DOES LOOK LIKE THE MANTLE FAMILY REUNION IS OVER, EITHER BY CHOICE OR BY A HIGHER POWER FINALLY GETTING THEM INTO THE SAME PLACE FOR EFFICIENT SMITING...
...AND WE STILL HAVE ALL THOSE BURGERS TO GRILL...

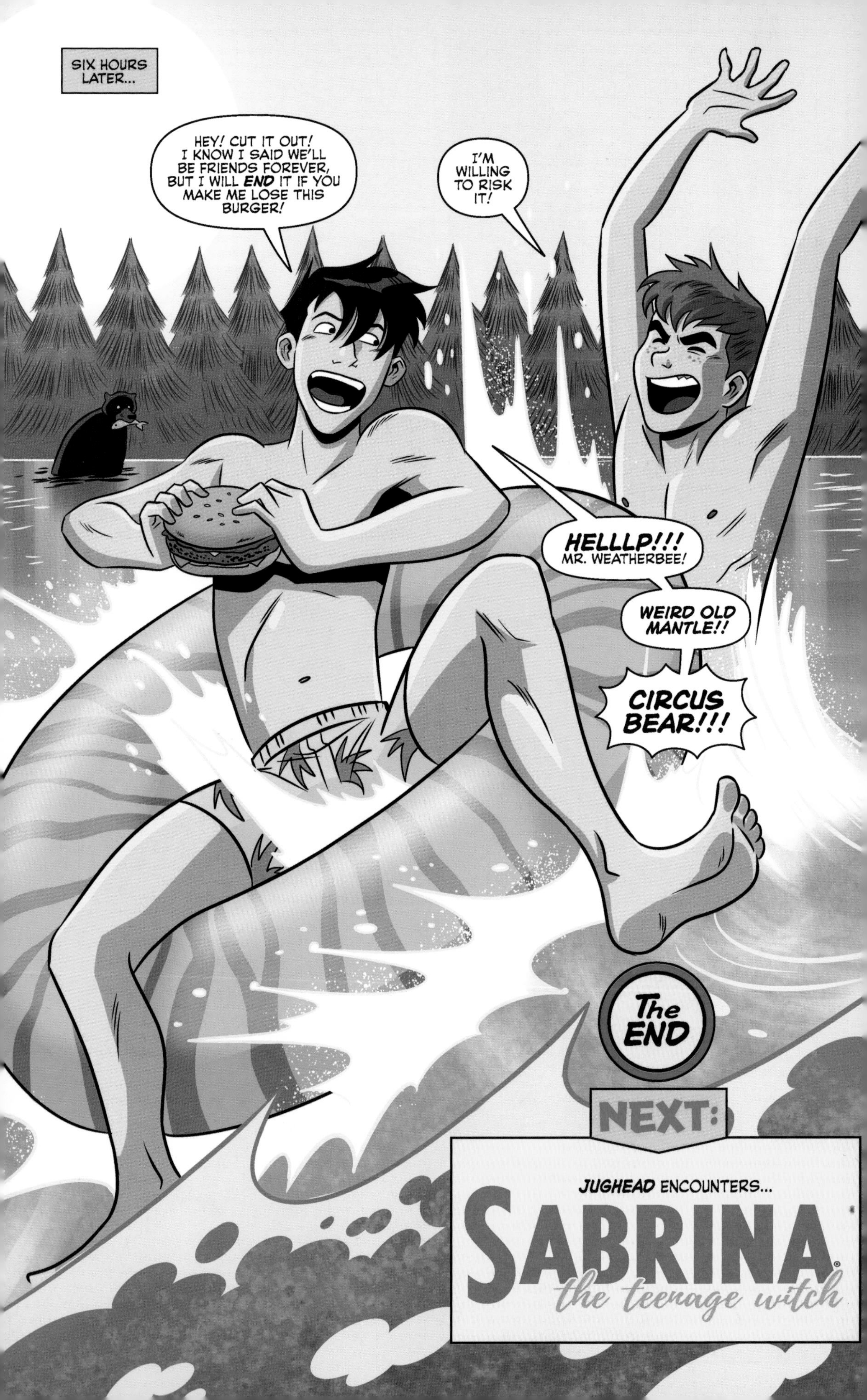
SIX HOURS LATER...
HEY! CUT IT OUT! I KNOW I SAID WE'LL BE FRIENDS FOREVER, BUT I WILL END IT IF YOU MAKE ME LOSE THIS BURGER!
I'M WILLING TO RISK IT!
HELLLP!!! MR. WEATHERBEE!
WEIRD OLD MANTLE!!
CIRCUS BEAR!!!
The END
NEXT:
JUGHEAD ENCOUNTERS...
SABRINA® the teenage witch

TO BE

CONTINUED...

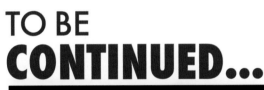

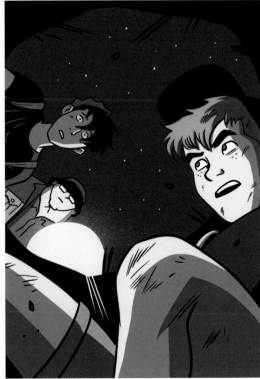

ISSUE NINE

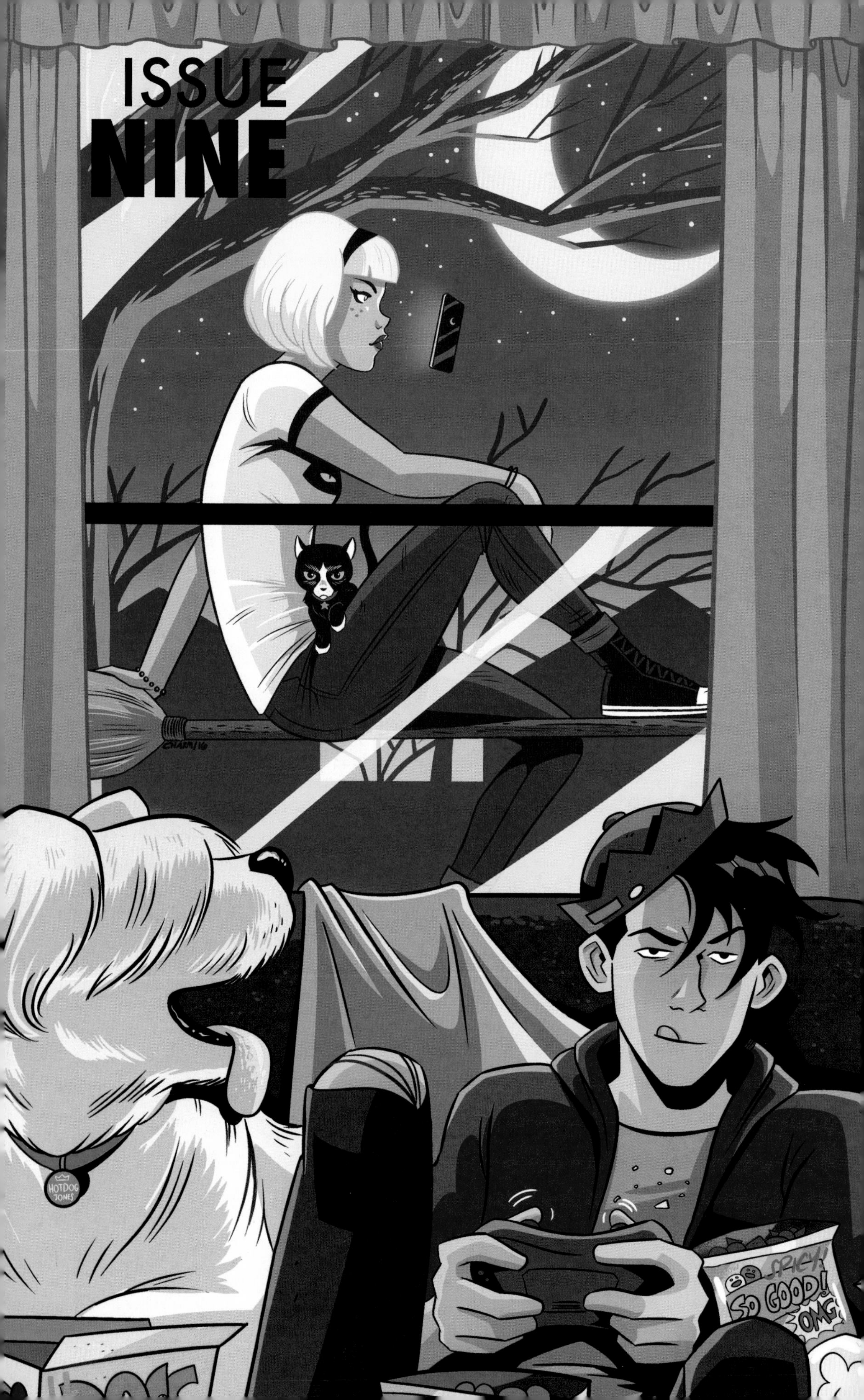
CHARM/16
HOTDOG JONES
SPICY!
SO GOOD!
OMG

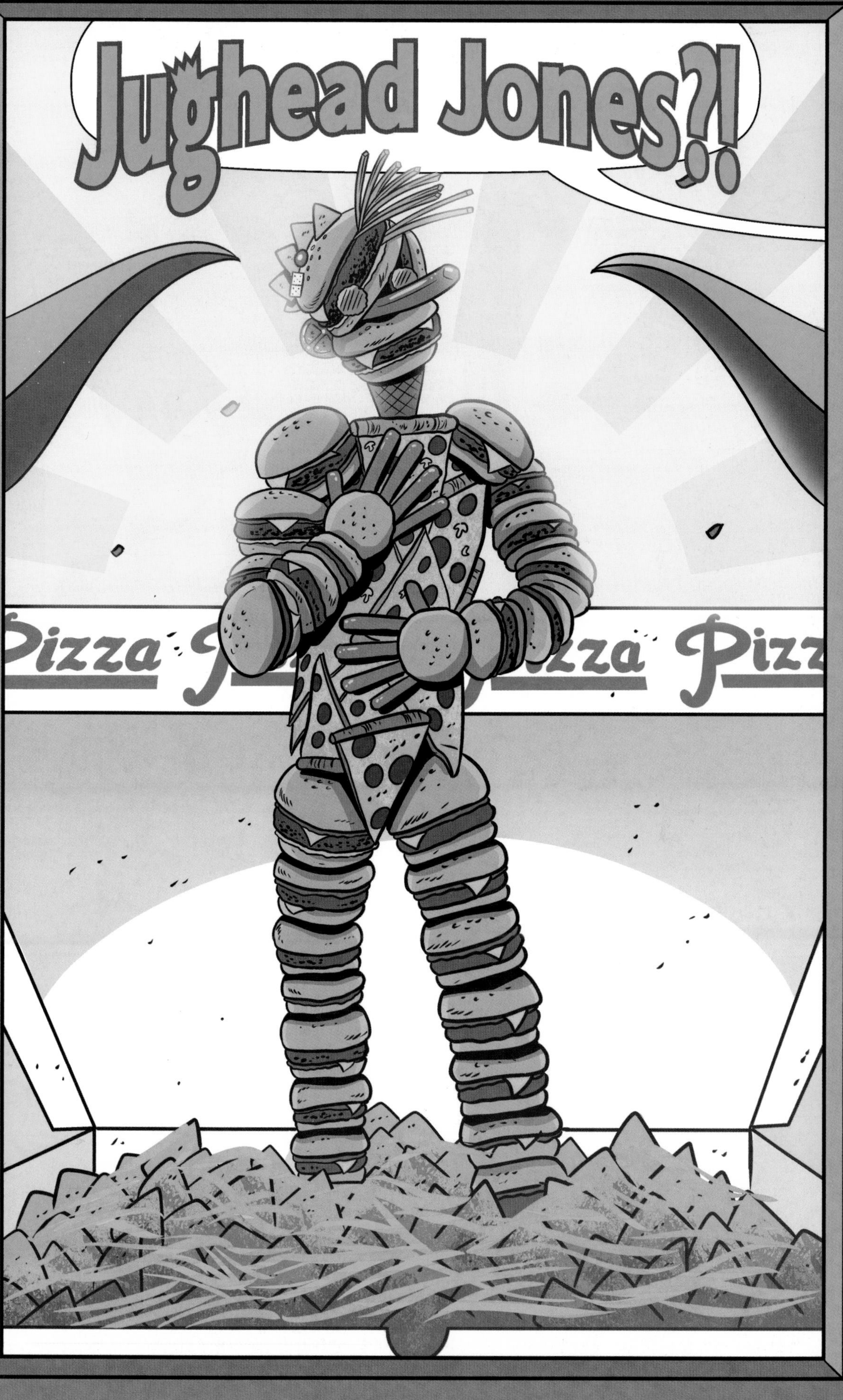
Jughead Jones?!
Pizza
Pizza
Pizz

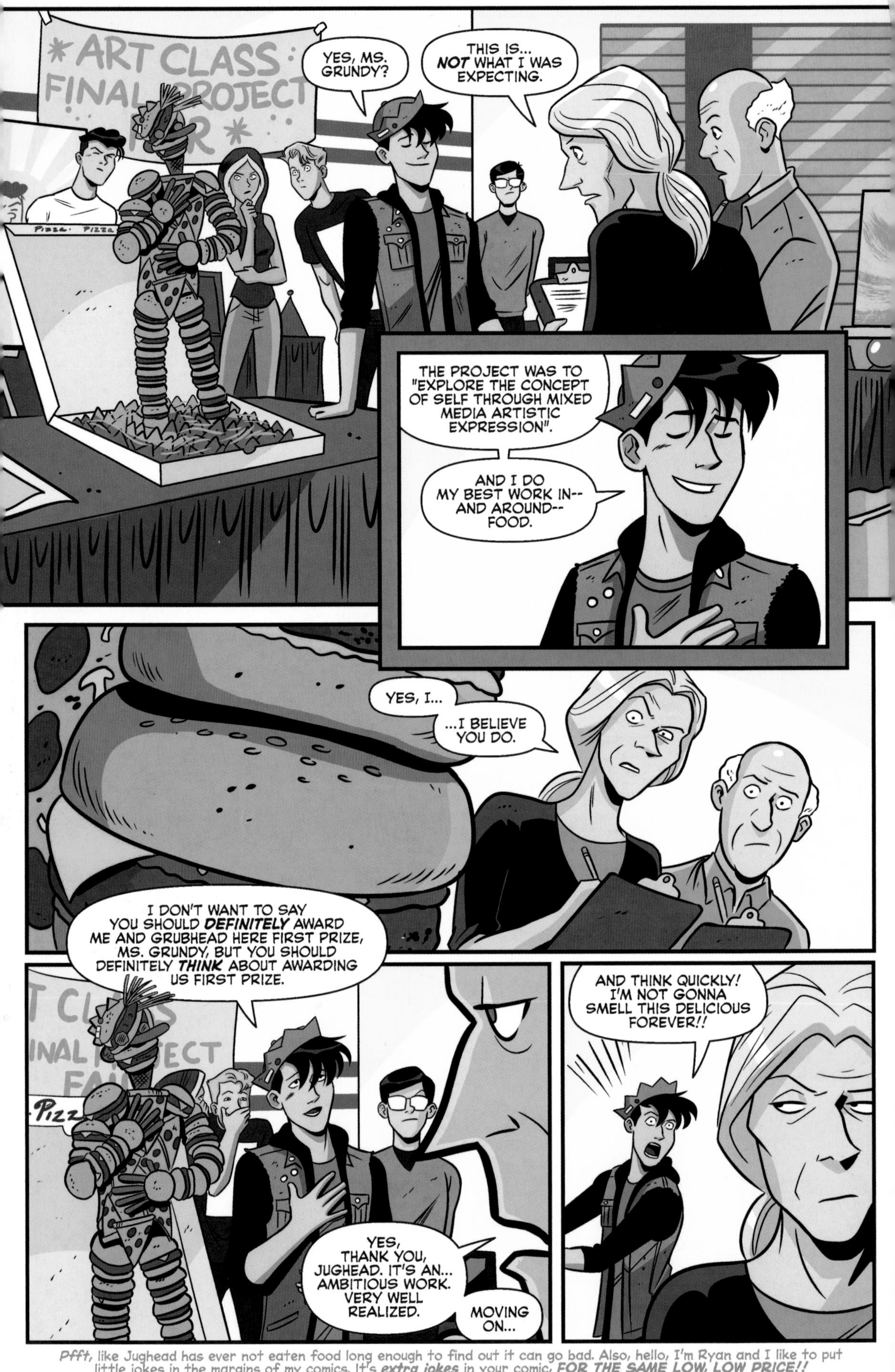
* ART CLASS: FINAL PROJECT FAIR *
PIZZA PIZZA
YES, MS. GRUNDY?
THIS IS... NOT WHAT I WAS EXPECTING.
THE PROJECT WAS TO "EXPLORE THE CONCEPT OF SELF THROUGH MIXED MEDIA ARTISTIC EXPRESSION".
AND I DO MY BEST WORK IN-- AND AROUND-- FOOD.
YES, I...
...I BELIEVE YOU DO.
I DON'T WANT TO SAY YOU SHOULD DEFINITELY AWARD ME AND GRUBHEAD HERE FIRST PRIZE, MS. GRUNDY, BUT YOU SHOULD DEFINITELY THINK ABOUT AWARDING US FIRST PRIZE.
YES, THANK YOU, JUGHEAD. IT'S AN... AMBITIOUS WORK. VERY WELL REALIZED.
MOVING ON...
AND THINK QUICKLY! I'M NOT GONNA SMELL THIS DELICIOUS FOREVER!!

Pfft, like Jughead has ever not eaten food long enough to find out it can go bad. Also, hello, I'm Ryan and I like to put little jokes in the margins of my comics. It's ***extra jokes*** in your comic, **FOR THE SAME LOW, LOW PRICE!!** That's right: Chip was **RIPPING YOU OFF**.

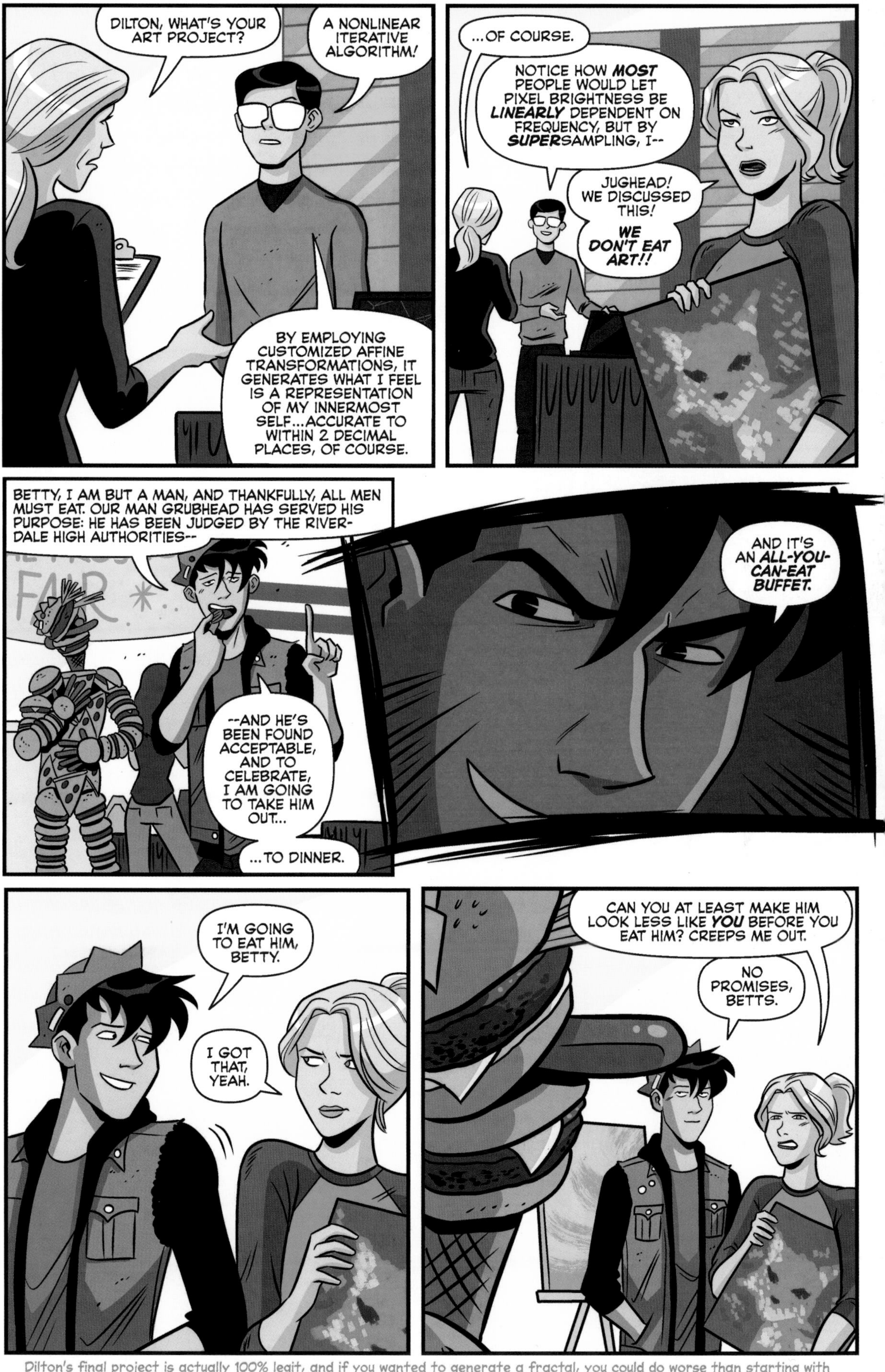
DILTON, WHAT'S YOUR ART PROJECT?
A NONLINEAR ITERATIVE ALGORITHM!
BY EMPLOYING CUSTOMIZED AFFINE TRANSFORMATIONS, IT GENERATES WHAT I FEEL IS A REPRESENTATION OF MY INNERMOST SELF...ACCURATE TO WITHIN 2 DECIMAL PLACES, OF COURSE.
...OF COURSE.
NOTICE HOW **MOST** PEOPLE WOULD LET PIXEL BRIGHTNESS BE **LINEARLY** DEPENDENT ON FREQUENCY, BUT BY **SUPER**SAMPLING, I--
JUGHEAD! WE DISCUSSED THIS!
WE DON'T EAT ART!!
BETTY, I AM BUT A MAN, AND THANKFULLY, ALL MEN MUST EAT. OUR MAN GRUBHEAD HAS SERVED HIS PURPOSE: HE HAS BEEN JUDGED BY THE RIVERDALE HIGH AUTHORITIES--
FAIR
--AND HE'S BEEN FOUND ACCEPTABLE, AND TO CELEBRATE, I AM GOING TO TAKE HIM OUT...
...TO DINNER.
AND IT'S AN **ALL-YOU-CAN-EAT BUFFET.**
I'M GOING TO EAT HIM, BETTY.
I GOT THAT, YEAH.
CAN YOU AT LEAST MAKE HIM LOOK LESS LIKE **YOU** BEFORE YOU EAT HIM? CREEPS ME OUT.
NO PROMISES, BETTS.

Dilton's final project is actually 100% legit, and if you wanted to generate a fractal, you could do worse than starting with a nonlinear iterative algorithm with affine transformations. Those of you big into both nonlinear iterative algorithms *and* teen comedy comics are nodding your heads right now. I can tell.

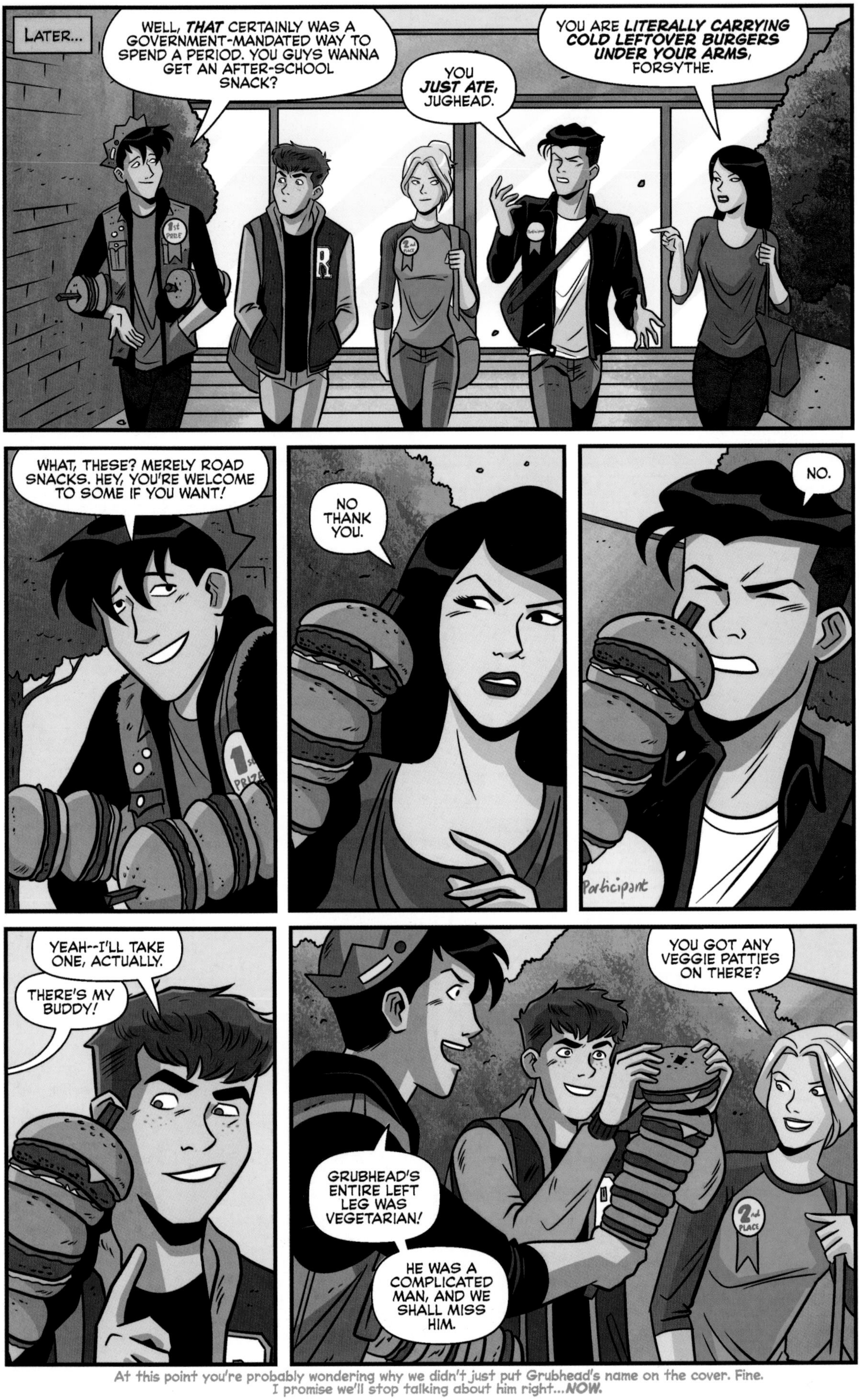
LATER...
WELL, **THAT** CERTAINLY WAS A GOVERNMENT-MANDATED WAY TO SPEND A PERIOD. YOU GUYS WANNA GET AN AFTER-SCHOOL SNACK?
YOU **JUST ATE,** JUGHEAD.
YOU ARE **LITERALLY CARRYING COLD LEFTOVER BURGERS UNDER YOUR ARMS,** FORSYTHE.
WHAT, THESE? MERELY ROAD SNACKS. HEY, YOU'RE WELCOME TO SOME IF YOU WANT!
NO THANK YOU.
NO.
Participant
YEAH--I'LL TAKE ONE, ACTUALLY.
THERE'S MY BUDDY!
YOU GOT ANY VEGGIE PATTIES ON THERE?
GRUBHEAD'S ENTIRE LEFT LEG WAS VEGETARIAN!
HE WAS A COMPLICATED MAN, AND WE SHALL MISS HIM.

At this point you're probably wondering why we didn't just put Grubhead's name on the cover. Fine.
I promise we'll stop talking about him right... ***NOW.***

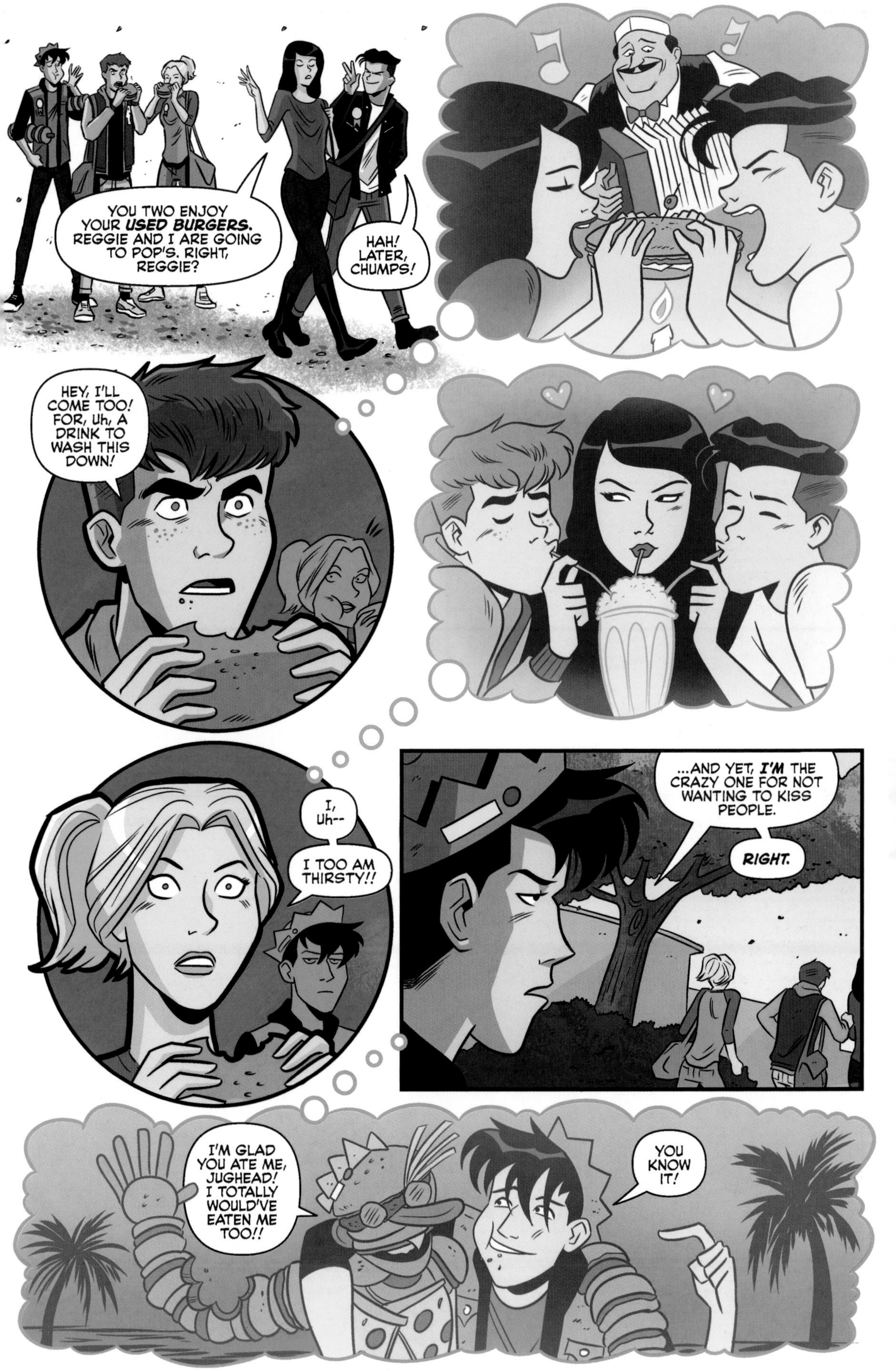
YOU TWO ENJOY YOUR USED BURGERS. REGGIE AND I ARE GOING TO POP'S. RIGHT, REGGIE?
HAH! LATER, CHUMPS!
HEY, I'LL COME TOO! FOR, Uh, A DRINK TO WASH THIS DOWN!
I, Uh--
I TOO AM THIRSTY!!
...AND YET, I'M THE CRAZY ONE FOR NOT WANTING TO KISS PEOPLE.
RIGHT.
I'M GLAD YOU ATE ME, JUGHEAD! I TOTALLY WOULD'VE EATEN ME TOO!!
YOU KNOW IT!

GRUBHEAD RETURNS, LOOKS LIKE I'M A UNRELIABLE NARRATOR!! HAH HAH HAH OH WELL

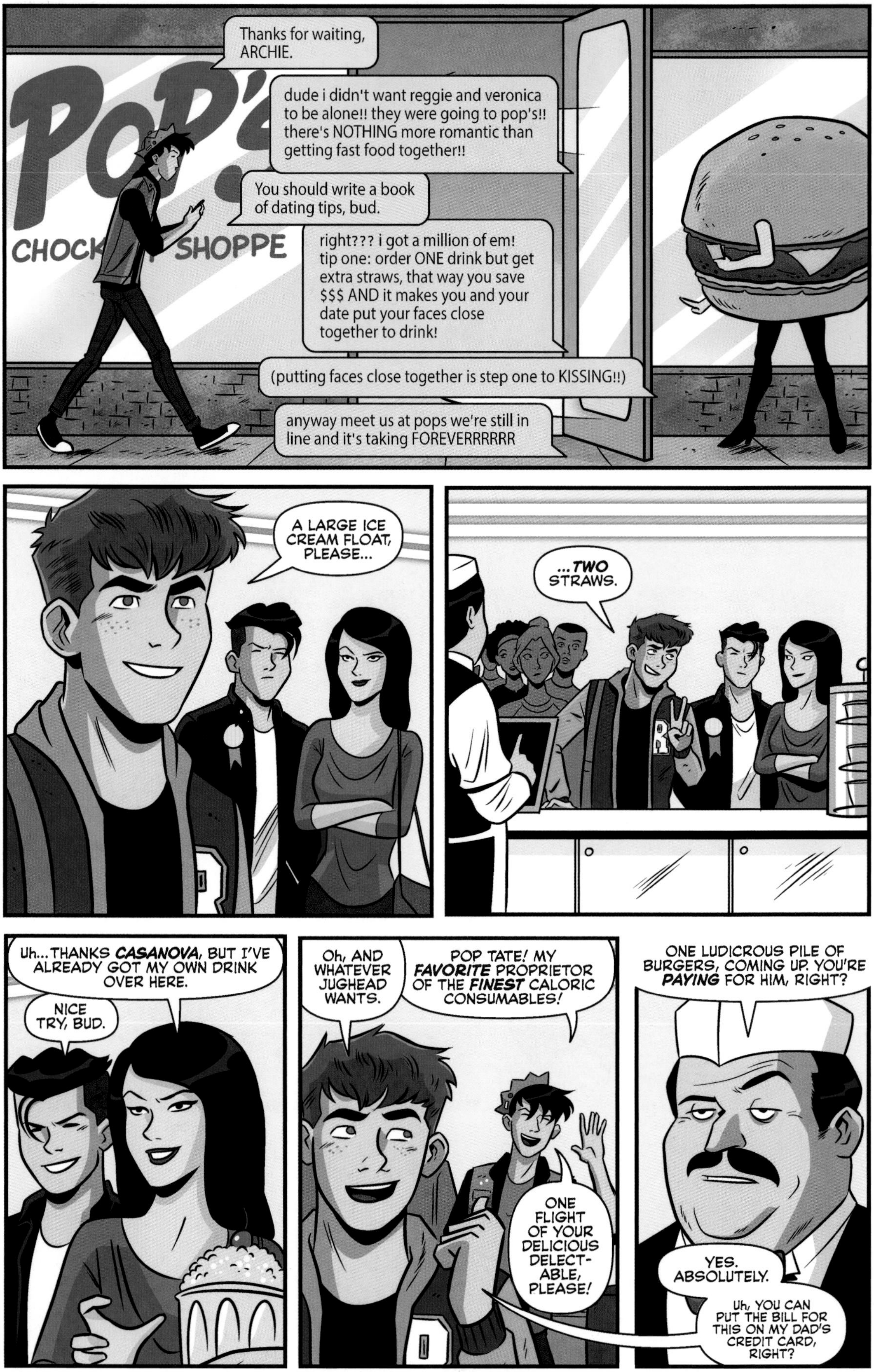
Thanks for waiting, ARCHIE.
dude i didn't want reggie and veronica to be alone!! they were going to pop's!! there's NOTHING more romantic than getting fast food together!!
You should write a book of dating tips, bud.
right??? i got a million of em! tip one: order ONE drink but get extra straws, that way you save $$$ AND it makes you and your date put your faces close together to drink!
(putting faces close together is step one to KISSING!!)
anyway meet us at pops we're still in line and it's taking FOREVERRRRRR
POP'S
CHOCK SHOPPE
A LARGE ICE CREAM FLOAT, PLEASE...
...TWO STRAWS.
Uh...THANKS CASANOVA, BUT I'VE ALREADY GOT MY OWN DRINK OVER HERE.
NICE TRY, BUD.
Oh, AND WHATEVER JUGHEAD WANTS.
POP TATE! MY FAVORITE PROPRIETOR OF THE FINEST CALORIC CONSUMABLES!
ONE FLIGHT OF YOUR DELICIOUS DELECTABLE, PLEASE!
ONE LUDICROUS PILE OF BURGERS, COMING UP. YOU'RE PAYING FOR HIM, RIGHT?
YES. ABSOLUTELY.
Uh, YOU CAN PUT THE BILL FOR THIS ON MY DAD'S CREDIT CARD, RIGHT?

Tip two in "The Archie Andrews Guide To Dating" is "If you accidentally invite two women to the same dance on the same night, wear a different outfit with each of them. This will prevent them from spotting you in the crowd, and is absolutely preferable to a forthright and mature apology and explanation about your error in scheduling."

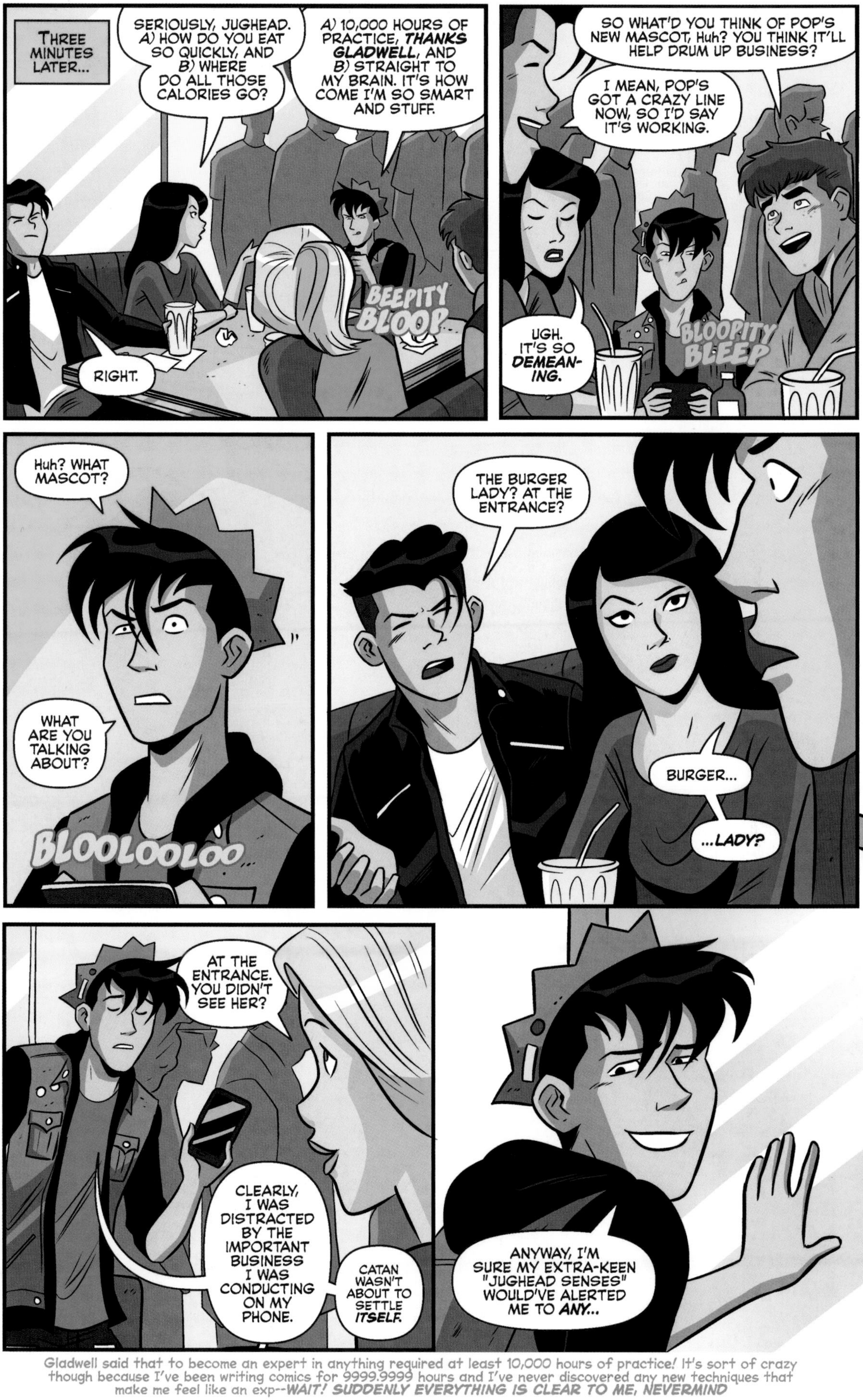
THREE MINUTES LATER...
SERIOUSLY, JUGHEAD. A) HOW DO YOU EAT SO QUICKLY, AND B) WHERE DO ALL THOSE CALORIES GO?
A) 10,000 HOURS OF PRACTICE, THANKS GLADWELL, AND B) STRAIGHT TO MY BRAIN. IT'S HOW COME I'M SO SMART AND STUFF.
RIGHT.
BEEPITY BLOOP
SO WHAT'D YOU THINK OF POP'S NEW MASCOT, Huh? YOU THINK IT'LL HELP DRUM UP BUSINESS?
I MEAN, POP'S GOT A CRAZY LINE NOW, SO I'D SAY IT'S WORKING.
UGH. IT'S SO DEMEAN-ING.
BLOOPITY BLEEP
Huh? WHAT MASCOT?
WHAT ARE YOU TALKING ABOUT?
BLOOLOOLOO
THE BURGER LADY? AT THE ENTRANCE?
BURGER...
...LADY?
AT THE ENTRANCE. YOU DIDN'T SEE HER?
CLEARLY, I WAS DISTRACTED BY THE IMPORTANT BUSINESS I WAS CONDUCTING ON MY PHONE.
CATAN WASN'T ABOUT TO SETTLE ITSELF.
ANYWAY, I'M SURE MY EXTRA-KEEN "JUGHEAD SENSES" WOULD'VE ALERTED ME TO ANY...

Gladwell said that to become an expert in anything required at least 10,000 hours of practice! It's sort of crazy though because I've been writing comics for 9999.9999 hours and I've never discovered any new techniques that make me feel like an exp--***WAIT! SUDDENLY EVERYTHING IS CLEAR TO ME, NEVERMIND***

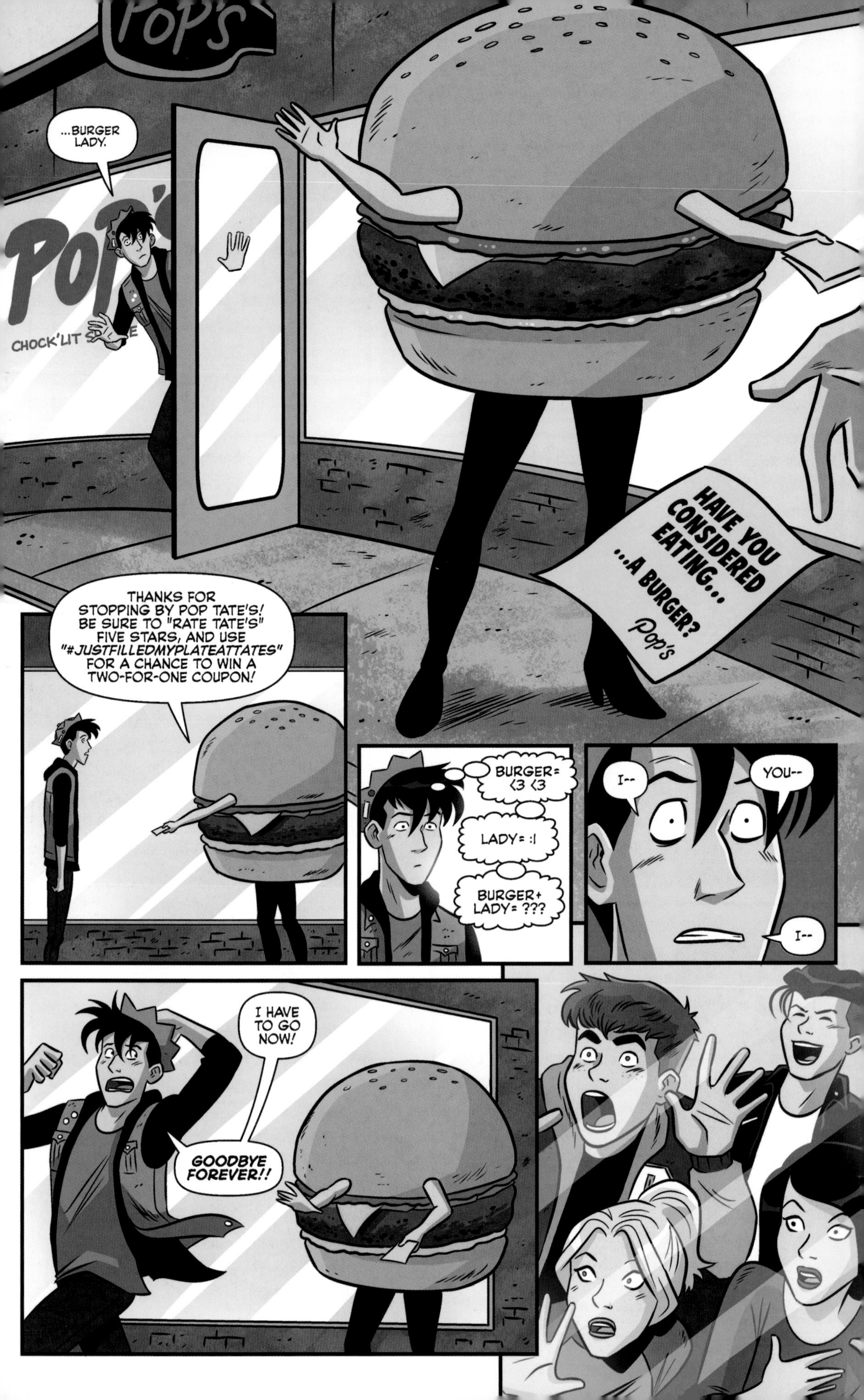
POP'S
...BURGER LADY.
POP'S
CHOCK'LIT S
HAVE YOU CONSIDERED EATING... ...A BURGER?
Pop's
THANKS FOR STOPPING BY POP TATE'S! BE SURE TO "RATE TATE'S" FIVE STARS, AND USE "#JUSTFILLEDMYPLATEATTATES" FOR A CHANCE TO WIN A TWO-FOR-ONE COUPON!
BURGER= <3 <3
LADY= :|
BURGER+ LADY= ???
I--
YOU--
I--
I HAVE TO GO NOW!
GOODBYE FOREVER!!

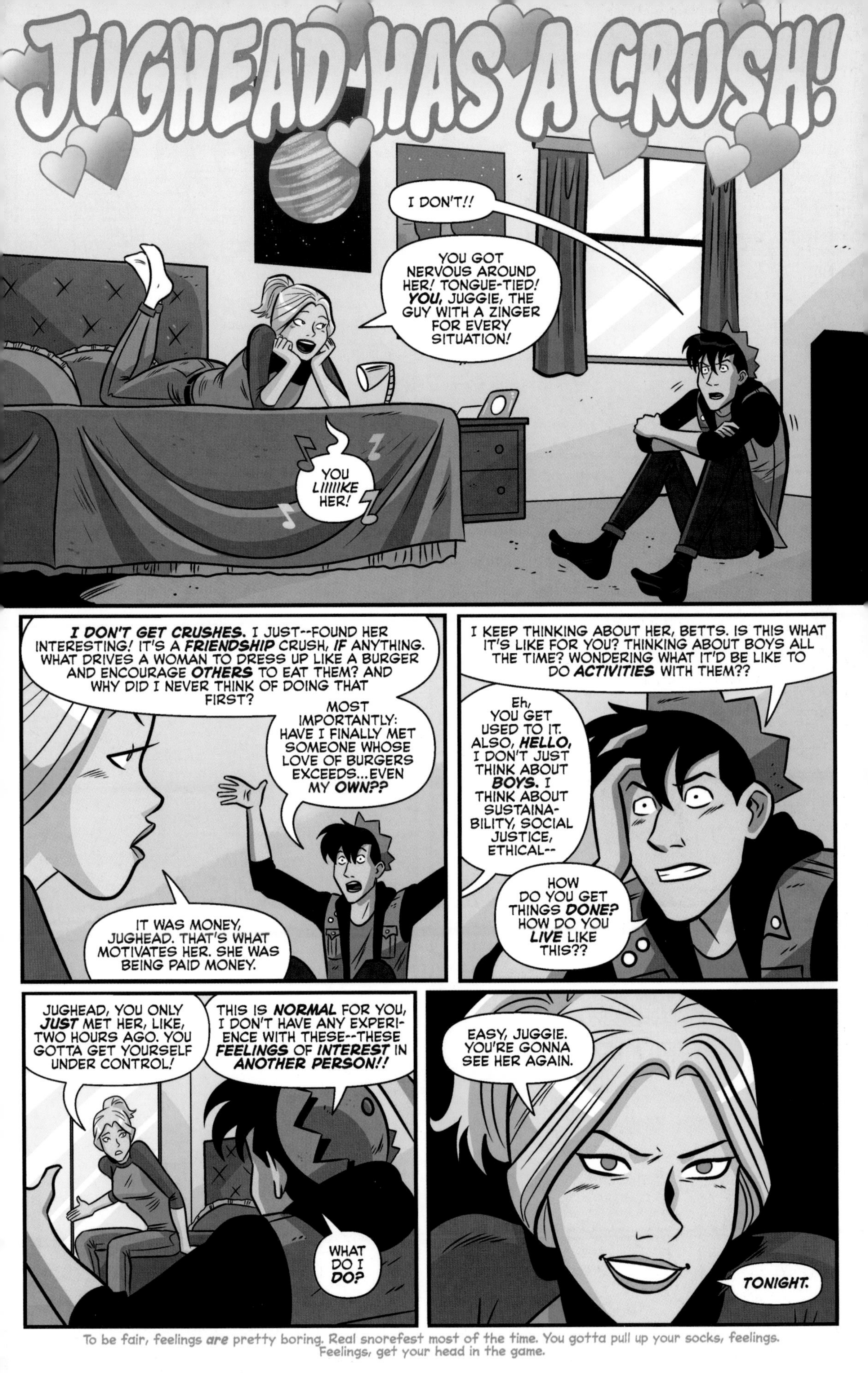
JUGHEAD HAS A CRUSH!
YOU GOT NERVOUS AROUND HER! TONGUE-TIED! YOU, JUGGIE, THE GUY WITH A ZINGER FOR EVERY SITUATION!
I DON'T!!
YOU LIIIIIKE HER!
I DON'T GET CRUSHES. I JUST--FOUND HER INTERESTING! IT'S A FRIENDSHIP CRUSH, IF ANYTHING. WHAT DRIVES A WOMAN TO DRESS UP LIKE A BURGER AND ENCOURAGE OTHERS TO EAT THEM? AND WHY DID I NEVER THINK OF DOING THAT FIRST?
MOST IMPORTANTLY: HAVE I FINALLY MET SOMEONE WHOSE LOVE OF BURGERS EXCEEDS...EVEN MY OWN??
IT WAS MONEY, JUGHEAD. THAT'S WHAT MOTIVATES HER. SHE WAS BEING PAID MONEY.
I KEEP THINKING ABOUT HER, BETTS. IS THIS WHAT IT'S LIKE FOR YOU? THINKING ABOUT BOYS ALL THE TIME? WONDERING WHAT IT'D BE LIKE TO DO ACTIVITIES WITH THEM??
Eh, YOU GET USED TO IT. ALSO, HELLO, I DON'T JUST THINK ABOUT BOYS. I THINK ABOUT SUSTAINA-BILITY, SOCIAL JUSTICE, ETHICAL--
HOW DO YOU GET THINGS DONE? HOW DO YOU LIVE LIKE THIS??
JUGHEAD, YOU ONLY JUST MET HER, LIKE, TWO HOURS AGO. YOU GOTTA GET YOURSELF UNDER CONTROL!
THIS IS NORMAL FOR YOU, I DON'T HAVE ANY EXPERI-ENCE WITH THESE--THESE FEELINGS OF INTEREST IN ANOTHER PERSON!!
WHAT DO I DO?
EASY, JUGGIE. YOU'RE GONNA SEE HER AGAIN.
TONIGHT.

To be fair, feelings *are* pretty boring. Real snorefest most of the time. You gotta pull up your socks, feelings. Feelings, get your head in the game.

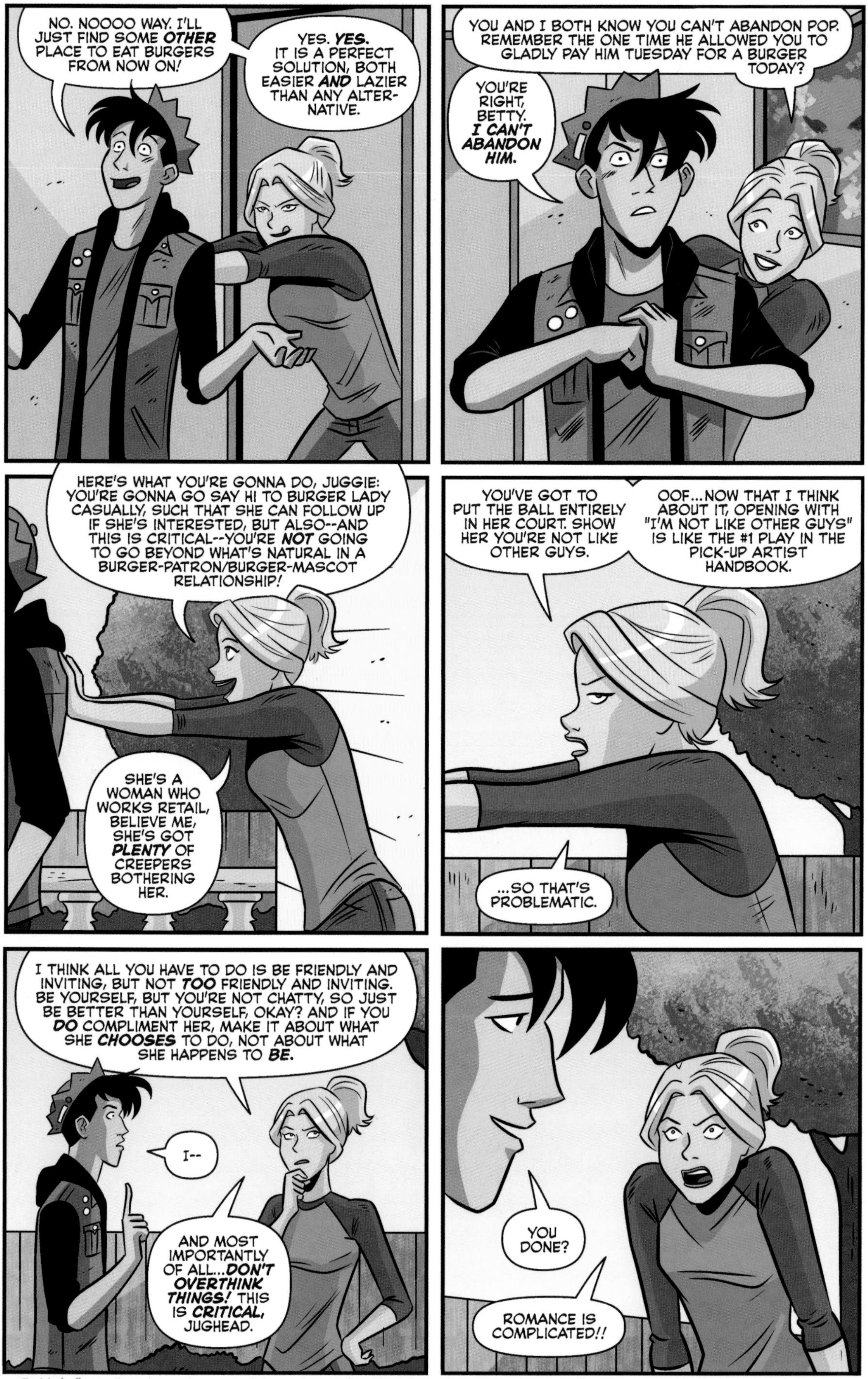
NO. NOOOO WAY. I'LL JUST FIND SOME **OTHER** PLACE TO EAT BURGERS FROM NOW ON!
YES. **YES.** IT IS A PERFECT SOLUTION, BOTH EASIER **AND** LAZIER THAN ANY ALTERNATIVE.
YOU AND I BOTH KNOW YOU CAN'T ABANDON POP. REMEMBER THE ONE TIME HE ALLOWED YOU TO GLADLY PAY HIM TUESDAY FOR A BURGER TODAY?
YOU'RE RIGHT, BETTY. ***I CAN'T ABANDON HIM.***
HERE'S WHAT YOU'RE GONNA DO, JUGGIE: YOU'RE GONNA GO SAY HI TO BURGER LADY CASUALLY, SUCH THAT SHE CAN FOLLOW UP IF SHE'S INTERESTED, BUT ALSO--AND THIS IS CRITICAL--YOU'RE **NOT** GOING TO GO BEYOND WHAT'S NATURAL IN A BURGER-PATRON/BURGER-MASCOT RELATIONSHIP!
SHE'S A WOMAN WHO WORKS RETAIL, BELIEVE ME, SHE'S GOT **PLENTY** OF CREEPERS BOTHERING HER.
YOU'VE GOT TO PUT THE BALL ENTIRELY IN HER COURT. SHOW HER YOU'RE NOT LIKE OTHER GUYS.
OOF...NOW THAT I THINK ABOUT IT, OPENING WITH "I'M NOT LIKE OTHER GUYS" IS LIKE THE #1 PLAY IN THE PICK-UP ARTIST HANDBOOK.
...SO THAT'S PROBLEMATIC.
I THINK ALL YOU HAVE TO DO IS BE FRIENDLY AND INVITING, BUT NOT **TOO** FRIENDLY AND INVITING. BE YOURSELF, BUT YOU'RE NOT CHATTY, SO JUST BE BETTER THAN YOURSELF, OKAY? AND IF YOU **DO** COMPLIMENT HER, MAKE IT ABOUT WHAT SHE **CHOOSES** TO DO, NOT ABOUT WHAT SHE HAPPENS TO **BE.**
I--
AND MOST IMPORTANTLY OF ALL...***DON'T OVERTHINK THINGS!*** THIS IS ***CRITICAL,*** JUGHEAD.
YOU DONE?
ROMANCE IS COMPLICATED!!

Betty's "compliment people on what they choose to do, not what they happen to be" is an actual, real-life, industrial-grade romance tip. Try it out! And when you're kissing on someone attractive down the road, think of me! ***CONSTANTLY.***

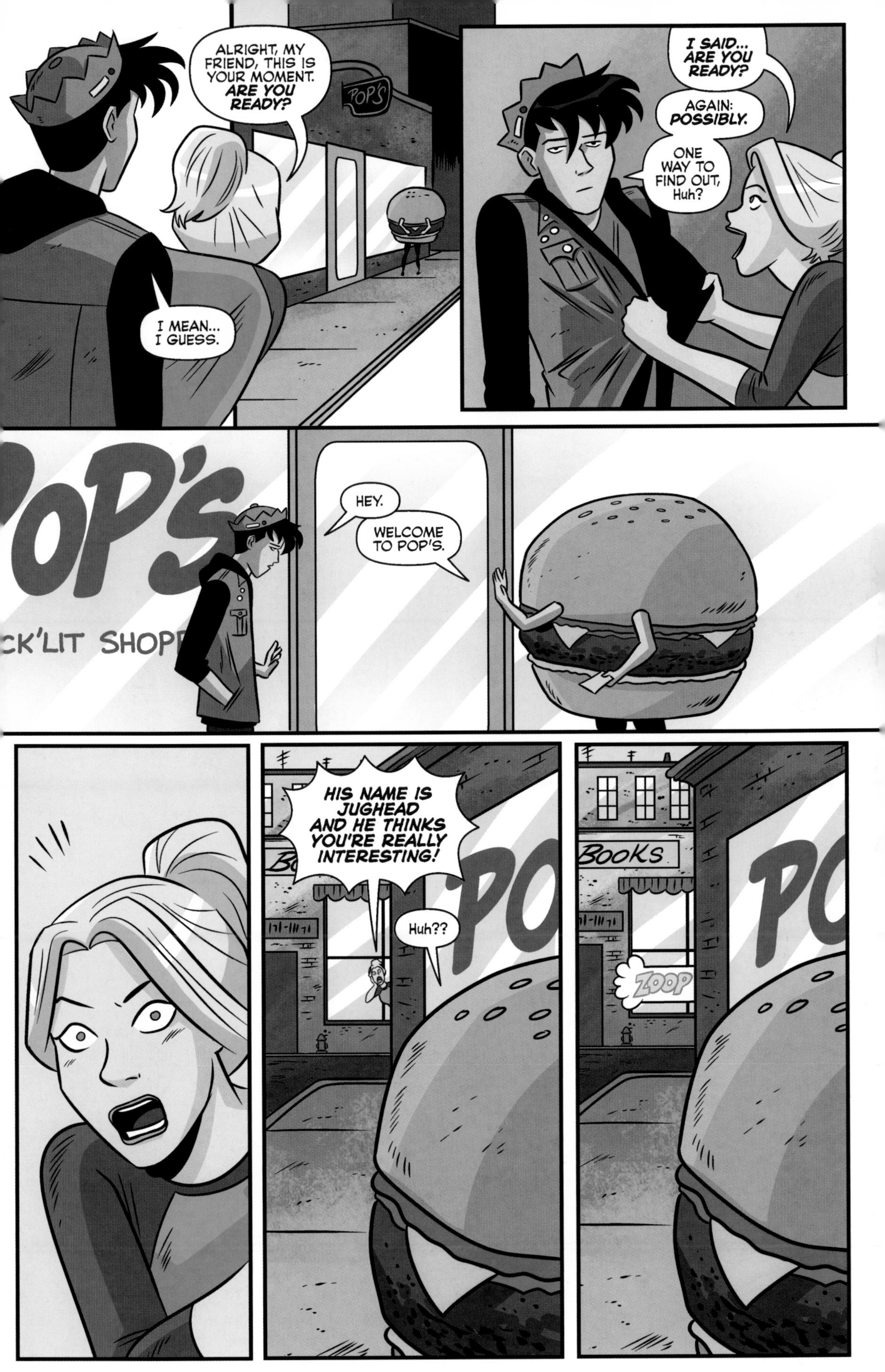
ALRIGHT, MY FRIEND, THIS IS YOUR MOMENT. ARE YOU READY?
POP'S
I MEAN... I GUESS.
I SAID... ARE YOU READY?
AGAIN: POSSIBLY.
ONE WAY TO FIND OUT, Huh?
POP'S
HEY.
WELCOME TO POP'S.
HIS NAME IS JUGHEAD AND HE THINKS YOU'RE REALLY INTERESTING!
Huh??
BOOKS
ZOOP

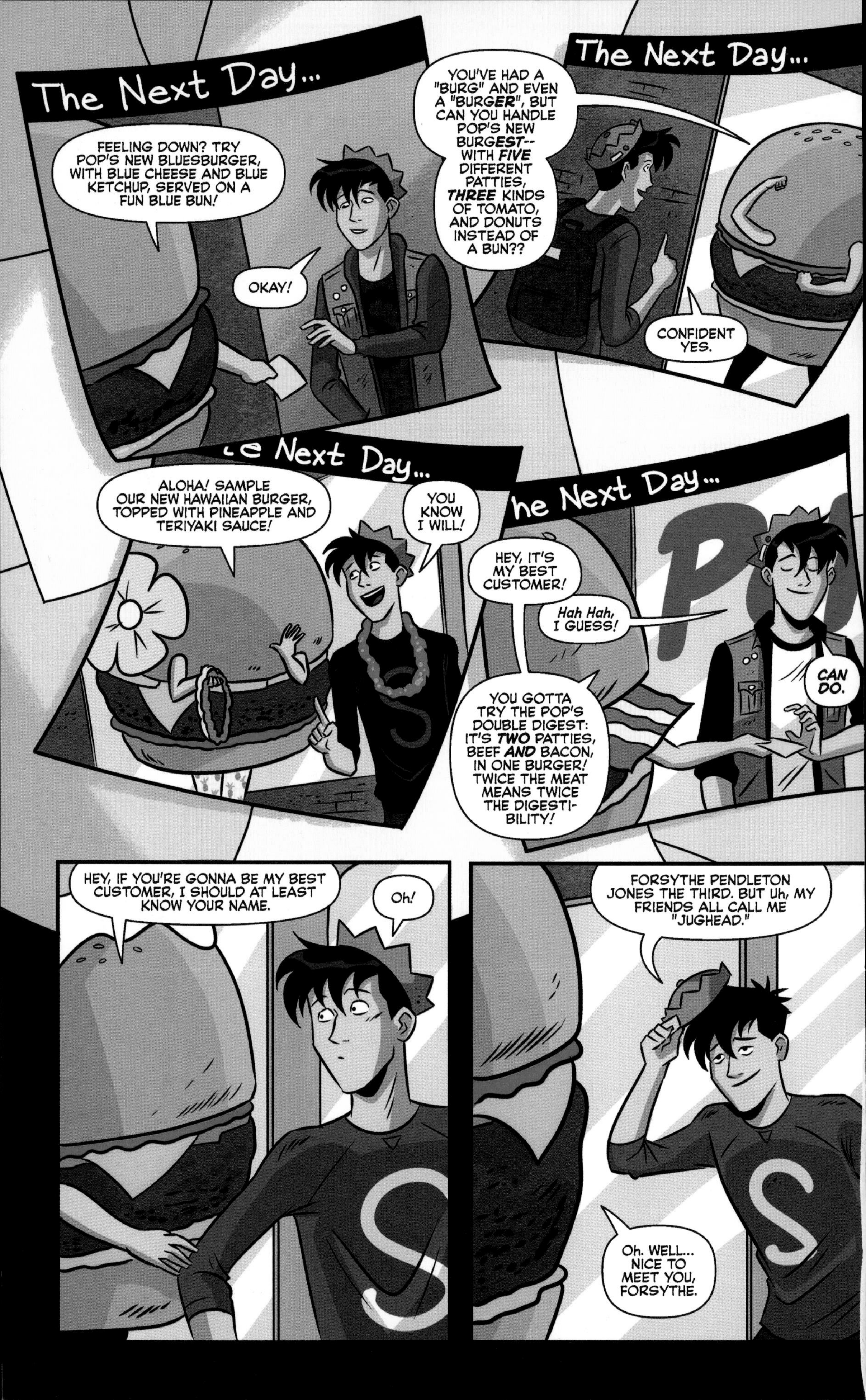
The Next Day...
FEELING DOWN? TRY POP'S NEW BLUESBURGER, WITH BLUE CHEESE AND BLUE KETCHUP, SERVED ON A FUN BLUE BUN!
OKAY!
The Next Day...
YOU'VE HAD A "BURG" AND EVEN A "BURGER", BUT CAN YOU HANDLE POP'S NEW BURGEST-- WITH FIVE DIFFERENT PATTIES, THREE KINDS OF TOMATO, AND DONUTS INSTEAD OF A BUN??
CONFIDENT YES.
e Next Day...
ALOHA! SAMPLE OUR NEW HAWAIIAN BURGER, TOPPED WITH PINEAPPLE AND TERIYAKI SAUCE!
YOU KNOW I WILL!
he Next Day...
HEY, IT'S MY BEST CUSTOMER!
Hah Hah, I GUESS!
YOU GOTTA TRY THE POP'S DOUBLE DIGEST: IT'S TWO PATTIES, BEEF AND BACON, IN ONE BURGER! TWICE THE MEAT MEANS TWICE THE DIGESTI-BILITY!
CAN DO.
HEY, IF YOU'RE GONNA BE MY BEST CUSTOMER, I SHOULD AT LEAST KNOW YOUR NAME.
Oh!
FORSYTHE PENDLETON JONES THE THIRD. BUT Uh, MY FRIENDS ALL CALL ME "JUGHEAD."
Oh. WELL... NICE TO MEET YOU, FORSYTHE.

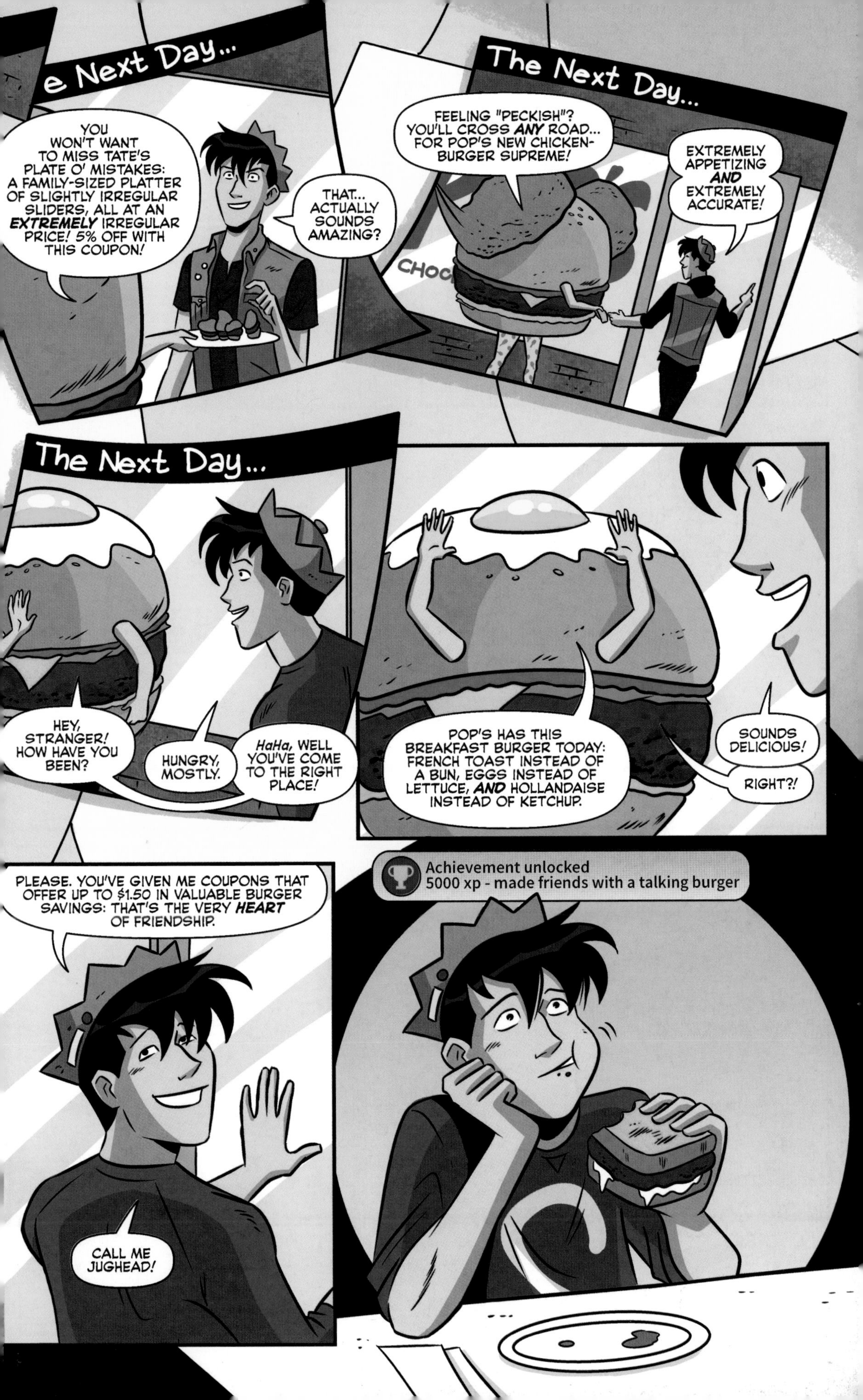
e Next Day...
YOU WON'T WANT TO MISS TATE'S PLATE O' MISTAKES: A FAMILY-SIZED PLATTER OF SLIGHTLY IRREGULAR SLIDERS, ALL AT AN EXTREMELY IRREGULAR PRICE! 5% OFF WITH THIS COUPON!
THAT... ACTUALLY SOUNDS AMAZING?
The Next Day...
FEELING "PECKISH"? YOU'LL CROSS ANY ROAD... FOR POP'S NEW CHICKEN-BURGER SUPREME!
CHOC
EXTREMELY APPETIZING AND EXTREMELY ACCURATE!
The Next Day...
HEY, STRANGER! HOW HAVE YOU BEEN?
HUNGRY, MOSTLY.
HaHa, WELL YOU'VE COME TO THE RIGHT PLACE!
POP'S HAS THIS BREAKFAST BURGER TODAY: FRENCH TOAST INSTEAD OF A BUN, EGGS INSTEAD OF LETTUCE, AND HOLLANDAISE INSTEAD OF KETCHUP.
SOUNDS DELICIOUS!
RIGHT?!
PLEASE. YOU'VE GIVEN ME COUPONS THAT OFFER UP TO $1.50 IN VALUABLE BURGER SAVINGS: THAT'S THE VERY HEART OF FRIENDSHIP.
CALL ME JUGHEAD!
Achievement unlocked
5000 xp - made friends with a talking burger

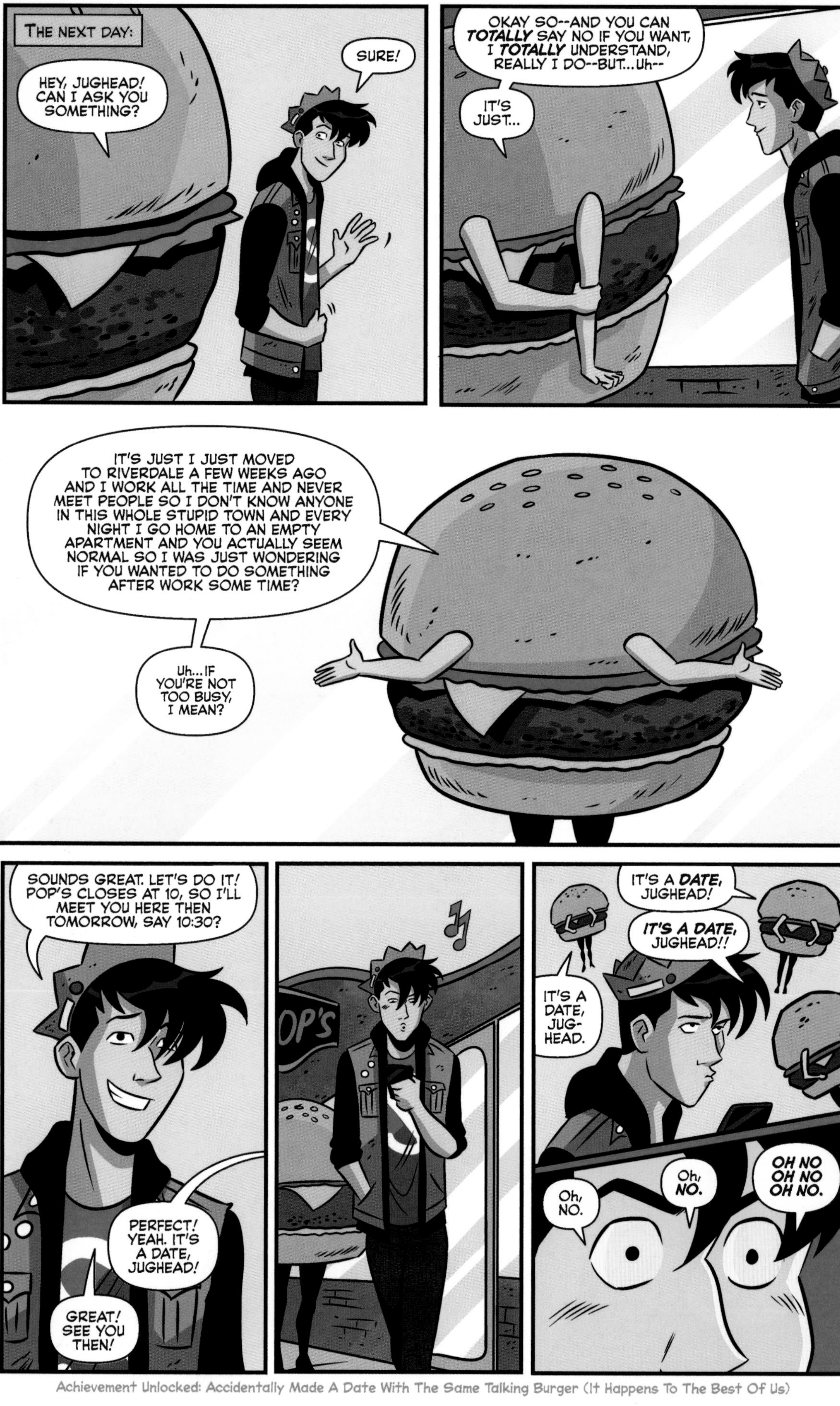
THE NEXT DAY:
HEY, JUGHEAD! CAN I ASK YOU SOMETHING?
SURE!
OKAY SO--AND YOU CAN TOTALLY SAY NO IF YOU WANT, I TOTALLY UNDERSTAND, REALLY I DO--BUT...Uh--
IT'S JUST...
IT'S JUST I JUST MOVED TO RIVERDALE A FEW WEEKS AGO AND I WORK ALL THE TIME AND NEVER MEET PEOPLE SO I DON'T KNOW ANYONE IN THIS WHOLE STUPID TOWN AND EVERY NIGHT I GO HOME TO AN EMPTY APARTMENT AND YOU ACTUALLY SEEM NORMAL SO I WAS JUST WONDERING IF YOU WANTED TO DO SOMETHING AFTER WORK SOME TIME?
Uh...IF YOU'RE NOT TOO BUSY, I MEAN?
SOUNDS GREAT. LET'S DO IT! POP'S CLOSES AT 10, SO I'LL MEET YOU HERE THEN TOMORROW, SAY 10:30?
PERFECT! YEAH. IT'S A DATE, JUGHEAD!
GREAT! SEE YOU THEN!
POP'S
IT'S A DATE, JUGHEAD!
IT'S A DATE, JUGHEAD!!
IT'S A DATE, JUG-HEAD.
Oh, NO.
Oh, NO.
OH NO OH NO OH NO.

Achievement Unlocked: Accidentally Made A Date With The Same Talking Burger (It Happens To The Best Of Us)

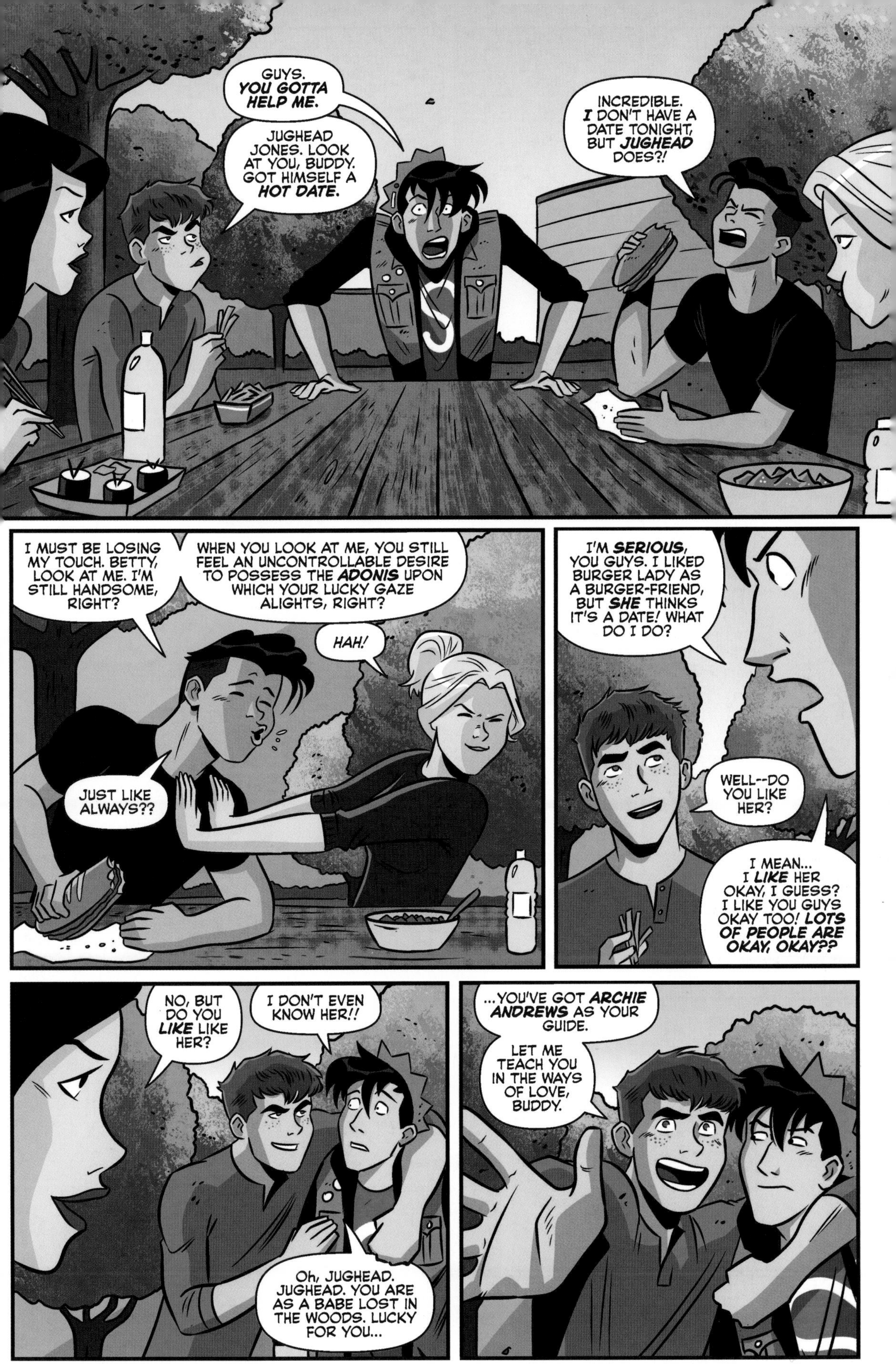
GUYS. YOU GOTTA HELP ME.
JUGHEAD JONES. LOOK AT YOU, BUDDY. GOT HIMSELF A HOT DATE.
INCREDIBLE. I DON'T HAVE A DATE TONIGHT, BUT JUGHEAD DOES?!
I MUST BE LOSING MY TOUCH. BETTY, LOOK AT ME. I'M STILL HANDSOME, RIGHT?
WHEN YOU LOOK AT ME, YOU STILL FEEL AN UNCONTROLLABLE DESIRE TO POSSESS THE ADONIS UPON WHICH YOUR LUCKY GAZE ALIGHTS, RIGHT?
HAH!
JUST LIKE ALWAYS??
I'M SERIOUS, YOU GUYS. I LIKED BURGER LADY AS A BURGER-FRIEND, BUT SHE THINKS IT'S A DATE! WHAT DO I DO?
WELL--DO YOU LIKE HER?
I MEAN... I LIKE HER OKAY, I GUESS? I LIKE YOU GUYS OKAY TOO! LOTS OF PEOPLE ARE OKAY, OKAY??
NO, BUT DO YOU LIKE LIKE HER?
I DON'T EVEN KNOW HER!!
Oh, JUGHEAD. JUGHEAD. YOU ARE AS A BABE LOST IN THE WOODS. LUCKY FOR YOU...
...YOU'VE GOT ARCHIE ANDREWS AS YOUR GUIDE.
LET ME TEACH YOU IN THE WAYS OF LOVE, BUDDY.

Reggie's lying, he has a hot date. He's taking a night off from going out to spend some quality time with himself! He's gonna read a book, maybe watch a movie, maybe draw a bath and throw some bath salts in there, swirl them around, get in, and just relax. Here's a Reggie's Recommendation™: you're never too busy for self-care!!

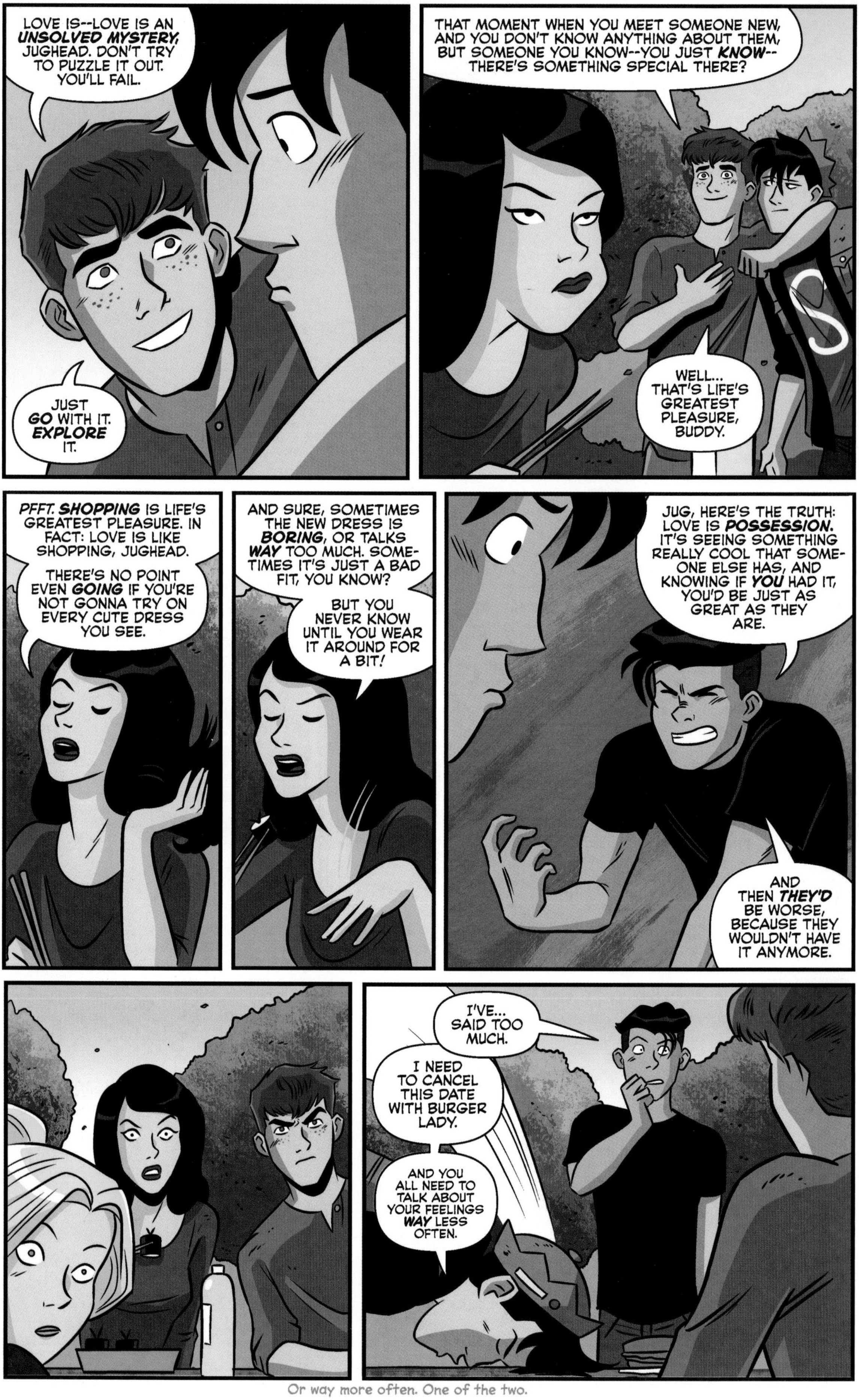
LOVE IS--LOVE IS AN UNSOLVED MYSTERY, JUGHEAD. DON'T TRY TO PUZZLE IT OUT. YOU'LL FAIL.
JUST GO WITH IT. EXPLORE IT.
THAT MOMENT WHEN YOU MEET SOMEONE NEW, AND YOU DON'T KNOW ANYTHING ABOUT THEM, BUT SOMEONE YOU KNOW--YOU JUST KNOW--THERE'S SOMETHING SPECIAL THERE?
WELL... THAT'S LIFE'S GREATEST PLEASURE, BUDDY.
PFFT. SHOPPING IS LIFE'S GREATEST PLEASURE. IN FACT: LOVE IS LIKE SHOPPING, JUGHEAD.
THERE'S NO POINT EVEN GOING IF YOU'RE NOT GONNA TRY ON EVERY CUTE DRESS YOU SEE.
AND SURE, SOMETIMES THE NEW DRESS IS BORING, OR TALKS WAY TOO MUCH. SOMETIMES IT'S JUST A BAD FIT, YOU KNOW?
BUT YOU NEVER KNOW UNTIL YOU WEAR IT AROUND FOR A BIT!
JUG, HERE'S THE TRUTH: LOVE IS POSSESSION. IT'S SEEING SOMETHING REALLY COOL THAT SOMEONE ELSE HAS, AND KNOWING IF YOU HAD IT, YOU'D BE JUST AS GREAT AS THEY ARE.
AND THEN THEY'D BE WORSE, BECAUSE THEY WOULDN'T HAVE IT ANYMORE.
I'VE... SAID TOO MUCH.
I NEED TO CANCEL THIS DATE WITH BURGER LADY.
AND YOU ALL NEED TO TALK ABOUT YOUR FEELINGS WAY LESS OFTEN.

Or way more often. One of the two.

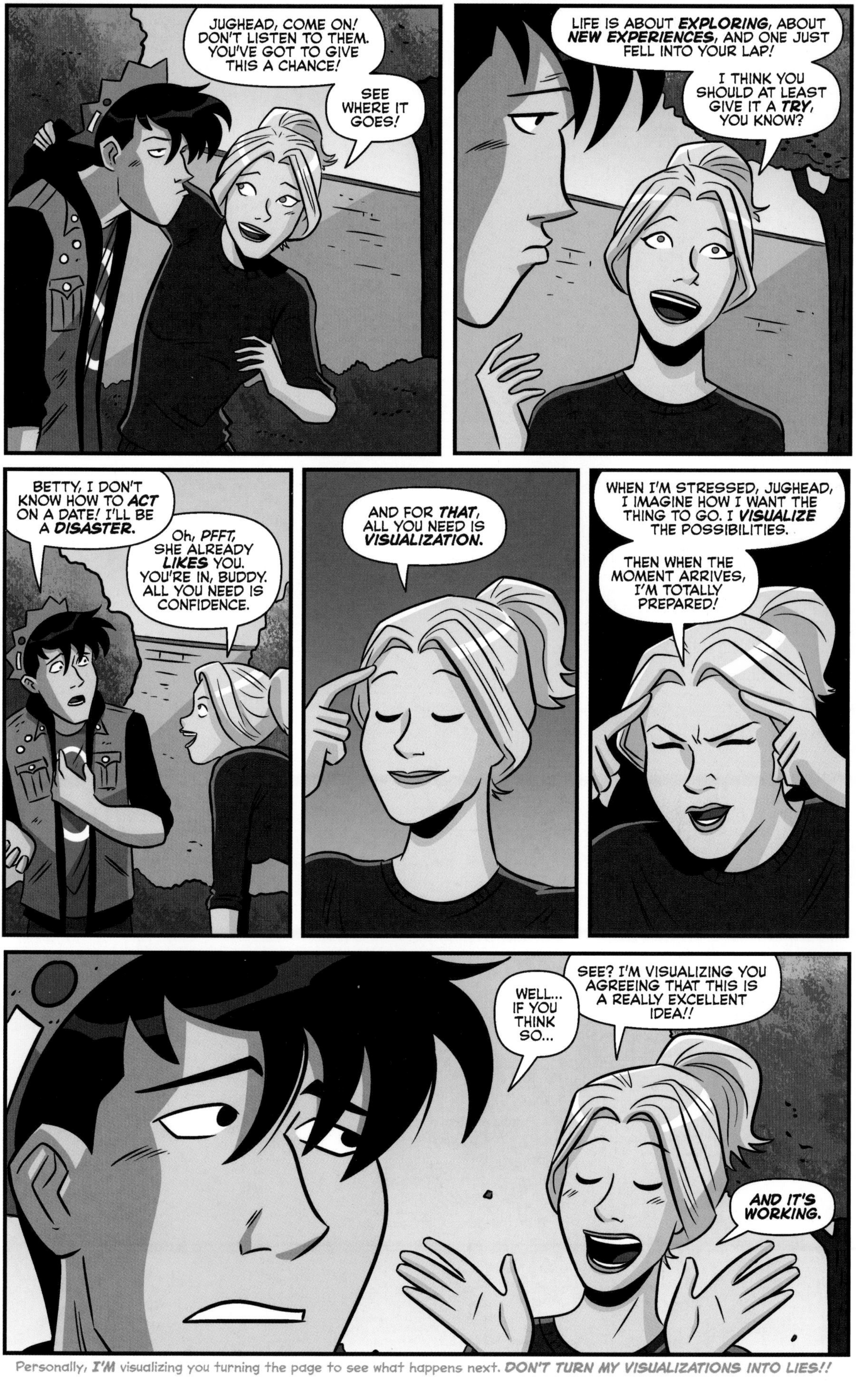
JUGHEAD, COME ON! DON'T LISTEN TO THEM. YOU'VE GOT TO GIVE THIS A CHANCE!
SEE WHERE IT GOES!
LIFE IS ABOUT EXPLORING, ABOUT NEW EXPERIENCES, AND ONE JUST FELL INTO YOUR LAP!
I THINK YOU SHOULD AT LEAST GIVE IT A TRY, YOU KNOW?
BETTY, I DON'T KNOW HOW TO ACT ON A DATE! I'LL BE A DISASTER.
Oh, PFFT, SHE ALREADY LIKES YOU. YOU'RE IN, BUDDY. ALL YOU NEED IS CONFIDENCE.
AND FOR THAT, ALL YOU NEED IS VISUALIZATION.
WHEN I'M STRESSED, JUGHEAD, I IMAGINE HOW I WANT THE THING TO GO. I VISUALIZE THE POSSIBILITIES.
THEN WHEN THE MOMENT ARRIVES, I'M TOTALLY PREPARED!
WELL... IF YOU THINK SO...
SEE? I'M VISUALIZING YOU AGREEING THAT THIS IS A REALLY EXCELLENT IDEA!!
AND IT'S WORKING.

Personally, ***I'M*** visualizing you turning the page to see what happens next. ***DON'T TURN MY VISUALIZATIONS INTO LIES!!***

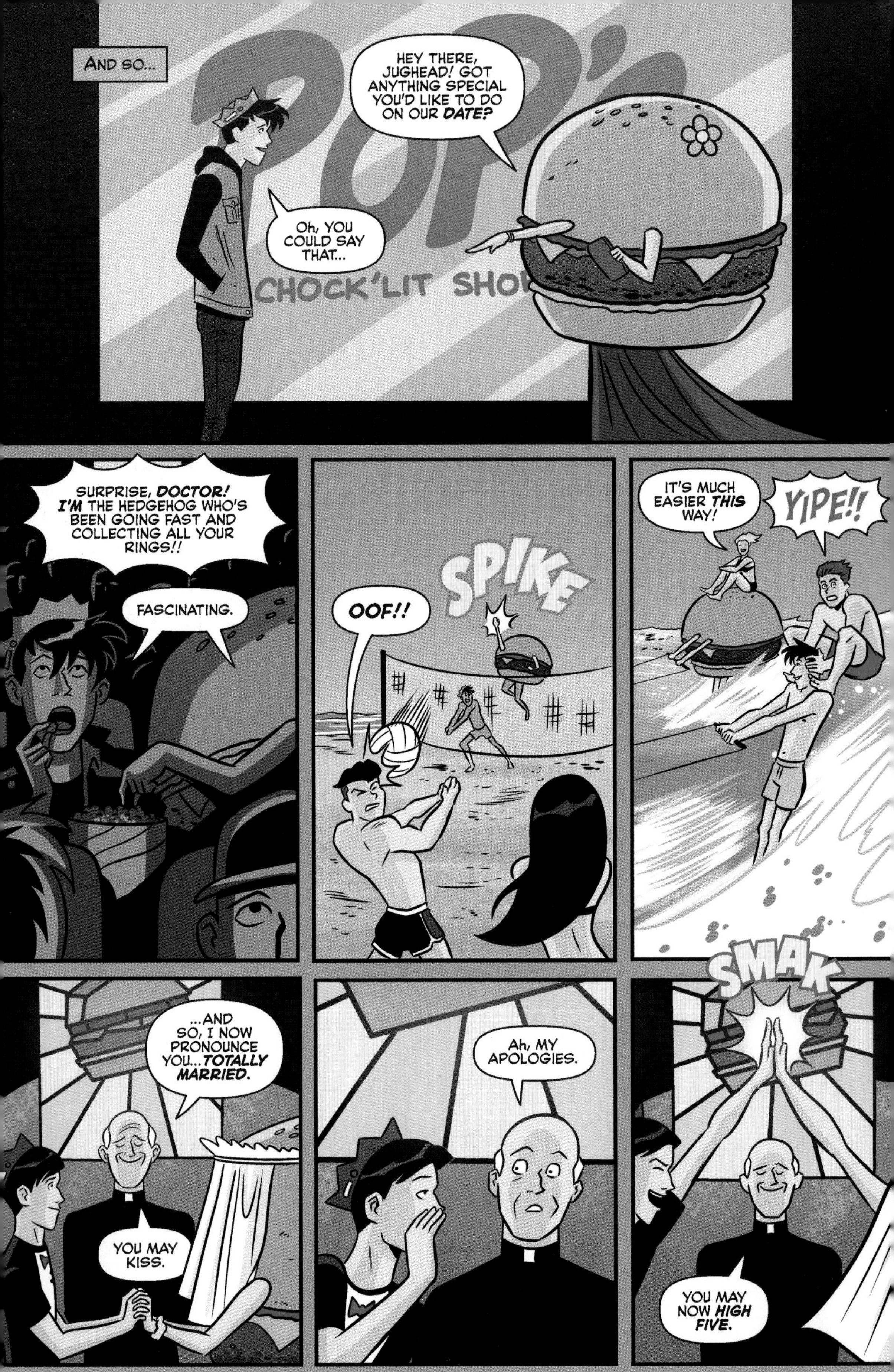
AND SO...
HEY THERE, JUGHEAD! GOT ANYTHING SPECIAL YOU'D LIKE TO DO ON OUR DATE?
Oh, YOU COULD SAY THAT...
POP'S
CHOCK'LIT SHOP
SURPRISE, DOCTOR! I'M THE HEDGEHOG WHO'S BEEN GOING FAST AND COLLECTING ALL YOUR RINGS!!
FASCINATING.
SPIKE
OOF!!
IT'S MUCH EASIER THIS WAY!
YIPE!!
...AND SO, I NOW PRONOUNCE YOU...TOTALLY MARRIED.
YOU MAY KISS.
Ah, MY APOLOGIES.
SMAK
YOU MAY NOW HIGH FIVE.

You may now wink and make finger guns at each other, and then do that thing where you mush perfectly good cake into each other's faces.

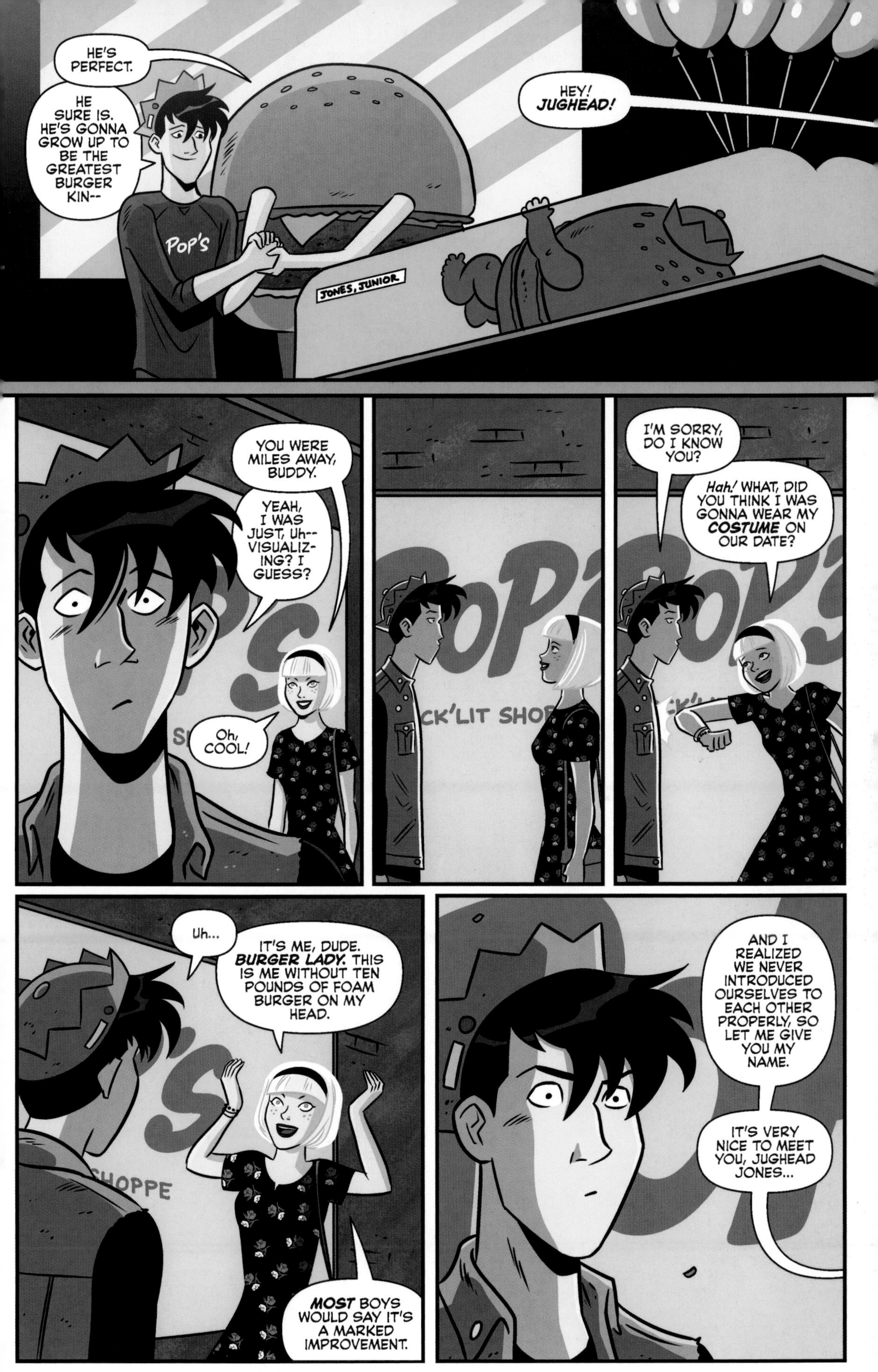
HE'S PERFECT.
HE SURE IS. HE'S GONNA GROW UP TO BE THE GREATEST BURGER KIN--
HEY! ***JUGHEAD!***
POP'S
JONES, JUNIOR
YOU WERE MILES AWAY, BUDDY.
YEAH, I WAS JUST, Uh-- VISUALIZ-ING? I GUESS?
Oh, COOL!
I'M SORRY, DO I KNOW YOU?
Hah! WHAT, DID YOU THINK I WAS GONNA WEAR MY ***COSTUME*** ON OUR DATE?
Uh...
IT'S ME, DUDE. ***BURGER LADY.*** THIS IS ME WITHOUT TEN POUNDS OF FOAM BURGER ON MY HEAD.
MOST BOYS WOULD SAY IT'S A MARKED IMPROVEMENT.
AND I REALIZED WE NEVER INTRODUCED OURSELVES TO EACH OTHER PROPERLY, SO LET ME GIVE YOU MY NAME.
IT'S VERY NICE TO MEET YOU, JUGHEAD JONES...

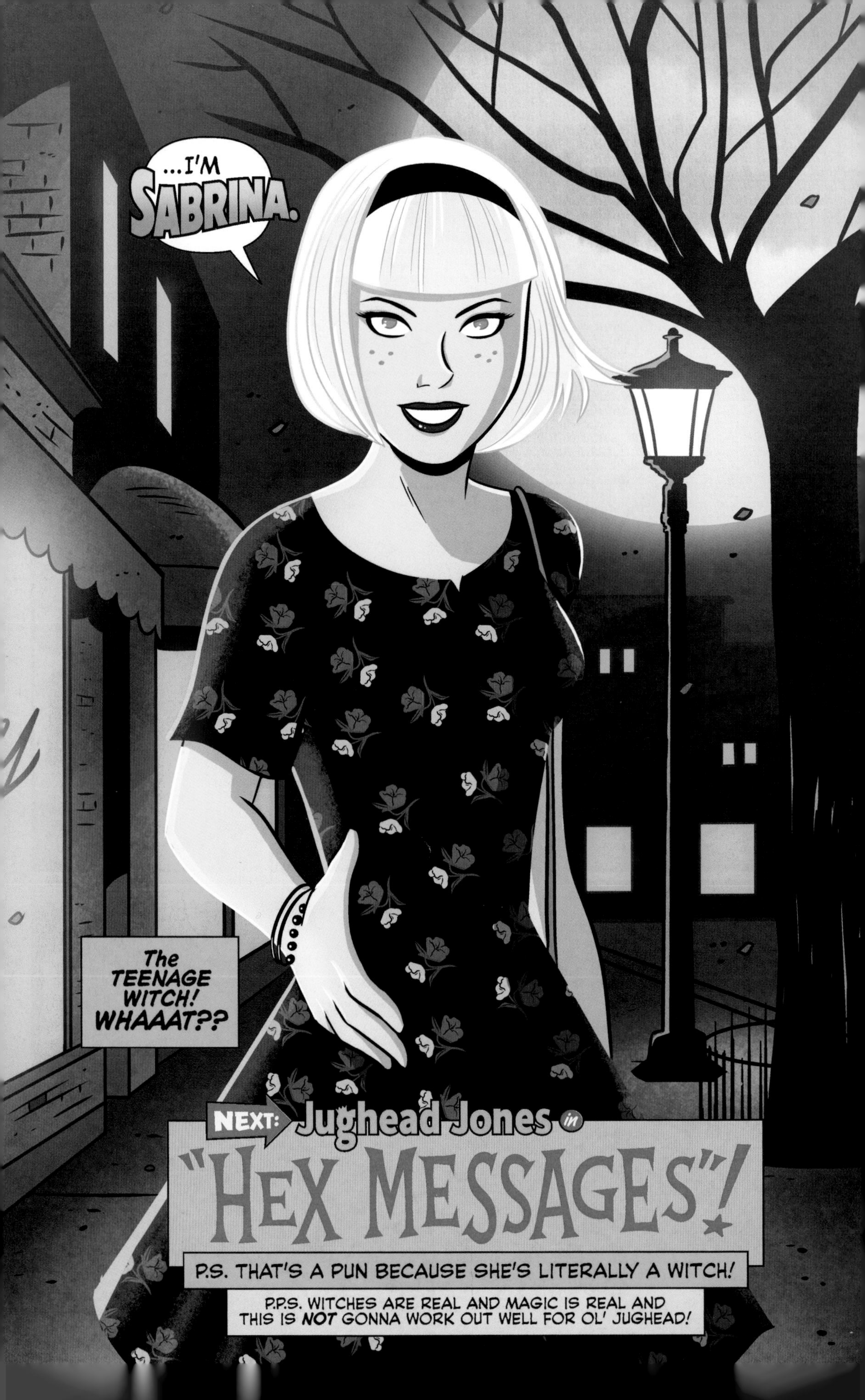

...I'M SABRINA.
The TEENAGE WITCH! WHAAAT??
NEXT: Jughead Jones in
"HEX MESSAGES"!
P.S. THAT'S A PUN BECAUSE SHE'S LITERALLY A WITCH!
P.P.S. WITCHES ARE REAL AND MAGIC IS REAL AND THIS IS NOT GONNA WORK OUT WELL FOR OL' JUGHEAD!

TO BE
CONTINUED...

ISSUE TEN

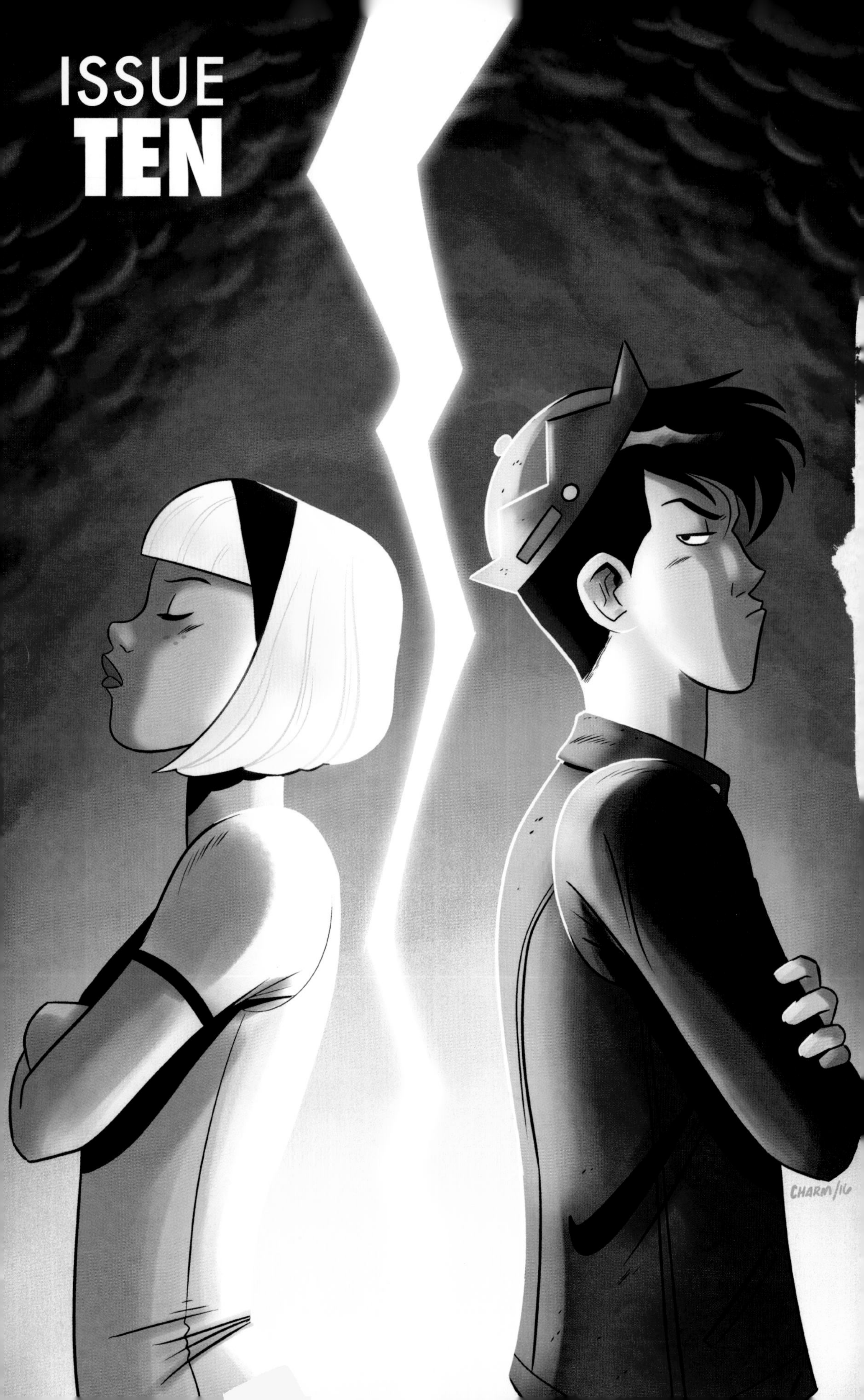
CHARM/16

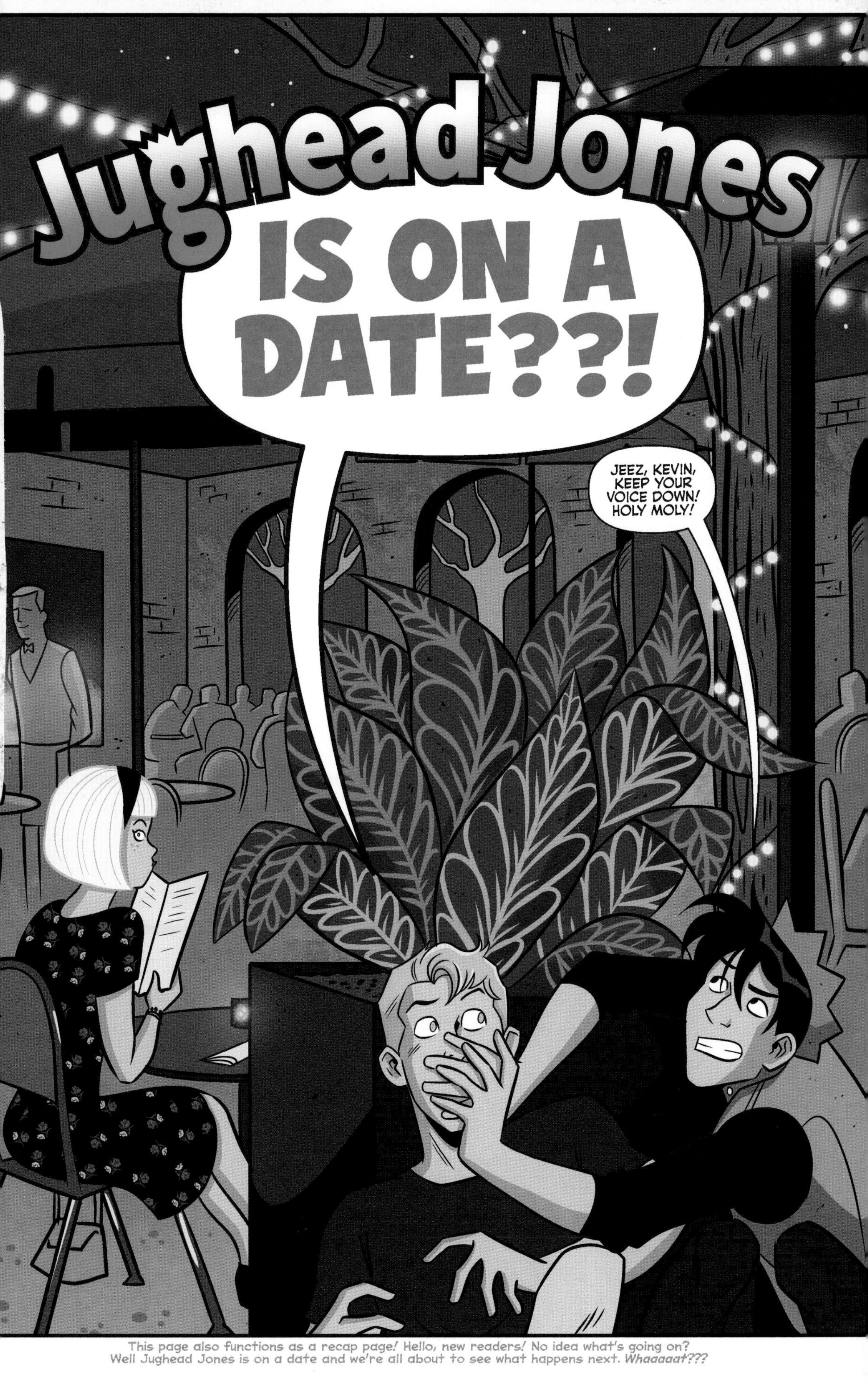
Jughead Jones
IS ON A DATE??!
JEEZ, KEVIN, KEEP YOUR VOICE DOWN! HOLY MOLY!

This page also functions as a recap page! Hello, new readers! No idea what's going on? Well Jughead Jones is on a date and we're all about to see what happens next. *Whaaaaat???*

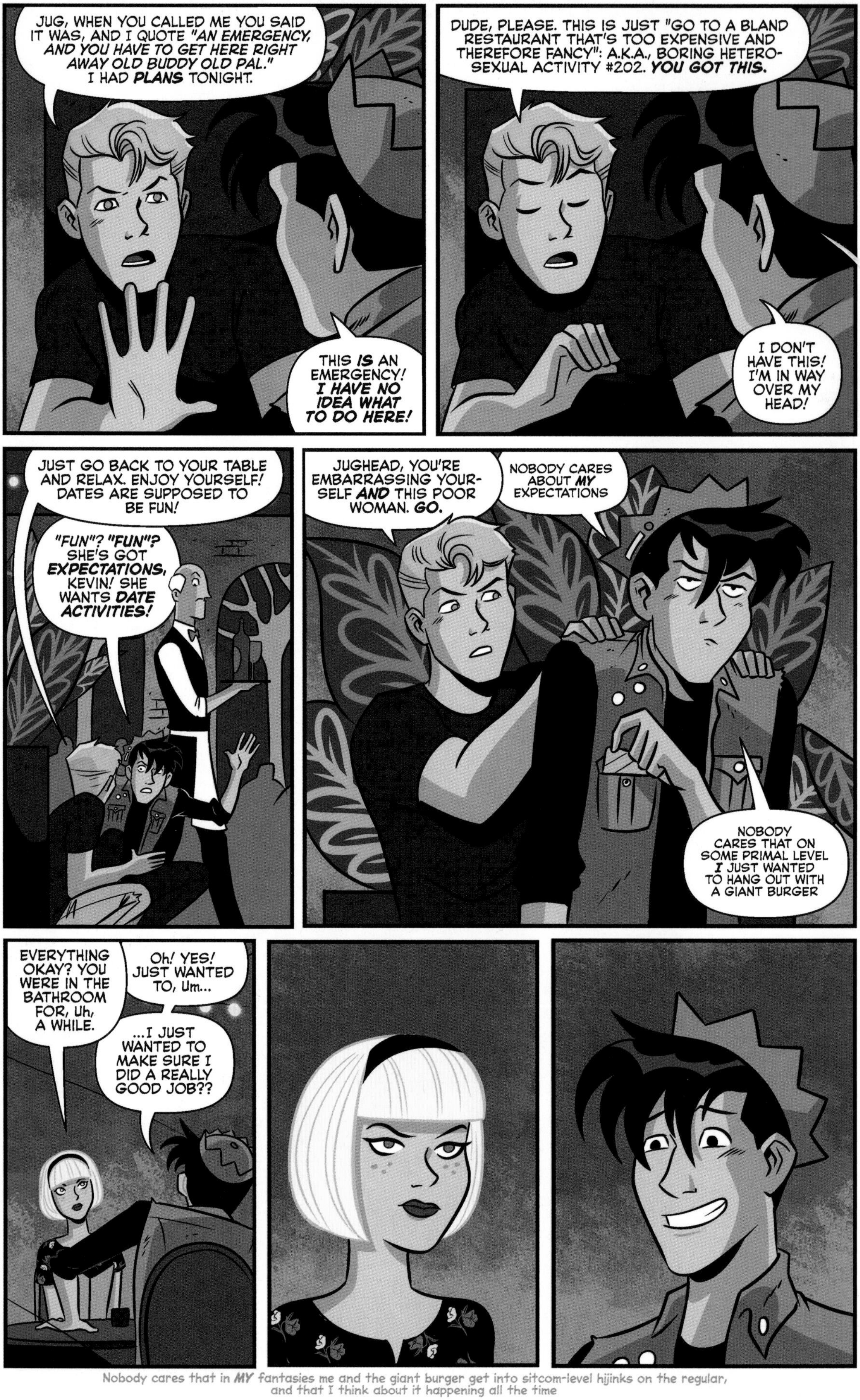
JUG, WHEN YOU CALLED ME YOU SAID IT WAS, AND I QUOTE "AN EMERGENCY, AND YOU HAVE TO GET HERE RIGHT AWAY OLD BUDDY OLD PAL." I HAD PLANS TONIGHT.
THIS IS AN EMERGENCY! I HAVE NO IDEA WHAT TO DO HERE!
DUDE, PLEASE. THIS IS JUST "GO TO A BLAND RESTAURANT THAT'S TOO EXPENSIVE AND THEREFORE FANCY": A.K.A., BORING HETERO-SEXUAL ACTIVITY #202. YOU GOT THIS.
I DON'T HAVE THIS! I'M IN WAY OVER MY HEAD!
JUST GO BACK TO YOUR TABLE AND RELAX. ENJOY YOURSELF! DATES ARE SUPPOSED TO BE FUN!
"FUN"? "FUN"? SHE'S GOT EXPECTATIONS, KEVIN! SHE WANTS DATE ACTIVITIES!
JUGHEAD, YOU'RE EMBARRASSING YOUR-SELF AND THIS POOR WOMAN. GO.
NOBODY CARES ABOUT MY EXPECTATIONS
NOBODY CARES THAT ON SOME PRIMAL LEVEL I JUST WANTED TO HANG OUT WITH A GIANT BURGER
EVERYTHING OKAY? YOU WERE IN THE BATHROOM FOR, Uh, A WHILE.
Oh! YES! JUST WANTED TO, Um...
...I JUST WANTED TO MAKE SURE I DID A REALLY GOOD JOB??
Nobody cares that in MY fantasies me and the giant burger get into sitcom-level hijinks on the regular, and that I think about it happening all the time

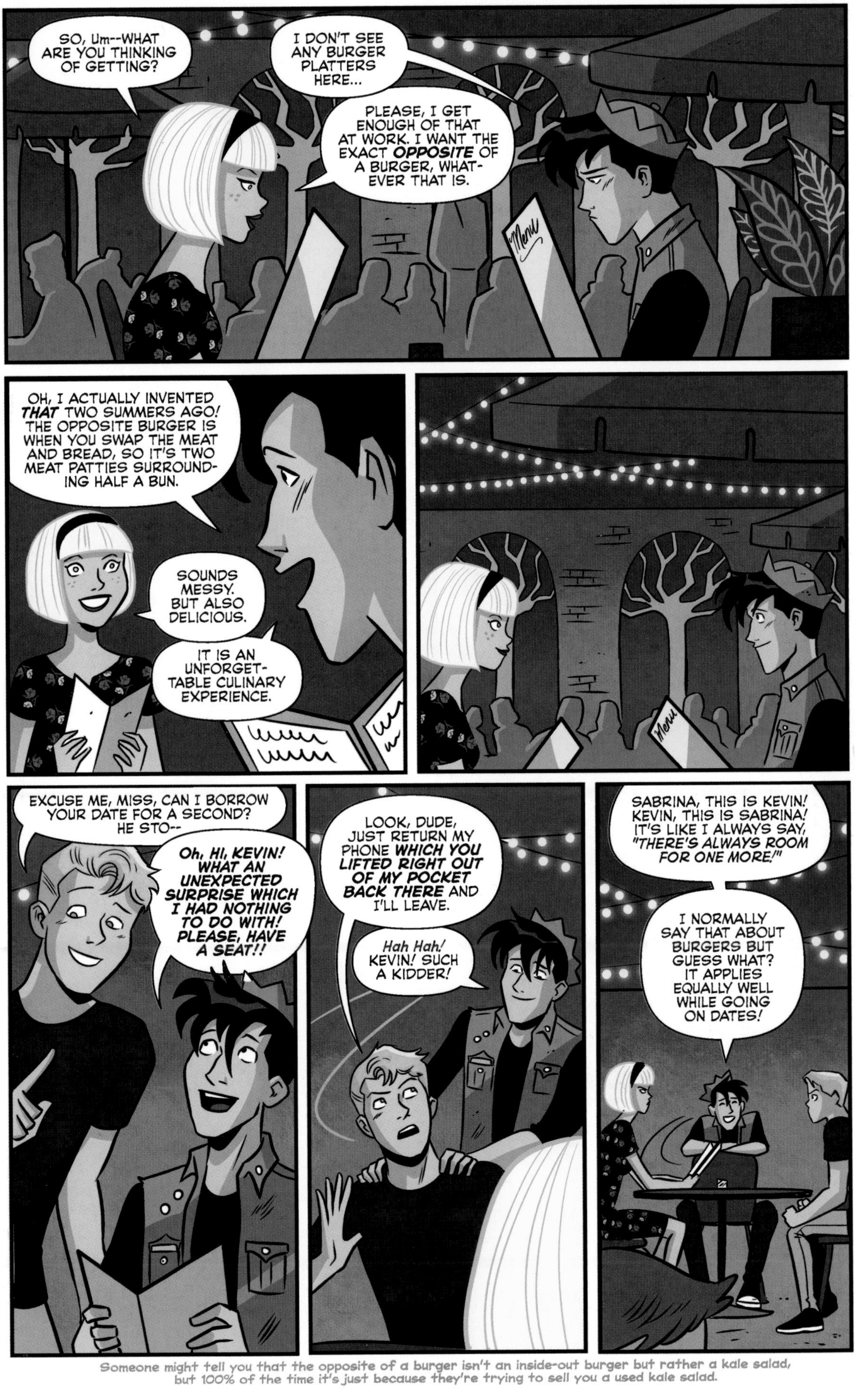
SO, Um--WHAT ARE YOU THINKING OF GETTING?
I DON'T SEE ANY BURGER PLATTERS HERE...
PLEASE, I GET ENOUGH OF THAT AT WORK. I WANT THE EXACT OPPOSITE OF A BURGER, WHAT-EVER THAT IS.
Menu
OH, I ACTUALLY INVENTED THAT TWO SUMMERS AGO! THE OPPOSITE BURGER IS WHEN YOU SWAP THE MEAT AND BREAD, SO IT'S TWO MEAT PATTIES SURROUND-ING HALF A BUN.
SOUNDS MESSY. BUT ALSO DELICIOUS.
IT IS AN UNFORGET-TABLE CULINARY EXPERIENCE.
Menu
EXCUSE ME, MISS, CAN I BORROW YOUR DATE FOR A SECOND? HE STO--
Oh, HI, KEVIN! WHAT AN UNEXPECTED SURPRISE WHICH I HAD NOTHING TO DO WITH! PLEASE, HAVE A SEAT!!
LOOK, DUDE, JUST RETURN MY PHONE WHICH YOU LIFTED RIGHT OUT OF MY POCKET BACK THERE AND I'LL LEAVE.
Hah Hah! KEVIN! SUCH A KIDDER!
SABRINA, THIS IS KEVIN! KEVIN, THIS IS SABRINA! IT'S LIKE I ALWAYS SAY, "THERE'S ALWAYS ROOM FOR ONE MORE!"
I NORMALLY SAY THAT ABOUT BURGERS BUT GUESS WHAT? IT APPLIES EQUALLY WELL WHILE GOING ON DATES!

Someone might tell you that the opposite of a burger isn't an inside-out burger but rather a kale salad, but 100% of the time it's just because they're trying to sell you a used kale salad.

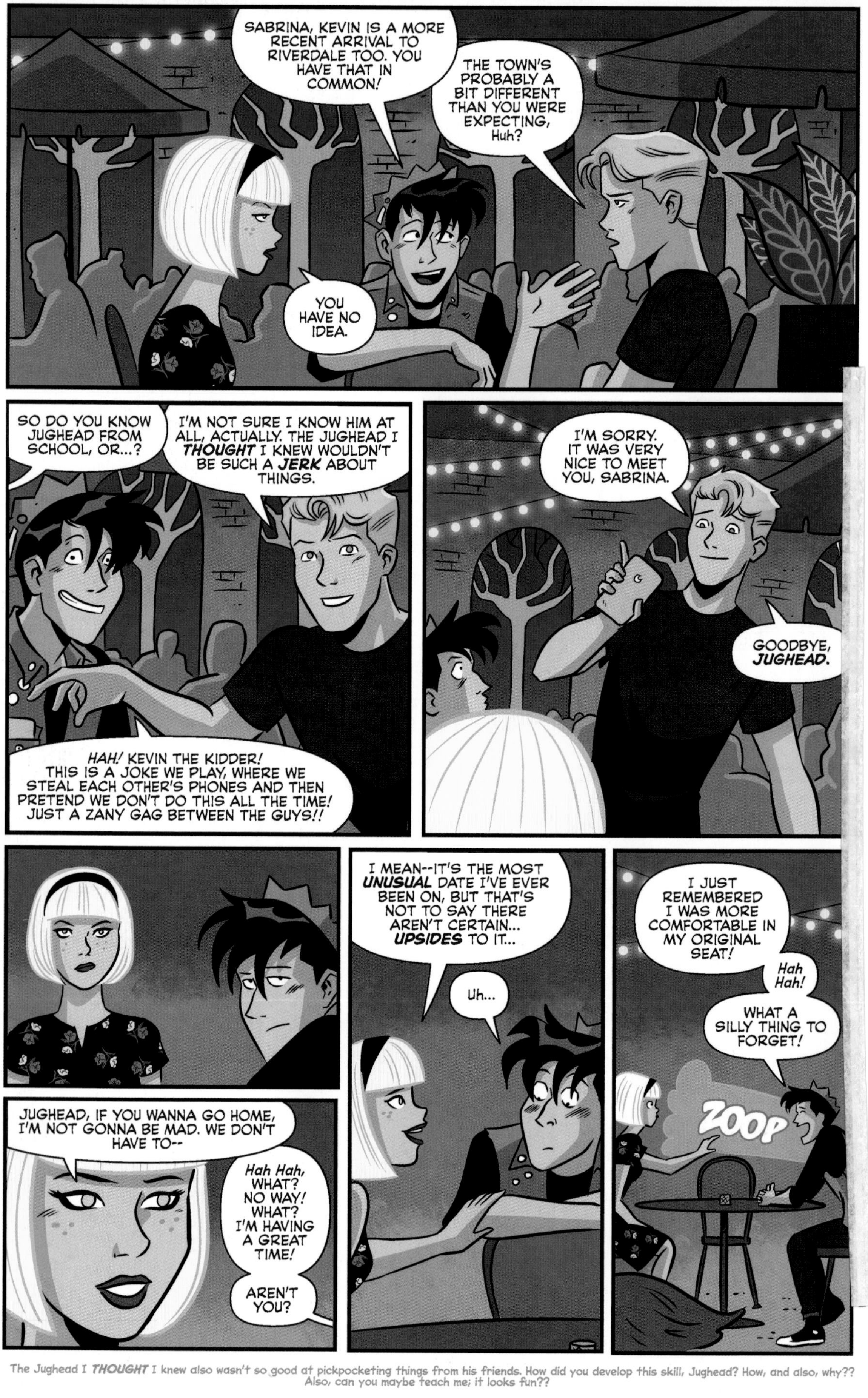
SABRINA, KEVIN IS A MORE RECENT ARRIVAL TO RIVERDALE TOO. YOU HAVE THAT IN COMMON!
THE TOWN'S PROBABLY A BIT DIFFERENT THAN YOU WERE EXPECTING, Huh?
YOU HAVE NO IDEA.
SO DO YOU KNOW JUGHEAD FROM SCHOOL, OR...?
I'M NOT SURE I KNOW HIM AT ALL, ACTUALLY. THE JUGHEAD I THOUGHT I KNEW WOULDN'T BE SUCH A JERK ABOUT THINGS.
HAH! KEVIN THE KIDDER! THIS IS A JOKE WE PLAY, WHERE WE STEAL EACH OTHER'S PHONES AND THEN PRETEND WE DON'T DO THIS ALL THE TIME! JUST A ZANY GAG BETWEEN THE GUYS!!
I'M SORRY. IT WAS VERY NICE TO MEET YOU, SABRINA.
GOODBYE, JUGHEAD.
JUGHEAD, IF YOU WANNA GO HOME, I'M NOT GONNA BE MAD. WE DON'T HAVE TO--
Hah Hah, WHAT? NO WAY! WHAT? I'M HAVING A GREAT TIME!
AREN'T YOU?
I MEAN--IT'S THE MOST UNUSUAL DATE I'VE EVER BEEN ON, BUT THAT'S NOT TO SAY THERE AREN'T CERTAIN... UPSIDES TO IT...
Uh...
I JUST REMEMBERED I WAS MORE COMFORTABLE IN MY ORIGINAL SEAT!
Hah Hah!
WHAT A SILLY THING TO FORGET!
ZOOP

The Jughead I ***THOUGHT*** I knew also wasn't so good at pickpocketing things from his friends. How did you develop this skill, Jughead? How, and also, why?? Also, can you maybe teach me; it looks fun??

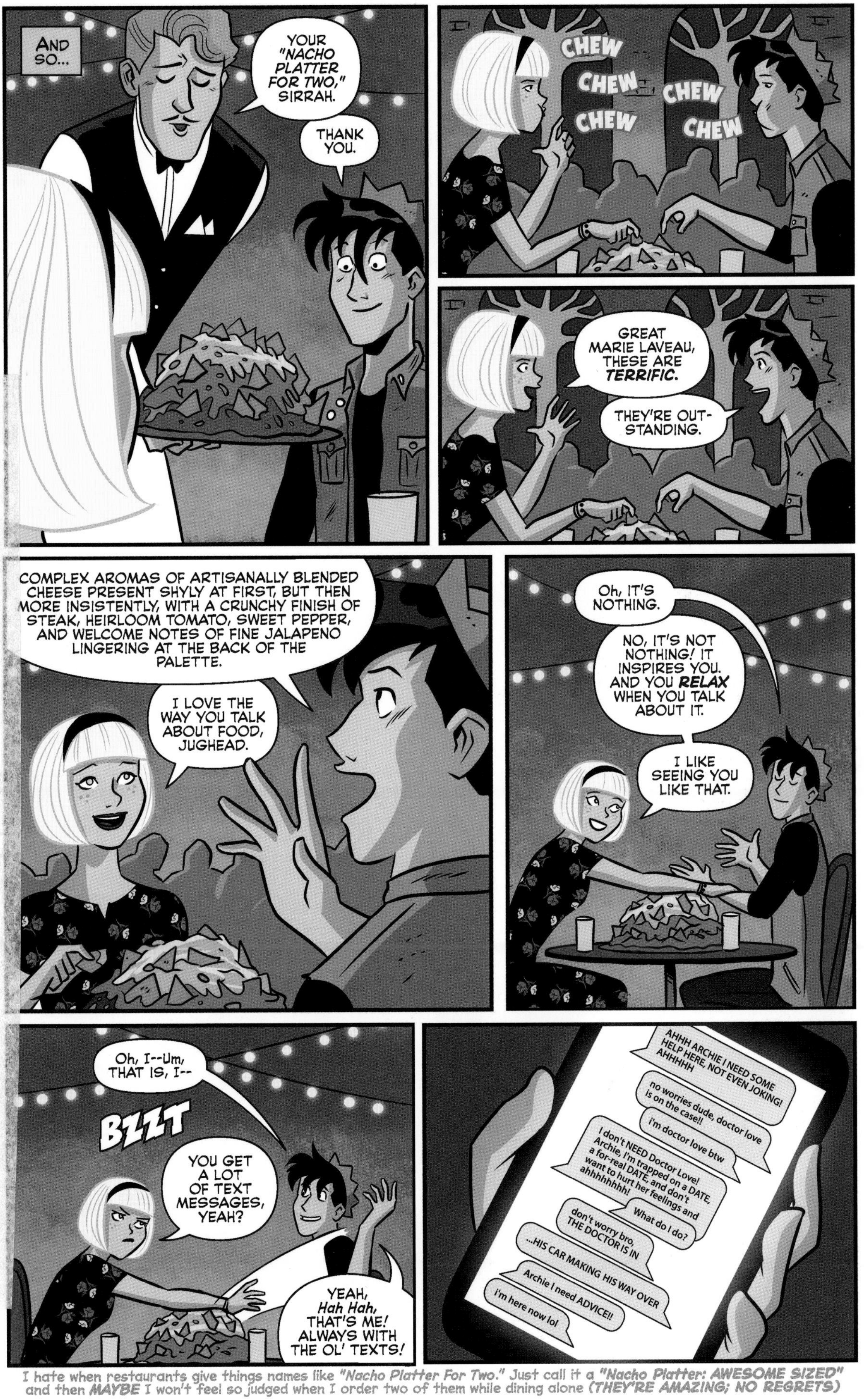
AND SO...
YOUR "NACHO PLATTER FOR TWO," SIRRAH.
THANK YOU.
CHEW
CHEW
CHEW
CHEW
CHEW
GREAT MARIE LAVEAU, THESE ARE TERRIFIC.
THEY'RE OUT-STANDING.
COMPLEX AROMAS OF ARTISANALLY BLENDED CHEESE PRESENT SHYLY AT FIRST, BUT THEN MORE INSISTENTLY, WITH A CRUNCHY FINISH OF STEAK, HEIRLOOM TOMATO, SWEET PEPPER, AND WELCOME NOTES OF FINE JALAPENO LINGERING AT THE BACK OF THE PALETTE.
I LOVE THE WAY YOU TALK ABOUT FOOD, JUGHEAD.
Oh, IT'S NOTHING.
NO, IT'S NOT NOTHING! IT INSPIRES YOU. AND YOU RELAX WHEN YOU TALK ABOUT IT.
I LIKE SEEING YOU LIKE THAT.
Oh, I--Um, THAT IS, I--
BZZT
YOU GET A LOT OF TEXT MESSAGES, YEAH?
YEAH, Hah Hah, THAT'S ME! ALWAYS WITH THE OL' TEXTS!
AHHH ARCHIE I NEED SOME HELP HERE, NOT EVEN JOKING! AHHHHH
no worries dude, doctor love is on the case!!
i'm doctor love btw
I don't NEED Doctor Love! Archie, I'm trapped on a DATE, a for-real DATE, and don't want to hurt her feelings and ahhhhhhhh!
What do I do?
don't worry bro, THE DOCTOR IS IN
...HIS CAR MAKING HIS WAY OVER
Archie I need ADVICE!!
i'm here now lol

I hate when restaurants give things names like *"Nacho Platter For Two."* Just call it a *"Nacho Platter: **AWESOME SIZED**"* and then ***MAYBE*** I won't feel so judged when I order two of them while dining alone ***(THEY'RE AMAZING; NO REGRETS)***

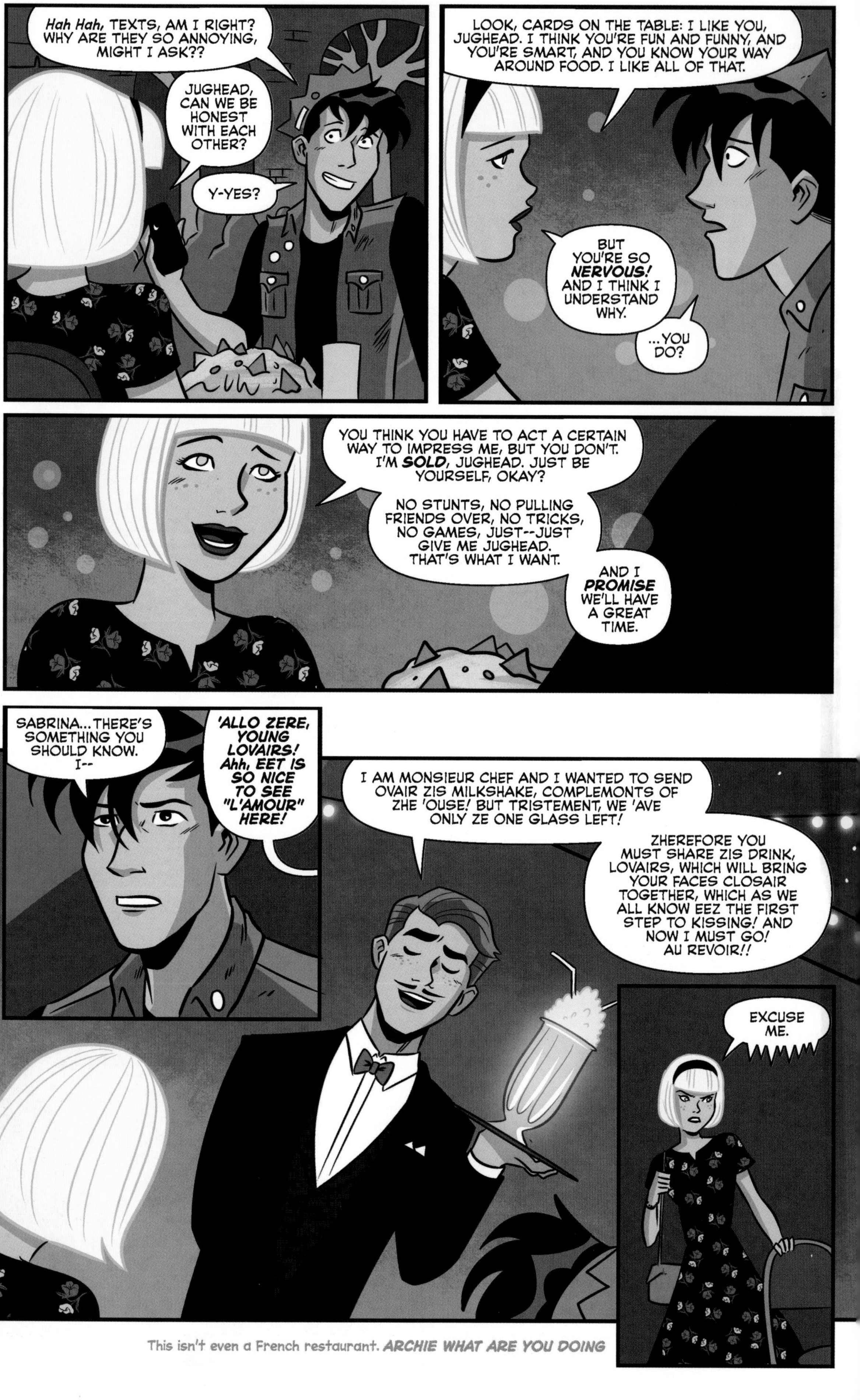
Hah Hah, TEXTS, AM I RIGHT? WHY ARE THEY SO ANNOYING, MIGHT I ASK??
JUGHEAD, CAN WE BE HONEST WITH EACH OTHER?
Y-YES?
LOOK, CARDS ON THE TABLE: I LIKE YOU, JUGHEAD. I THINK YOU'RE FUN AND FUNNY, AND YOU'RE SMART, AND YOU KNOW YOUR WAY AROUND FOOD. I LIKE ALL OF THAT.
BUT YOU'RE SO NERVOUS! AND I THINK I UNDERSTAND WHY.
...YOU DO?
YOU THINK YOU HAVE TO ACT A CERTAIN WAY TO IMPRESS ME, BUT YOU DON'T. I'M SOLD, JUGHEAD. JUST BE YOURSELF, OKAY?
NO STUNTS, NO PULLING FRIENDS OVER, NO TRICKS, NO GAMES, JUST--JUST GIVE ME JUGHEAD. THAT'S WHAT I WANT.
AND I PROMISE WE'LL HAVE A GREAT TIME.
SABRINA...THERE'S SOMETHING YOU SHOULD KNOW. I--
'ALLO ZERE, YOUNG LOVAIRS! Ahh, EET IS SO NICE TO SEE "L'AMOUR" HERE!
I AM MONSIEUR CHEF AND I WANTED TO SEND OVAIR ZIS MILKSHAKE, COMPLEMONTS OF ZHE 'OUSE! BUT TRISTEMENT, WE 'AVE ONLY ZE ONE GLASS LEFT!
ZHEREFORE YOU MUST SHARE ZIS DRINK, LOVAIRS, WHICH WILL BRING YOUR FACES CLOSAIR TOGETHER, WHICH AS WE ALL KNOW EEZ THE FIRST STEP TO KISSING! AND NOW I MUST GO! AU REVOIR!!
EXCUSE ME.

This isn't even a French restaurant. ***ARCHIE WHAT ARE YOU DOING***

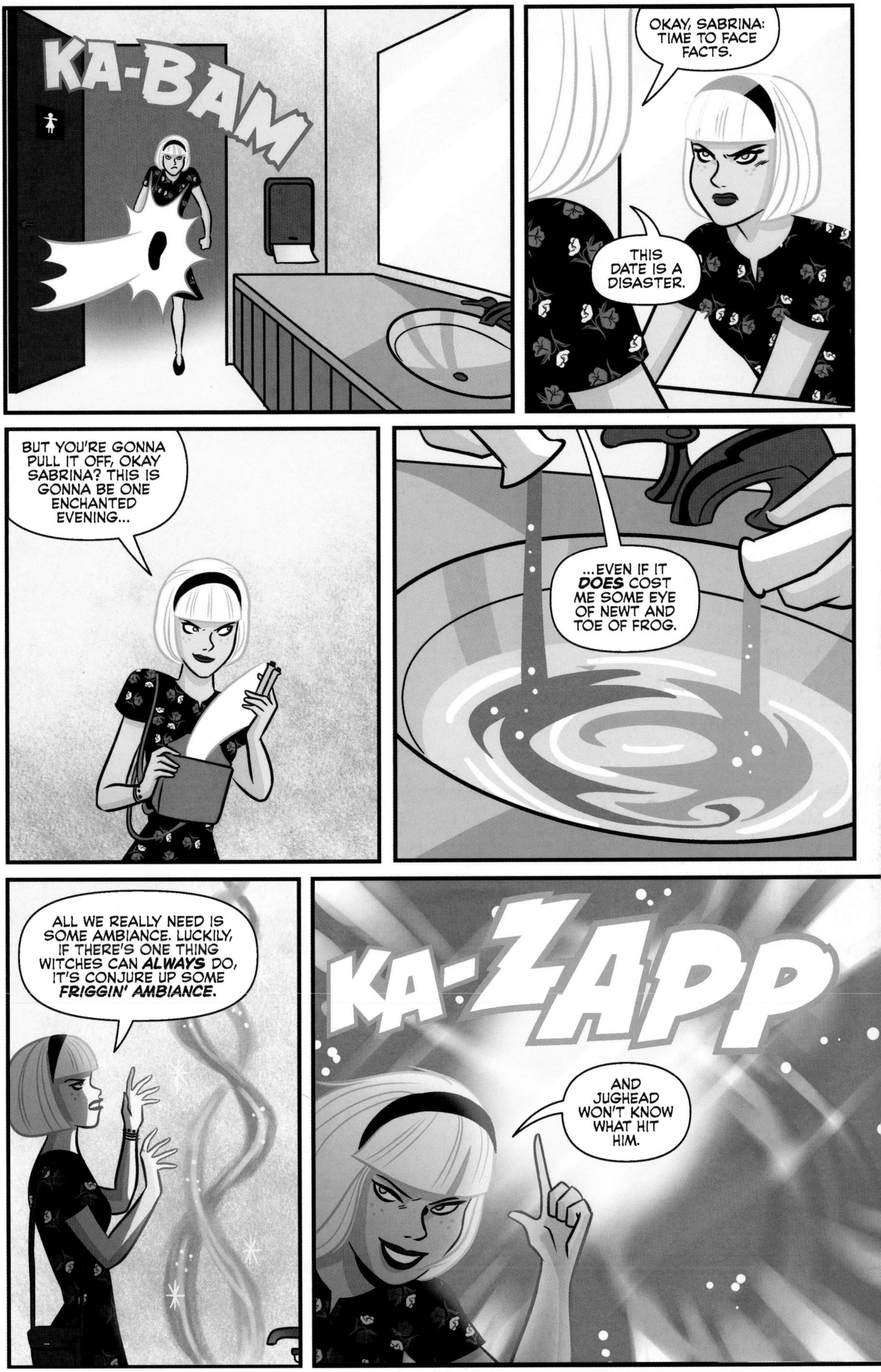
KA-BAM
OKAY, SABRINA: TIME TO FACE FACTS.
THIS DATE IS A DISASTER.
BUT YOU'RE GONNA PULL IT OFF, OKAY SABRINA? THIS IS GONNA BE ONE ENCHANTED EVENING...
...EVEN IF IT *DOES* COST ME SOME EYE OF NEWT AND TOE OF FROG.
ALL WE REALLY NEED IS SOME AMBIANCE. LUCKILY, IF THERE'S ONE THING WITCHES CAN *ALWAYS* DO, IT'S CONJURE UP SOME *FRIGGIN' AMBIANCE*.
KA-ZAPP
AND JUGHEAD WON'T KNOW WHAT HIT HIM.

Oh, if this is your first Archie comic I should mention that Sabrina is a witch! She is a *TEENAGE WITCH* and yes, nothing could possibly go wrong by combining supernatural power and teenage feelings. *NOTHING*

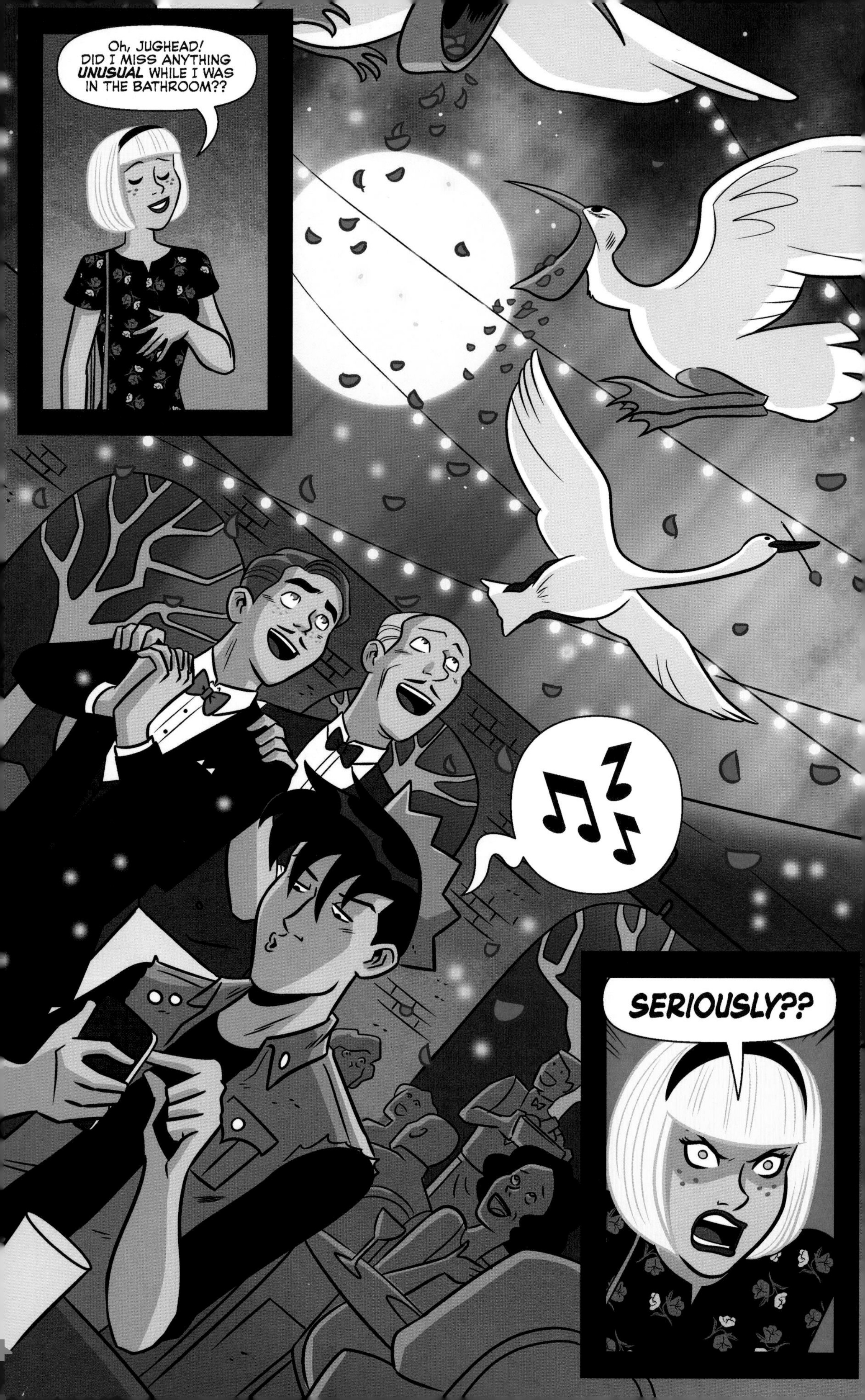

Oh, JUGHEAD! DID I MISS ANYTHING UNUSUAL WHILE I WAS IN THE BATHROOM??
SERIOUSLY??

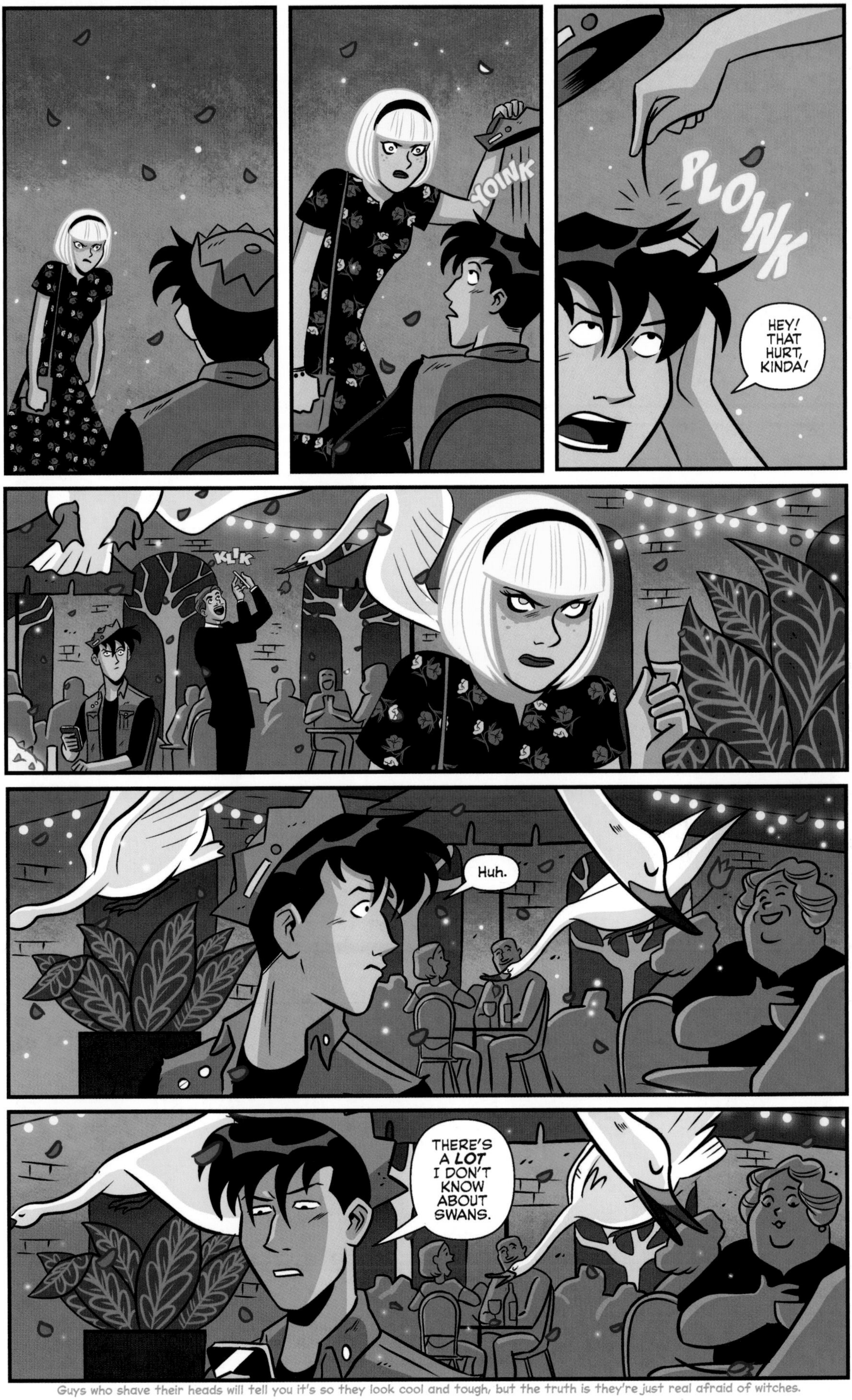
YOINK
PLOINK
HEY! THAT HURT, KINDA!
KLIK
Huh.
THERE'S A **LOT** I DON'T KNOW ABOUT SWANS.

Guys who shave their heads will tell you it's so they look cool and tough, but the truth is they're just real afraid of witches.

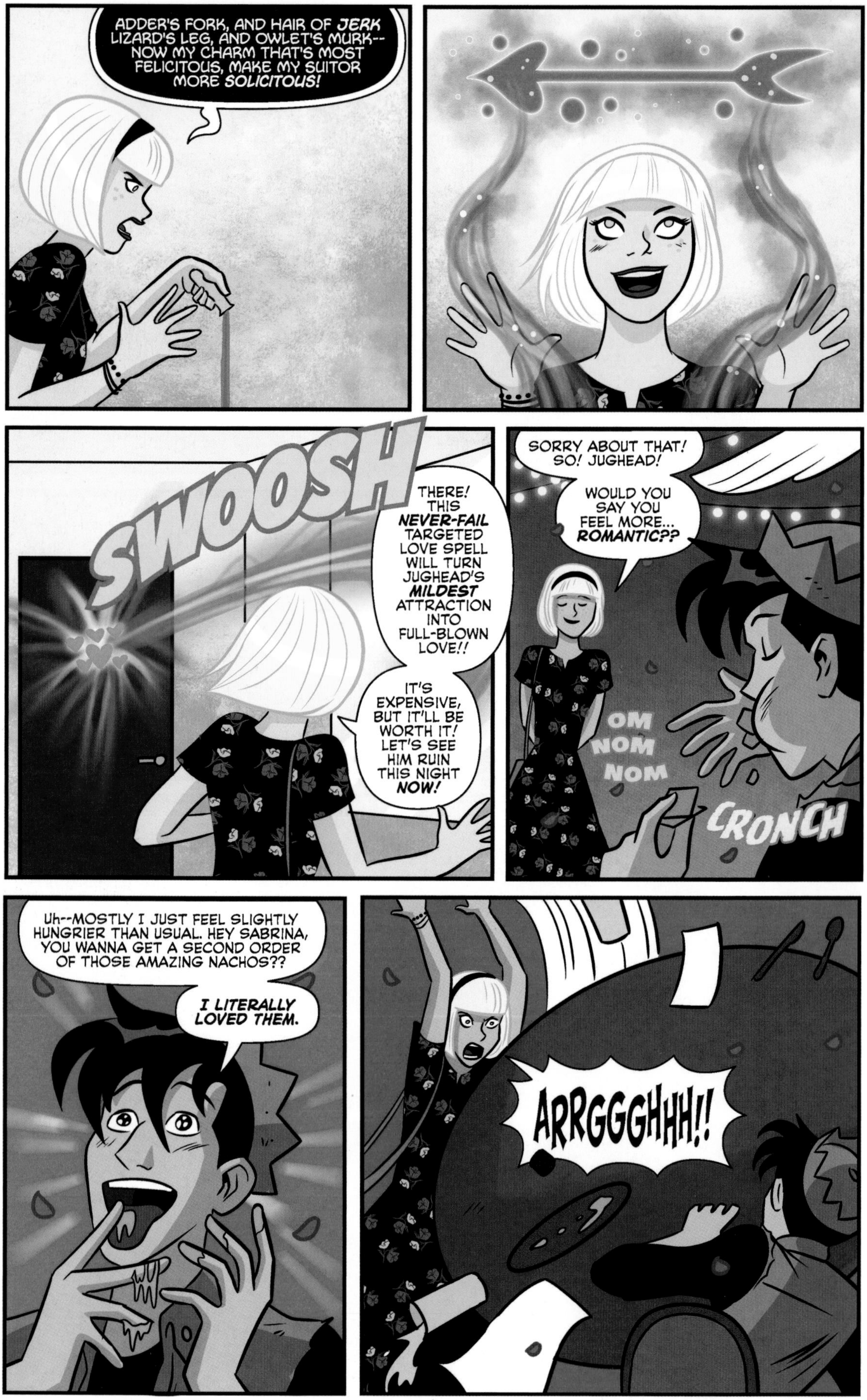
ADDER'S FORK, AND HAIR OF JERK LIZARD'S LEG, AND OWLET'S MURK-- NOW MY CHARM THAT'S MOST FELICITOUS, MAKE MY SUITOR MORE SOLICITOUS!
SWOOSH
THERE! THIS NEVER-FAIL TARGETED LOVE SPELL WILL TURN JUGHEAD'S MILDEST ATTRACTION INTO FULL-BLOWN LOVE!!
IT'S EXPENSIVE, BUT IT'LL BE WORTH IT! LET'S SEE HIM RUIN THIS NIGHT NOW!
SORRY ABOUT THAT! SO! JUGHEAD!
WOULD YOU SAY YOU FEEL MORE... ROMANTIC??
OM NOM NOM
CRONCH
Uh--MOSTLY I JUST FEEL SLIGHTLY HUNGRIER THAN USUAL. HEY SABRINA, YOU WANNA GET A SECOND ORDER OF THOSE AMAZING NACHOS??
I LITERALLY LOVED THEM.
ARRGGGHHH!!

So we'll, uh...get them in a to-go bag then?

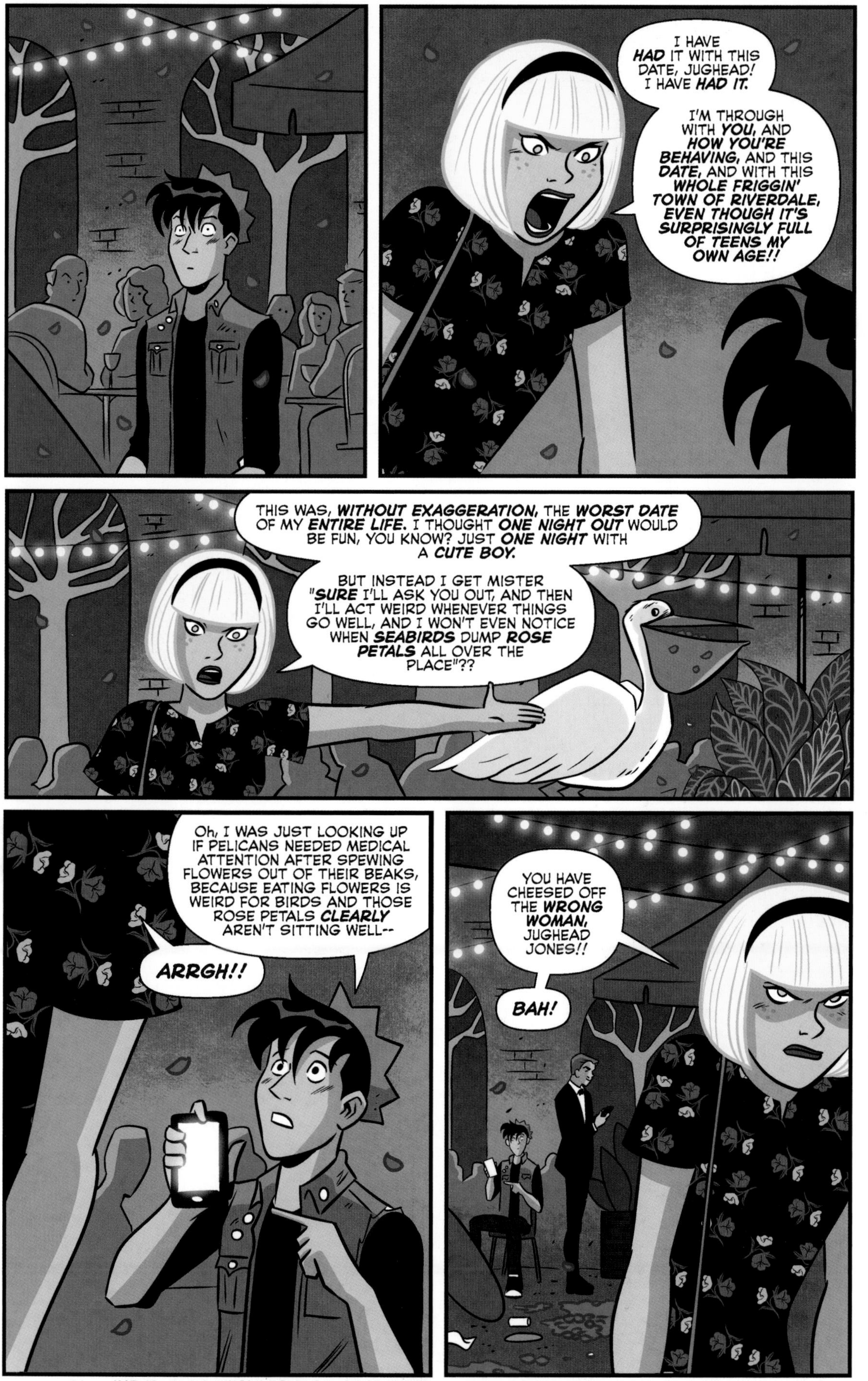
I HAVE HAD IT WITH THIS DATE, JUGHEAD! I HAVE HAD IT.
I'M THROUGH WITH YOU, AND HOW YOU'RE BEHAVING, AND THIS DATE, AND WITH THIS WHOLE FRIGGIN' TOWN OF RIVERDALE, EVEN THOUGH IT'S SURPRISINGLY FULL OF TEENS MY OWN AGE!!
THIS WAS, WITHOUT EXAGGERATION, THE WORST DATE OF MY ENTIRE LIFE. I THOUGHT ONE NIGHT OUT WOULD BE FUN, YOU KNOW? JUST ONE NIGHT WITH A CUTE BOY.
BUT INSTEAD I GET MISTER "SURE I'LL ASK YOU OUT, AND THEN I'LL ACT WEIRD WHENEVER THINGS GO WELL, AND I WON'T EVEN NOTICE WHEN SEABIRDS DUMP ROSE PETALS ALL OVER THE PLACE"??
Oh, I WAS JUST LOOKING UP IF PELICANS NEEDED MEDICAL ATTENTION AFTER SPEWING FLOWERS OUT OF THEIR BEAKS, BECAUSE EATING FLOWERS IS WEIRD FOR BIRDS AND THOSE ROSE PETALS CLEARLY AREN'T SITTING WELL--
ARRGH!!
YOU HAVE CHEESED OFF THE WRONG WOMAN, JUGHEAD JONES!!
BAH!

I have **HAD IT** with this **WHOLE TOWN** full of **RAD TEENS**, any number of which could sustain books detailing their **OWN UNIQUE ADVENTURES** for at least 75 years, **MINIMUM??**

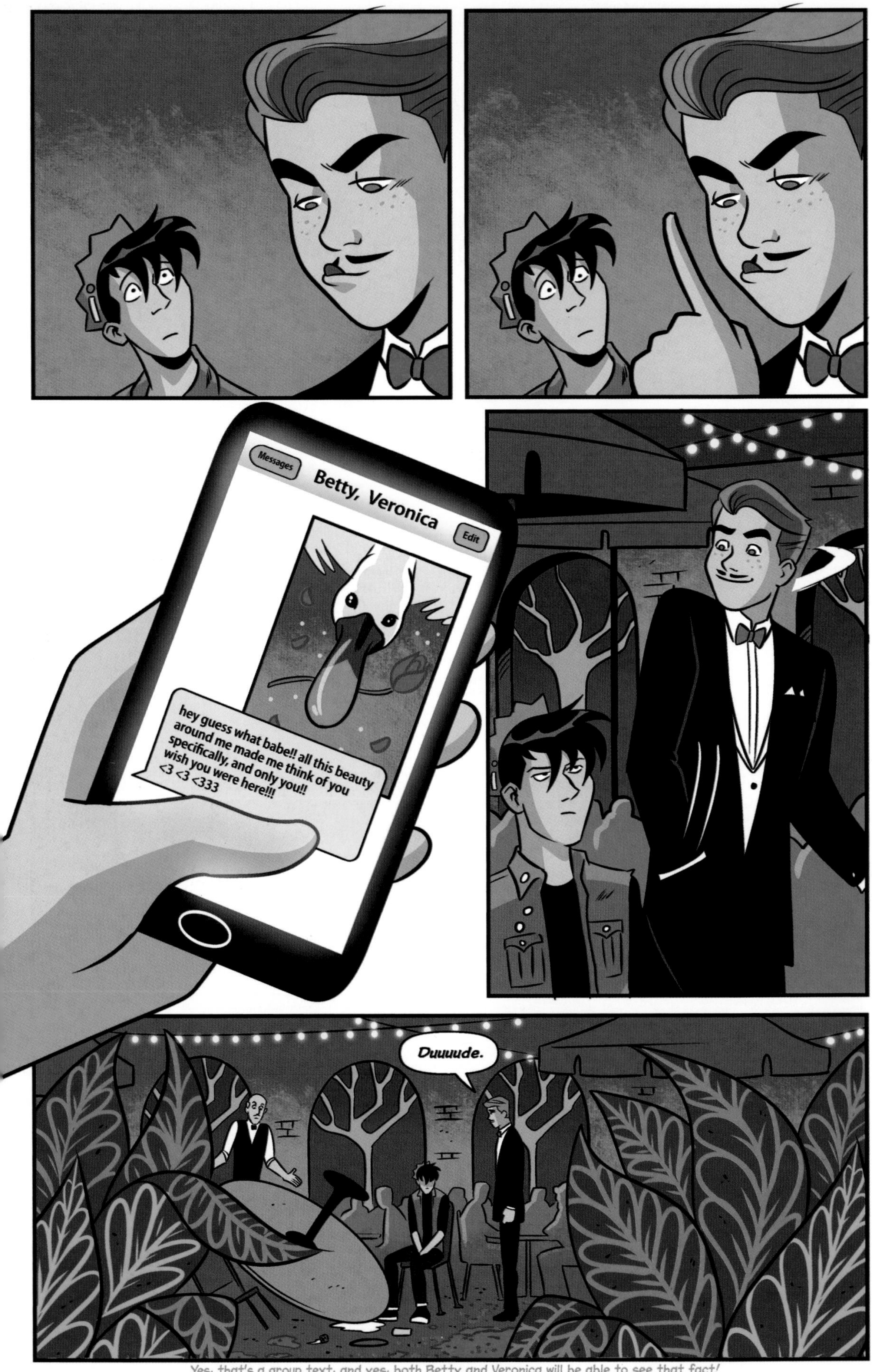
Messages
Betty, Veronica
Edit
hey guess what babe!! all this beauty around me made me think of you specifically, and only you!! wish you were here!!!
<3 <3 <333
Duuuude.
Yes, that's a group text, and yes, both Betty and Veronica will be able to see that fact!
ARCHIE, AGAIN I AM REDUCED TO ASKING: WHAT ARE YOU EVEN DOING

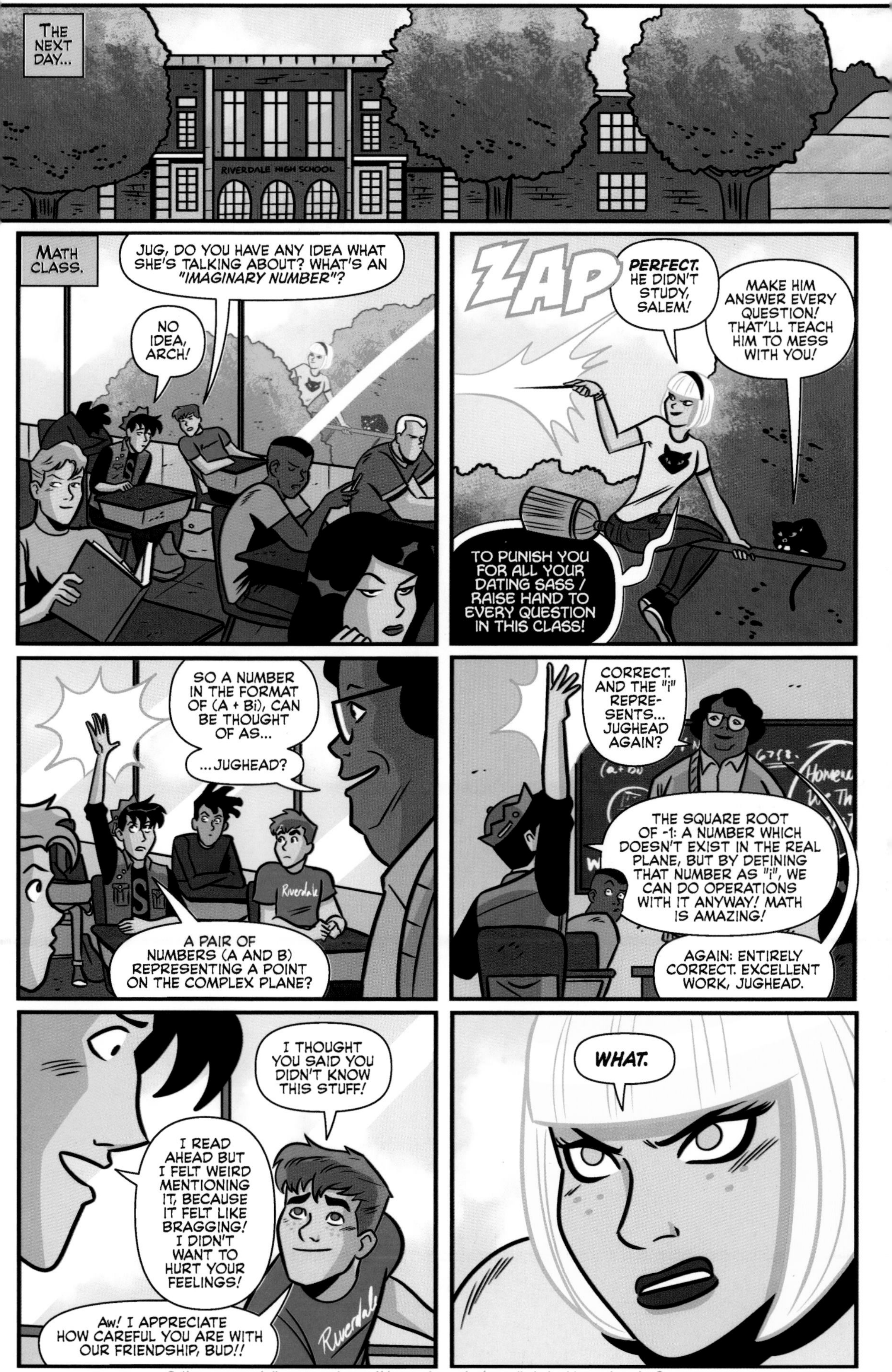
THE NEXT DAY...
RIVERDALE HIGH SCHOOL
MATH CLASS.
JUG, DO YOU HAVE ANY IDEA WHAT SHE'S TALKING ABOUT? WHAT'S AN "IMAGINARY NUMBER"?
NO IDEA, ARCH!
ZAP
PERFECT. HE DIDN'T STUDY, SALEM!
MAKE HIM ANSWER EVERY QUESTION! THAT'LL TEACH HIM TO MESS WITH YOU!
TO PUNISH YOU FOR ALL YOUR DATING SASS / RAISE HAND TO EVERY QUESTION IN THIS CLASS!
SO A NUMBER IN THE FORMAT OF (A + Bi), CAN BE THOUGHT OF AS...
...JUGHEAD?
A PAIR OF NUMBERS (A AND B) REPRESENTING A POINT ON THE COMPLEX PLANE?
CORRECT. AND THE "i" REPRESENTS... JUGHEAD AGAIN?
THE SQUARE ROOT OF -1: A NUMBER WHICH DOESN'T EXIST IN THE REAL PLANE, BUT BY DEFINING THAT NUMBER AS "i", WE CAN DO OPERATIONS WITH IT ANYWAY! MATH IS AMAZING!
AGAIN: ENTIRELY CORRECT. EXCELLENT WORK, JUGHEAD.
I THOUGHT YOU SAID YOU DIDN'T KNOW THIS STUFF!
I READ AHEAD BUT I FELT WEIRD MENTIONING IT, BECAUSE IT FELT LIKE BRAGGING! I DIDN'T WANT TO HURT YOUR FEELINGS!
AW! I APPRECIATE HOW CAREFUL YOU ARE WITH OUR FRIENDSHIP, BUD!!
WHAT.

Q: How can you tell someone has written a character's spells in iambic pentameter?
A: ***DON'T WORRY, THEY'LL TELL YOU***

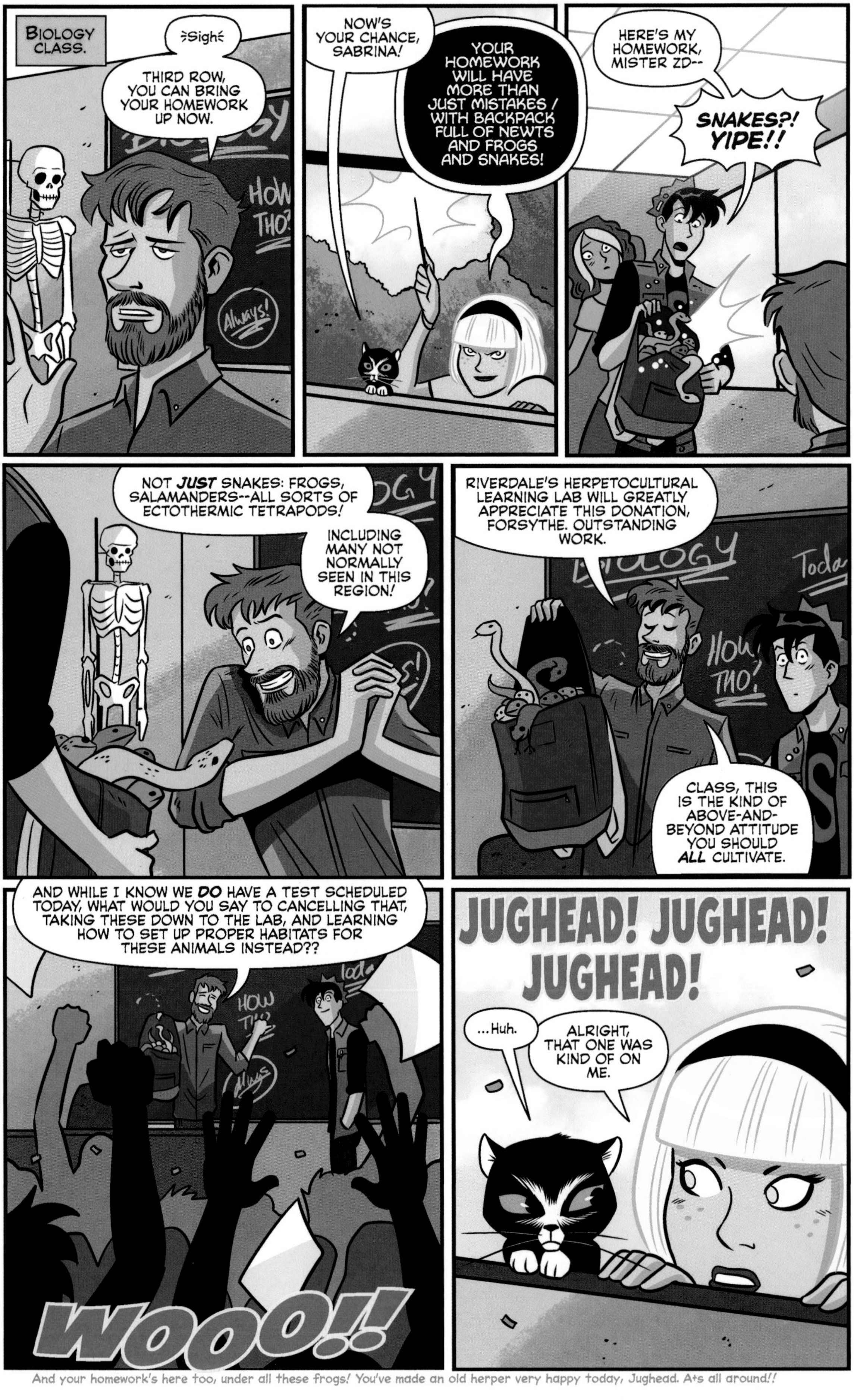
BIOLOGY CLASS.
⪼Sigh⪻
THIRD ROW, YOU CAN BRING YOUR HOMEWORK UP NOW.
NOW'S YOUR CHANCE, SABRINA!
YOUR HOMEWORK WILL HAVE MORE THAN JUST MISTAKES / WITH BACKPACK FULL OF NEWTS AND FROGS AND SNAKES!
HERE'S MY HOMEWORK, MISTER ZD--
SNAKES?! YIPE!!
NOT JUST SNAKES: FROGS, SALAMANDERS--ALL SORTS OF ECTOTHERMIC TETRAPODS!
INCLUDING MANY NOT NORMALLY SEEN IN THIS REGION!
RIVERDALE'S HERPETOCULTURAL LEARNING LAB WILL GREATLY APPRECIATE THIS DONATION, FORSYTHE. OUTSTANDING WORK.
CLASS, THIS IS THE KIND OF ABOVE-AND-BEYOND ATTITUDE YOU SHOULD ALL CULTIVATE.
AND WHILE I KNOW WE DO HAVE A TEST SCHEDULED TODAY, WHAT WOULD YOU SAY TO CANCELLING THAT, TAKING THESE DOWN TO THE LAB, AND LEARNING HOW TO SET UP PROPER HABITATS FOR THESE ANIMALS INSTEAD??
WOOO!!
JUGHEAD! JUGHEAD! JUGHEAD!
...Huh.
ALRIGHT, THAT ONE WAS KIND OF ON ME.

And your homework's here too, under all these frogs! You've made an old herper very happy today, Jughead. A+s all around!!

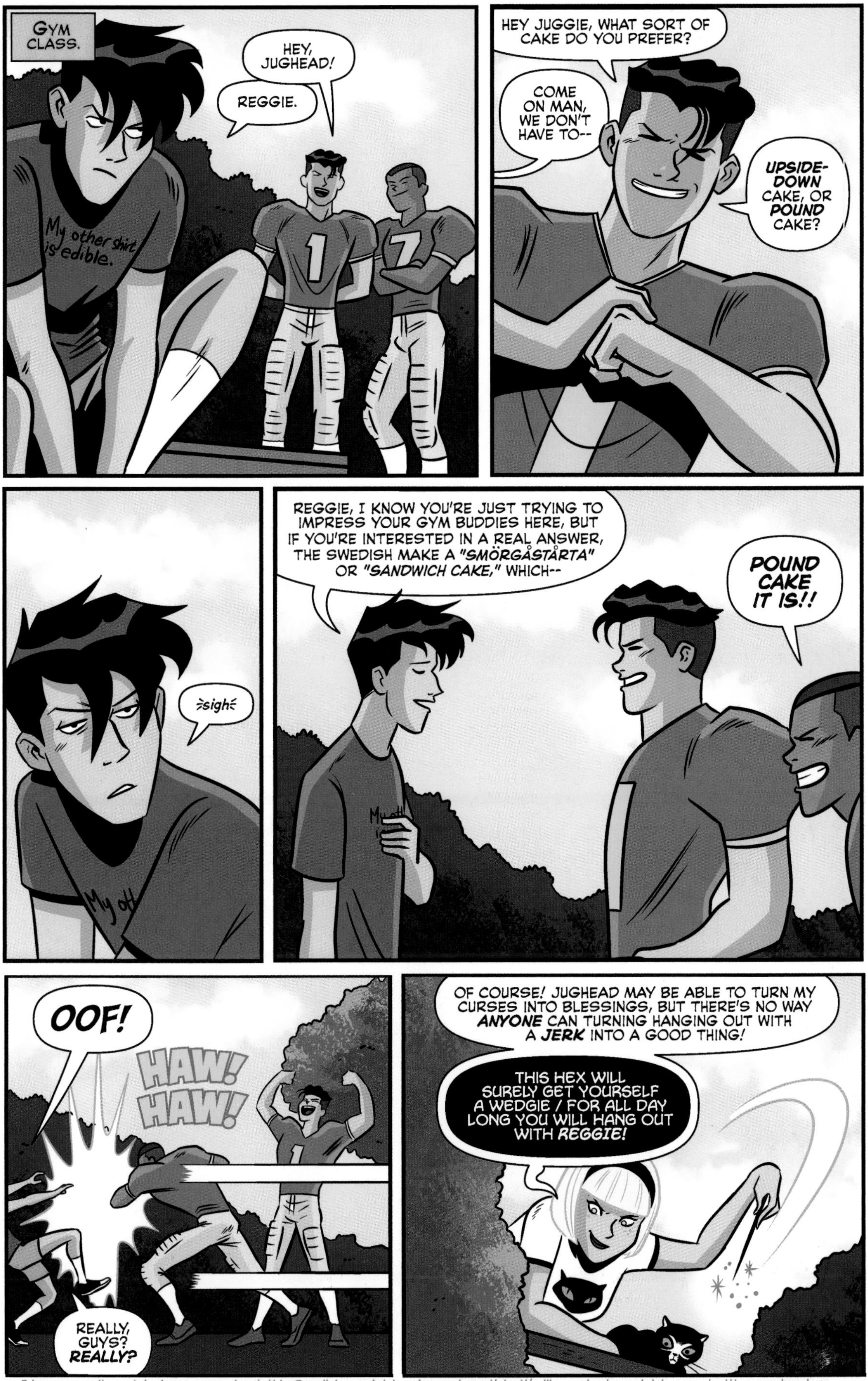
GYM CLASS.
HEY, JUGHEAD!
REGGIE.
My other shirt is edible.
HEY JUGGIE, WHAT SORT OF CAKE DO YOU PREFER?
COME ON MAN, WE DON'T HAVE TO--
UPSIDE-DOWN CAKE, OR POUND CAKE?
sigh
REGGIE, I KNOW YOU'RE JUST TRYING TO IMPRESS YOUR GYM BUDDIES HERE, BUT IF YOU'RE INTERESTED IN A REAL ANSWER, THE SWEDISH MAKE A "SMÖRGÅSTÅRTA" OR "SANDWICH CAKE," WHICH--
POUND CAKE IT IS!!
OOF!
HAW! HAW!
REALLY, GUYS? REALLY?
OF COURSE! JUGHEAD MAY BE ABLE TO TURN MY CURSES INTO BLESSINGS, BUT THERE'S NO WAY ANYONE CAN TURNING HANGING OUT WITH A JERK INTO A GOOD THING!
THIS HEX WILL SURELY GET YOURSELF A WEDGIE / FOR ALL DAY LONG YOU WILL HANG OUT WITH REGGIE!

I know you all want to hear more about this Swedish sandwich cake, so here it is: it's like a giant sandwich except with more toppings, you cut it like a cake, and you sprinkle the top of the cake with some extra toppings so everyone knows what kind of sandwich cake they're about to eat. ***IT'S AMAZING.***

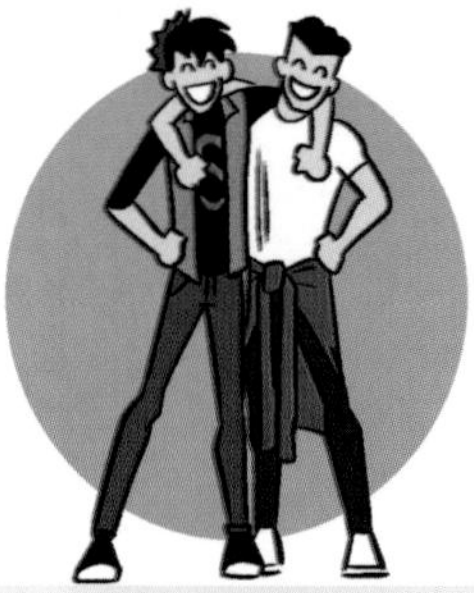

BUT THEN IT TURNED INTO A JUGHEAD/REGGIE

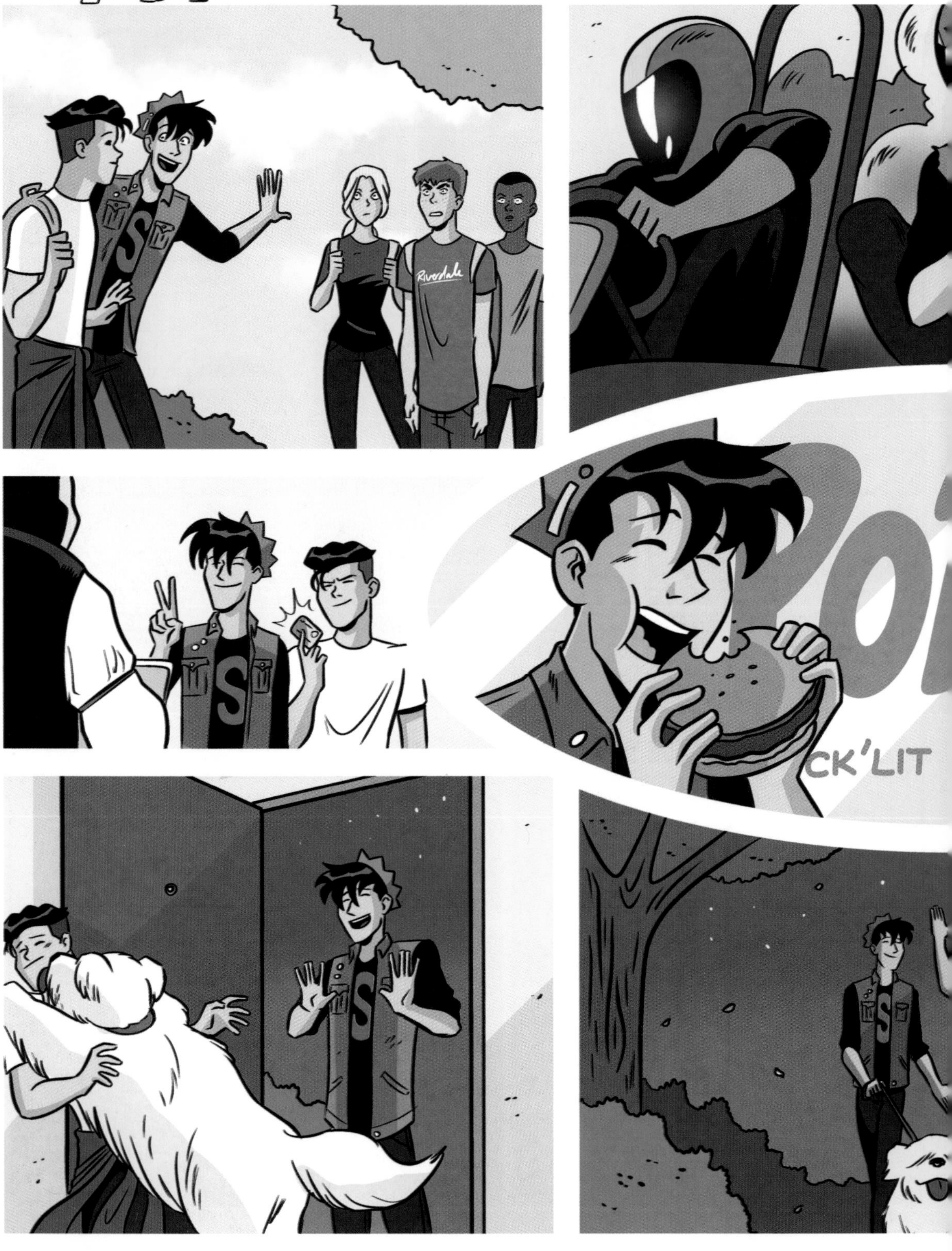
Riverdale
CK'LIT

FRIENDSHIP MONTAGE INSTEAD

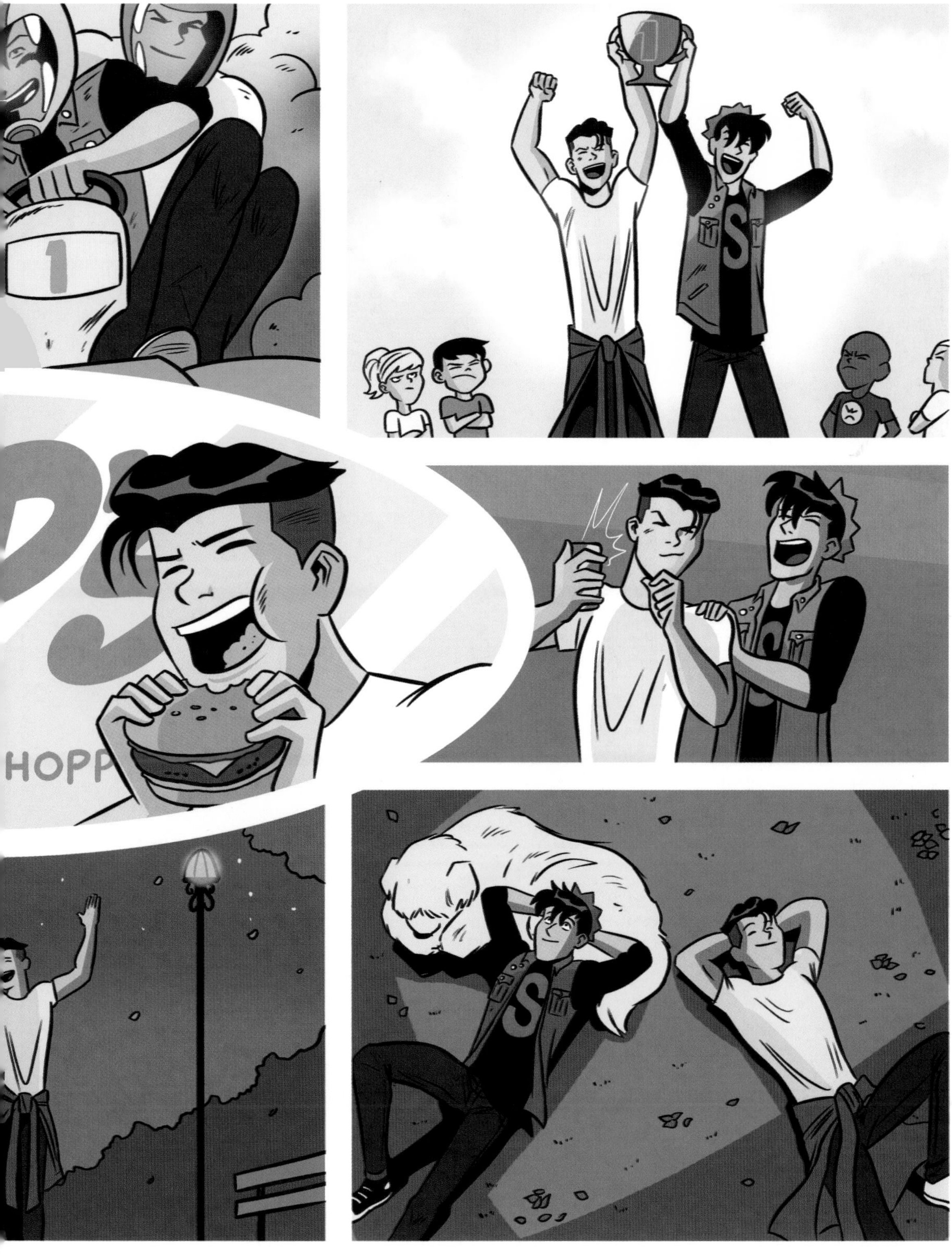

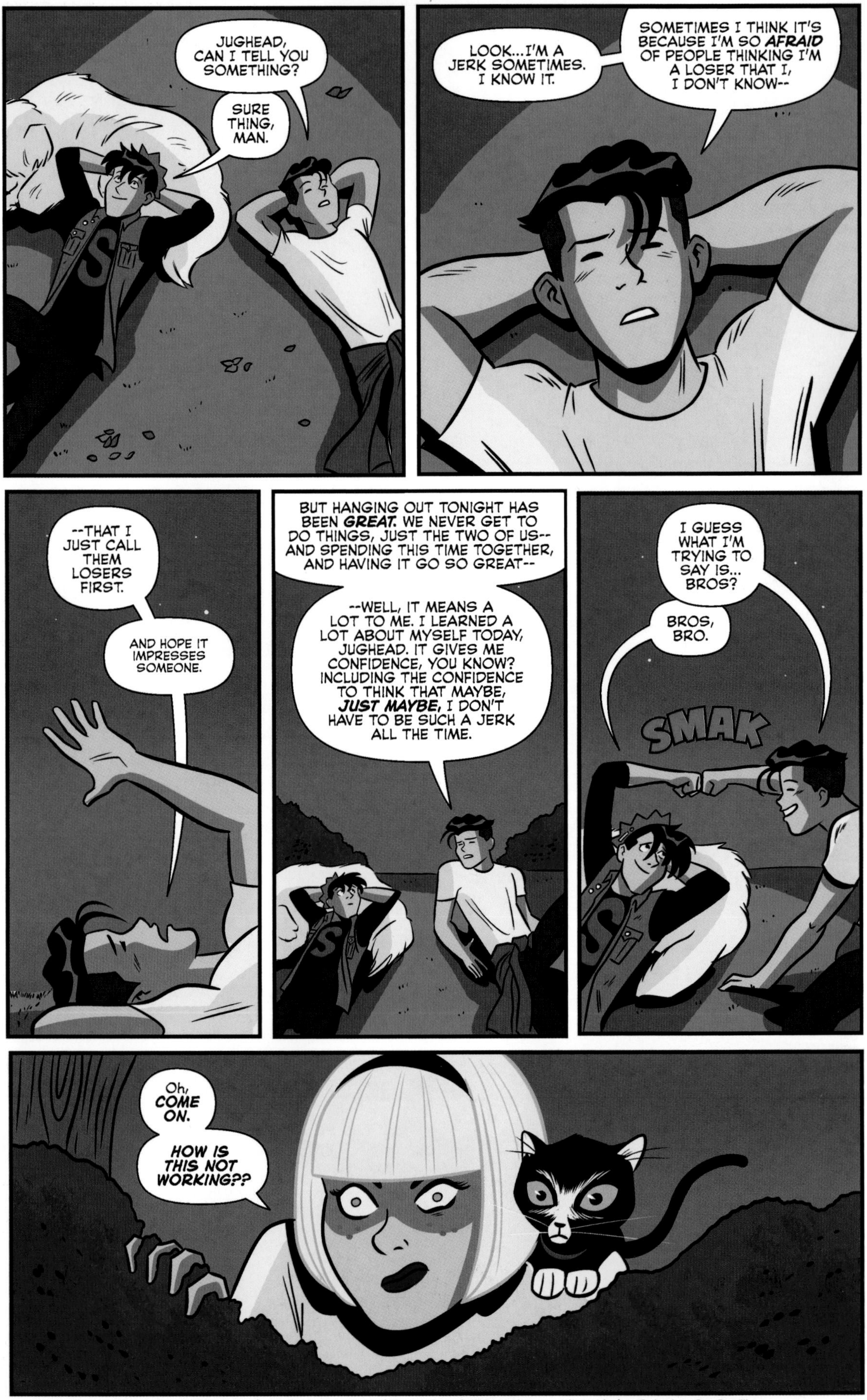
JUGHEAD, CAN I TELL YOU SOMETHING?
SURE THING, MAN.
LOOK...I'M A JERK SOMETIMES. I KNOW IT.
SOMETIMES I THINK IT'S BECAUSE I'M SO AFRAID OF PEOPLE THINKING I'M A LOSER THAT I, I DON'T KNOW--
--THAT I JUST CALL THEM LOSERS FIRST.
AND HOPE IT IMPRESSES SOMEONE.
BUT HANGING OUT TONIGHT HAS BEEN GREAT. WE NEVER GET TO DO THINGS, JUST THE TWO OF US--AND SPENDING THIS TIME TOGETHER, AND HAVING IT GO SO GREAT--
--WELL, IT MEANS A LOT TO ME. I LEARNED A LOT ABOUT MYSELF TODAY, JUGHEAD. IT GIVES ME CONFIDENCE, YOU KNOW? INCLUDING THE CONFIDENCE TO THINK THAT MAYBE, JUST MAYBE, I DON'T HAVE TO BE SUCH A JERK ALL THE TIME.
I GUESS WHAT I'M TRYING TO SAY IS... BROS?
BROS, BRO.
SMAK
Oh, COME ON.
HOW IS THIS NOT WORKING??

Great things happen when you're relaxing on a dog! Dogs: Great Things Happen When You're Relaxing On One™.

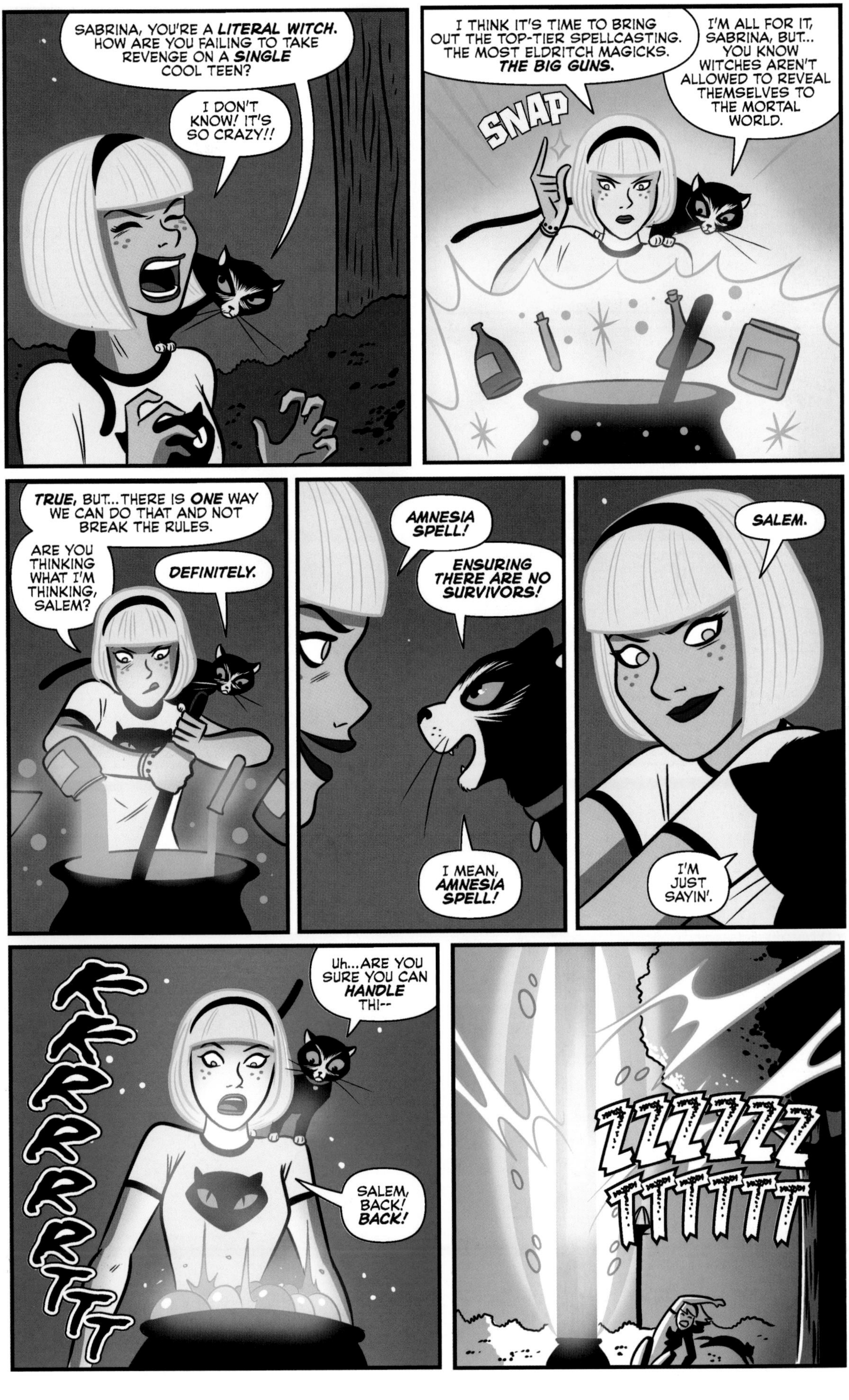
SABRINA, YOU'RE A *LITERAL WITCH.* HOW ARE YOU FAILING TO TAKE REVENGE ON A *SINGLE* COOL TEEN?
I DON'T KNOW! IT'S SO CRAZY!!
I THINK IT'S TIME TO BRING OUT THE TOP-TIER SPELLCASTING. THE MOST ELDRITCH MAGICKS. ***THE BIG GUNS.***
SNAP
I'M ALL FOR IT, SABRINA, BUT... YOU KNOW WITCHES AREN'T ALLOWED TO REVEAL THEMSELVES TO THE MORTAL WORLD.
TRUE, BUT...THERE IS ***ONE*** WAY WE CAN DO THAT AND NOT BREAK THE RULES.
ARE YOU THINKING WHAT I'M THINKING, SALEM?
DEFINITELY.
AMNESIA SPELL!
ENSURING THERE ARE NO SURVIVORS!
I MEAN, ***AMNESIA SPELL!***
SALEM.
I'M JUST SAYIN'.
KKRRRRTTT
UH...ARE YOU SURE YOU CAN ***HANDLE*** THI--
SALEM, BACK! ***BACK!***
ZZZZZZ
TTTTTT

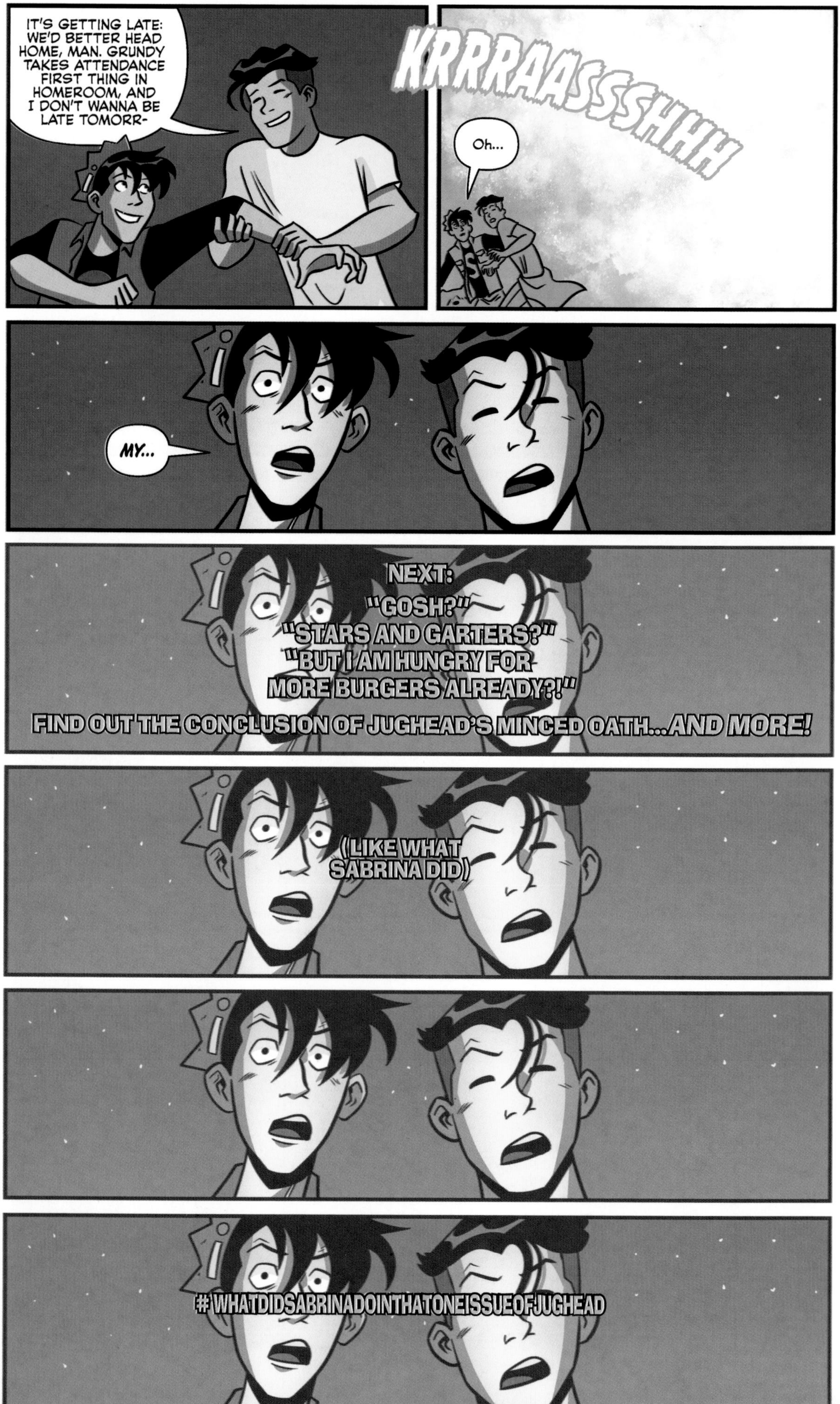
IT'S GETTING LATE: WE'D BETTER HEAD HOME, MAN. GRUNDY TAKES ATTENDANCE FIRST THING IN HOMEROOM, AND I DON'T WANNA BE LATE TOMORR-
KRRRAASSSHHH
Oh...
MY...
NEXT:
"GOSH?"
"STARS AND GARTERS?"
"BUT I AM HUNGRY FOR MORE BURGERS ALREADY?!"
FIND OUT THE CONCLUSION OF JUGHEAD'S MINCED OATH...AND MORE!
(LIKE WHAT SABRINA DID)
#WHATDIDSABRINADOINTHATONEISSUEOFJUGHEAD

TO BE
CONTINUED...

ISSUE **ELEVEN**

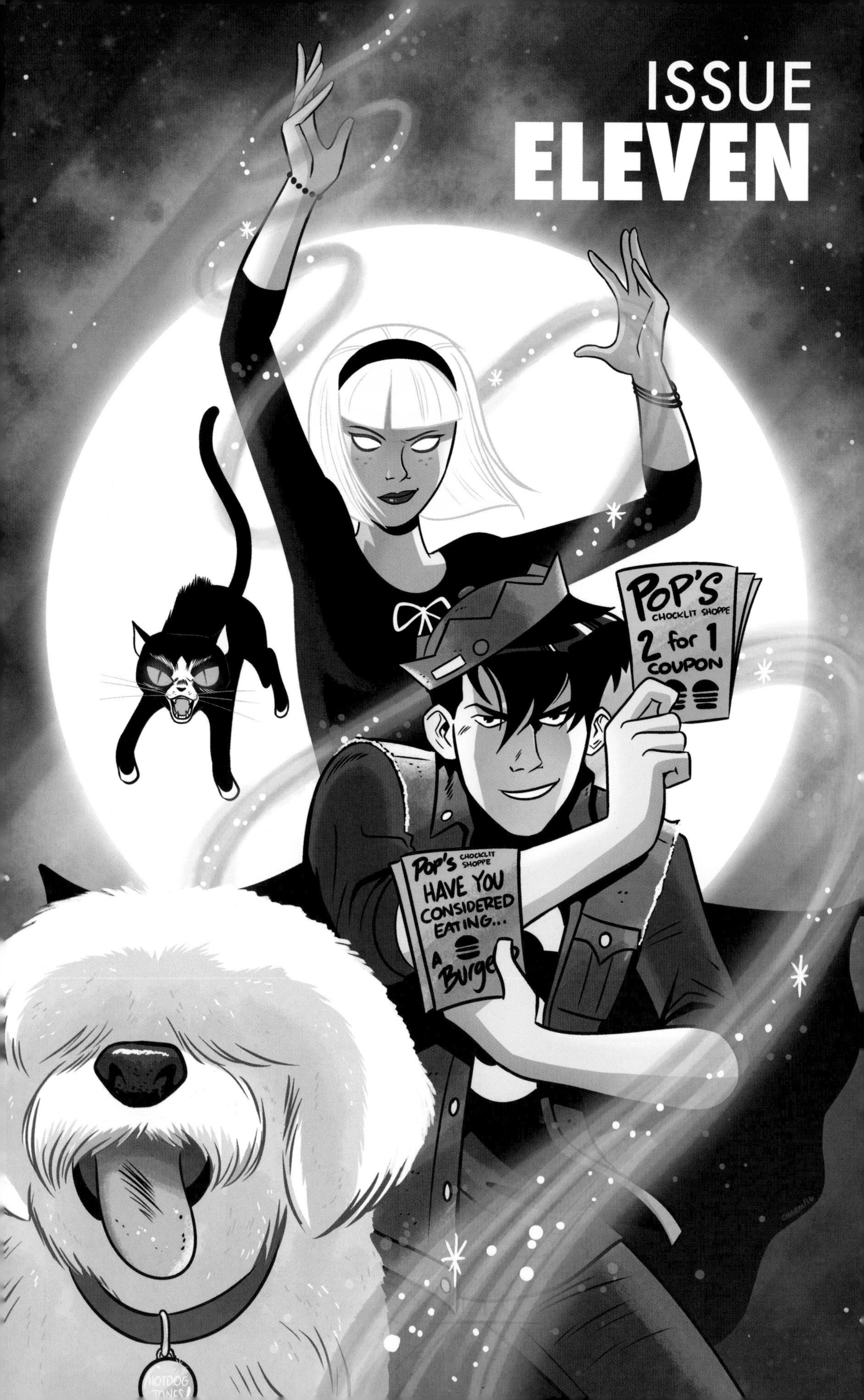

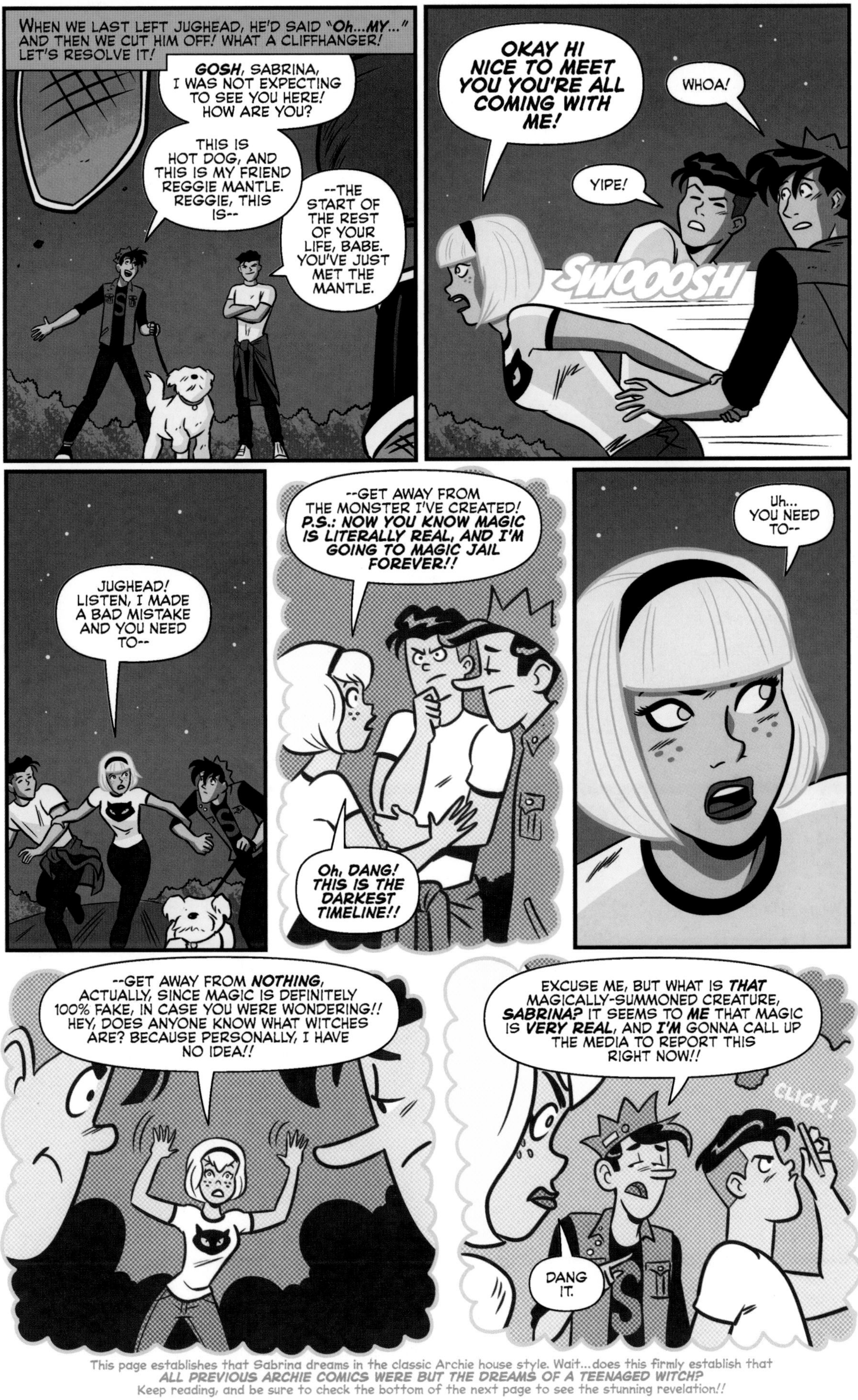
WHEN WE LAST LEFT JUGHEAD, HE'D SAID "Oh...MY..." AND THEN WE CUT HIM OFF! WHAT A CLIFFHANGER! LET'S RESOLVE IT!
GOSH, SABRINA, I WAS NOT EXPECTING TO SEE YOU HERE! HOW ARE YOU?
THIS IS HOT DOG, AND THIS IS MY FRIEND REGGIE MANTLE. REGGIE, THIS IS--
--THE START OF THE REST OF YOUR LIFE, BABE. YOU'VE JUST MET THE MANTLE.
OKAY HI NICE TO MEET YOU YOU'RE ALL COMING WITH ME!
WHOA!
YIPE!
SWOOOSH
JUGHEAD! LISTEN, I MADE A BAD MISTAKE AND YOU NEED TO--
--GET AWAY FROM THE MONSTER I'VE CREATED! P.S.: NOW YOU KNOW MAGIC IS LITERALLY REAL, AND I'M GOING TO MAGIC JAIL FOREVER!!
Oh, DANG! THIS IS THE DARKEST TIMELINE!!
Uh... YOU NEED TO--
--GET AWAY FROM NOTHING, ACTUALLY, SINCE MAGIC IS DEFINITELY 100% FAKE, IN CASE YOU WERE WONDERING!! HEY, DOES ANYONE KNOW WHAT WITCHES ARE? BECAUSE PERSONALLY, I HAVE NO IDEA!!
EXCUSE ME, BUT WHAT IS THAT MAGICALLY-SUMMONED CREATURE, SABRINA? IT SEEMS TO ME THAT MAGIC IS VERY REAL, AND I'M GONNA CALL UP THE MEDIA TO REPORT THIS RIGHT NOW!!
CLICK!
DANG IT.

This page establishes that Sabrina dreams in the classic Archie house style. Wait...does this firmly establish that
ALL PREVIOUS ARCHIE COMICS WERE BUT THE DREAMS OF A TEENAGED WITCH?
Keep reading, and be sure to check the bottom of the next page to see the stunning revelation!!

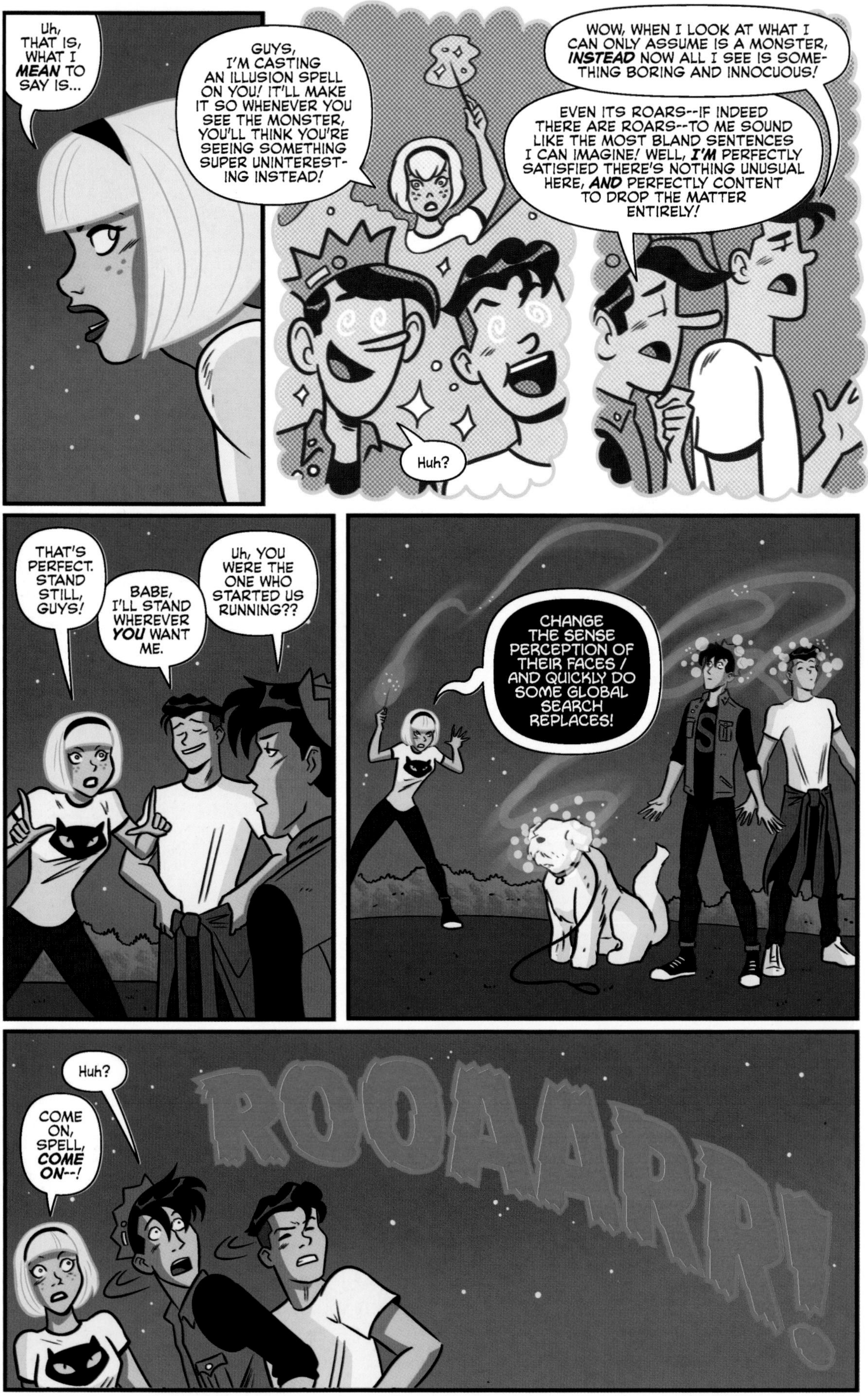
Uh, THAT IS, WHAT I **MEAN** TO SAY IS...
GUYS, I'M CASTING AN ILLUSION SPELL ON YOU! IT'LL MAKE IT SO WHENEVER YOU SEE THE MONSTER, YOU'LL THINK YOU'RE SEEING SOMETHING SUPER UNINTERESTING INSTEAD!
Huh?
WOW, WHEN I LOOK AT WHAT I CAN ONLY ASSUME IS A MONSTER, ***INSTEAD*** NOW ALL I SEE IS SOMETHING BORING AND INNOCUOUS!
EVEN ITS ROARS--IF INDEED THERE ARE ROARS--TO ME SOUND LIKE THE MOST BLAND SENTENCES I CAN IMAGINE! WELL, ***I'M*** PERFECTLY SATISFIED THERE'S NOTHING UNUSUAL HERE, ***AND*** PERFECTLY CONTENT TO DROP THE MATTER ENTIRELY!
THAT'S PERFECT. STAND STILL, GUYS!
BABE, I'LL STAND WHEREVER ***YOU*** WANT ME.
Uh, YOU WERE THE ONE WHO STARTED US RUNNING??
CHANGE THE SENSE PERCEPTION OF THEIR FACES / AND QUICKLY DO SOME GLOBAL SEARCH REPLACES!
Huh?
COME ON, SPELL, ***COME ON***--!
ROOAARR!

Hey, welcome back from the previous page! Anyway the answer is "no, that's crazy, all the adventures actually happened and were documented in comics form, let's all be sensible and stop asking questions about it right now."

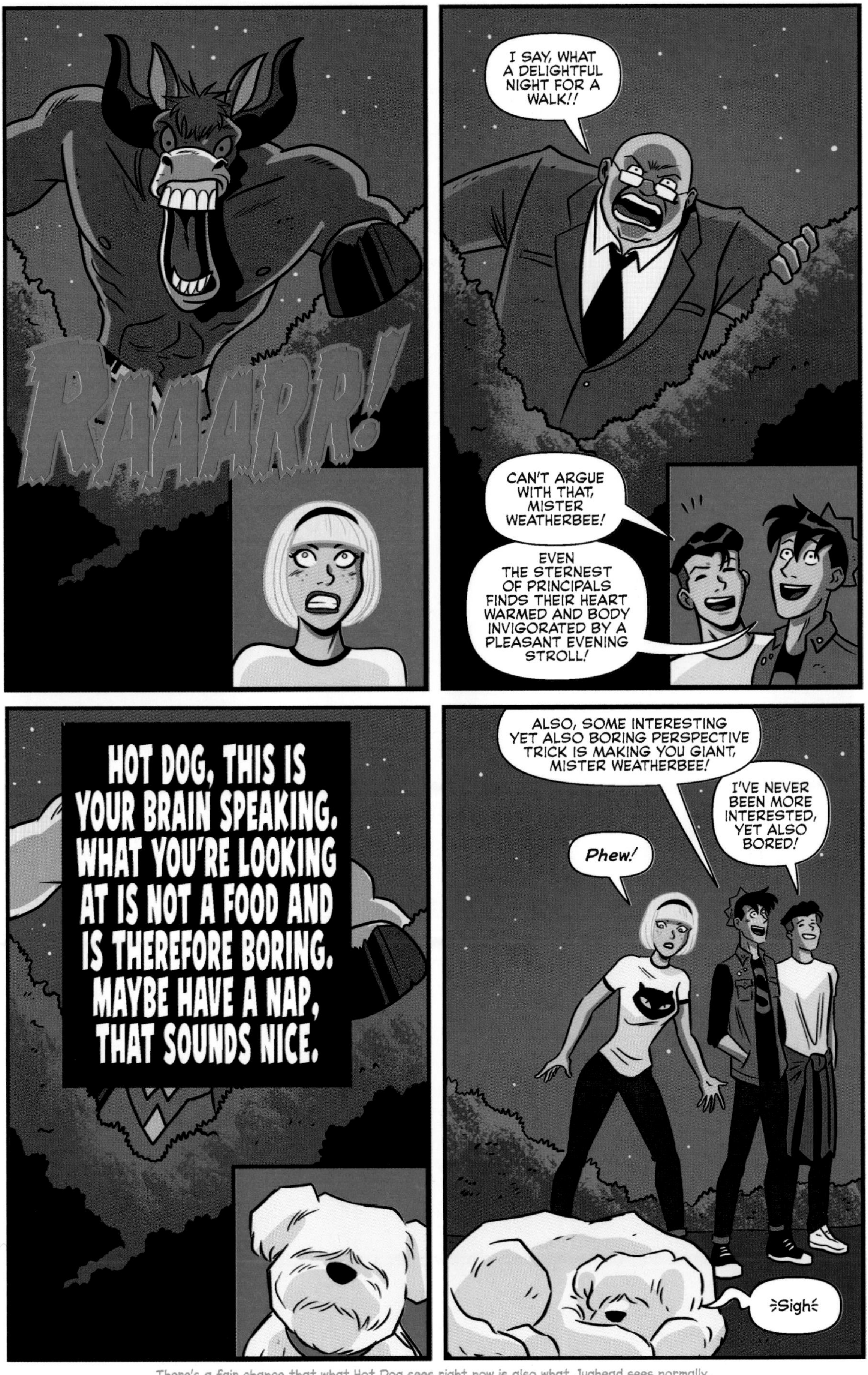
RAAARR!
I SAY, WHAT A DELIGHTFUL NIGHT FOR A WALK!!
CAN'T ARGUE WITH THAT, MISTER WEATHERBEE!
EVEN THE STERNEST OF PRINCIPALS FINDS THEIR HEART WARMED AND BODY INVIGORATED BY A PLEASANT EVENING STROLL!
HOT DOG, THIS IS YOUR BRAIN SPEAKING. WHAT YOU'RE LOOKING AT IS NOT A FOOD AND IS THEREFORE BORING. MAYBE HAVE A NAP, THAT SOUNDS NICE.
ALSO, SOME INTERESTING YET ALSO BORING PERSPECTIVE TRICK IS MAKING YOU GIANT, MISTER WEATHERBEE!
I'VE NEVER BEEN MORE INTERESTED, YET ALSO BORED!
Phew!
Sigh

There's a fair chance that what Hot Dog sees right now is also what Jughead sees normally.
Honestly, there's a fair chance that what Hot Dog sees right now is what *I* see all the time too.

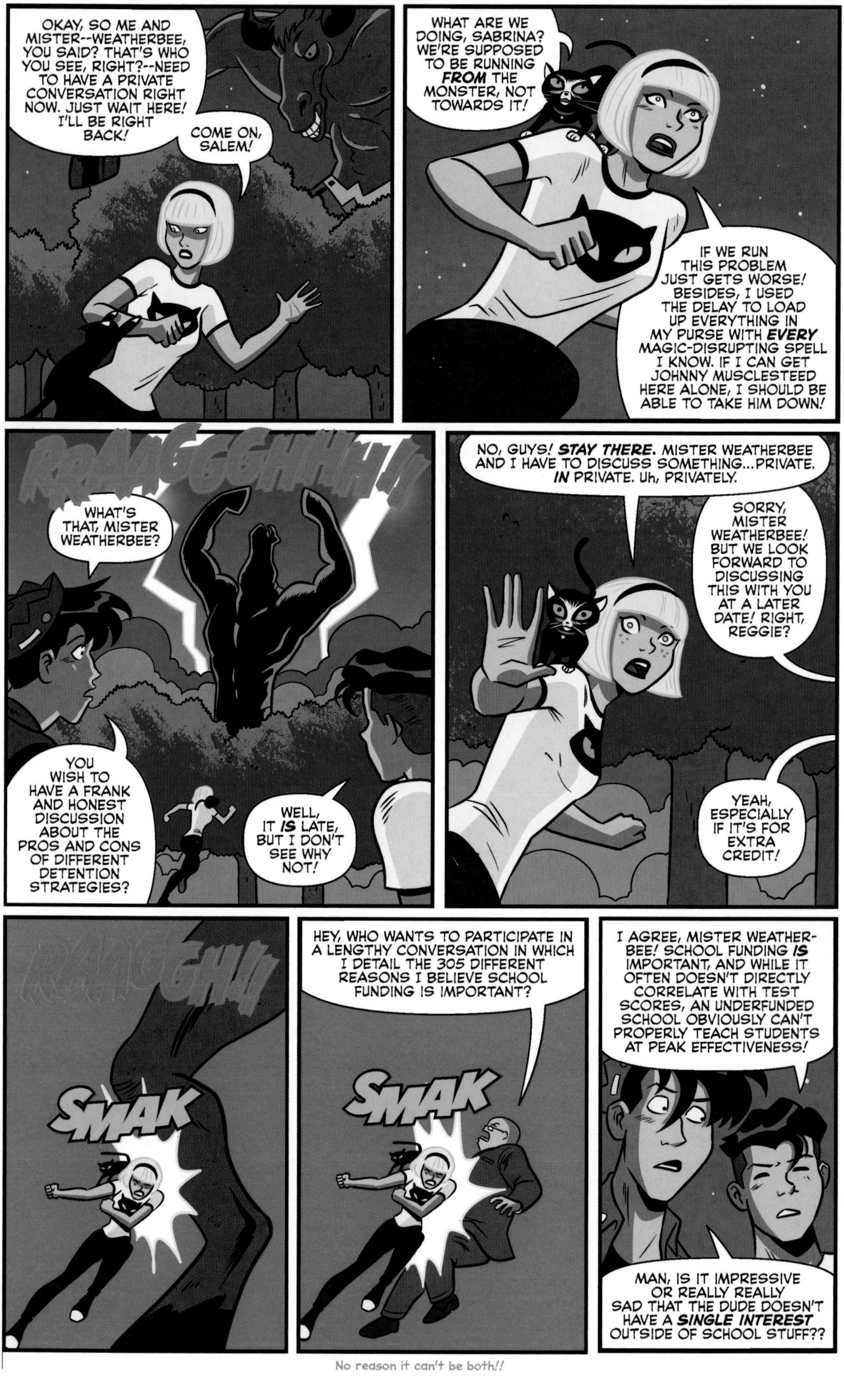
OKAY, SO ME AND MISTER--WEATHERBEE, YOU SAID? THAT'S WHO YOU SEE, RIGHT?--NEED TO HAVE A PRIVATE CONVERSATION RIGHT NOW. JUST WAIT HERE! I'LL BE RIGHT BACK!
COME ON, SALEM!
WHAT ARE WE DOING, SABRINA? WE'RE SUPPOSED TO BE RUNNING FROM THE MONSTER, NOT TOWARDS IT!
IF WE RUN THIS PROBLEM JUST GETS WORSE! BESIDES, I USED THE DELAY TO LOAD UP EVERYTHING IN MY PURSE WITH EVERY MAGIC-DISRUPTING SPELL I KNOW. IF I CAN GET JOHNNY MUSCLESTEED HERE ALONE, I SHOULD BE ABLE TO TAKE HIM DOWN!
RRAAGGGHHHH!!
WHAT'S THAT, MISTER WEATHERBEE?
YOU WISH TO HAVE A FRANK AND HONEST DISCUSSION ABOUT THE PROS AND CONS OF DIFFERENT DETENTION STRATEGIES?
WELL, IT IS LATE, BUT I DON'T SEE WHY NOT!
NO, GUYS! STAY THERE. MISTER WEATHERBEE AND I HAVE TO DISCUSS SOMETHING...PRIVATE. IN PRIVATE. Uh, PRIVATELY.
SORRY, MISTER WEATHERBEE! BUT WE LOOK FORWARD TO DISCUSSING THIS WITH YOU AT A LATER DATE! RIGHT, REGGIE?
YEAH, ESPECIALLY IF IT'S FOR EXTRA CREDIT!
RAAGGH!!
SMAK
HEY, WHO WANTS TO PARTICIPATE IN A LENGTHY CONVERSATION IN WHICH I DETAIL THE 305 DIFFERENT REASONS I BELIEVE SCHOOL FUNDING IS IMPORTANT?
SMAK
I AGREE, MISTER WEATHER-BEE! SCHOOL FUNDING IS IMPORTANT, AND WHILE IT OFTEN DOESN'T DIRECTLY CORRELATE WITH TEST SCORES, AN UNDERFUNDED SCHOOL OBVIOUSLY CAN'T PROPERLY TEACH STUDENTS AT PEAK EFFECTIVENESS!
MAN, IS IT IMPRESSIVE OR REALLY REALLY SAD THAT THE DUDE DOESN'T HAVE A SINGLE INTEREST OUTSIDE OF SCHOOL STUFF??
No reason it can't be both!!

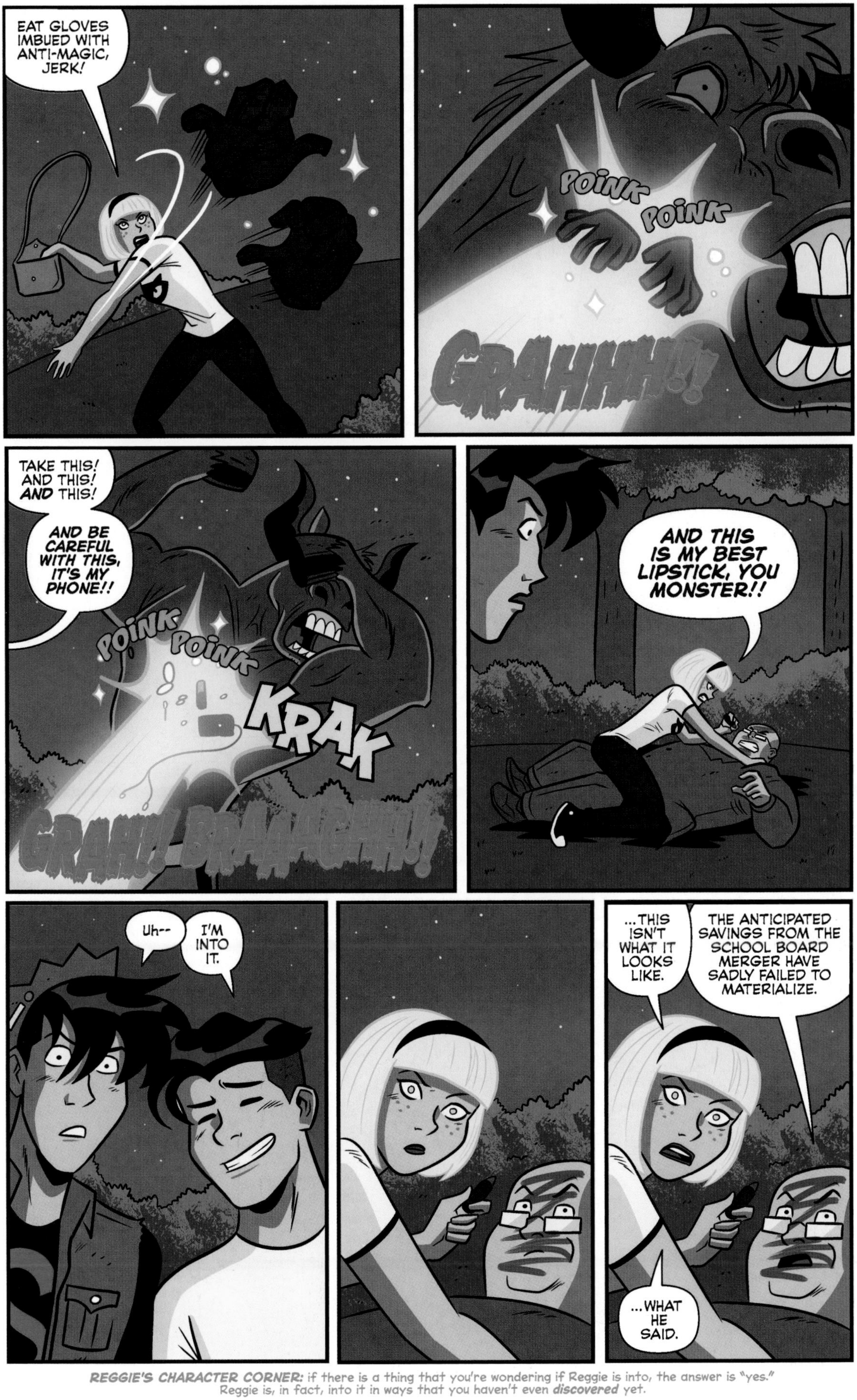
EAT GLOVES IMBUED WITH ANTI-MAGIC, JERK!
POINK
POINK
GRAHHH!!
TAKE THIS! AND THIS! AND THIS!
AND BE CAREFUL WITH THIS, IT'S MY PHONE!!
POINK
POINK
KRAK
GRAH! BRAAAGHH!!
AND THIS IS MY BEST LIPSTICK, YOU MONSTER!!
Uh--
I'M INTO IT.
...THIS ISN'T WHAT IT LOOKS LIKE.
THE ANTICIPATED SAVINGS FROM THE SCHOOL BOARD MERGER HAVE SADLY FAILED TO MATERIALIZE.
...WHAT HE SAID.

REGGIE'S CHARACTER CORNER: if there is a thing that you're wondering if Reggie is into, the answer is "yes." Reggie is, in fact, into it in ways that you haven't even ***discovered*** yet.

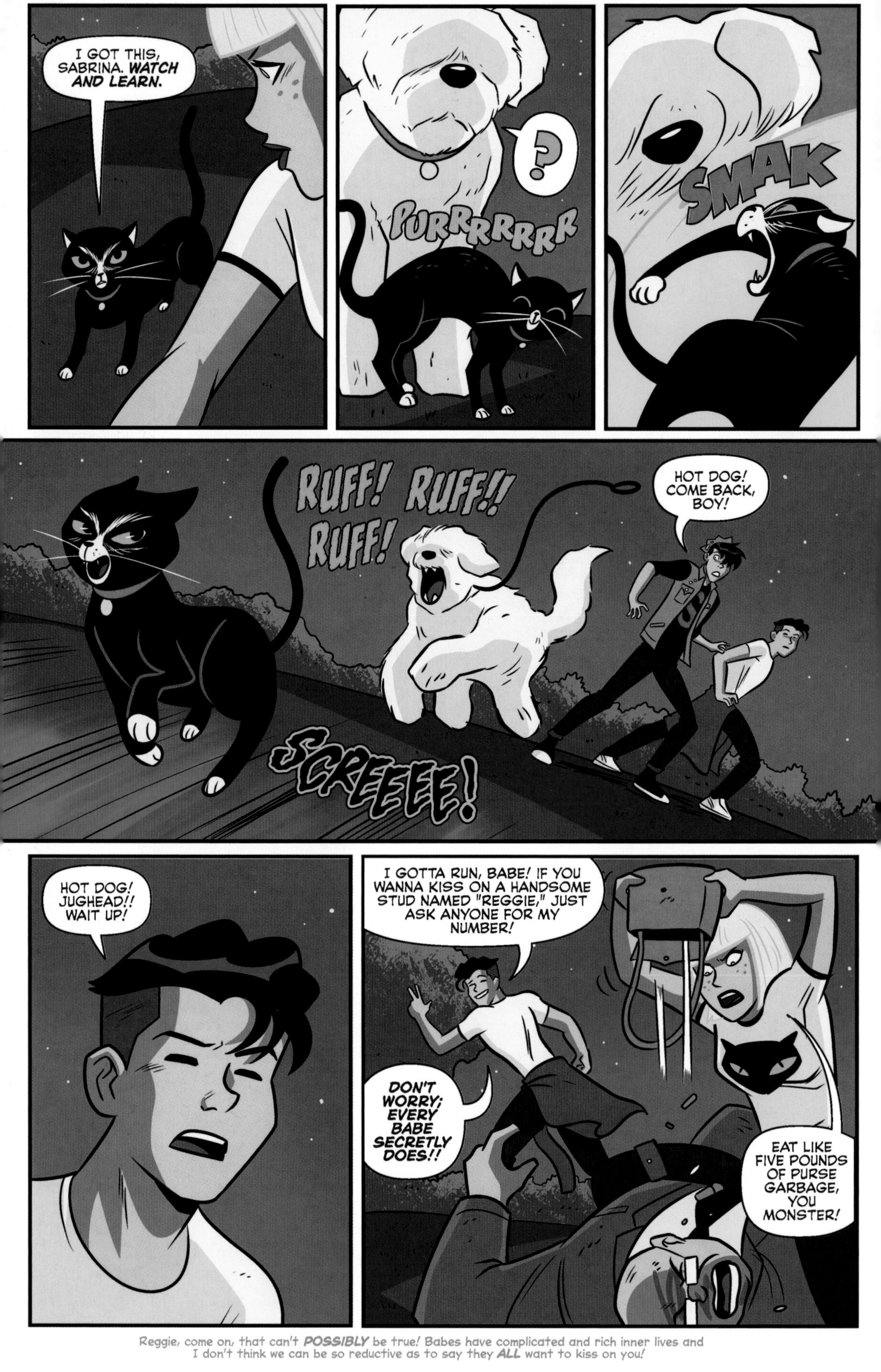
I GOT THIS, SABRINA. WATCH AND LEARN.
?
PURRRRRRRR
SMAK
RUFF! RUFF!! RUFF!
HOT DOG! COME BACK, BOY!
SCREEEE!
HOT DOG! JUGHEAD!! WAIT UP!
I GOTTA RUN, BABE! IF YOU WANNA KISS ON A HANDSOME STUD NAMED "REGGIE," JUST ASK ANYONE FOR MY NUMBER!
DON'T WORRY; EVERY BABE SECRETLY DOES!!
EAT LIKE FIVE POUNDS OF PURSE GARBAGE, YOU MONSTER!

Reggie, come on, that can't ***POSSIBLY*** be true! Babes have complicated and rich inner lives and I don't think we can be so reductive as to say they ***ALL*** want to kiss on you!

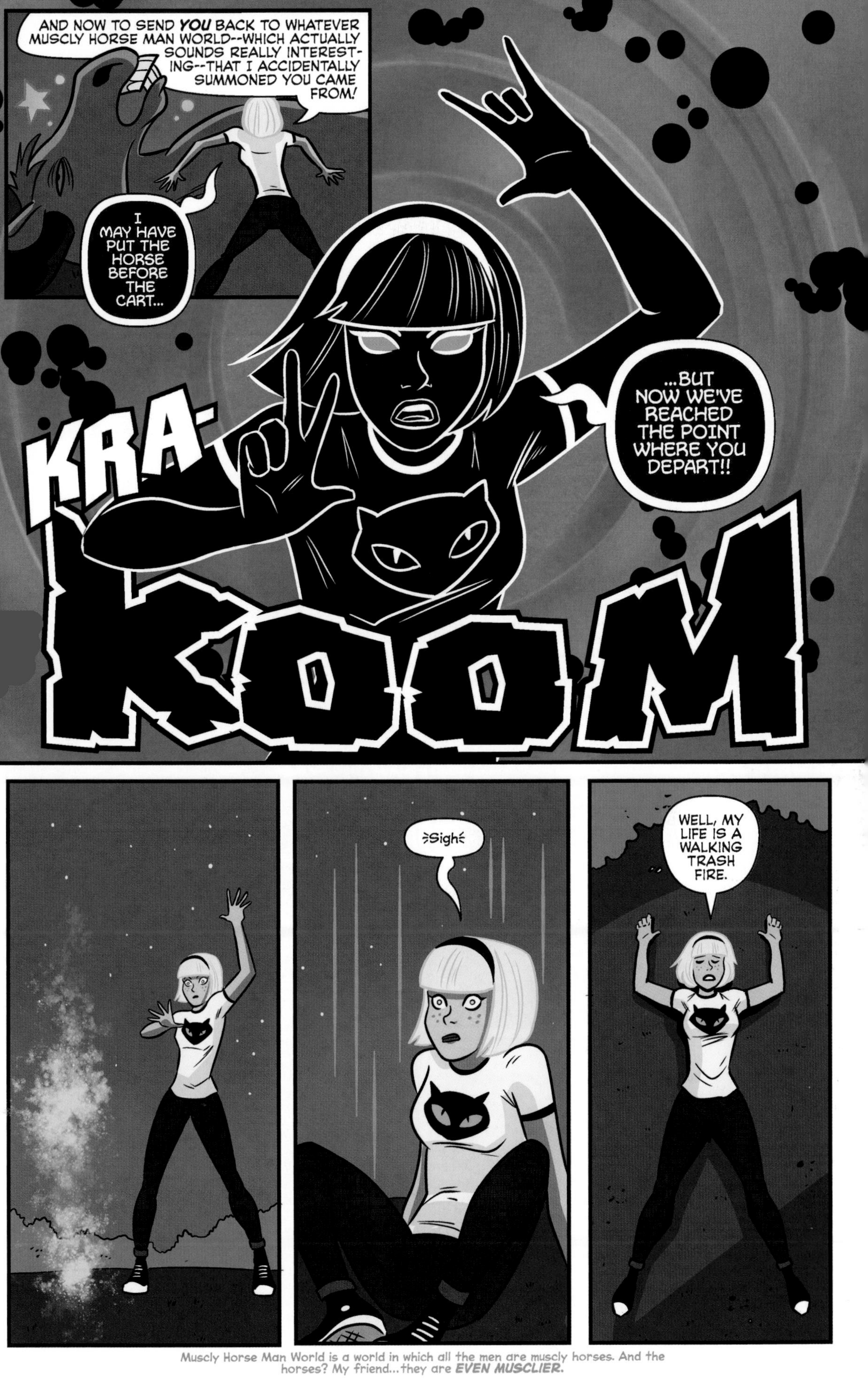
AND NOW TO SEND *YOU* BACK TO WHATEVER MUSCLY HORSE MAN WORLD--WHICH ACTUALLY SOUNDS REALLY INTERESTING--THAT I ACCIDENTALLY SUMMONED YOU CAME FROM!
I MAY HAVE PUT THE HORSE BEFORE THE CART...
...BUT NOW WE'VE REACHED THE POINT WHERE YOU DEPART!!
KRA-KOOM
Sigh
WELL, MY LIFE IS A WALKING TRASH FIRE.

Muscly Horse Man World is a world in which all the men are muscly horses. And the horses? My friend...they are ***EVEN MUSCLIER.***

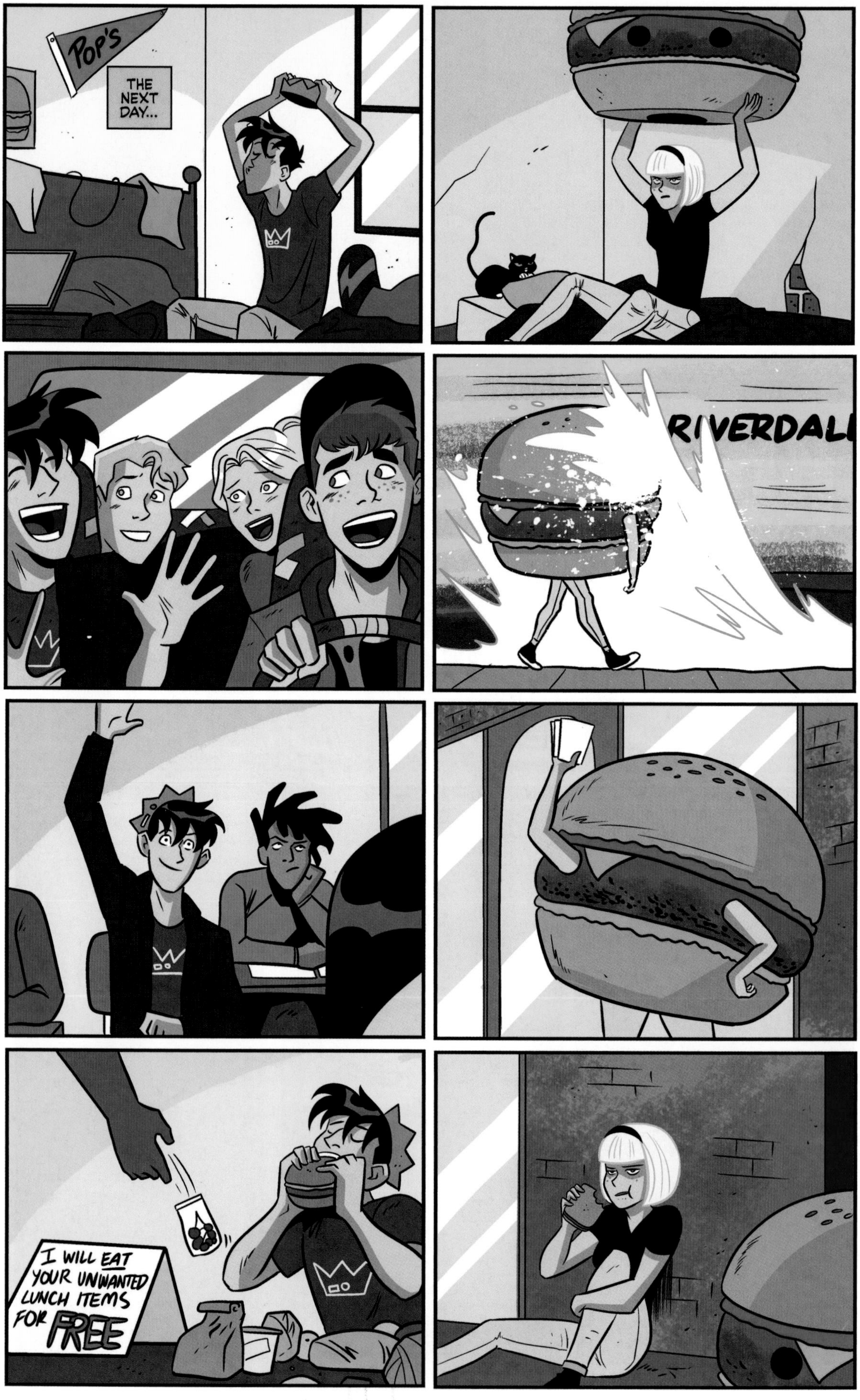
POP'S
THE NEXT DAY...
RIVERDALE
I WILL EAT YOUR UNWANTED LUNCH ITEMS FOR FREE

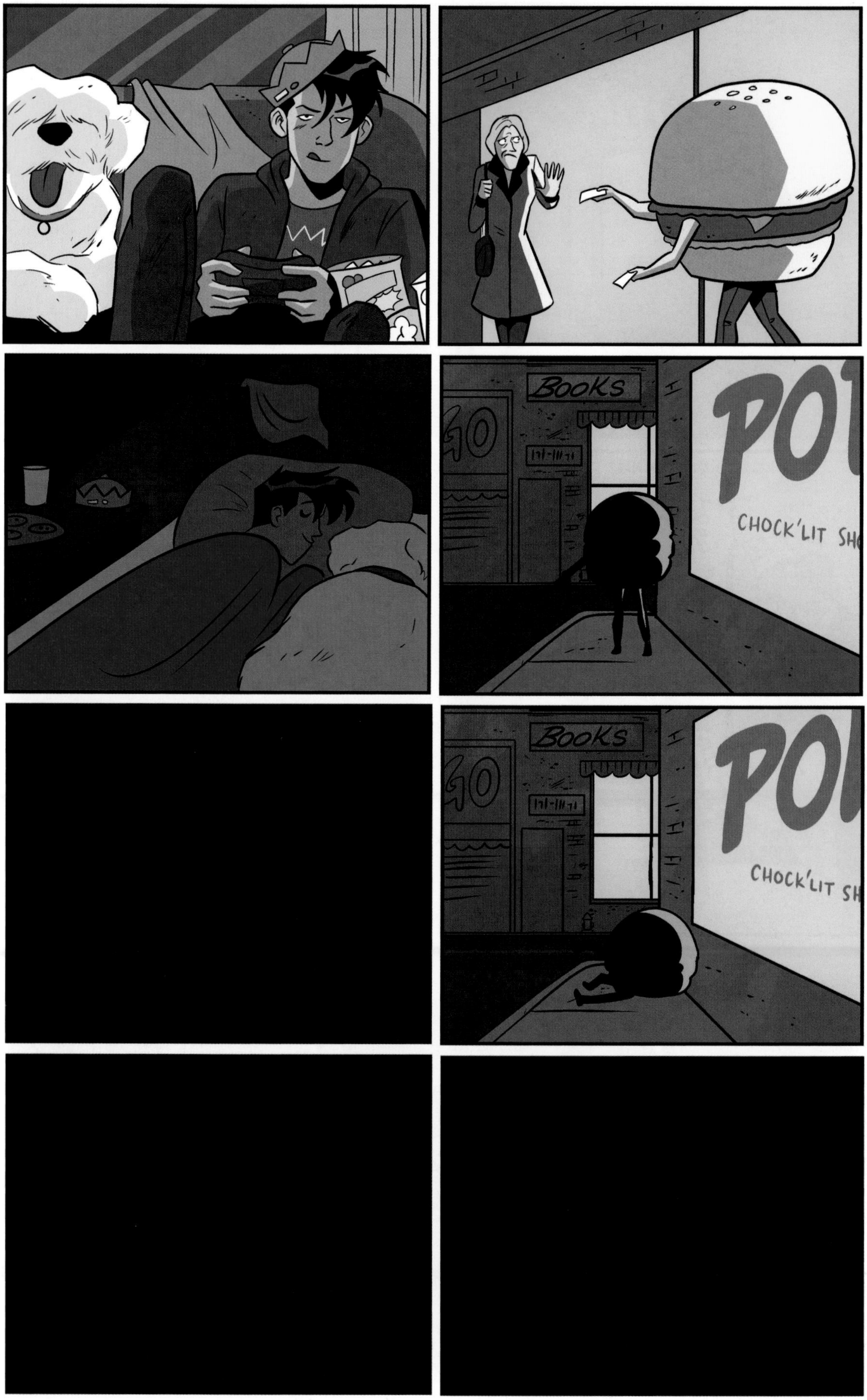
Books
CHOCK'LIT

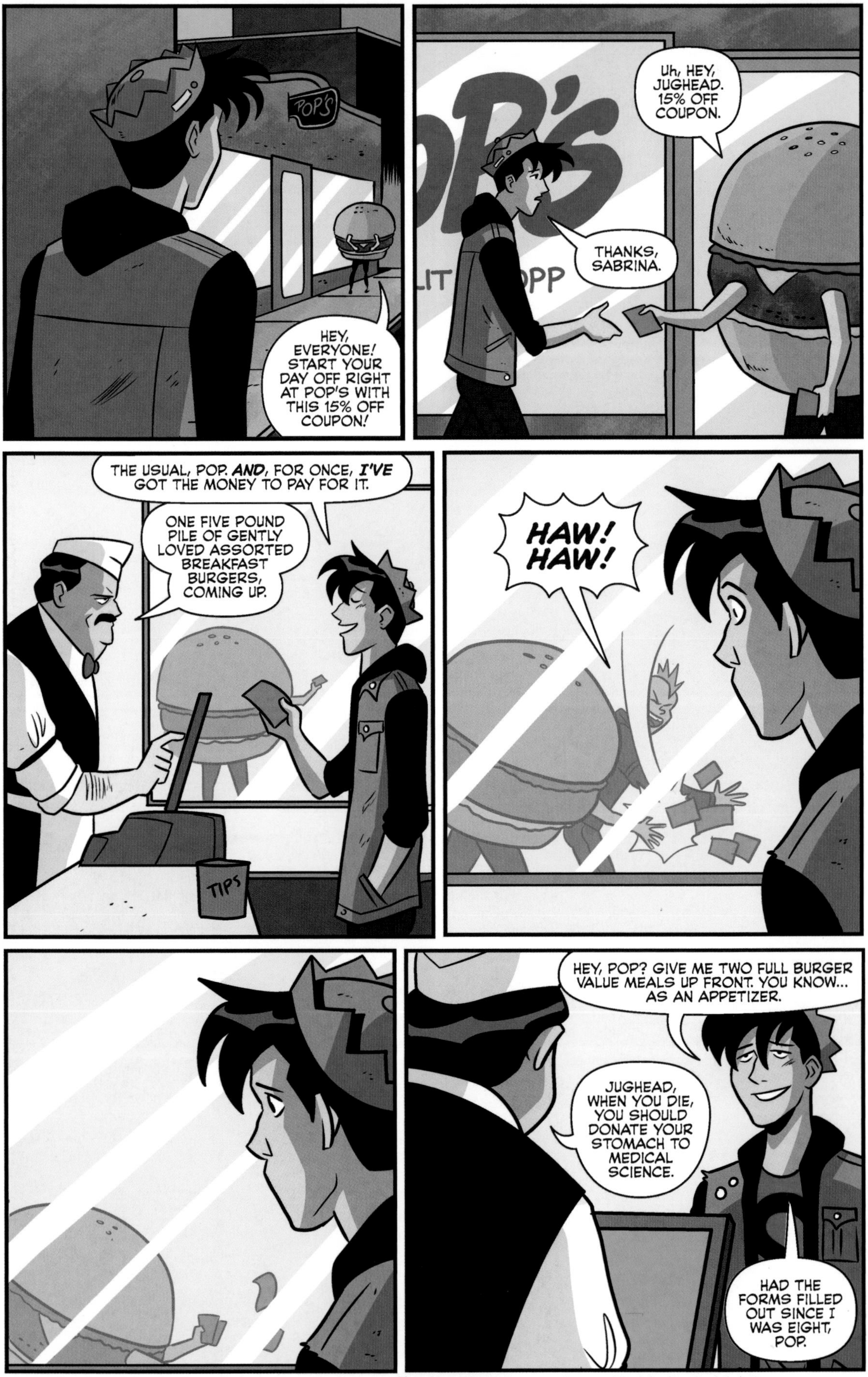
POP'S
HEY, EVERYONE! START YOUR DAY OFF RIGHT AT POP'S WITH THIS 15% OFF COUPON!
UH, HEY, JUGHEAD. 15% OFF COUPON.
THANKS, SABRINA.
THE USUAL, POP. AND, FOR ONCE, I'VE GOT THE MONEY TO PAY FOR IT.
ONE FIVE POUND PILE OF GENTLY LOVED ASSORTED BREAKFAST BURGERS, COMING UP.
TIPS
HAW! HAW!
HEY, POP? GIVE ME TWO FULL BURGER VALUE MEALS UP FRONT. YOU KNOW... AS AN APPETIZER.
JUGHEAD, WHEN YOU DIE, YOU SHOULD DONATE YOUR STOMACH TO MEDICAL SCIENCE.
HAD THE FORMS FILLED OUT SINCE I WAS EIGHT, POP.

My stomach is going to medical science, my brain to a different medical science, and my cool hat to the Cool Hat Museum, which I can only assume will be willed into existence on the strength of my cool hat alone.

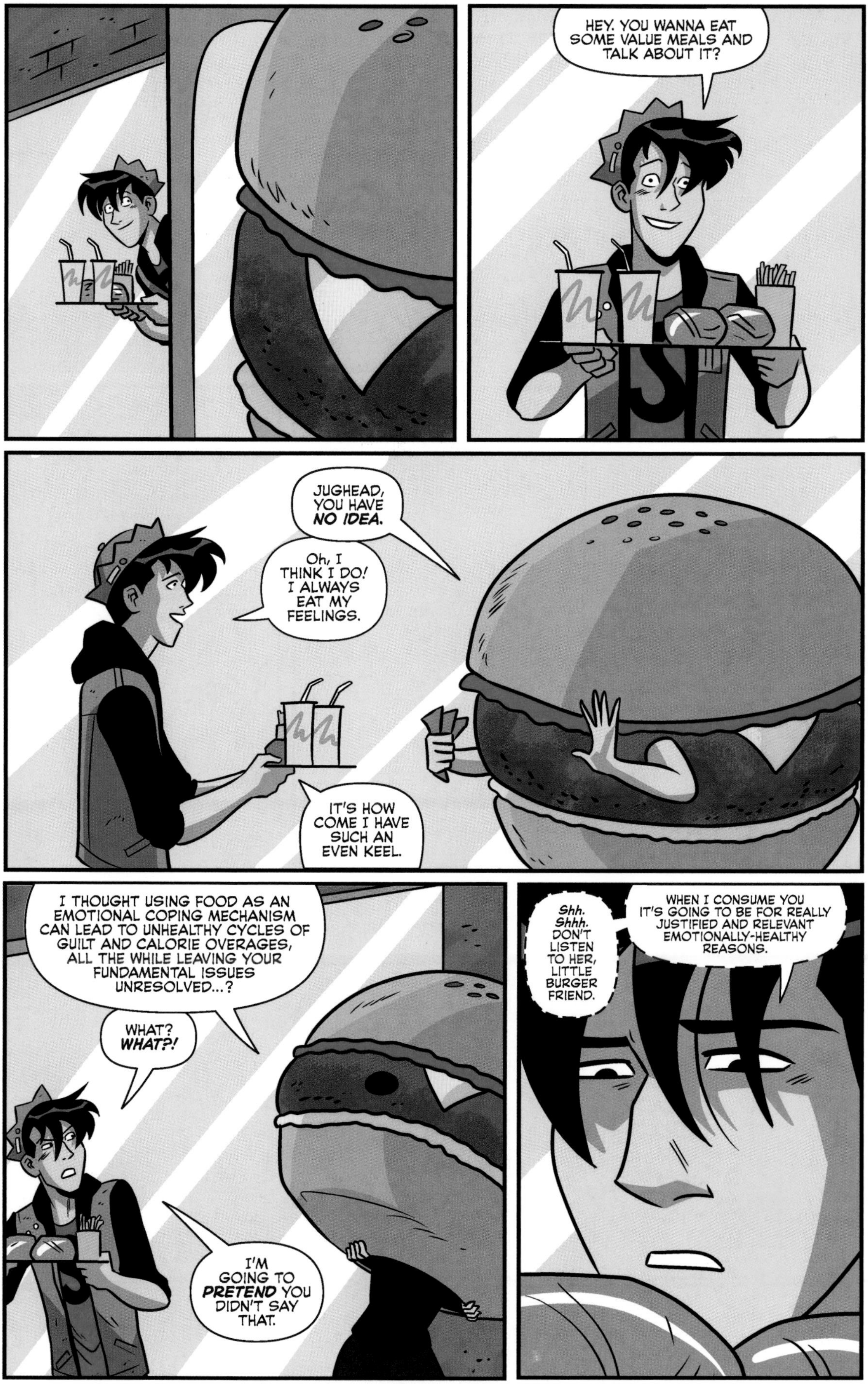
HEY. YOU WANNA EAT SOME VALUE MEALS AND TALK ABOUT IT?
JUGHEAD, YOU HAVE **NO IDEA.**
Oh, I THINK I DO! I ALWAYS EAT MY FEELINGS.
IT'S HOW COME I HAVE SUCH AN EVEN KEEL.
I THOUGHT USING FOOD AS AN EMOTIONAL COPING MECHANISM CAN LEAD TO UNHEALTHY CYCLES OF GUILT AND CALORIE OVERAGES, ALL THE WHILE LEAVING YOUR FUNDAMENTAL ISSUES UNRESOLVED...?
WHAT? **WHAT?!**
I'M GOING TO **PRETEND** YOU DIDN'T SAY THAT.
Shh. Shhh. DON'T LISTEN TO HER, LITTLE BURGER FRIEND.
WHEN I CONSUME YOU IT'S GOING TO BE FOR REALLY JUSTIFIED AND RELEVANT EMOTIONALLY-HEALTHY REASONS.

Everyone eating a burger while reading this comic ***(WHICH HOPEFULLY INCLUDES YOU)*** is looking at their burger suspiciously right now. It's fine! I'm sure your emotions are ***FINE.***

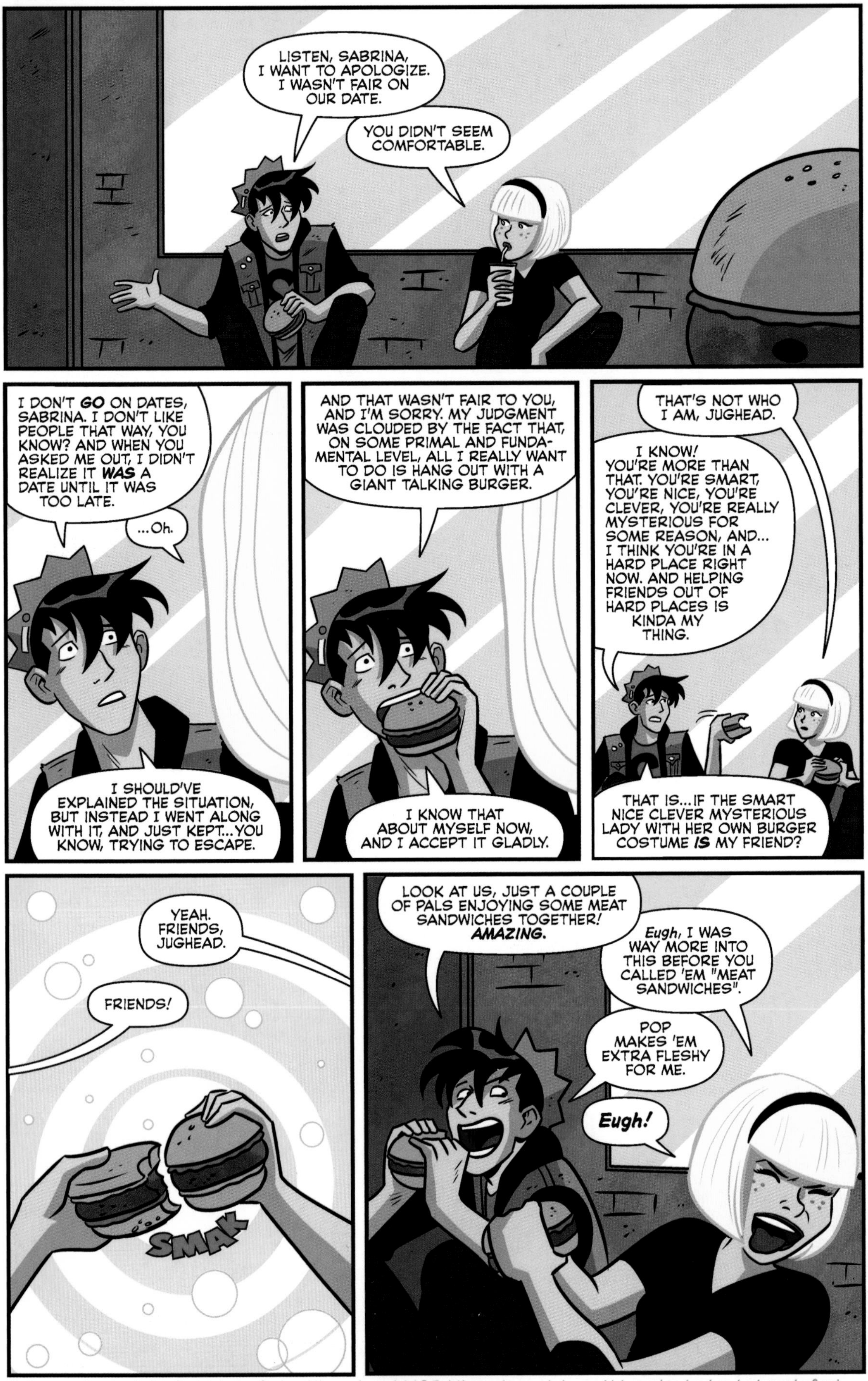
LISTEN, SABRINA, I WANT TO APOLOGIZE. I WASN'T FAIR ON OUR DATE.
YOU DIDN'T SEEM COMFORTABLE.
I DON'T **GO** ON DATES, SABRINA. I DON'T LIKE PEOPLE THAT WAY, YOU KNOW? AND WHEN YOU ASKED ME OUT, I DIDN'T REALIZE IT **WAS** A DATE UNTIL IT WAS TOO LATE.
...Oh.
I SHOULD'VE EXPLAINED THE SITUATION, BUT INSTEAD I WENT ALONG WITH IT, AND JUST KEPT...YOU KNOW, TRYING TO ESCAPE.
AND THAT WASN'T FAIR TO YOU, AND I'M SORRY. MY JUDGMENT WAS CLOUDED BY THE FACT THAT, ON SOME PRIMAL AND FUNDAMENTAL LEVEL, ALL I REALLY WANT TO DO IS HANG OUT WITH A GIANT TALKING BURGER.
I KNOW THAT ABOUT MYSELF NOW, AND I ACCEPT IT GLADLY.
THAT'S NOT WHO I AM, JUGHEAD.
I KNOW! YOU'RE MORE THAN THAT. YOU'RE SMART, YOU'RE NICE, YOU'RE CLEVER, YOU'RE REALLY MYSTERIOUS FOR SOME REASON, AND... I THINK YOU'RE IN A HARD PLACE RIGHT NOW. AND HELPING FRIENDS OUT OF HARD PLACES IS KINDA MY THING.
THAT IS...IF THE SMART NICE CLEVER MYSTERIOUS LADY WITH HER OWN BURGER COSTUME **IS** MY FRIEND?
YEAH. FRIENDS, JUGHEAD.
FRIENDS!
SMAK
LOOK AT US, JUST A COUPLE OF PALS ENJOYING SOME MEAT SANDWICHES TOGETHER! ***AMAZING.***
Eugh, I WAS WAY MORE INTO THIS BEFORE YOU CALLED 'EM "MEAT SANDWICHES".
POP MAKES 'EM EXTRA FLESHY FOR ME.
Eugh!

Yo Pop, can I get a double-flesh interior-flesh cattle meat sandwich? Put it on a bun made by combining water, heat and eukaryote fungi with the edible portion of grasses, okay? No I will **NOT** lower my voice, Pop. No Pop, ***YOU'RE*** scaring away the other customers.

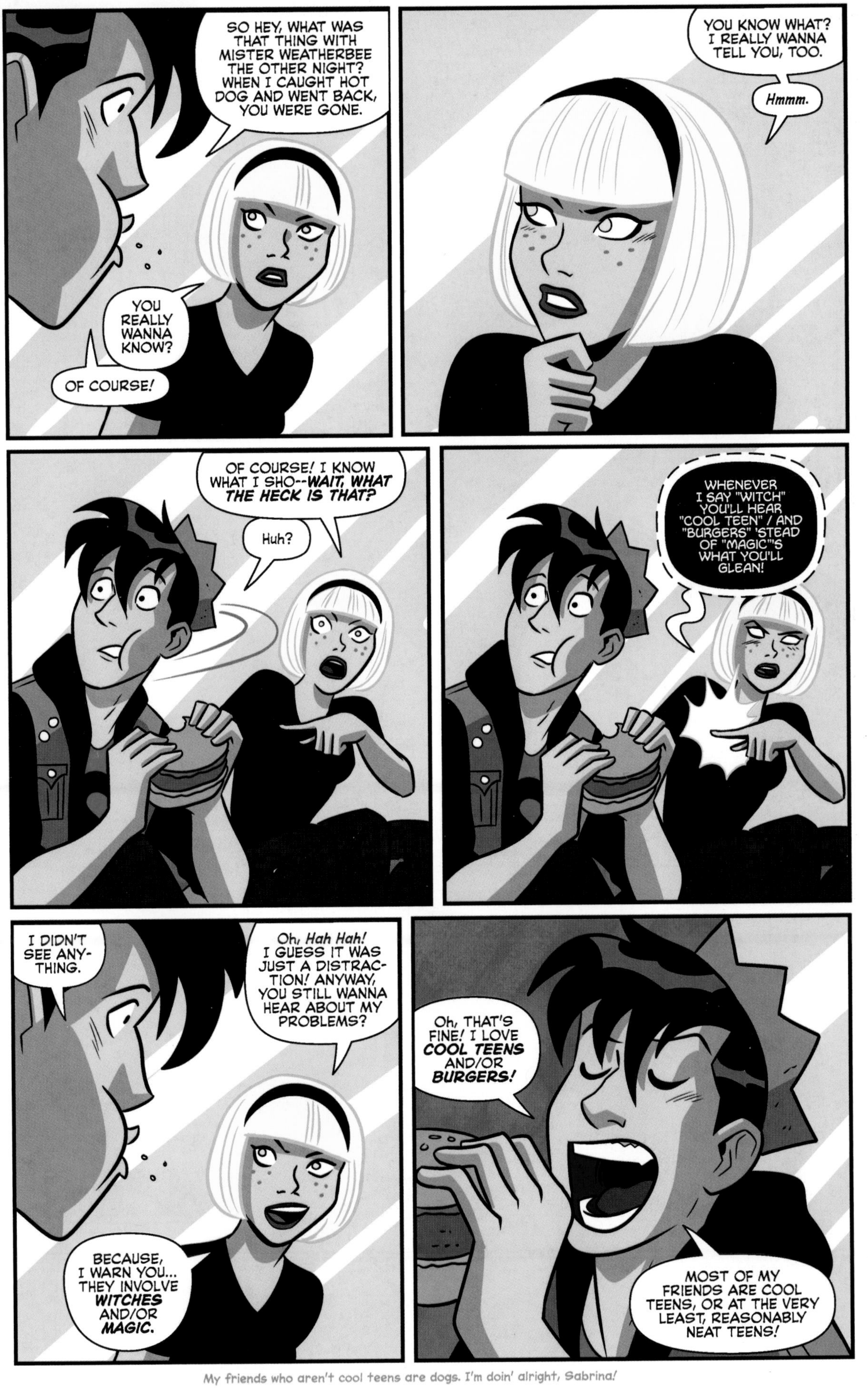
SO HEY, WHAT WAS THAT THING WITH MISTER WEATHERBEE THE OTHER NIGHT? WHEN I CAUGHT HOT DOG AND WENT BACK, YOU WERE GONE.
YOU REALLY WANNA KNOW?
OF COURSE!
YOU KNOW WHAT? I REALLY WANNA TELL YOU, TOO.
Hmmm.
OF COURSE! I KNOW WHAT I SHO--WAIT, WHAT THE HECK IS THAT?
Huh?
WHENEVER I SAY "WITCH" YOU'LL HEAR "COOL TEEN" / AND "BURGERS" 'STEAD OF "MAGIC"'S WHAT YOU'LL GLEAN!
I DIDN'T SEE ANY-THING.
Oh, Hah Hah! I GUESS IT WAS JUST A DISTRAC-TION! ANYWAY, YOU STILL WANNA HEAR ABOUT MY PROBLEMS?
BECAUSE, I WARN YOU... THEY INVOLVE WITCHES AND/OR MAGIC.
Oh, THAT'S FINE! I LOVE COOL TEENS AND/OR BURGERS!
MOST OF MY FRIENDS ARE COOL TEENS, OR AT THE VERY LEAST, REASONABLY NEAT TEENS!

My friends who aren't cool teens are dogs. I'm doin' alright, Sabrina!

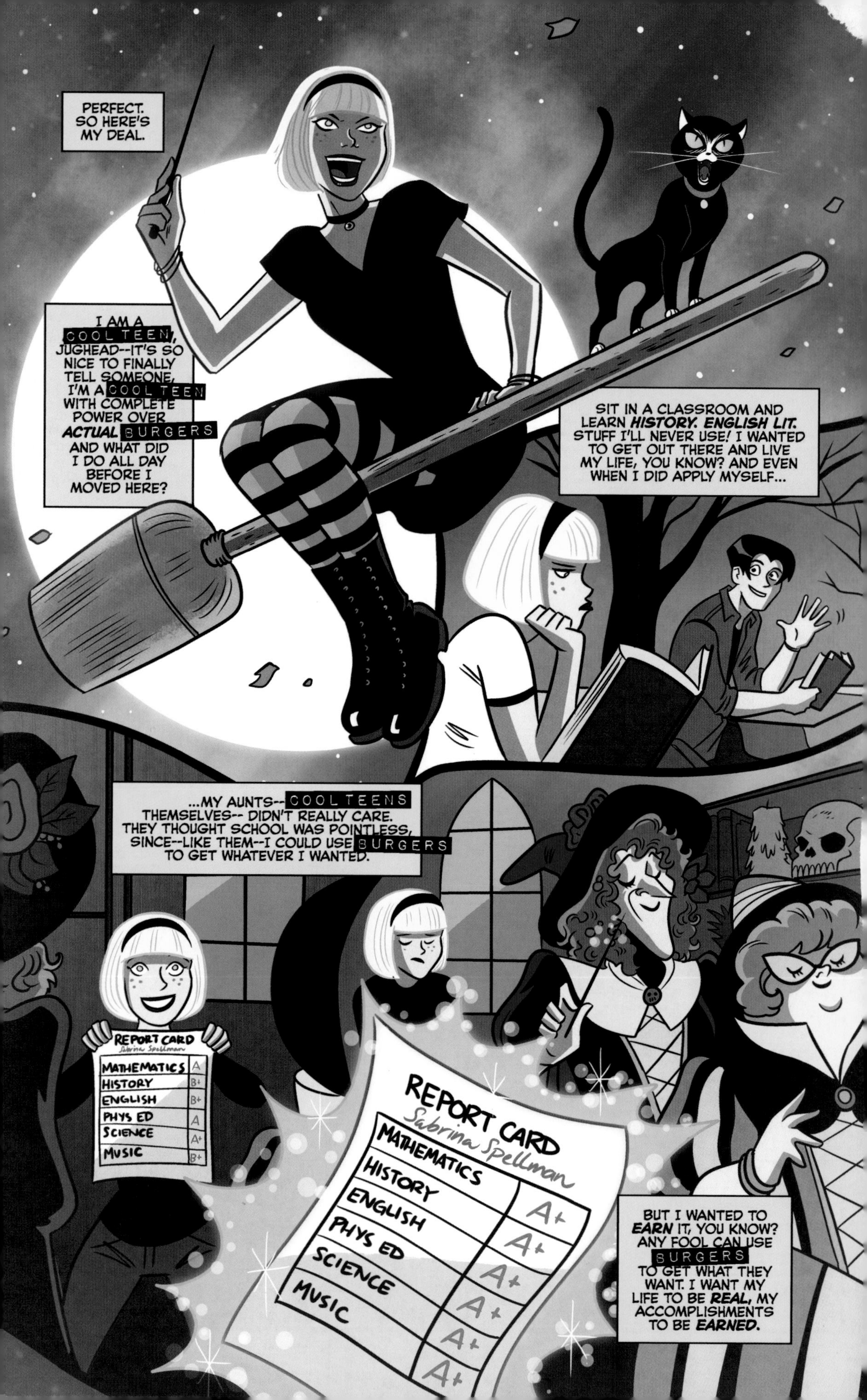
PERFECT. SO HERE'S MY DEAL.
I AM A COOL TEEN, JUGHEAD--IT'S SO NICE TO FINALLY TELL SOMEONE. I'M A COOL TEEN WITH COMPLETE POWER OVER ACTUAL BURGERS AND WHAT DID I DO ALL DAY BEFORE I MOVED HERE?
SIT IN A CLASSROOM AND LEARN HISTORY. ENGLISH LIT. STUFF I'LL NEVER USE! I WANTED TO GET OUT THERE AND LIVE MY LIFE, YOU KNOW? AND EVEN WHEN I DID APPLY MYSELF...
...MY AUNTS--COOL TEENS THEMSELVES-- DIDN'T REALLY CARE. THEY THOUGHT SCHOOL WAS POINTLESS, SINCE--LIKE THEM--I COULD USE BURGERS TO GET WHATEVER I WANTED.
REPORT CARD
Sabrina Spellman
MATHEMATICS A
HISTORY B+
ENGLISH B+
PHYS ED A
SCIENCE A+
MUSIC B+
REPORT CARD
Sabrina Spellman
MATHEMATICS A+
HISTORY A+
ENGLISH A+
PHYS ED A+
SCIENCE A+
MUSIC A+
BUT I WANTED TO EARN IT, YOU KNOW? ANY FOOL CAN USE BURGERS TO GET WHAT THEY WANT. I WANT MY LIFE TO BE REAL, MY ACCOMPLISHMENTS TO BE EARNED.

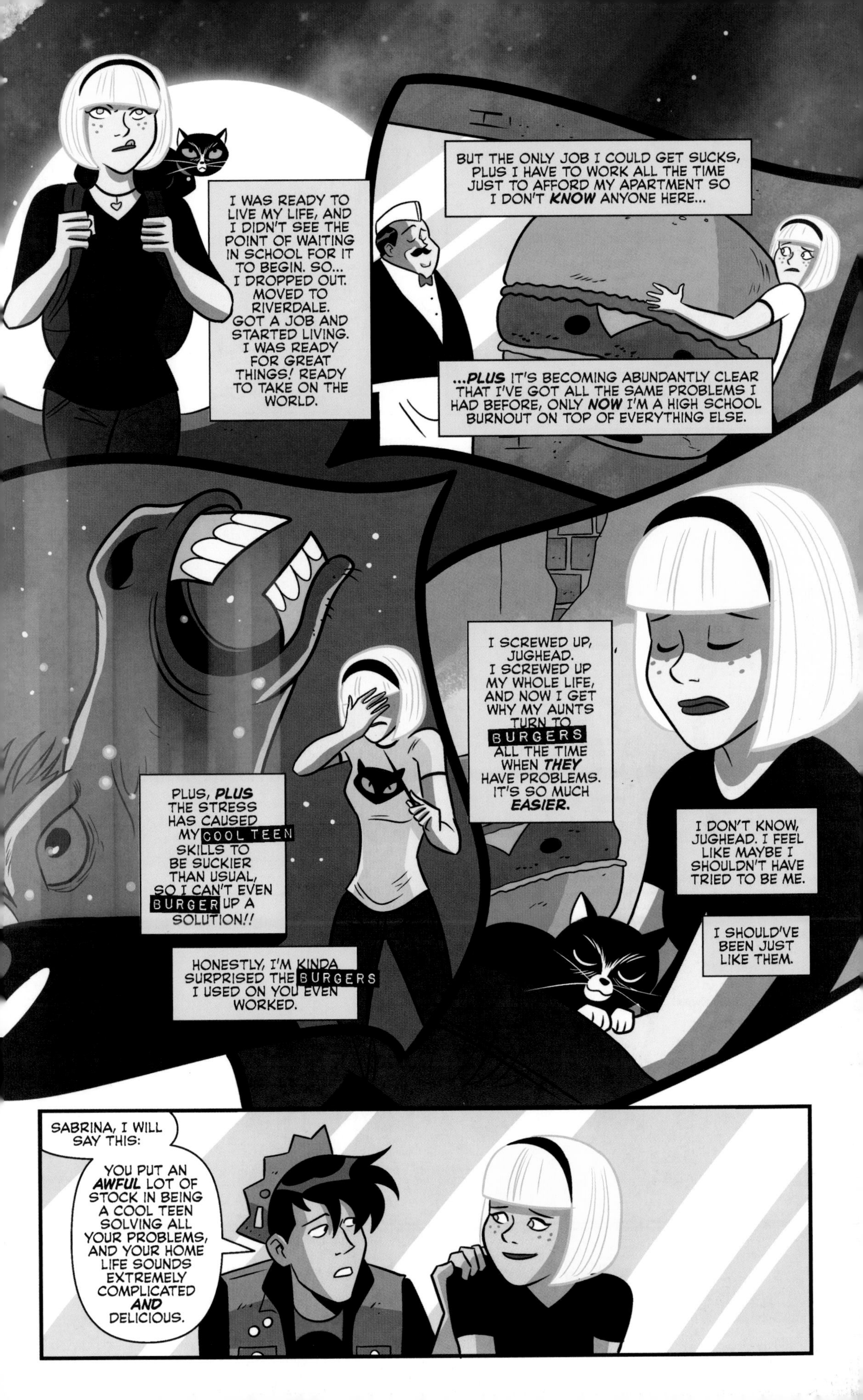

I WAS READY TO LIVE MY LIFE, AND I DIDN'T SEE THE POINT OF WAITING IN SCHOOL FOR IT TO BEGIN. SO... I DROPPED OUT. MOVED TO RIVERDALE. GOT A JOB AND STARTED LIVING. I WAS READY FOR GREAT THINGS! READY TO TAKE ON THE WORLD.
BUT THE ONLY JOB I COULD GET SUCKS, PLUS I HAVE TO WORK ALL THE TIME JUST TO AFFORD MY APARTMENT SO I DON'T **KNOW** ANYONE HERE...
...PLUS IT'S BECOMING ABUNDANTLY CLEAR THAT I'VE GOT ALL THE SAME PROBLEMS I HAD BEFORE, ONLY **NOW** I'M A HIGH SCHOOL BURNOUT ON TOP OF EVERYTHING ELSE.
PLUS, **PLUS** THE STRESS HAS CAUSED MY COOL TEEN SKILLS TO BE SUCKIER THAN USUAL, SO I CAN'T EVEN BURGER UP A SOLUTION!!
HONESTLY, I'M KINDA SURPRISED THE BURGERS I USED ON YOU EVEN WORKED.
I SCREWED UP, JUGHEAD. I SCREWED UP MY WHOLE LIFE, AND NOW I GET WHY MY AUNTS TURN TO BURGERS ALL THE TIME WHEN **THEY** HAVE PROBLEMS. IT'S SO MUCH **EASIER.**
I DON'T KNOW, JUGHEAD. I FEEL LIKE MAYBE I SHOULDN'T HAVE TRIED TO BE ME.
I SHOULD'VE BEEN JUST LIKE THEM.
SABRINA, I WILL SAY THIS:
YOU PUT AN **AWFUL** LOT OF STOCK IN BEING A COOL TEEN SOLVING ALL YOUR PROBLEMS, AND YOUR HOME LIFE SOUNDS EXTREMELY COMPLICATED **AND** DELICIOUS.

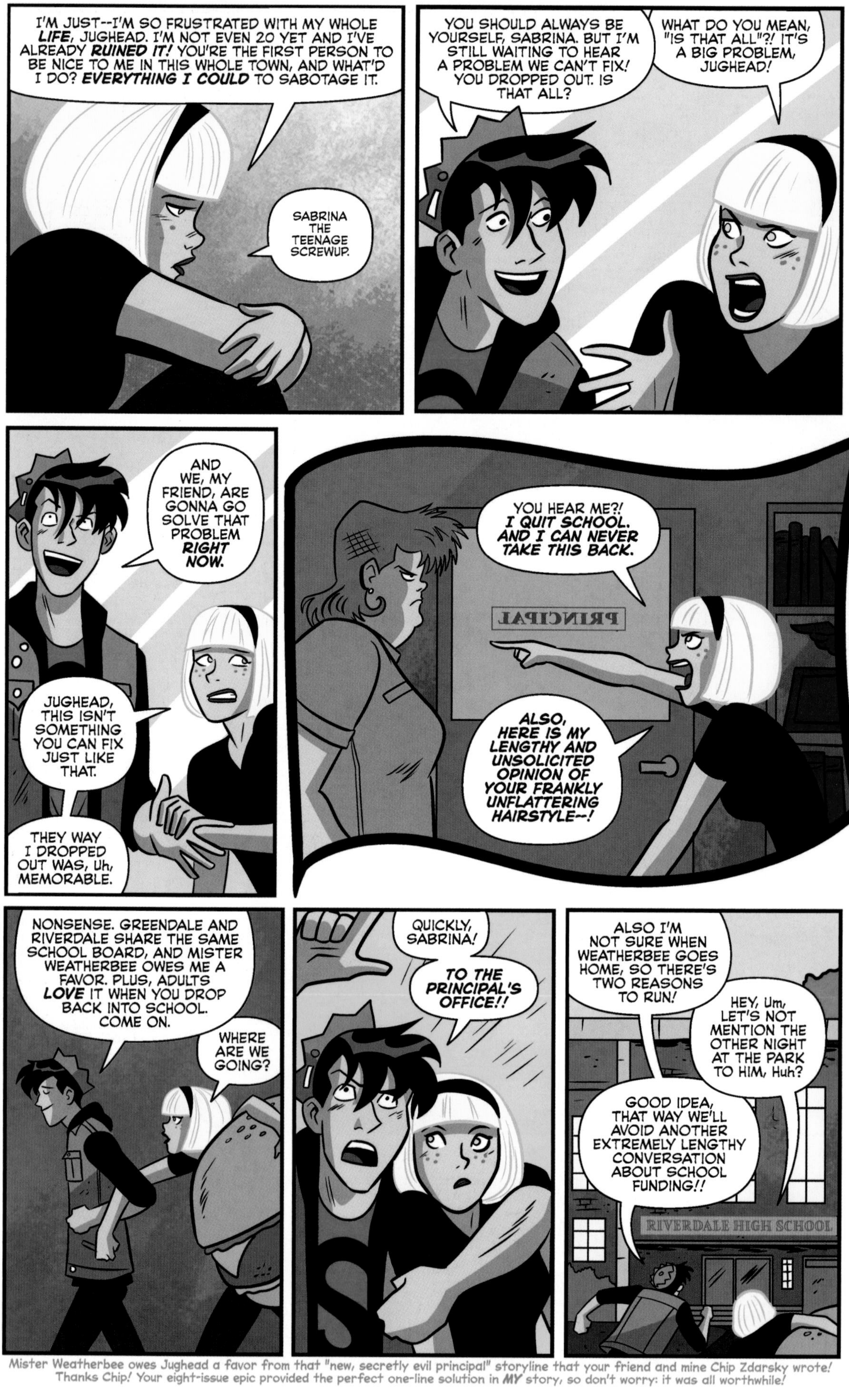

I'M JUST--I'M SO FRUSTRATED WITH MY WHOLE **LIFE**, JUGHEAD. I'M NOT EVEN 20 YET AND I'VE ALREADY ***RUINED IT!*** YOU'RE THE FIRST PERSON TO BE NICE TO ME IN THIS WHOLE TOWN, AND WHAT'D I DO? ***EVERYTHING I COULD*** TO SABOTAGE IT.
SABRINA THE TEENAGE SCREWUP.
YOU SHOULD ALWAYS BE YOURSELF, SABRINA. BUT I'M STILL WAITING TO HEAR A PROBLEM WE CAN'T FIX! YOU DROPPED OUT. IS THAT ALL?
WHAT DO YOU MEAN, "IS THAT ALL"?! IT'S A BIG PROBLEM, JUGHEAD!
AND WE, MY FRIEND, ARE GONNA GO SOLVE THAT PROBLEM ***RIGHT NOW.***
JUGHEAD, THIS ISN'T SOMETHING YOU CAN FIX JUST LIKE THAT.
THEY WAY I DROPPED OUT WAS, Uh, MEMORABLE.
YOU HEAR ME?! ***I QUIT SCHOOL. AND I CAN NEVER TAKE THIS BACK.***
PRINCIPAL
ALSO, HERE IS MY LENGTHY AND UNSOLICITED OPINION OF YOUR FRANKLY UNFLATTERING HAIRSTYLE--!
NONSENSE. GREENDALE AND RIVERDALE SHARE THE SAME SCHOOL BOARD, AND MISTER WEATHERBEE OWES ME A FAVOR. PLUS, ADULTS ***LOVE*** IT WHEN YOU DROP BACK INTO SCHOOL. COME ON.
WHERE ARE WE GOING?
QUICKLY, SABRINA!
TO THE PRINCIPAL'S OFFICE!!
ALSO I'M NOT SURE WHEN WEATHERBEE GOES HOME, SO THERE'S TWO REASONS TO RUN!
HEY, Um, LET'S NOT MENTION THE OTHER NIGHT AT THE PARK TO HIM, Huh?
GOOD IDEA, THAT WAY WE'LL AVOID ANOTHER EXTREMELY LENGTHY CONVERSATION ABOUT SCHOOL FUNDING!!
RIVERDALE HIGH SCHOOL

Mister Weatherbee owes Jughead a favor from that "new, secretly evil principal" storyline that your friend and mine Chip Zdarsky wrote! Thanks Chip! Your eight-issue epic provided the perfect one-line solution in ***MY*** story, so don't worry: it was all worthwhile!

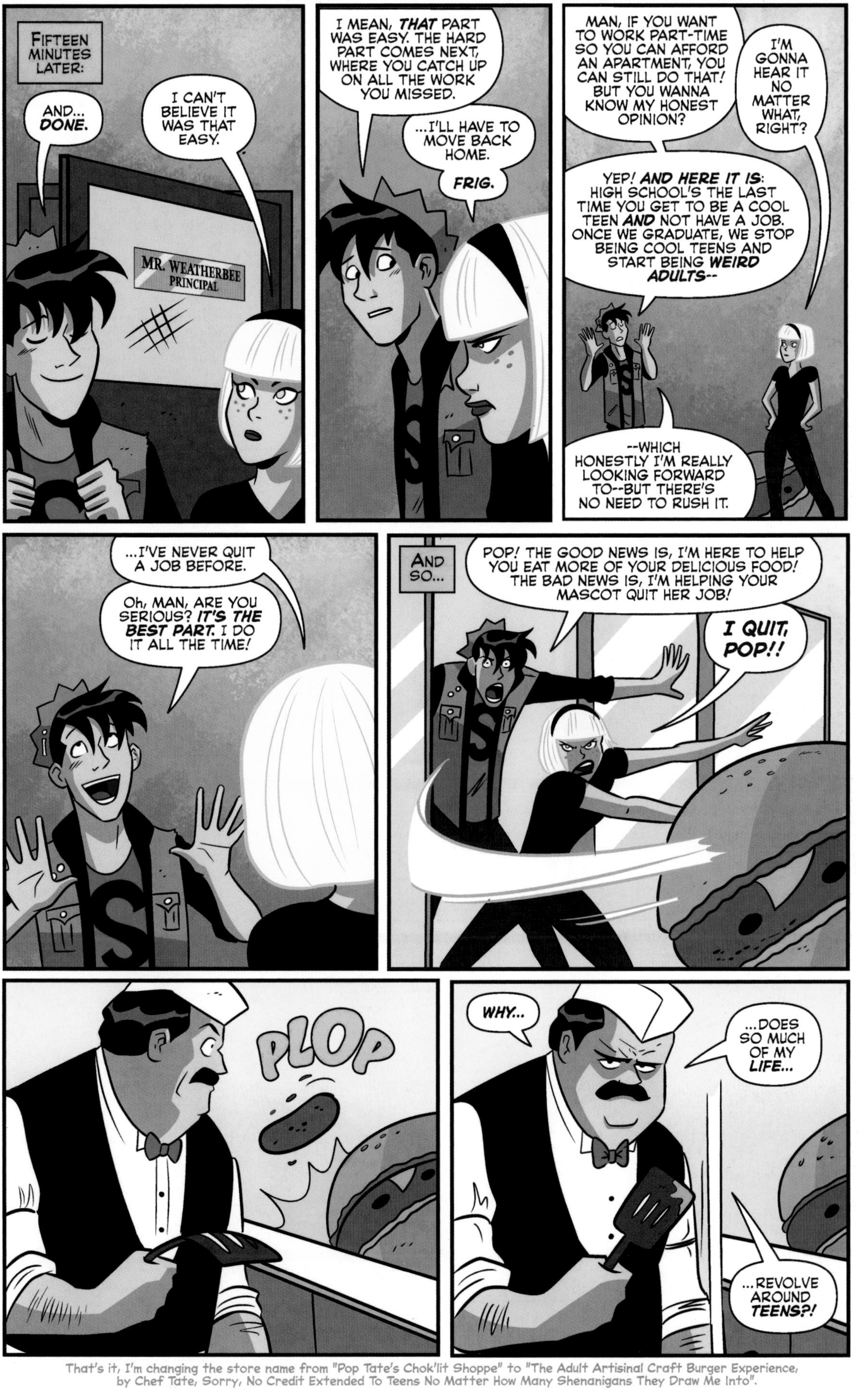
FIFTEEN MINUTES LATER:
AND... DONE.
I CAN'T BELIEVE IT WAS THAT EASY.
MR. WEATHERBEE PRINCIPAL
I MEAN, THAT PART WAS EASY. THE HARD PART COMES NEXT, WHERE YOU CATCH UP ON ALL THE WORK YOU MISSED.
...I'LL HAVE TO MOVE BACK HOME.
FRIG.
MAN, IF YOU WANT TO WORK PART-TIME SO YOU CAN AFFORD AN APARTMENT, YOU CAN STILL DO THAT! BUT YOU WANNA KNOW MY HONEST OPINION?
I'M GONNA HEAR IT NO MATTER WHAT, RIGHT?
YEP! AND HERE IT IS: HIGH SCHOOL'S THE LAST TIME YOU GET TO BE A COOL TEEN AND NOT HAVE A JOB. ONCE WE GRADUATE, WE STOP BEING COOL TEENS AND START BEING WEIRD ADULTS--
--WHICH HONESTLY I'M REALLY LOOKING FORWARD TO--BUT THERE'S NO NEED TO RUSH IT.
...I'VE NEVER QUIT A JOB BEFORE.
Oh, MAN, ARE YOU SERIOUS? IT'S THE BEST PART. I DO IT ALL THE TIME!
AND SO...
POP! THE GOOD NEWS IS, I'M HERE TO HELP YOU EAT MORE OF YOUR DELICIOUS FOOD! THE BAD NEWS IS, I'M HELPING YOUR MASCOT QUIT HER JOB!
I QUIT, POP!!
PLOP
WHY...
...DOES SO MUCH OF MY LIFE...
...REVOLVE AROUND TEENS?!

That's it, I'm changing the store name from "Pop Tate's Chok'lit Shoppe" to "The Adult Artisinal Craft Burger Experience, by Chef Tate, Sorry, No Credit Extended To Teens No Matter How Many Shenanigans They Draw Me Into".

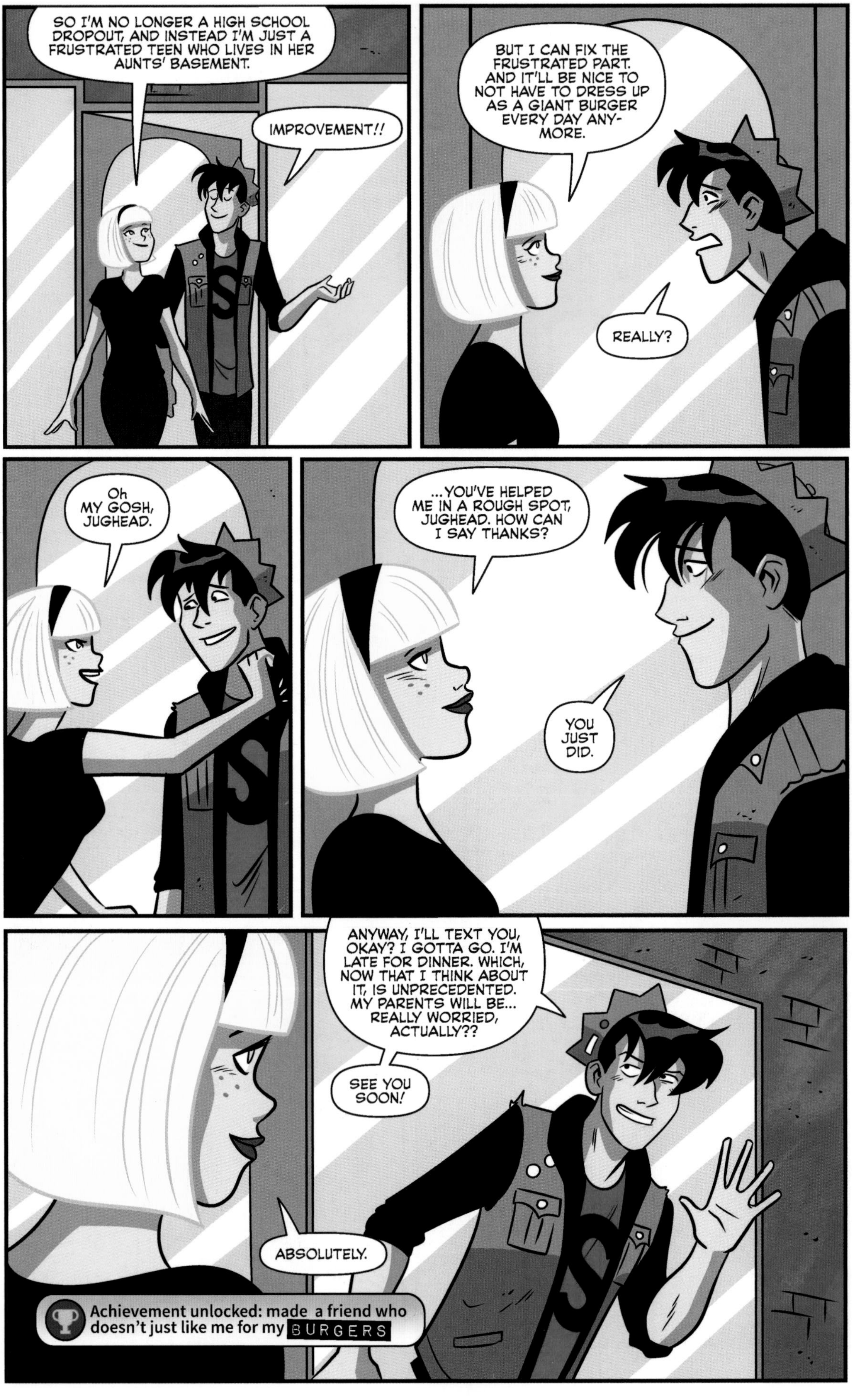
SO I'M NO LONGER A HIGH SCHOOL DROPOUT, AND INSTEAD I'M JUST A FRUSTRATED TEEN WHO LIVES IN HER AUNTS' BASEMENT.
IMPROVEMENT!!
BUT I CAN FIX THE FRUSTRATED PART. AND IT'LL BE NICE TO NOT HAVE TO DRESS UP AS A GIANT BURGER EVERY DAY ANY-MORE.
REALLY?
Oh MY GOSH, JUGHEAD.
...YOU'VE HELPED ME IN A ROUGH SPOT, JUGHEAD. HOW CAN I SAY THANKS?
YOU JUST DID.
ANYWAY, I'LL TEXT YOU, OKAY? I GOTTA GO. I'M LATE FOR DINNER. WHICH, NOW THAT I THINK ABOUT IT, IS UNPRECEDENTED. MY PARENTS WILL BE... REALLY WORRIED, ACTUALLY??
SEE YOU SOON!
ABSOLUTELY.
Achievement unlocked: made a friend who doesn't just like me for my BURGERS

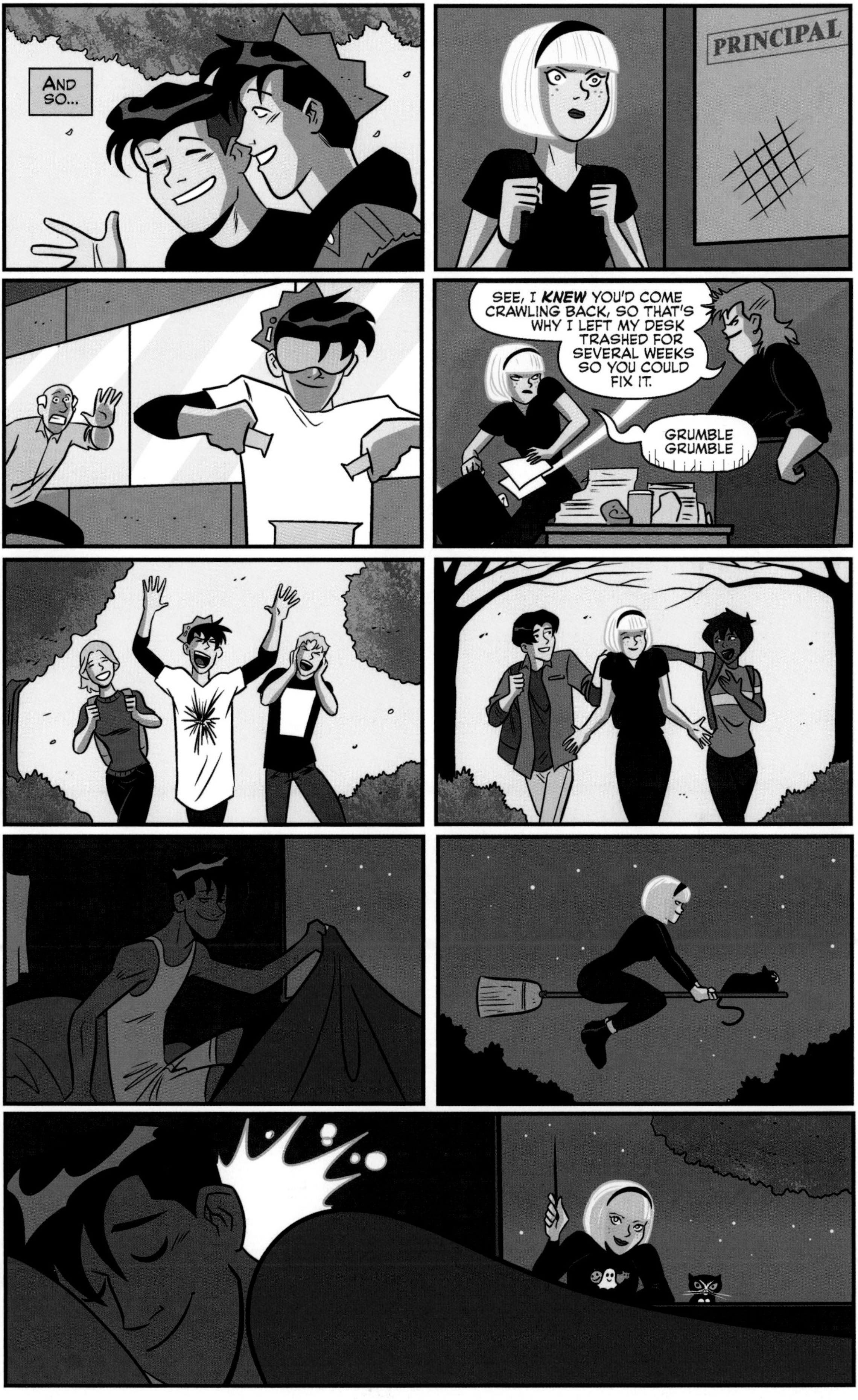
AND SO...
PRINCIPAL
SEE, I KNEW YOU'D COME CRAWLING BACK, SO THAT'S WHY I LEFT MY DESK TRASHED FOR SEVERAL WEEKS SO YOU COULD FIX IT.
GRUMBLE GRUMBLE

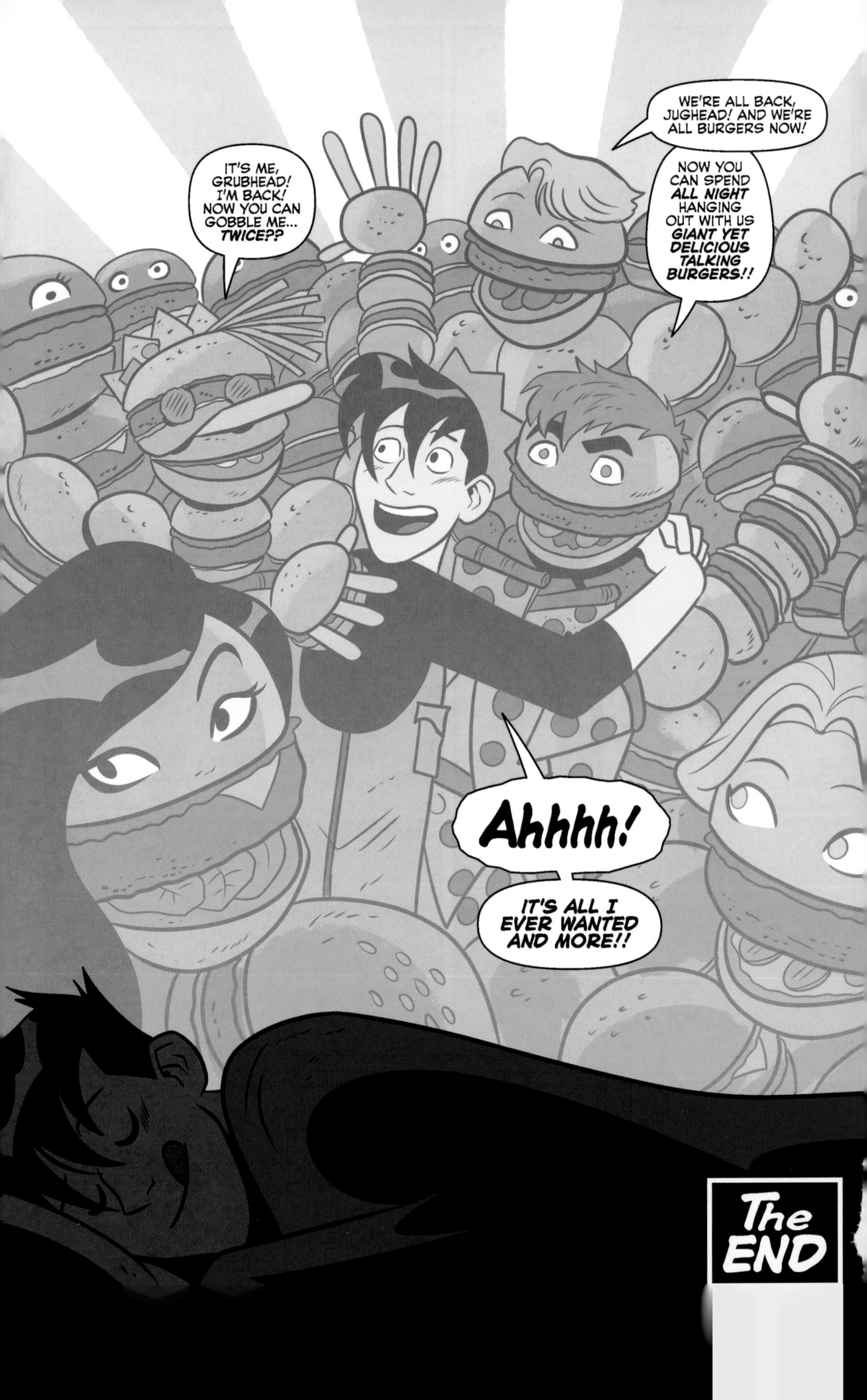
IT'S ME, GRUBHEAD! I'M BACK! NOW YOU CAN GOBBLE ME... *TWICE??*
WE'RE ALL BACK, JUGHEAD! AND WE'RE ALL BURGERS NOW!
NOW YOU CAN SPEND *ALL NIGHT* HANGING OUT WITH US *GIANT YET DELICIOUS TALKING BURGERS!!*
Ahhhh!
IT'S ALL I EVER WANTED AND MORE!!
The END

Jughead®

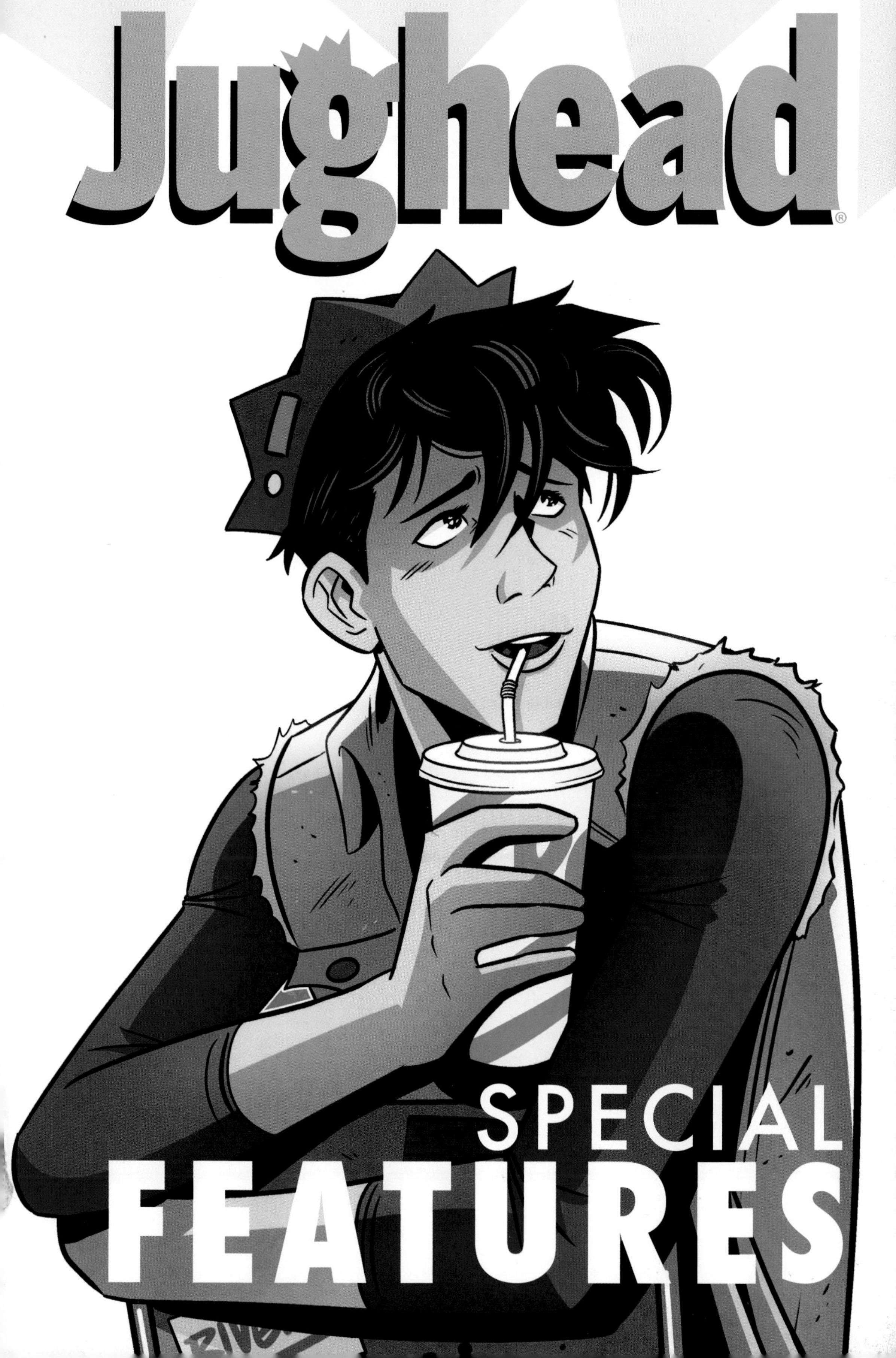

SPECIAL FEATURES

Jughead®

COVER **GALLERY**

In addition to the amazing main covers we have for each issue, we feature special variant covers from a variety of talented artists. Here are all of the main and variant covers for each of the five issues in *Jughead Volume Two*.

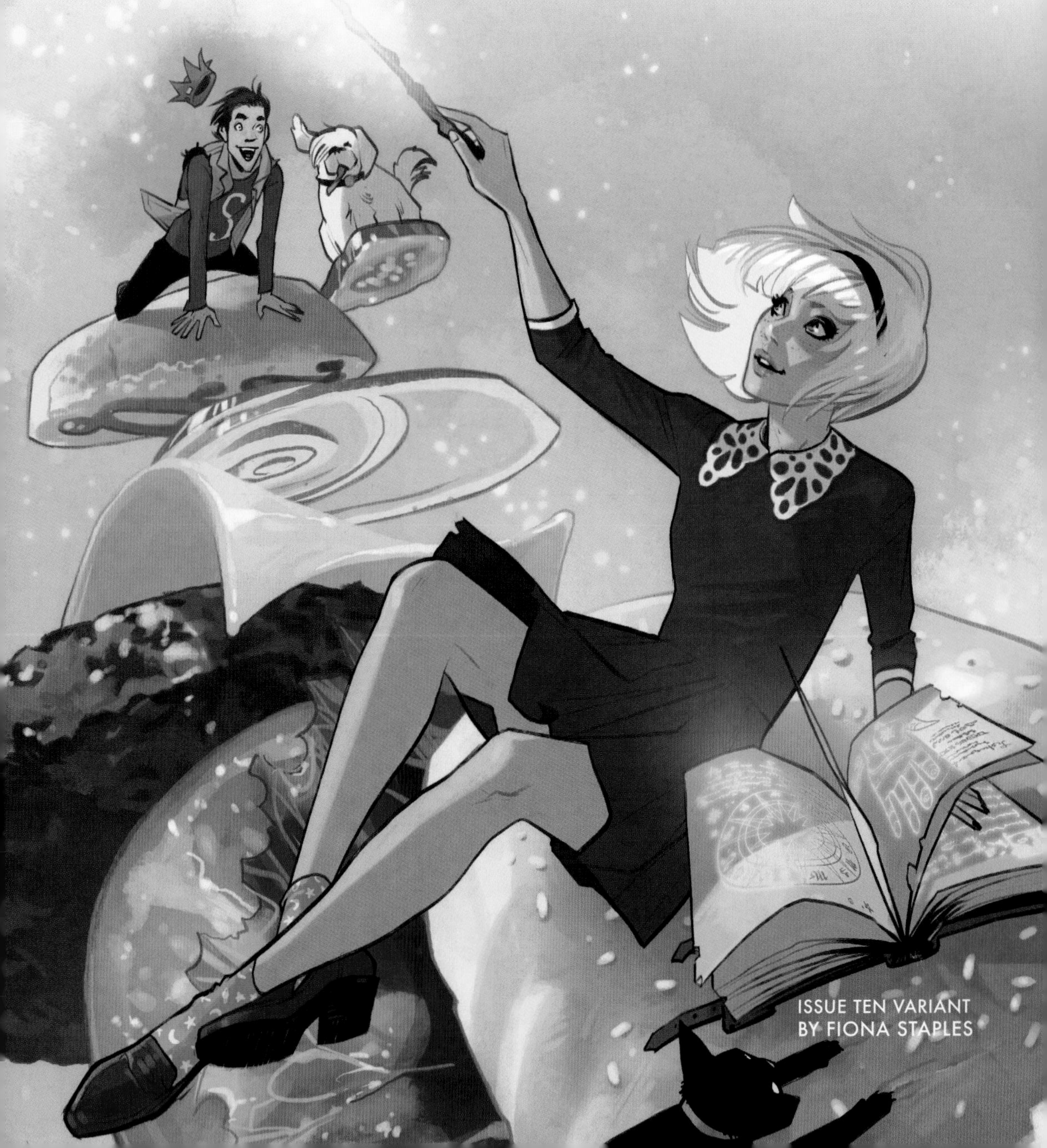

ISSUE TEN VARIANT
BY FIONA STAPLES

ISSUE **SEVEN**

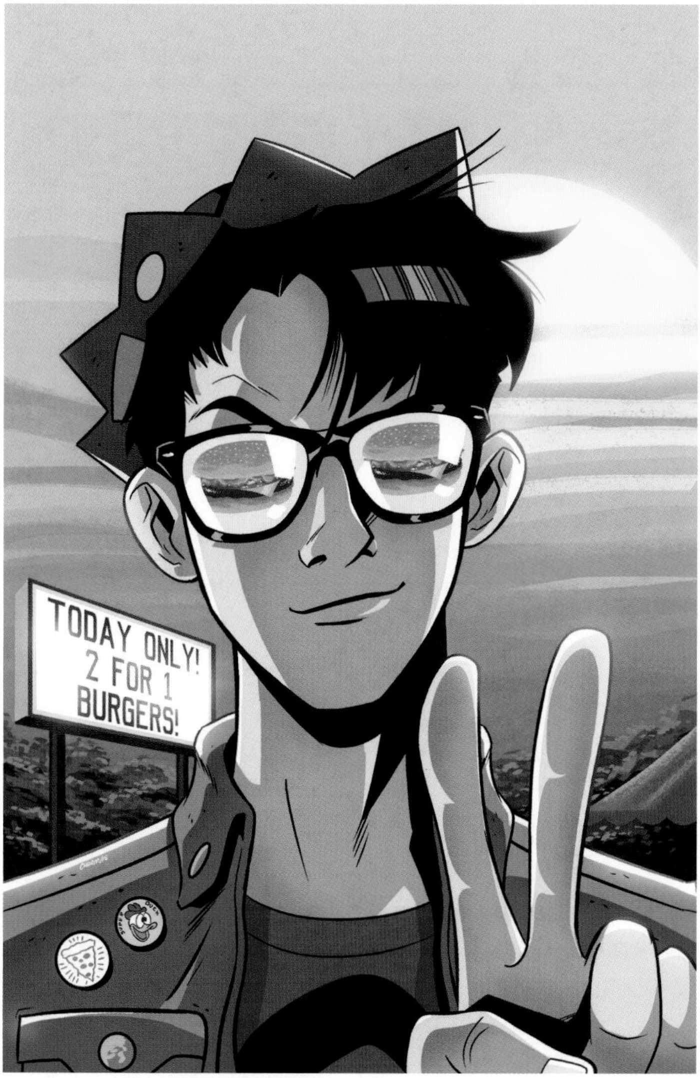
TODAY ONLY!
2 FOR 1
BURGERS!

DEREK CHARM

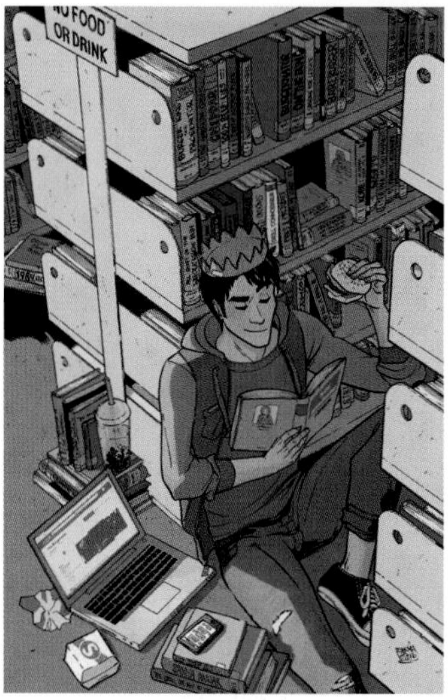
NO FOOD
OR DRINK

SANYA ANWAR

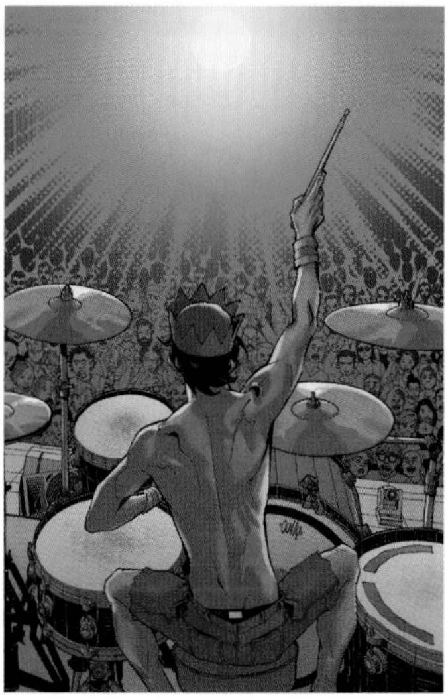

CULLY HAMNER

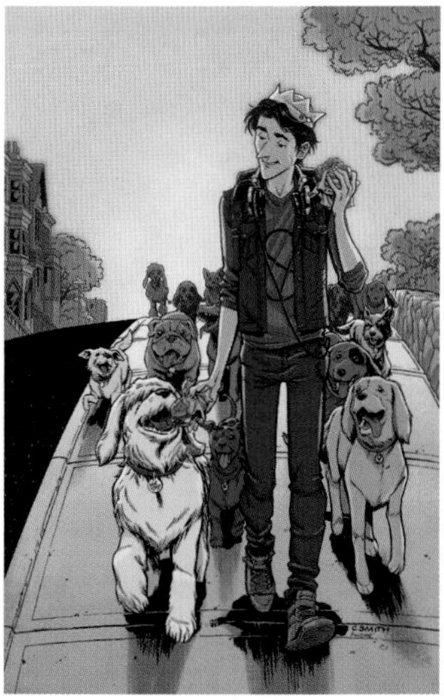

CORY SMITH

ISSUE **EIGHT**

DEREK CHARM

WALT SIMONSON

ANDRE SZYMANOWICZ

ISSUE **NINE**

DEREK CHARM

VERONICA FISH

AUDREY MOK

ISSUE **TEN**

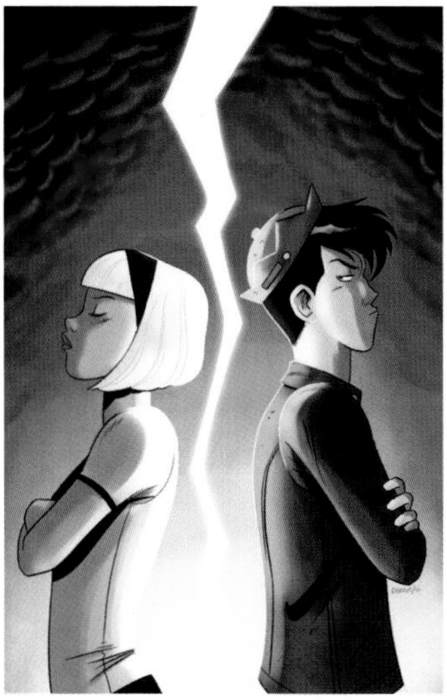

DEREK CHARM

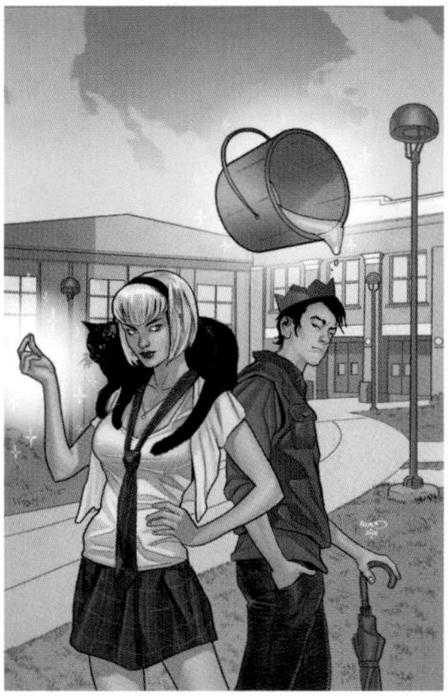

PAUL RENAUD

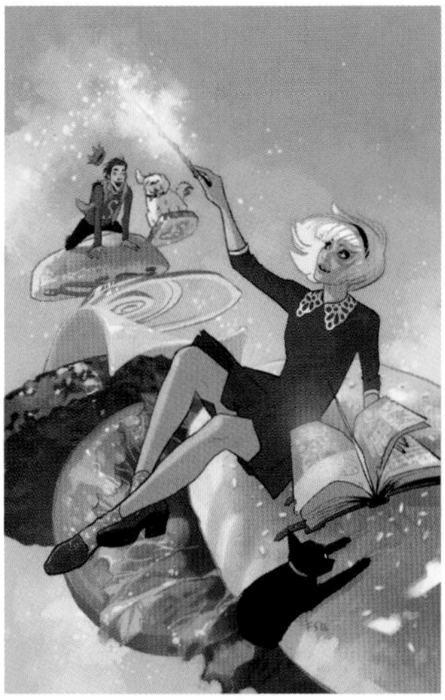

FIONA STAPLES

ISSUE **ELEVEN**

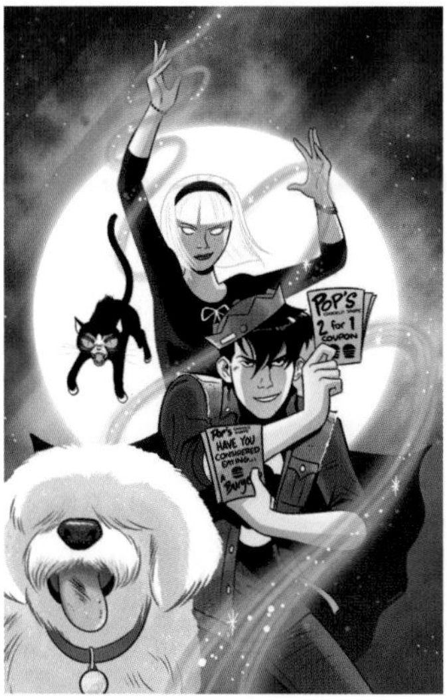
POP'S
2 for 1
COUPON

DEREK CHARM

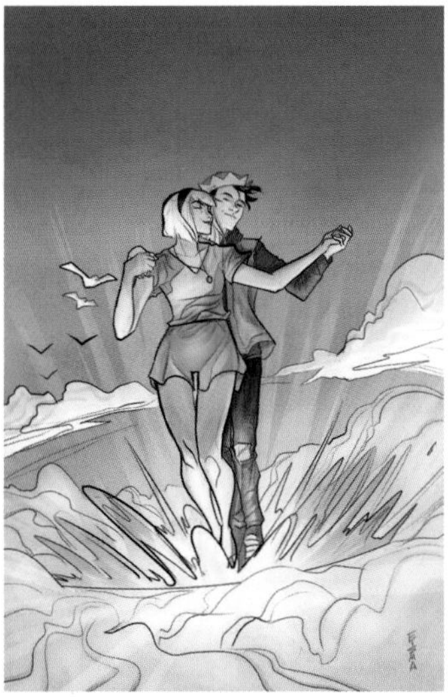

JOE EISMA

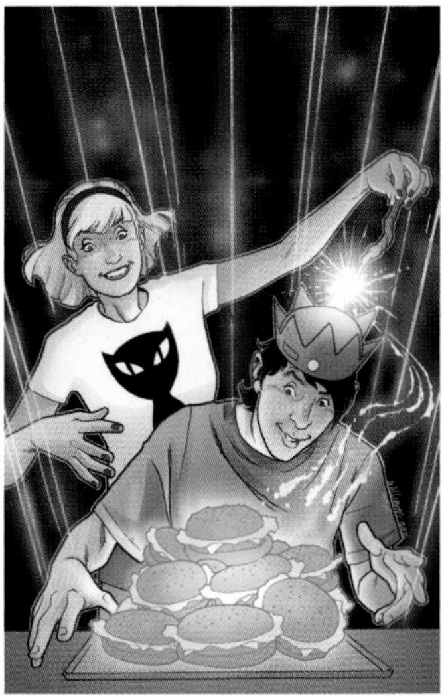

DAVID WILLIAMS

Jughead

ORIGINAL SKETCHES

Before Derek Charm came on board as the new interior artist for *Jughead*, he sent in some stellar character sketches that guaranteed him the position. Take a look at the sketches and samples for the very first time right here!

It's not only important to just get an idea of how each character looks, but to also get a glimpse at how their personalities and interests will be portrayed. Derek did an awesome job of doing just that!

CHARM/16

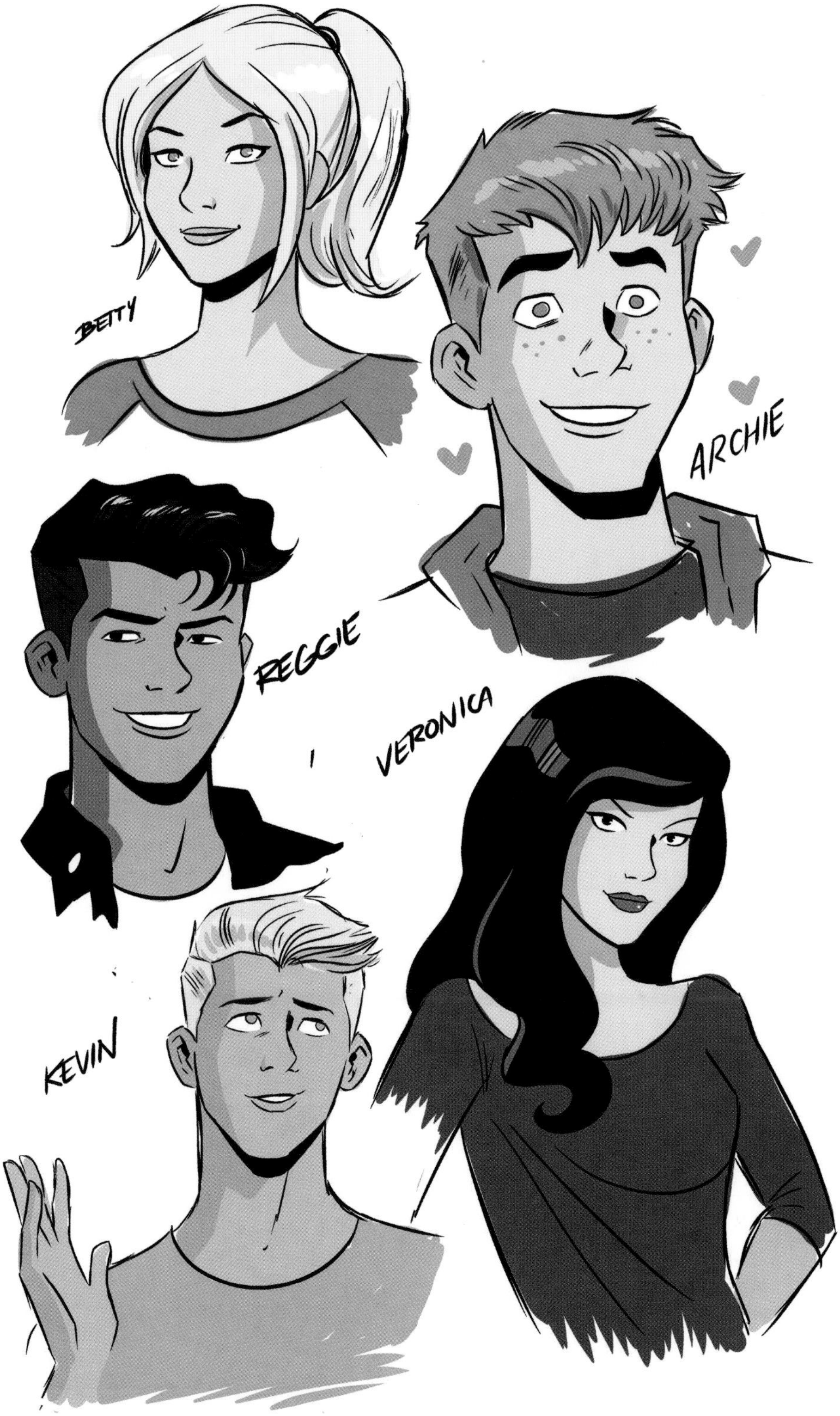
BETTY
ARCHIE
REGGIE
VERONICA
KEVIN

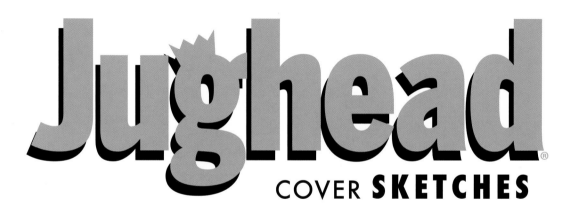

Jughead® COVER SKETCHES

Before each issue goes through the Diamond Previews solicitation process, our esteemed writers give us a synopsis of what will occur in each upcoming issue, and from that our talented interior artist will come up with some main cover ideas and send in rough drafts of how they would like the cover to appear. Then the Editor/President will choose one of the options, and then a finalized version will be routed to Archie Comics Publisher/Co-CEO for final approval.

Here are a few of DEREK CHARM's brilliant cover sketch options along with how they appeared in the final versions.

ISSUE SEVEN

COVER SKETCHES

Jughead
Jughead
Jughead
TODAY ONLY
2 for 1
BURGERS

FINAL COVER

Archie COMICS #7
ALL NEW!
Jughead
CHIP ZDARSKY
DEREK CHARM
TODAY ONLY!
2 FOR 1
BURGERS!

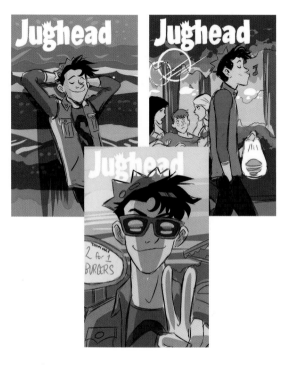

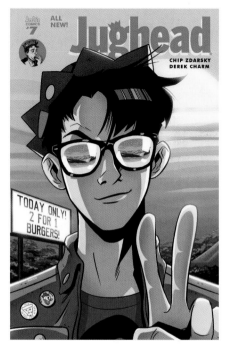

ISSUE **EIGHT**

COVER SKETCHES

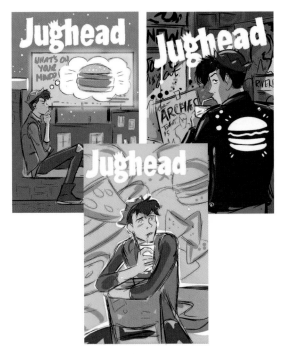

Jughead
WHAT'S ON YOUR MIND?
Jughead
ARCHIES
TONIGHT!
$5
Jughead

FINAL COVER

Archie COMICS #8
CHIP ZDARSKY
DEREK CHARM
ALL NEW!
Jughead
REGGIE RULE$

ISSUE **NINE**

COVER SKETCHES

Jughead

Jughead

FINAL COVER

Archie COMICS #9
Jughead
(IT'S KINDA LIKE A)
BRAND NEW #1
EXCEPT IT'S ISSUE #9
RYAN NORTH
DEREK CHARM

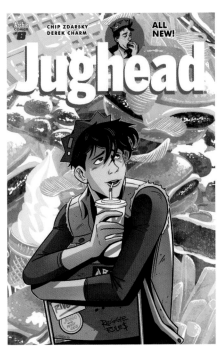

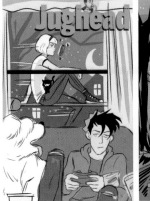

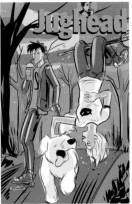

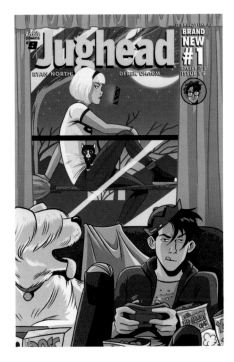

ISSUE **TEN**

COVER SKETCHES

Jughead
Jughead
Jughead

FINAL COVER

Archie COMICS
#10
RYAN NORTH
DEREK CHARM
ALL NEW!
Jughead
GUEST STARRING:
SABRINA
the teenage witch

ISSUE **ELEVEN**

COVER SKETCHES

Jughead
Jughead

FINAL COVER

Archie COMICS
#11
RYAN NORTH
DEREK CHARM
ALL NEW!
Jughead
POP'S
2 for 1
COUPON
HAVE YOU CONSIDERED EATING...
GUEST STARRING:
SABRINA
the teenage witch

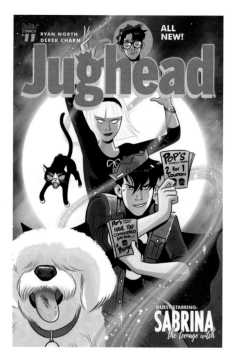

SPECIAL **BONUS ISSUE**

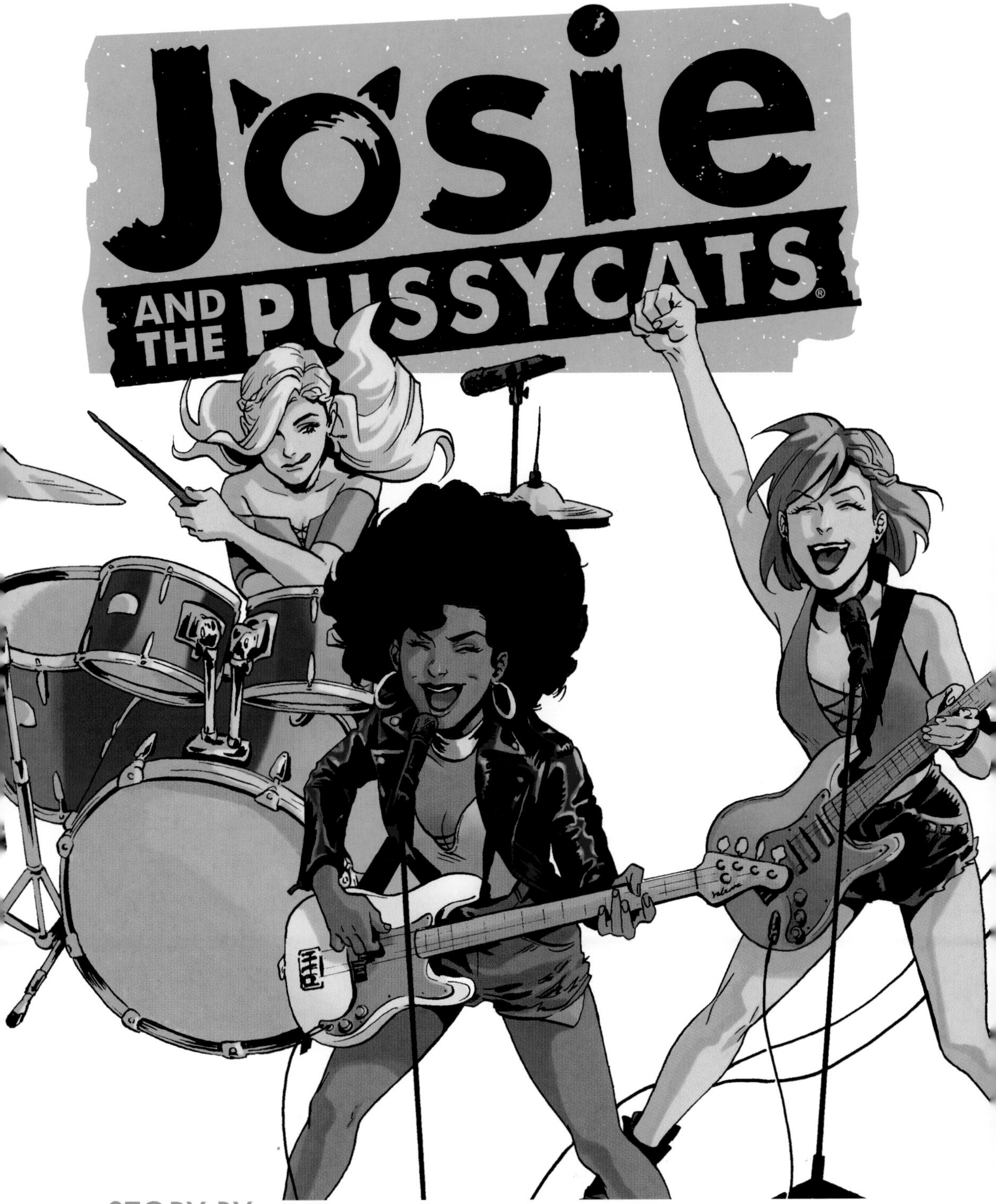
JOSIE
AND THE PUSSYCATS®

STORY BY
MARGUERITE BENNETT
& **CAMERON DEORDIO**

ART BY
AUDREY MOK

COLORING BY
ANDRE SZYMANOWICZ

LETTERING BY
JACK MORELLI

ISSUE
ONE

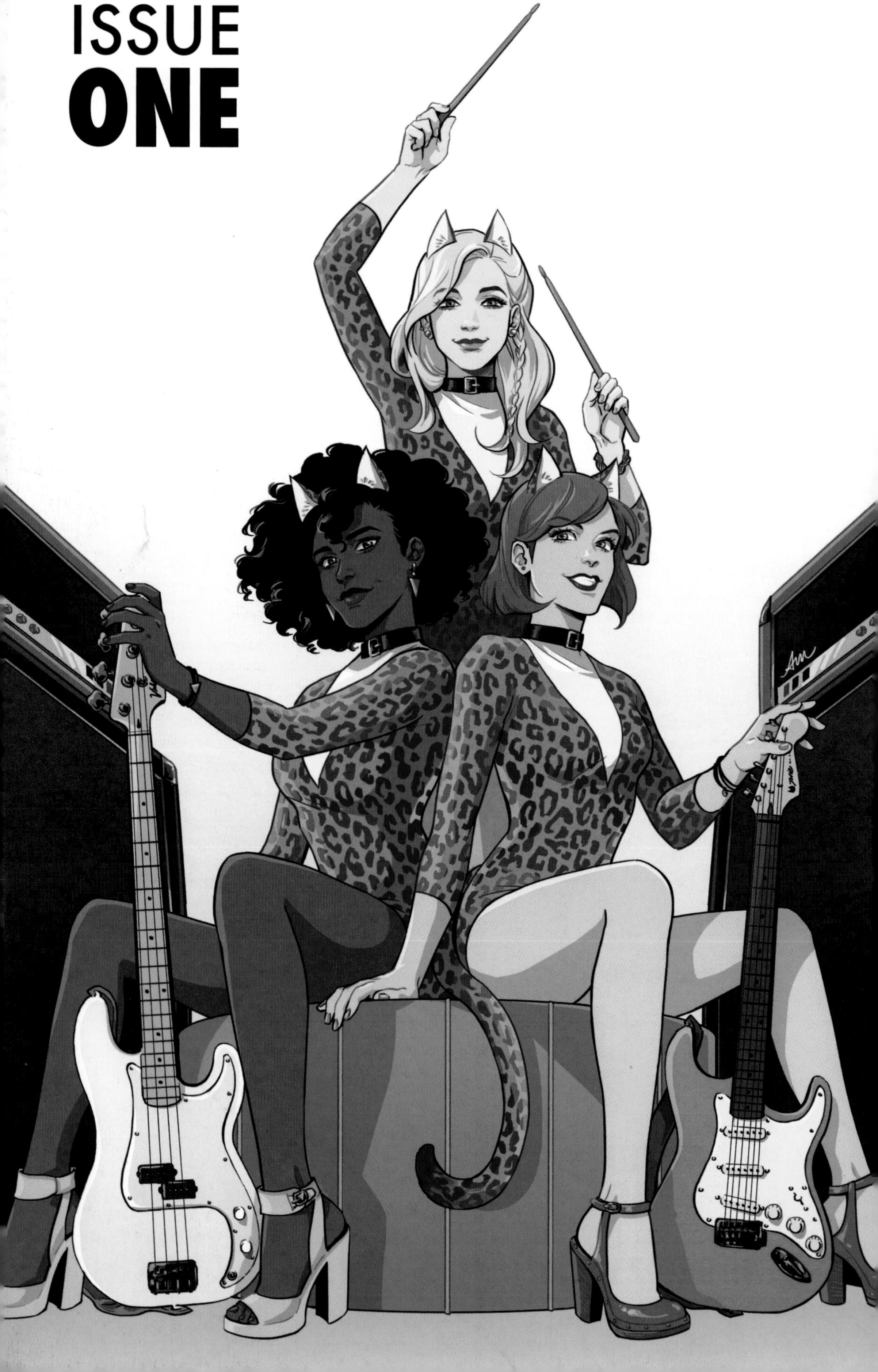

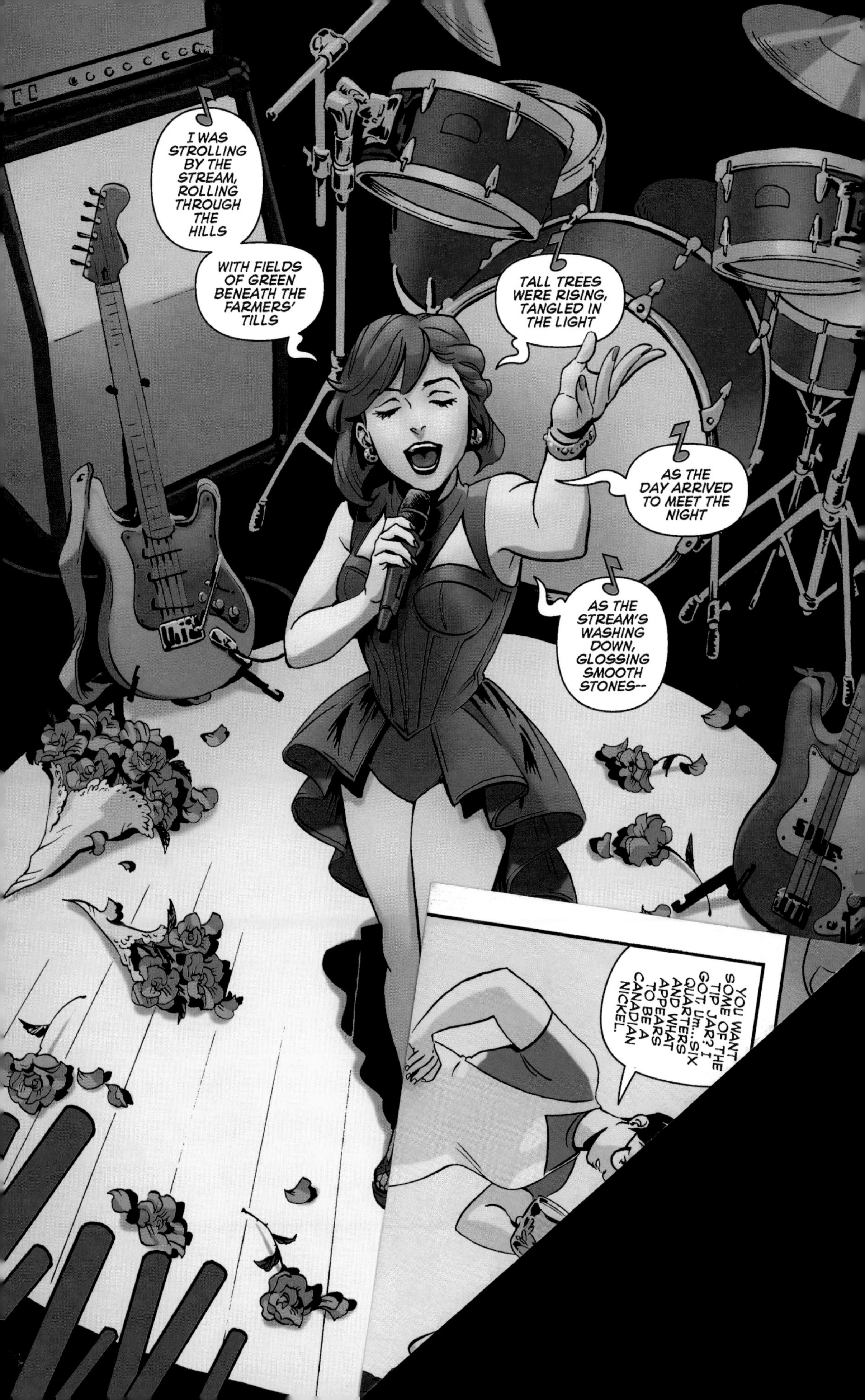
I WAS STROLLING BY THE STREAM, ROLLING THROUGH THE HILLS
WITH FIELDS OF GREEN BENEATH THE FARMERS' TILLS
TALL TREES WERE RISING, TANGLED IN THE LIGHT
AS THE DAY ARRIVED TO MEET THE NIGHT
AS THE STREAM'S WASHING DOWN, GLOSSING SMOOTH STONES--
YOU WANT SOME OF THE TIP JAR? I GOT, Um...SIX QUARTERS AND WHAT APPEARS TO BE A CANADIAN NICKEL.

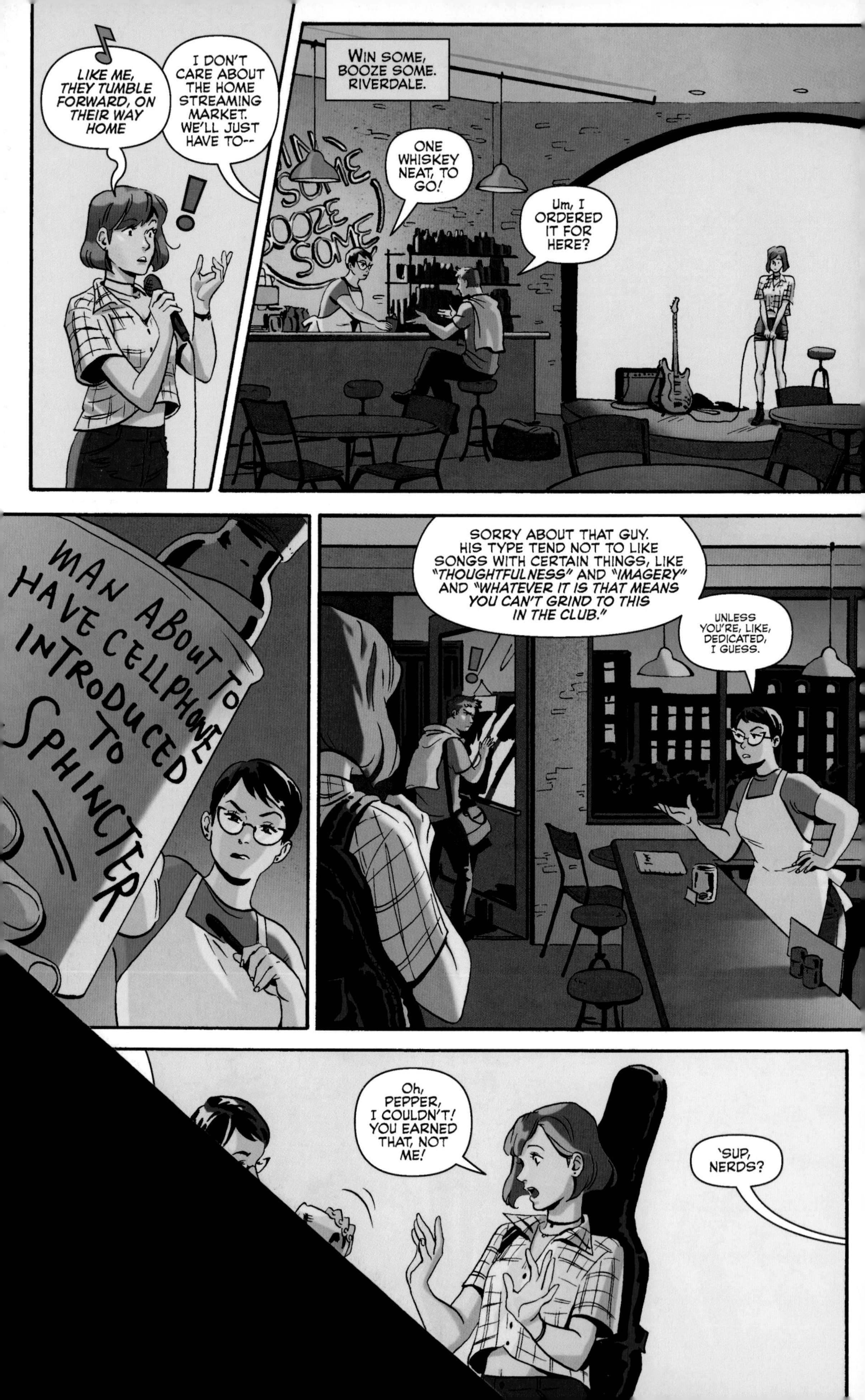
LIKE ME, THEY TUMBLE FORWARD, ON THEIR WAY HOME
I DON'T CARE ABOUT THE HOME STREAMING MARKET. WE'LL JUST HAVE TO--
WIN SOME, BOOZE SOME. RIVERDALE.
ONE WHISKEY NEAT, TO GO!
Um, I ORDERED IT FOR HERE?
MAN ABOUT TO HAVE CELLPHONE INTRODUCED TO SPHINCTER
SORRY ABOUT THAT GUY. HIS TYPE TEND NOT TO LIKE SONGS WITH CERTAIN THINGS, LIKE "THOUGHTFULNESS" AND "IMAGERY" AND "WHATEVER IT IS THAT MEANS YOU CAN'T GRIND TO THIS IN THE CLUB."
UNLESS YOU'RE, LIKE, DEDICATED, I GUESS.
Oh, PEPPER, I COULDN'T! YOU EARNED THAT, NOT ME!
'SUP, NERDS?

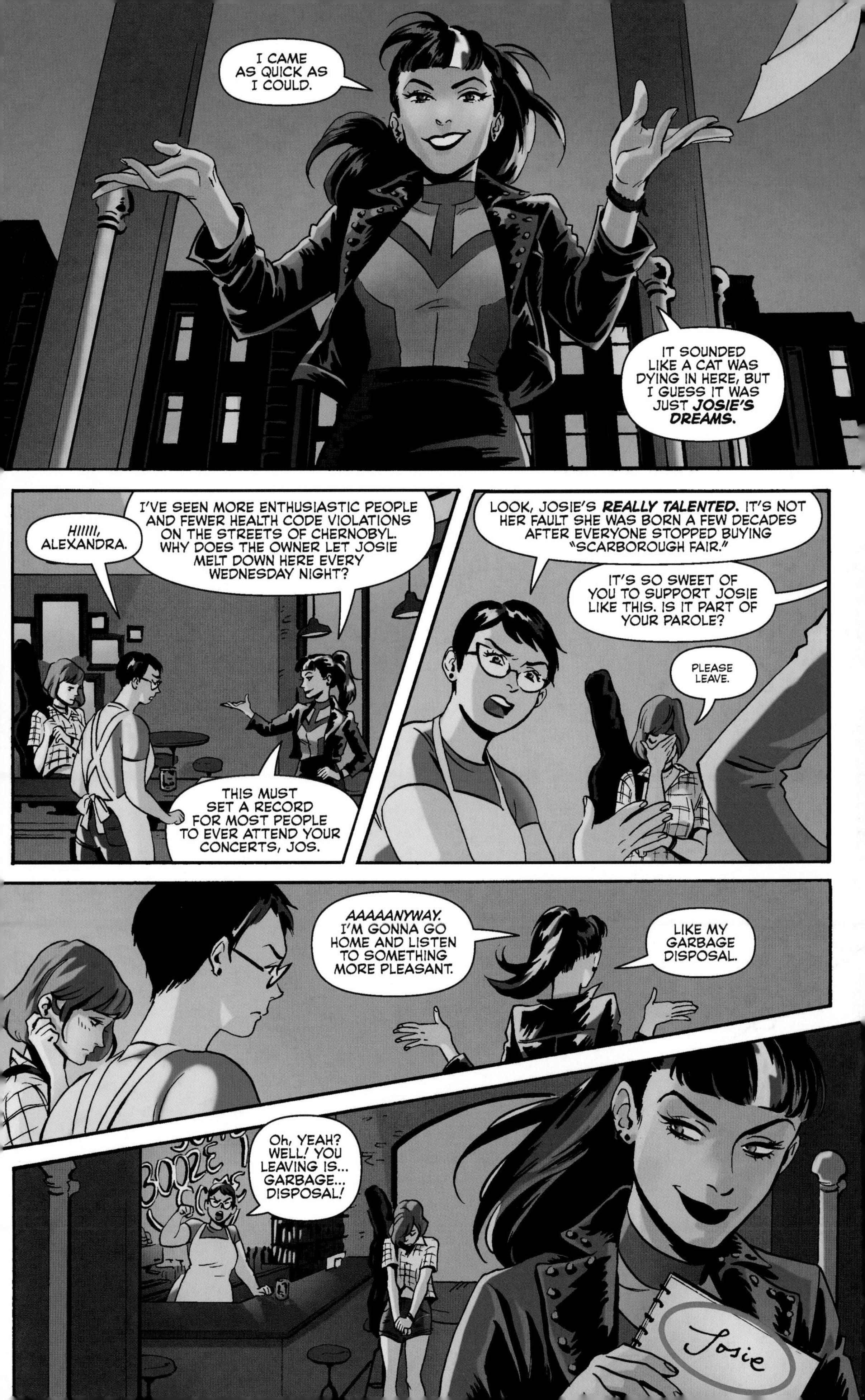
I CAME AS QUICK AS I COULD.
IT SOUNDED LIKE A CAT WAS DYING IN HERE, BUT I GUESS IT WAS JUST ***JOSIE'S DREAMS.***
HIIIII, ALEXANDRA.
I'VE SEEN MORE ENTHUSIASTIC PEOPLE AND FEWER HEALTH CODE VIOLATIONS ON THE STREETS OF CHERNOBYL. WHY DOES THE OWNER LET JOSIE MELT DOWN HERE EVERY WEDNESDAY NIGHT?
THIS MUST SET A RECORD FOR MOST PEOPLE TO EVER ATTEND YOUR CONCERTS, JOS.
LOOK, JOSIE'S ***REALLY TALENTED.*** IT'S NOT HER FAULT SHE WAS BORN A FEW DECADES AFTER EVERYONE STOPPED BUYING "SCARBOROUGH FAIR."
IT'S SO SWEET OF YOU TO SUPPORT JOSIE LIKE THIS. IS IT PART OF YOUR PAROLE?
PLEASE LEAVE.
AAAAANYWAY. I'M GONNA GO HOME AND LISTEN TO SOMETHING MORE PLEASANT.
LIKE MY GARBAGE DISPOSAL.
Oh, YEAH? WELL! YOU LEAVING IS... GARBAGE... DISPOSAL!
Josie

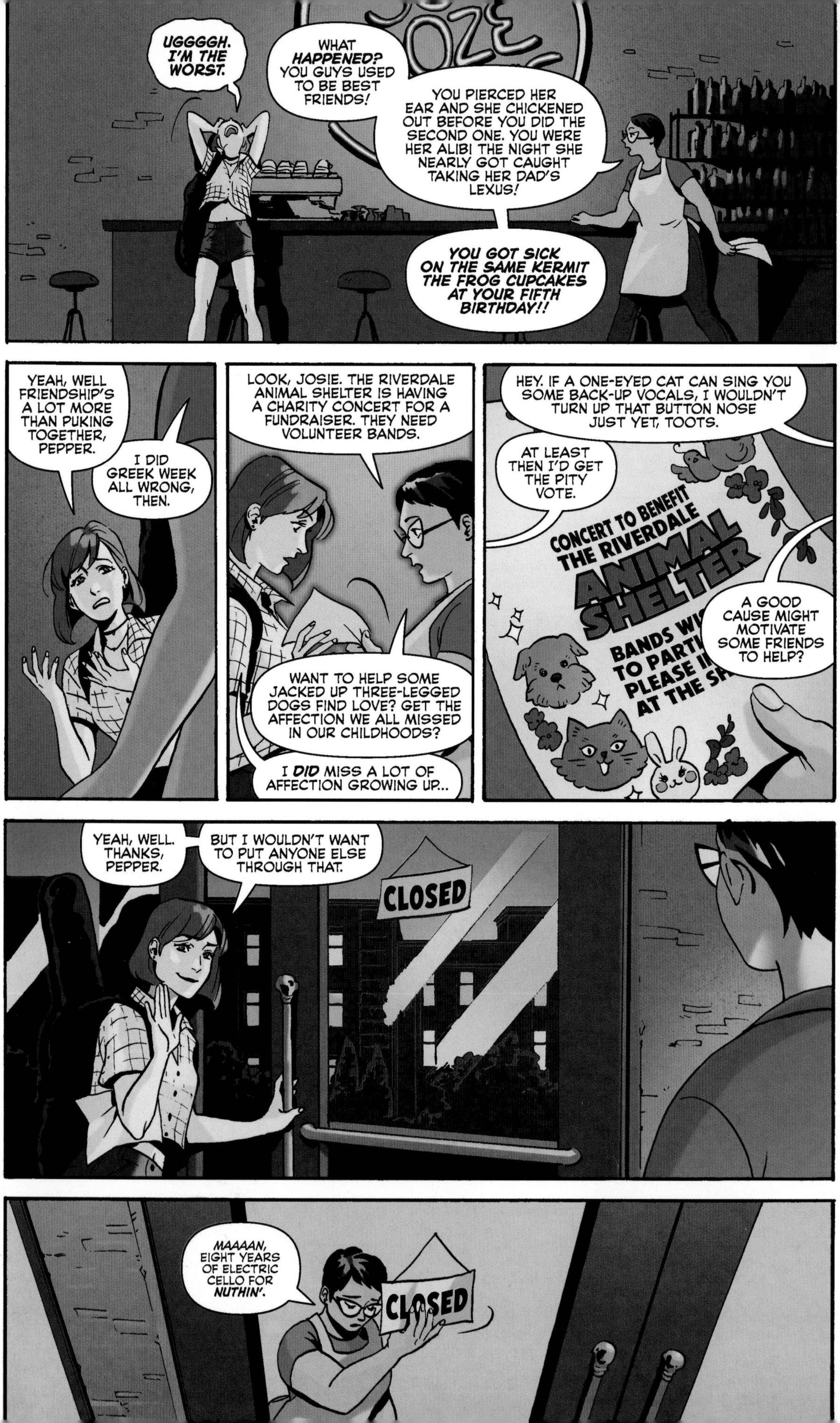
UGGGGH. I'M THE WORST.
WHAT HAPPENED? YOU GUYS USED TO BE BEST FRIENDS!
YOU PIERCED HER EAR AND SHE CHICKENED OUT BEFORE YOU DID THE SECOND ONE. YOU WERE HER ALIBI THE NIGHT SHE NEARLY GOT CAUGHT TAKING HER DAD'S LEXUS!
YOU GOT SICK ON THE SAME KERMIT THE FROG CUPCAKES AT YOUR FIFTH BIRTHDAY!!
YEAH, WELL FRIENDSHIP'S A LOT MORE THAN PUKING TOGETHER, PEPPER.
I DID GREEK WEEK ALL WRONG, THEN.
LOOK, JOSIE. THE RIVERDALE ANIMAL SHELTER IS HAVING A CHARITY CONCERT FOR A FUNDRAISER. THEY NEED VOLUNTEER BANDS.
WANT TO HELP SOME JACKED UP THREE-LEGGED DOGS FIND LOVE? GET THE AFFECTION WE ALL MISSED IN OUR CHILDHOODS?
I DID MISS A LOT OF AFFECTION GROWING UP...
HEY. IF A ONE-EYED CAT CAN SING YOU SOME BACK-UP VOCALS, I WOULDN'T TURN UP THAT BUTTON NOSE JUST YET, TOOTS.
AT LEAST THEN I'D GET THE PITY VOTE.
CONCERT TO BENEFIT THE RIVERDALE ANIMAL SHELTER
A GOOD CAUSE MIGHT MOTIVATE SOME FRIENDS TO HELP?
YEAH, WELL. THANKS, PEPPER.
BUT I WOULDN'T WANT TO PUT ANYONE ELSE THROUGH THAT.
CLOSED
MAAAAN, EIGHT YEARS OF ELECTRIC CELLO FOR NUTHIN'.
CLOSED

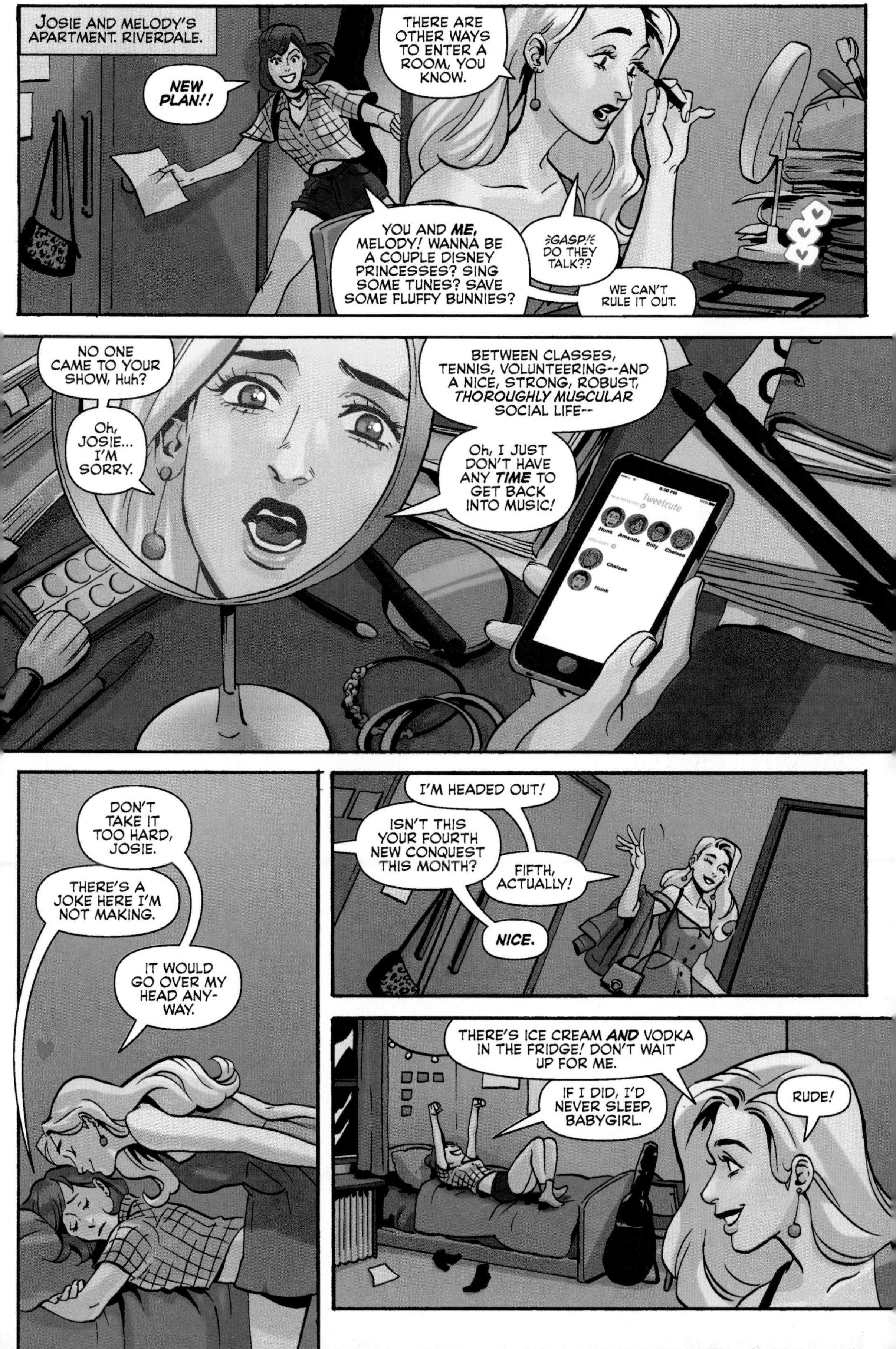
JOSIE AND MELODY'S APARTMENT. RIVERDALE.
NEW PLAN!!
THERE ARE OTHER WAYS TO ENTER A ROOM, YOU KNOW.
YOU AND ME, MELODY! WANNA BE A COUPLE DISNEY PRINCESSES? SING SOME TUNES? SAVE SOME FLUFFY BUNNIES?
GASP! DO THEY TALK??
WE CAN'T RULE IT OUT.
NO ONE CAME TO YOUR SHOW, Huh?
Oh, JOSIE... I'M SORRY.
BETWEEN CLASSES, TENNIS, VOLUNTEERING--AND A NICE, STRONG, ROBUST, THOROUGHLY MUSCULAR SOCIAL LIFE--
Oh, I JUST DON'T HAVE ANY TIME TO GET BACK INTO MUSIC!
Tweetcute
Hunk
Amanda
Billy
Chelsea
Chelsea
Hunk
DON'T TAKE IT TOO HARD, JOSIE.
THERE'S A JOKE HERE I'M NOT MAKING.
IT WOULD GO OVER MY HEAD ANY-WAY.
I'M HEADED OUT!
ISN'T THIS YOUR FOURTH NEW CONQUEST THIS MONTH?
FIFTH, ACTUALLY!
NICE.
THERE'S ICE CREAM AND VODKA IN THE FRIDGE! DON'T WAIT UP FOR ME.
IF I DID, I'D NEVER SLEEP, BABYGIRL.
RUDE!

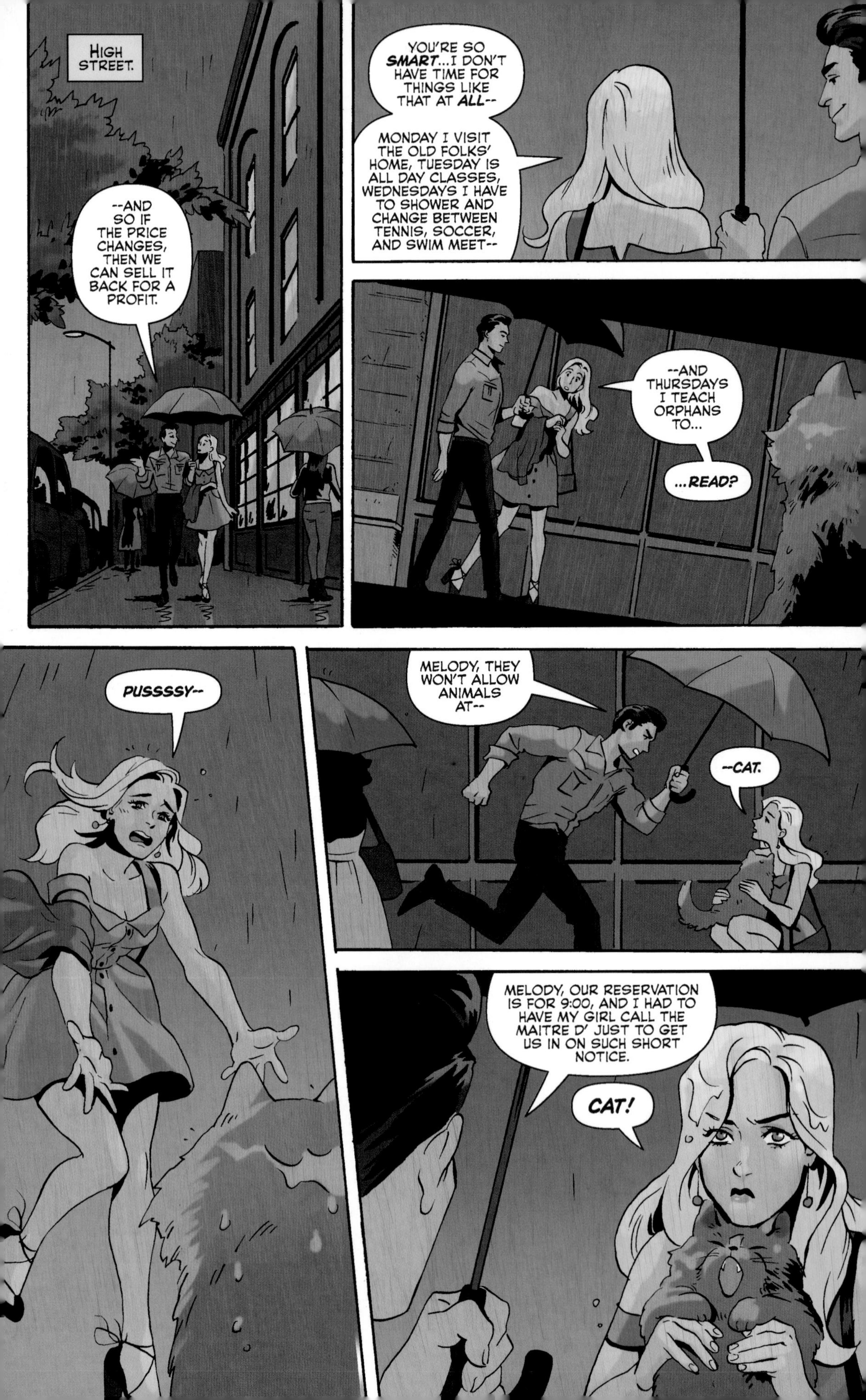
HIGH STREET.
--AND SO IF THE PRICE CHANGES, THEN WE CAN SELL IT BACK FOR A PROFIT.
YOU'RE SO SMART...I DON'T HAVE TIME FOR THINGS LIKE THAT AT ALL--
MONDAY I VISIT THE OLD FOLKS' HOME, TUESDAY IS ALL DAY CLASSES, WEDNESDAYS I HAVE TO SHOWER AND CHANGE BETWEEN TENNIS, SOCCER, AND SWIM MEET--
--AND THURSDAYS I TEACH ORPHANS TO...
...READ?
PUSSSSY--
MELODY, THEY WON'T ALLOW ANIMALS AT--
--CAT.
MELODY, OUR RESERVATION IS FOR 9:00, AND I HAD TO HAVE MY GIRL CALL THE MAITRE D' JUST TO GET US IN ON SUCH SHORT NOTICE.
CAT!

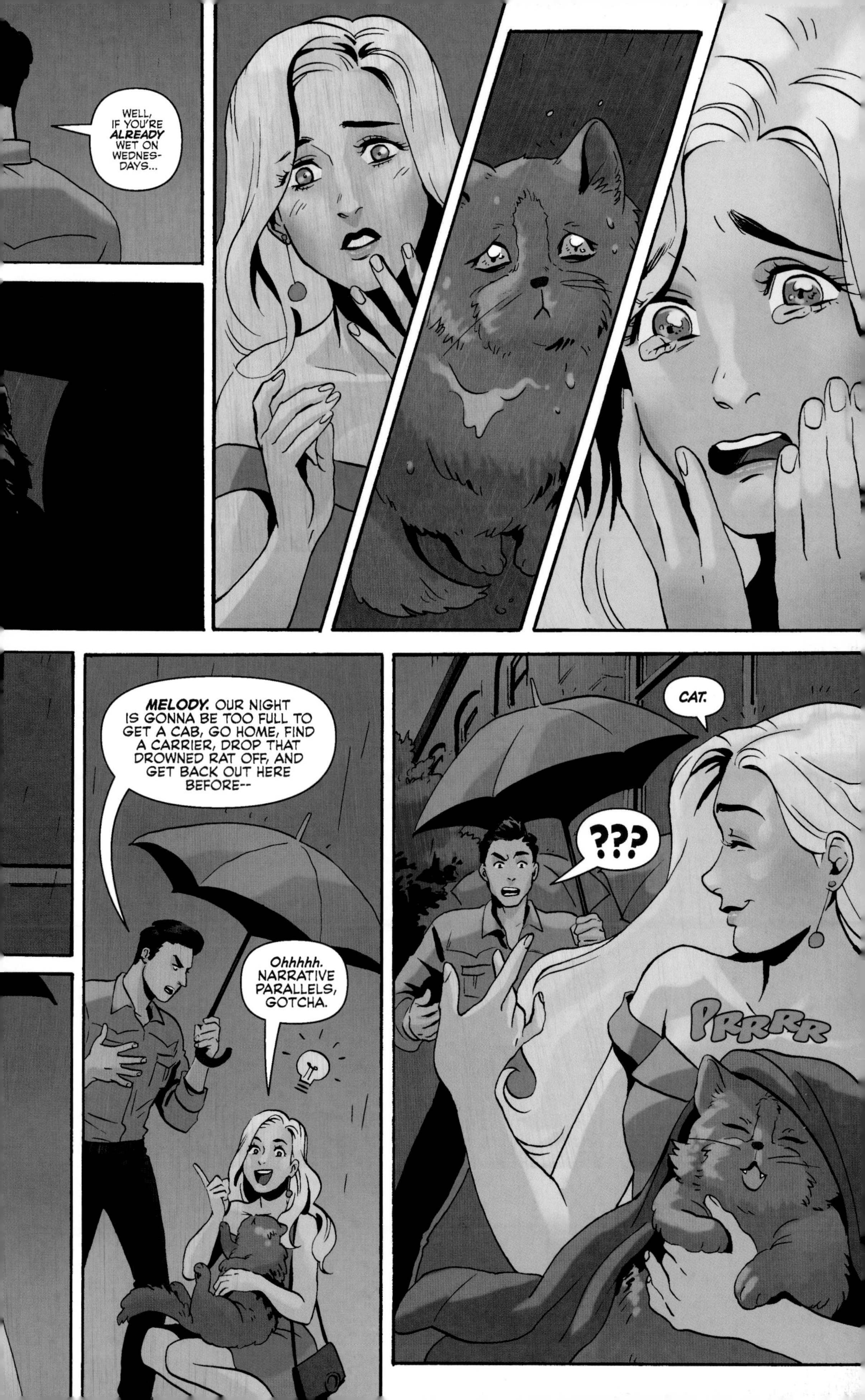
WELL, IF YOU'RE ALREADY WET ON WEDNES-DAYS...
MELODY. OUR NIGHT IS GONNA BE TOO FULL TO GET A CAB, GO HOME, FIND A CARRIER, DROP THAT DROWNED RAT OFF, AND GET BACK OUT HERE BEFORE--
Ohhhhh. NARRATIVE PARALLELS, GOTCHA.
CAT.
???
PRRRR

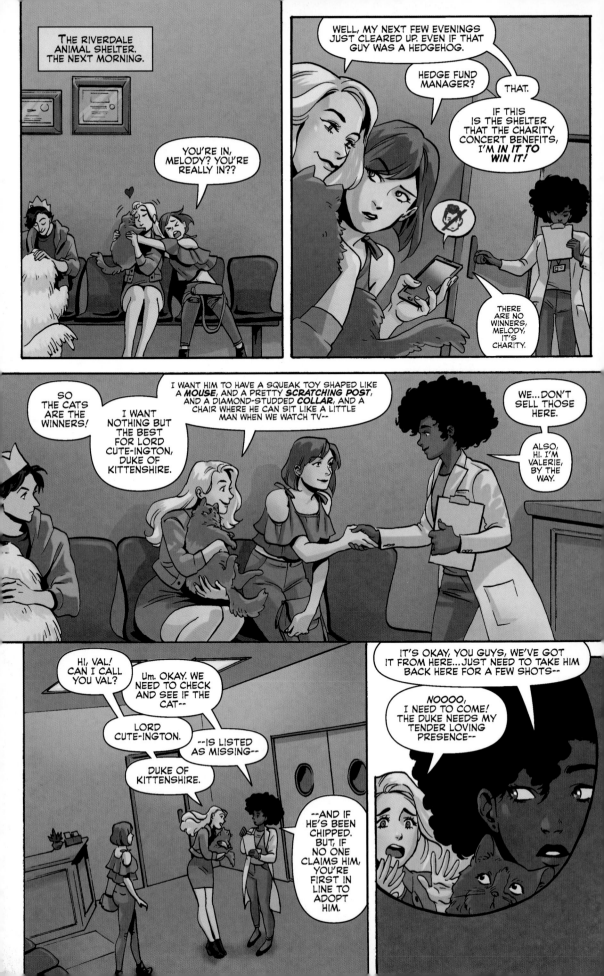

THE RIVERDALE ANIMAL SHELTER. THE NEXT MORNING.

YOU'RE IN, MELODY? YOU'RE REALLY IN??

WELL, MY NEXT FEW EVENINGS JUST CLEARED UP. EVEN IF THAT GUY WAS A HEDGEHOG.

HEDGE FUND MANAGER?

THAT.

IF THIS IS THE SHELTER THAT THE CHARITY CONCERT BENEFITS, I'M *IN IT TO WIN IT!*

THERE ARE NO WINNERS, MELODY, IT'S CHARITY.

SO THE CATS ARE THE WINNERS!

I WANT NOTHING BUT THE BEST FOR LORD CUTE-INGTON, DUKE OF KITTENSHIRE.

I WANT HIM TO HAVE A SQUEAK TOY SHAPED LIKE A *MOUSE*, AND A PRETTY *SCRATCHING POST*, AND A DIAMOND-STUDDED *COLLAR*, AND A CHAIR WHERE HE CAN SIT LIKE A LITTLE MAN WHEN WE WATCH TV--

WE...DON'T SELL THOSE HERE.

ALSO, HI. I'M VALERIE, BY THE WAY.

HI, VAL! CAN I CALL YOU VAL?

Um. OKAY. WE NEED TO CHECK AND SEE IF THE CAT--

LORD CUTE-INGTON.

--IS LISTED AS MISSING--

DUKE OF KITTENSHIRE.

--AND IF HE'S BEEN CHIPPED. BUT, IF NO ONE CLAIMS HIM, YOU'RE FIRST IN LINE TO ADOPT HIM.

IT'S OKAY, YOU GUYS, WE'VE GOT IT FROM HERE...JUST NEED TO TAKE HIM BACK HERE FOR A FEW SHOTS--

NOOOO, I NEED TO COME! THE DUKE NEEDS MY TENDER LOVING PRESENCE--

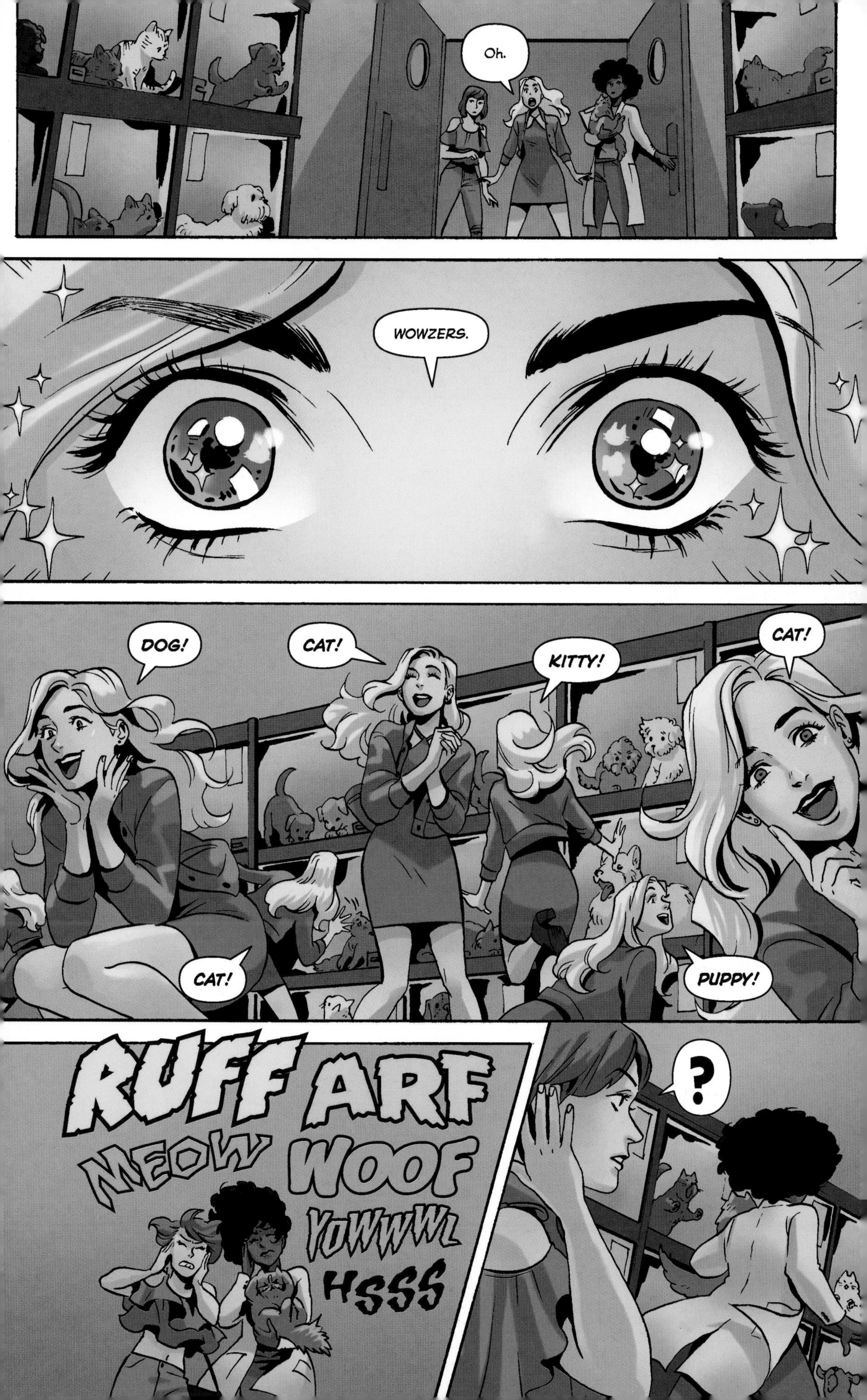
Oh.
WOWZERS.
DOG!
CAT!
KITTY!
CAT!
CAT!
PUPPY!
RUFF ARF
MEOW WOOF
YOWWWL
HSSS
?

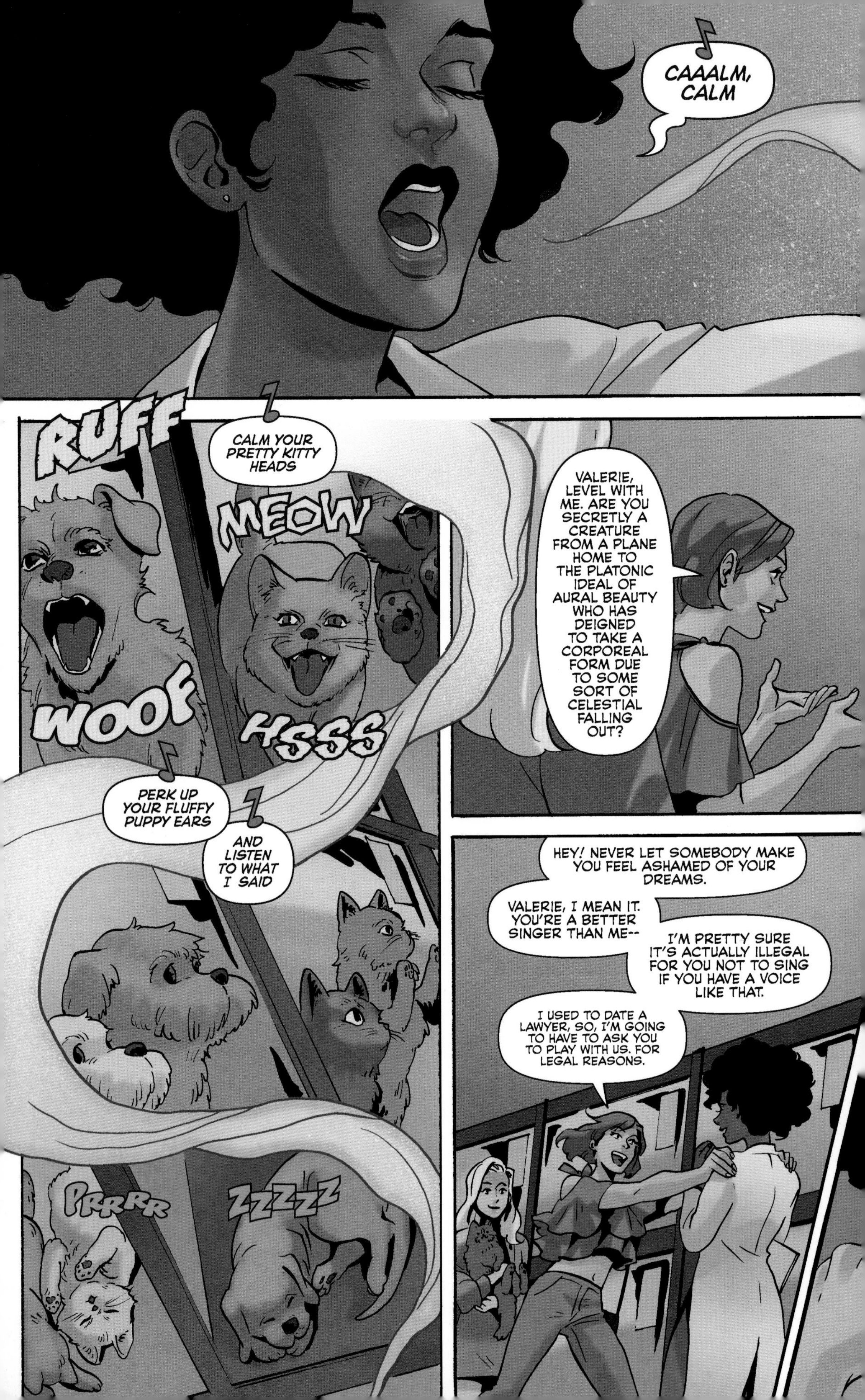
CAAALM, CALM
RUFF
CALM YOUR PRETTY KITTY HEADS
MEOW
WOOF
HSSS
PERK UP YOUR FLUFFY PUPPY EARS
AND LISTEN TO WHAT I SAID
PRRRRR
ZZZZZ
VALERIE, LEVEL WITH ME. ARE YOU SECRETLY A CREATURE FROM A PLANE HOME TO THE PLATONIC IDEAL OF AURAL BEAUTY WHO HAS DEIGNED TO TAKE A CORPOREAL FORM DUE TO SOME SORT OF CELESTIAL FALLING OUT?
HEY! NEVER LET SOMEBODY MAKE YOU FEEL ASHAMED OF YOUR DREAMS.
VALERIE, I MEAN IT. YOU'RE A BETTER SINGER THAN ME--
I'M PRETTY SURE IT'S ACTUALLY ILLEGAL FOR YOU NOT TO SING IF YOU HAVE A VOICE LIKE THAT.
I USED TO DATE A LAWYER, SO, I'M GOING TO HAVE TO ASK YOU TO PLAY WITH US. FOR LEGAL REASONS.

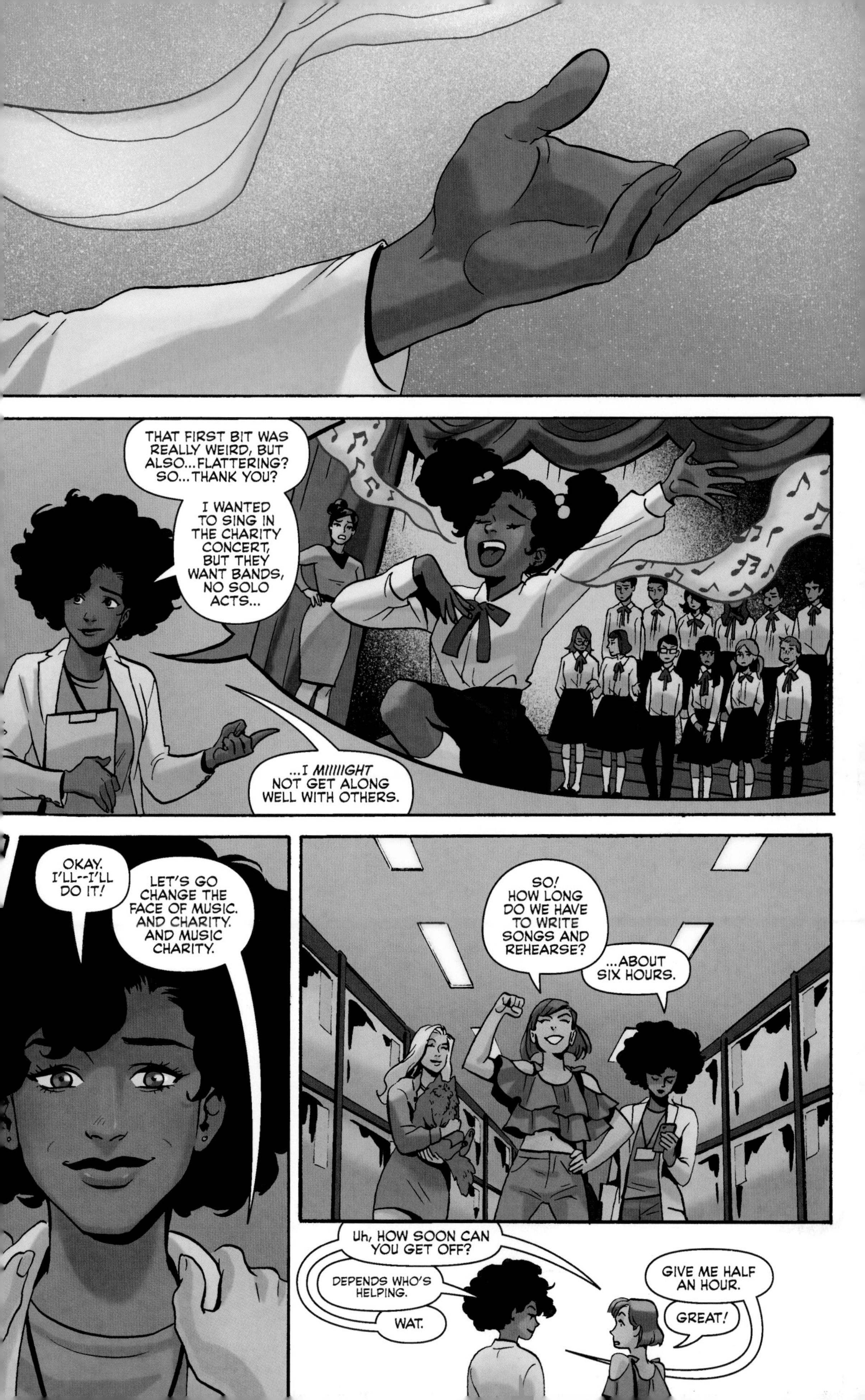
THAT FIRST BIT WAS REALLY WEIRD, BUT ALSO...FLATTERING? SO...THANK YOU?
I WANTED TO SING IN THE CHARITY CONCERT, BUT THEY WANT BANDS, NO SOLO ACTS...
...I *MIIIIIGHT* NOT GET ALONG WELL WITH OTHERS.
OKAY. I'LL--I'LL DO IT!
LET'S GO CHANGE THE FACE OF MUSIC. AND CHARITY. AND MUSIC CHARITY.
SO! HOW LONG DO WE HAVE TO WRITE SONGS AND REHEARSE?
...ABOUT SIX HOURS.
Uh, HOW SOON CAN YOU GET OFF?
DEPENDS WHO'S HELPING.
WAT.
GIVE ME HALF AN HOUR.
GREAT!

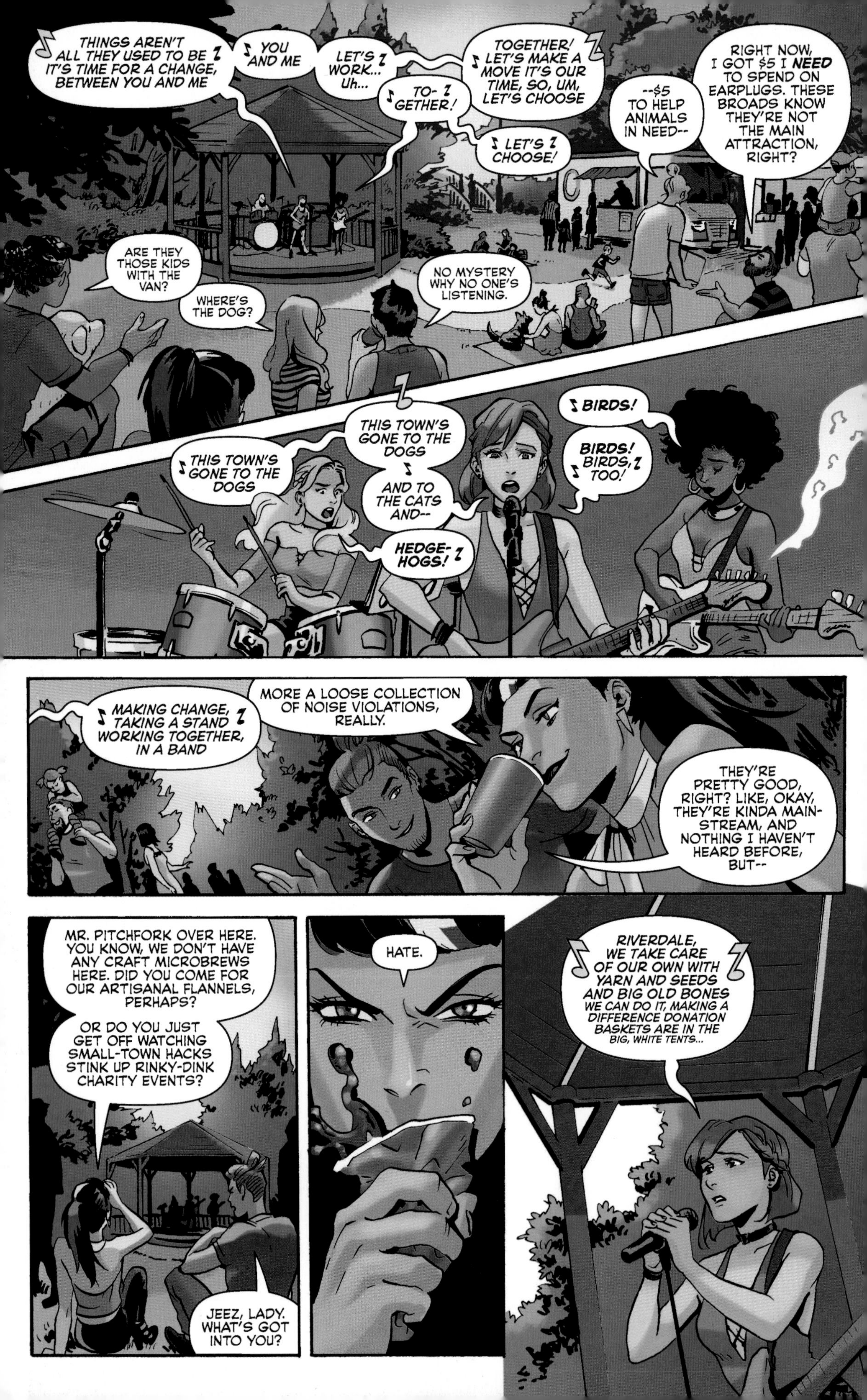
THINGS AREN'T ALL THEY USED TO BE IT'S TIME FOR A CHANGE, BETWEEN YOU AND ME
YOU AND ME
LET'S WORK... Uh...
TO-GETHER!
TOGETHER! LET'S MAKE A MOVE IT'S OUR TIME, SO, UM, LET'S CHOOSE
LET'S CHOOSE!
--$5 TO HELP ANIMALS IN NEED--
RIGHT NOW, I GOT $5 I NEED TO SPEND ON EARPLUGS. THESE BROADS KNOW THEY'RE NOT THE MAIN ATTRACTION, RIGHT?
ARE THEY THOSE KIDS WITH THE VAN?
WHERE'S THE DOG?
NO MYSTERY WHY NO ONE'S LISTENING.
THIS TOWN'S GONE TO THE DOGS
THIS TOWN'S GONE TO THE DOGS
AND TO THE CATS AND--
HEDGE-HOGS!
BIRDS!
BIRDS! BIRDS, TOO!
MAKING CHANGE, TAKING A STAND WORKING TOGETHER, IN A BAND
MORE A LOOSE COLLECTION OF NOISE VIOLATIONS, REALLY.
THEY'RE PRETTY GOOD, RIGHT? LIKE, OKAY, THEY'RE KINDA MAIN-STREAM, AND NOTHING I HAVEN'T HEARD BEFORE, BUT--
MR. PITCHFORK OVER HERE. YOU KNOW, WE DON'T HAVE ANY CRAFT MICROBREWS HERE. DID YOU COME FOR OUR ARTISANAL FLANNELS, PERHAPS?
OR DO YOU JUST GET OFF WATCHING SMALL-TOWN HACKS STINK UP RINKY-DINK CHARITY EVENTS?
JEEZ, LADY. WHAT'S GOT INTO YOU?
HATE.
RIVERDALE, WE TAKE CARE OF OUR OWN WITH YARN AND SEEDS AND BIG OLD BONES WE CAN DO IT, MAKING A DIFFERENCE DONATION BASKETS ARE IN THE BIG, WHITE TENTS...

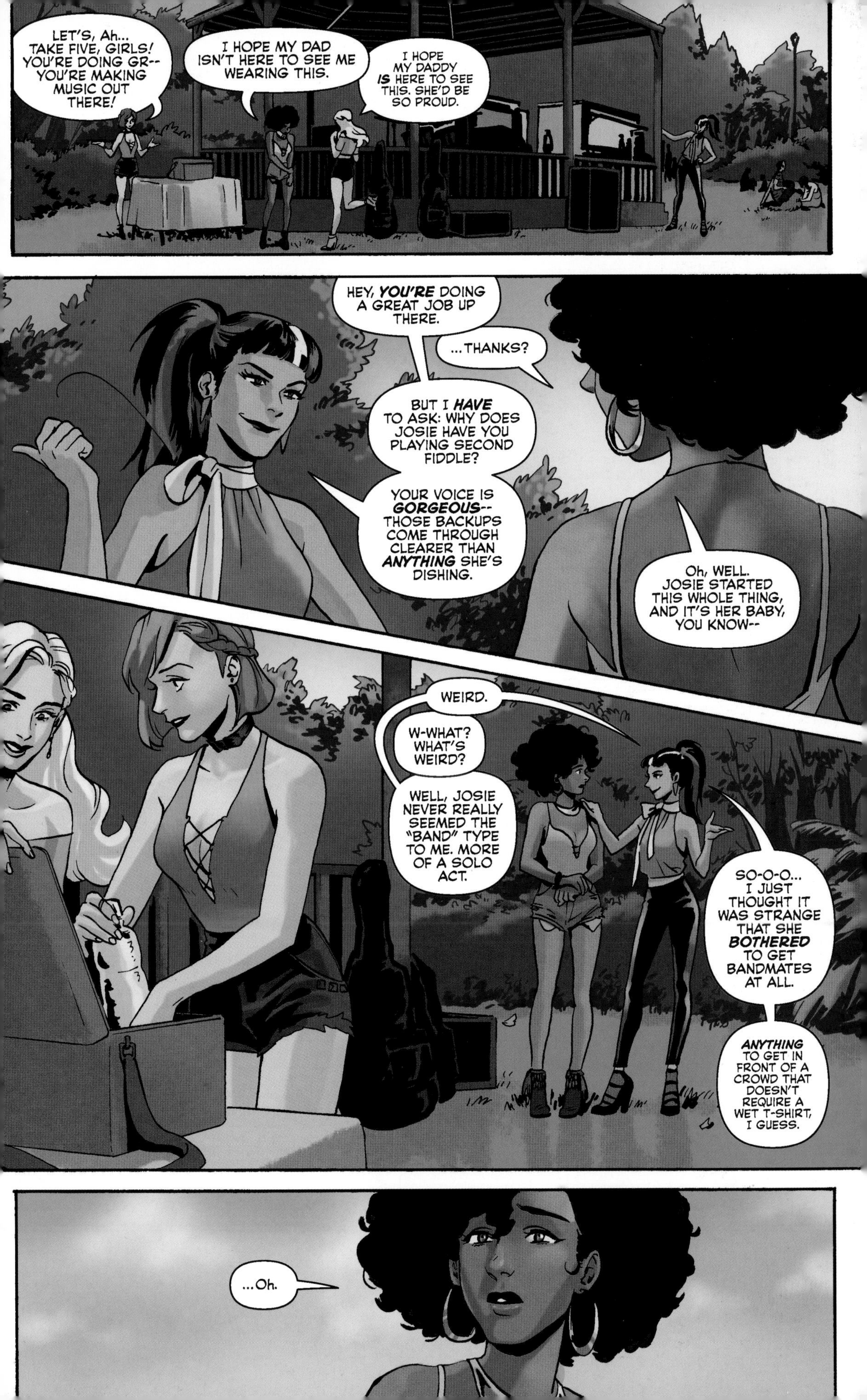
LET'S, Ah... TAKE FIVE, GIRLS! YOU'RE DOING GR-- YOU'RE MAKING MUSIC OUT THERE!
I HOPE MY DAD ISN'T HERE TO SEE ME WEARING THIS.
I HOPE MY DADDY IS HERE TO SEE THIS. SHE'D BE SO PROUD.
HEY, YOU'RE DOING A GREAT JOB UP THERE.
...THANKS?
BUT I HAVE TO ASK: WHY DOES JOSIE HAVE YOU PLAYING SECOND FIDDLE?
YOUR VOICE IS GORGEOUS-- THOSE BACKUPS COME THROUGH CLEARER THAN ANYTHING SHE'S DISHING.
Oh, WELL. JOSIE STARTED THIS WHOLE THING, AND IT'S HER BABY, YOU KNOW--
WEIRD.
W-WHAT? WHAT'S WEIRD?
WELL, JOSIE NEVER REALLY SEEMED THE "BAND" TYPE TO ME. MORE OF A SOLO ACT.
SO-O-O... I JUST THOUGHT IT WAS STRANGE THAT SHE BOTHERED TO GET BANDMATES AT ALL.
ANYTHING TO GET IN FRONT OF A CROWD THAT DOESN'T REQUIRE A WET T-SHIRT, I GUESS.
...Oh.

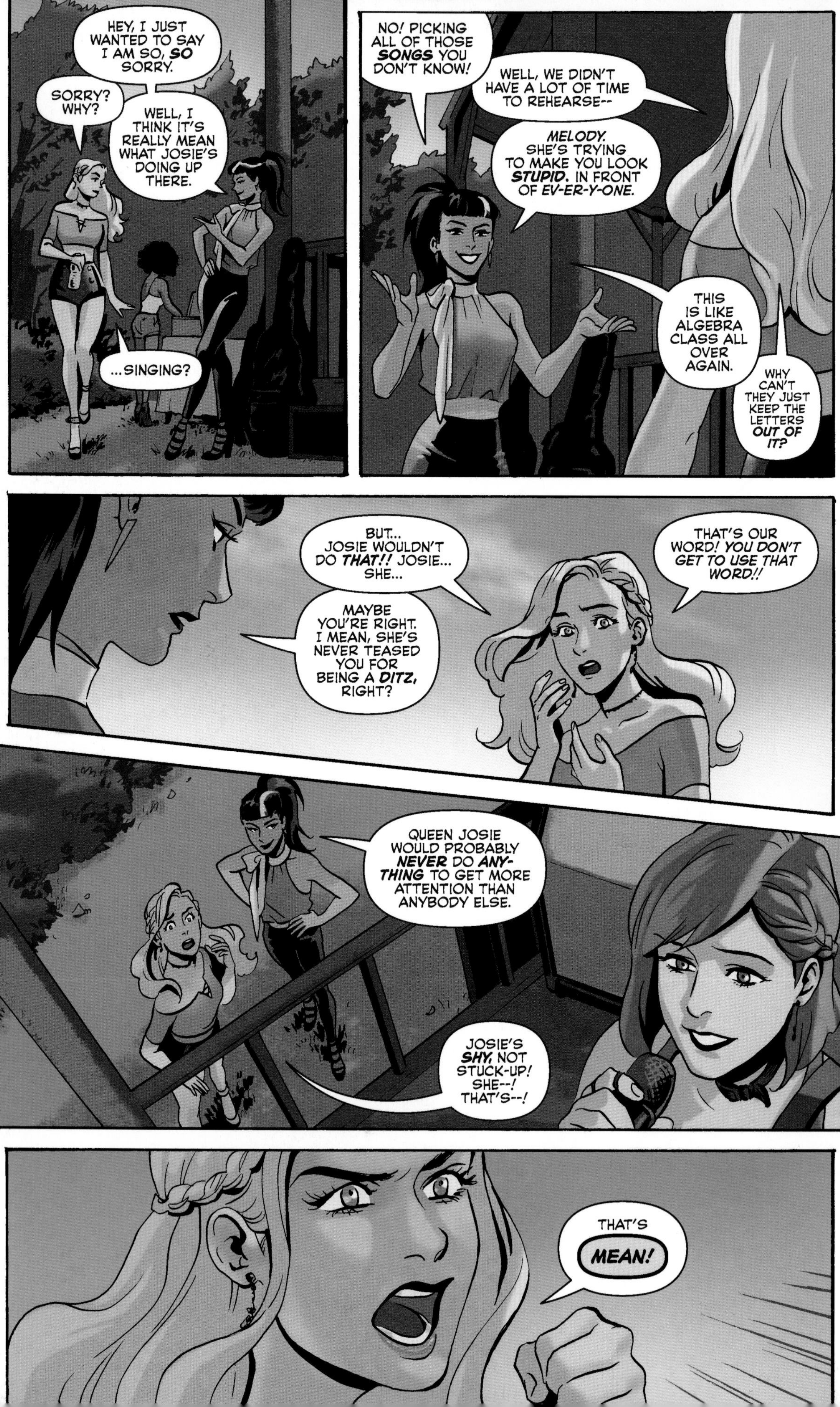
HEY, I JUST WANTED TO SAY I AM SO, **SO** SORRY.
SORRY? WHY?
WELL, I THINK IT'S REALLY MEAN WHAT JOSIE'S DOING UP THERE.
...SINGING?
NO! PICKING ALL OF THOSE **SONGS** YOU DON'T KNOW!
WELL, WE DIDN'T HAVE A LOT OF TIME TO REHEARSE--
MELODY. SHE'S TRYING TO MAKE YOU LOOK **STUPID.** IN FRONT OF ***EV-ER-Y-ONE.***
THIS IS LIKE ALGEBRA CLASS ALL OVER AGAIN.
WHY CAN'T THEY JUST KEEP THE LETTERS ***OUT OF IT?***
BUT... JOSIE WOULDN'T DO ***THAT!!*** JOSIE... SHE...
MAYBE YOU'RE RIGHT. I MEAN, SHE'S NEVER TEASED YOU FOR BEING A ***DITZ,*** RIGHT?
THAT'S OUR WORD! ***YOU DON'T GET TO USE THAT WORD!!***
QUEEN JOSIE WOULD PROBABLY ***NEVER*** DO ***ANY-THING*** TO GET MORE ATTENTION THAN ANYBODY ELSE.
JOSIE'S ***SHY,*** NOT STUCK-UP! SHE--! THAT'S--!
THAT'S ***MEAN!***

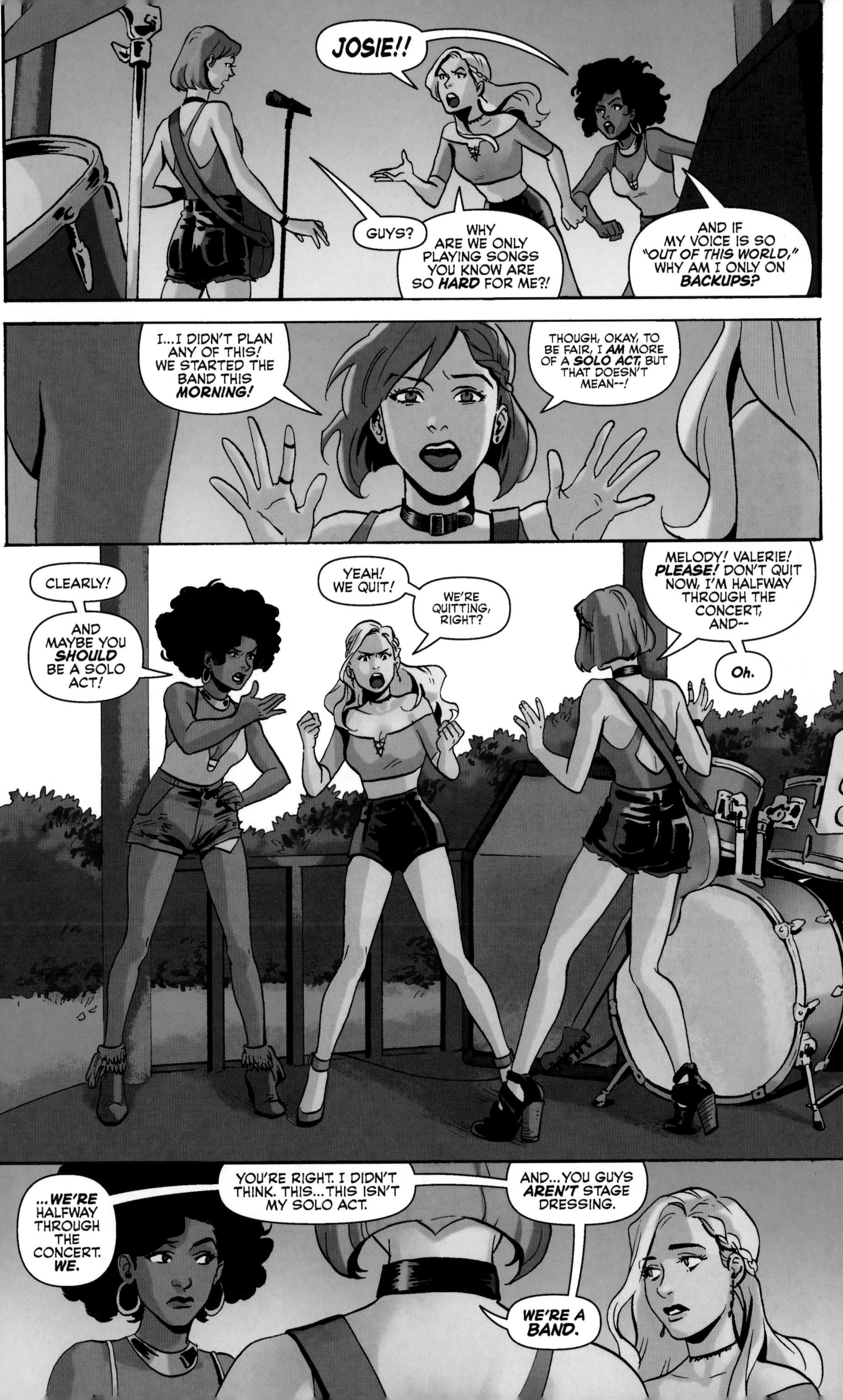
JOSIE!!
GUYS?
WHY ARE WE ONLY PLAYING SONGS YOU KNOW ARE SO **HARD** FOR ME?!
AND IF MY VOICE IS SO *"OUT OF THIS WORLD,"* WHY AM I ONLY ON **BACKUPS?**
I...I DIDN'T PLAN ANY OF THIS! WE STARTED THE BAND THIS **MORNING!**
THOUGH, OKAY, TO BE FAIR, I **AM** MORE OF A **SOLO ACT,** BUT THAT DOESN'T MEAN--!
CLEARLY!
AND MAYBE YOU **SHOULD** BE A SOLO ACT!
YEAH! WE QUIT!
WE'RE QUITTING, RIGHT?
MELODY! VALERIE! **PLEASE!** DON'T QUIT NOW, I'M HALFWAY THROUGH THE CONCERT, AND--
Oh.
...**WE'RE** HALFWAY THROUGH THE CONCERT. **WE.**
YOU'RE RIGHT. I DIDN'T THINK. THIS...THIS ISN'T MY SOLO ACT.
AND...YOU GUYS **AREN'T** STAGE DRESSING.
WE'RE A BAND.

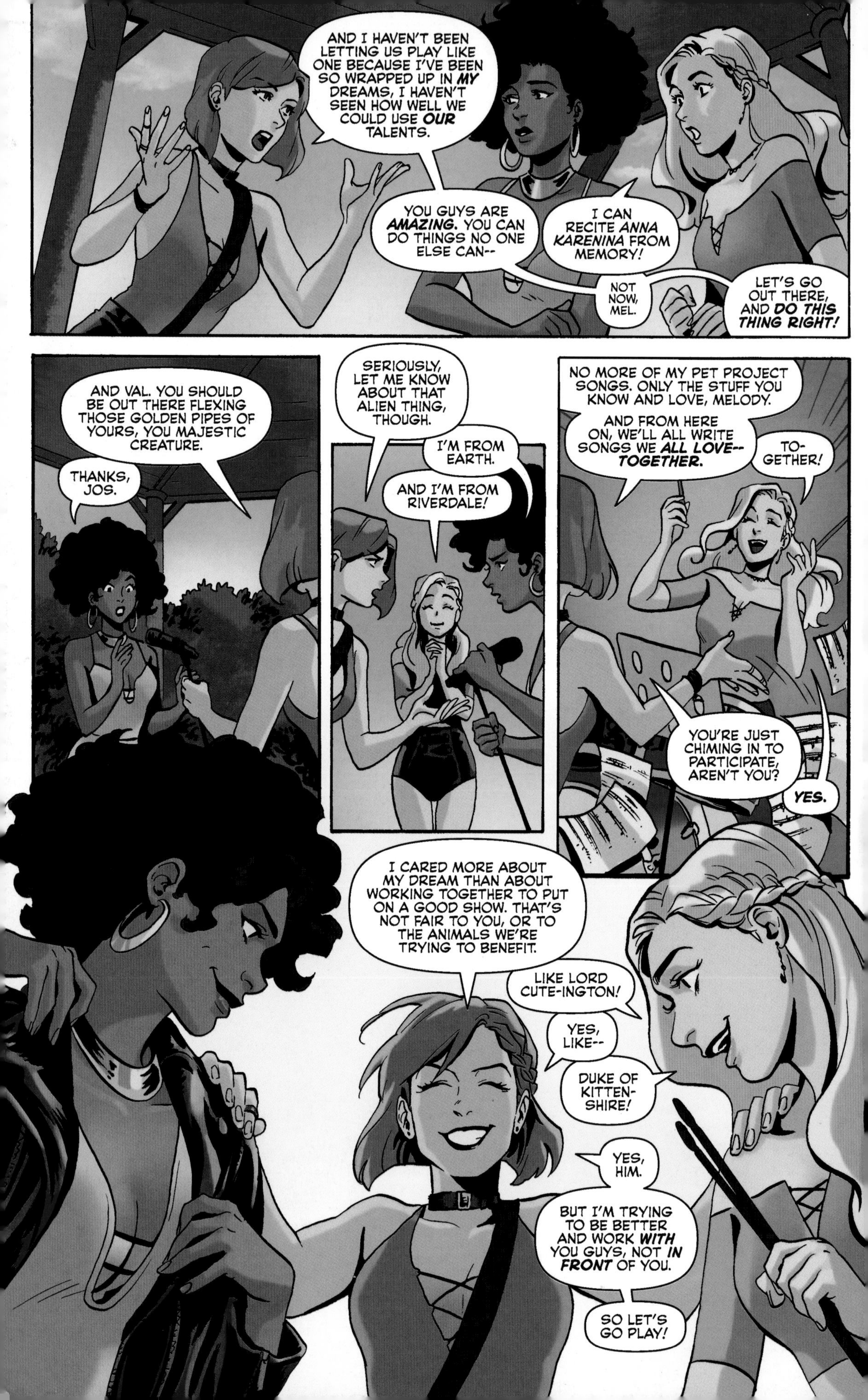
AND I HAVEN'T BEEN LETTING US PLAY LIKE ONE BECAUSE I'VE BEEN SO WRAPPED UP IN *MY* DREAMS, I HAVEN'T SEEN HOW WELL WE COULD USE *OUR* TALENTS.
YOU GUYS ARE *AMAZING.* YOU CAN DO THINGS NO ONE ELSE CAN--
I CAN RECITE *ANNA KARENINA* FROM MEMORY!
NOT NOW, MEL.
LET'S GO OUT THERE, AND *DO THIS THING RIGHT!*
AND VAL. YOU SHOULD BE OUT THERE FLEXING THOSE GOLDEN PIPES OF YOURS, YOU MAJESTIC CREATURE.
THANKS, JOS.
SERIOUSLY, LET ME KNOW ABOUT THAT ALIEN THING, THOUGH.
I'M FROM EARTH.
AND I'M FROM RIVERDALE!
NO MORE OF MY PET PROJECT SONGS. ONLY THE STUFF YOU KNOW AND LOVE, MELODY.
AND FROM HERE ON, WE'LL ALL WRITE SONGS WE *ALL LOVE-- TOGETHER.*
TO-GETHER!
YOU'RE JUST CHIMING IN TO PARTICIPATE, AREN'T YOU?
YES.
I CARED MORE ABOUT MY DREAM THAN ABOUT WORKING TOGETHER TO PUT ON A GOOD SHOW. THAT'S NOT FAIR TO YOU, OR TO THE ANIMALS WE'RE TRYING TO BENEFIT.
LIKE LORD CUTE-INGTON!
YES, LIKE--
DUKE OF KITTEN-SHIRE!
YES, HIM.
BUT I'M TRYING TO BE BETTER AND WORK *WITH* YOU GUYS, NOT *IN FRONT* OF YOU.
SO LET'S GO PLAY!

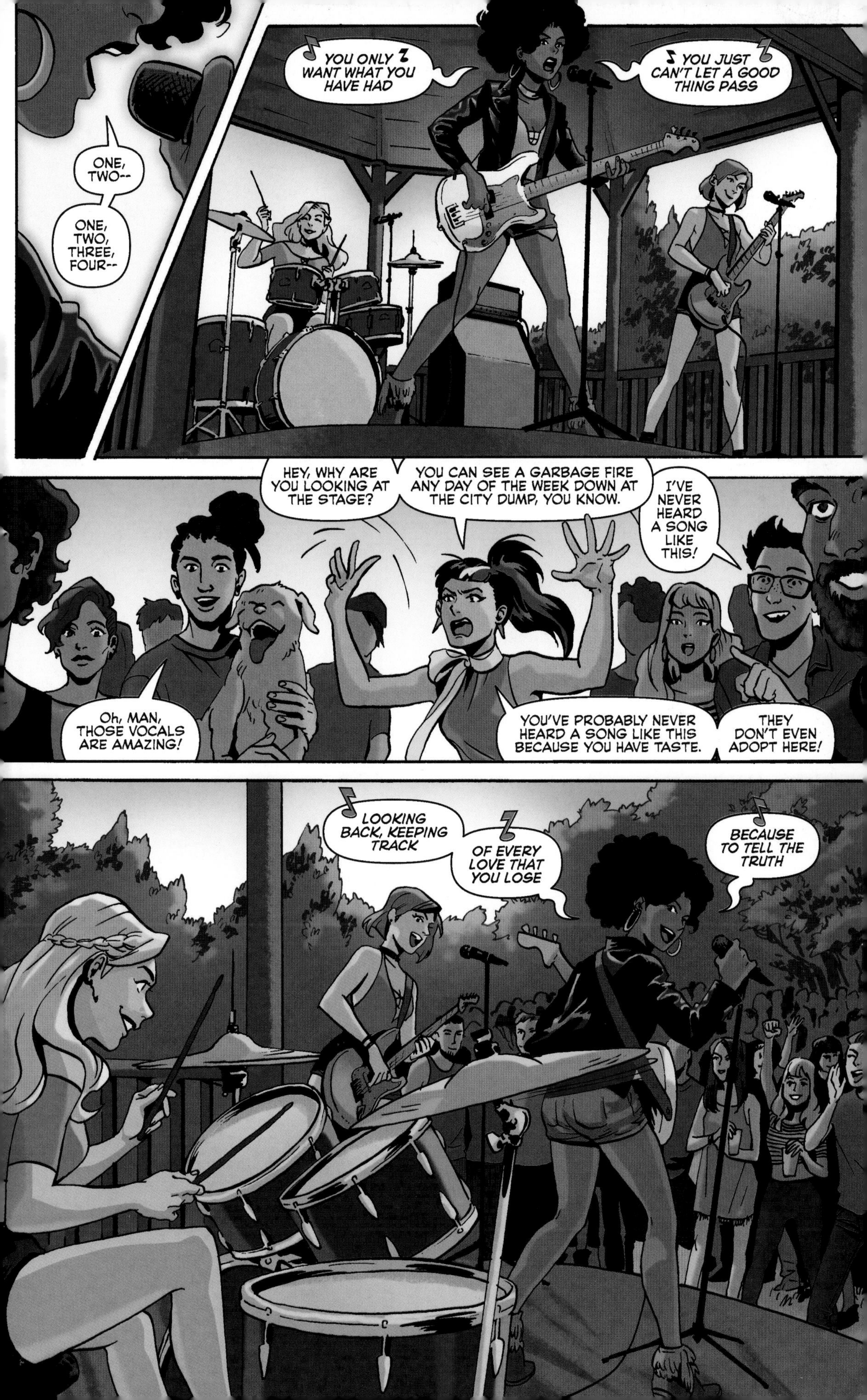
ONE, TWO--
ONE, TWO, THREE, FOUR--
YOU ONLY WANT WHAT YOU HAVE HAD
YOU JUST CAN'T LET A GOOD THING PASS
HEY, WHY ARE YOU LOOKING AT THE STAGE?
YOU CAN SEE A GARBAGE FIRE ANY DAY OF THE WEEK DOWN AT THE CITY DUMP, YOU KNOW.
I'VE NEVER HEARD A SONG LIKE THIS!
Oh, MAN, THOSE VOCALS ARE AMAZING!
YOU'VE PROBABLY NEVER HEARD A SONG LIKE THIS BECAUSE YOU HAVE TASTE.
THEY DON'T EVEN ADOPT HERE!
LOOKING BACK, KEEPING TRACK
OF EVERY LOVE THAT YOU LOSE
BECAUSE TO TELL THE TRUTH

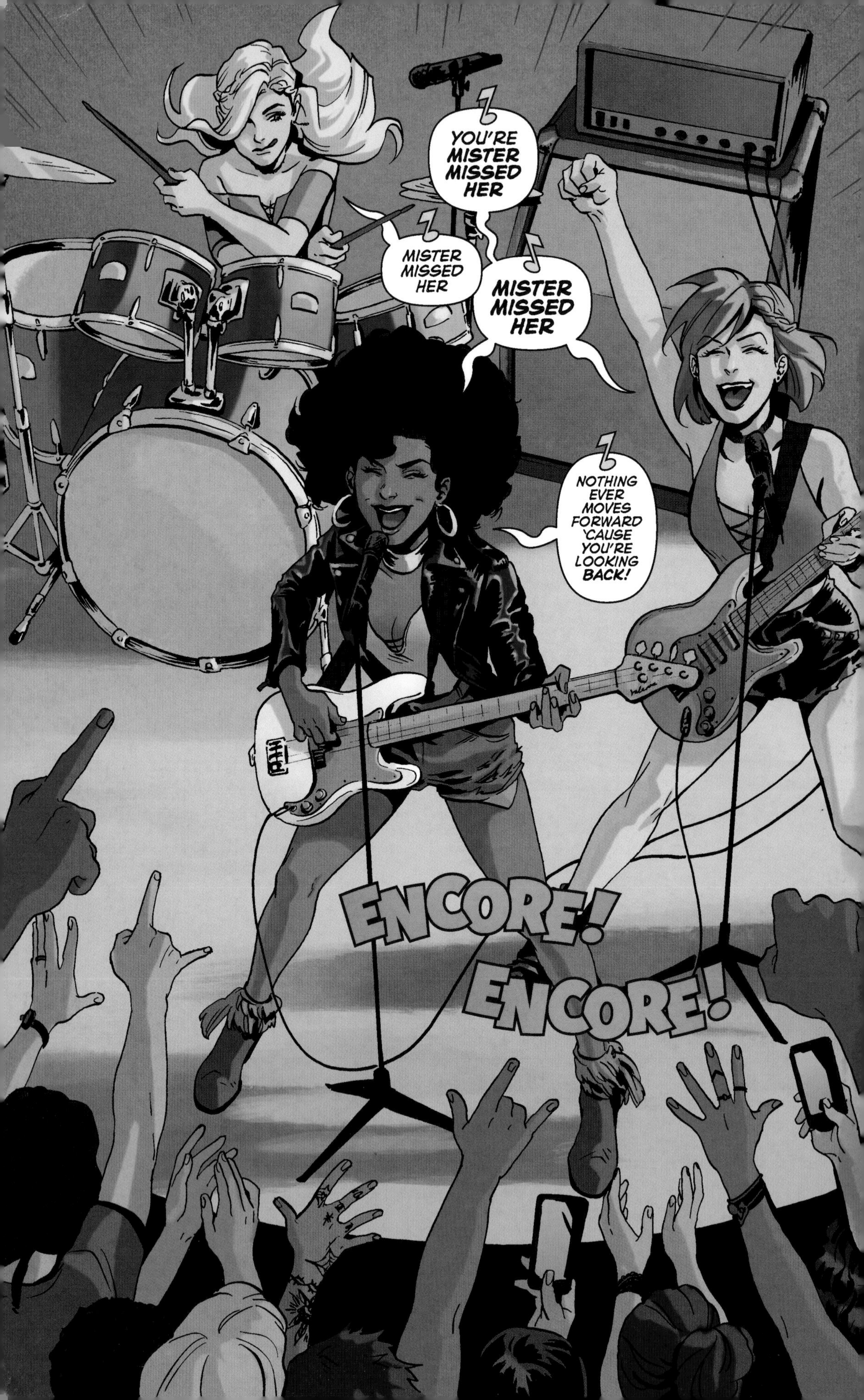
YOU'RE MISTER MISSED HER
MISTER MISSED HER
MISTER MISSED HER
NOTHING EVER MOVES FORWARD 'CAUSE YOU'RE LOOKING BACK!
ENCORE!
ENCORE!

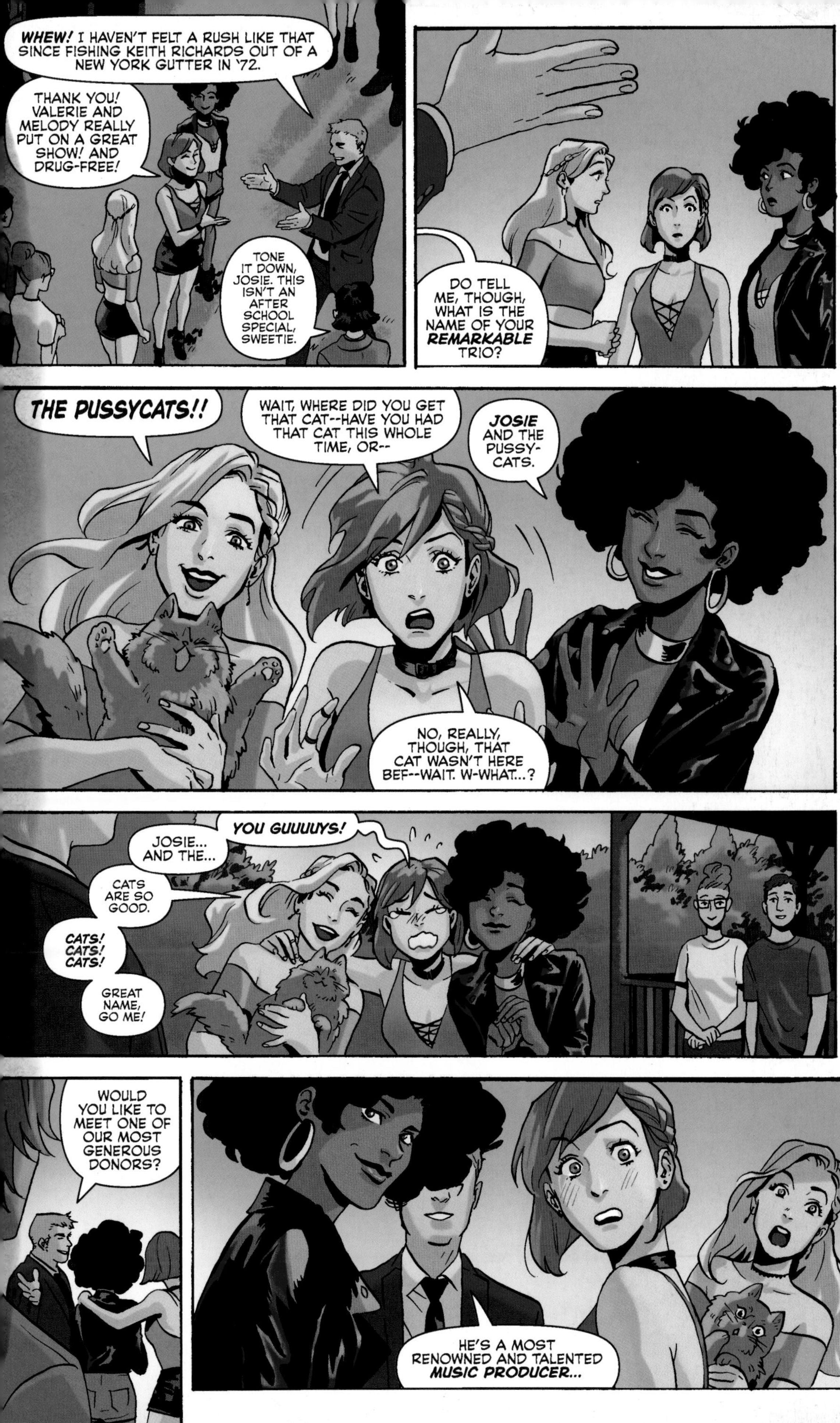

WHEW! I HAVEN'T FELT A RUSH LIKE THAT SINCE FISHING KEITH RICHARDS OUT OF A NEW YORK GUTTER IN '72.
THANK YOU! VALERIE AND MELODY REALLY PUT ON A GREAT SHOW! AND DRUG-FREE!
TONE IT DOWN, JOSIE. THIS ISN'T AN AFTER SCHOOL SPECIAL, SWEETIE.
DO TELL ME, THOUGH, WHAT IS THE NAME OF YOUR REMARKABLE TRIO?
THE PUSSYCATS!!
WAIT, WHERE DID YOU GET THAT CAT--HAVE YOU HAD THAT CAT THIS WHOLE TIME, OR--
JOSIE AND THE PUSSY-CATS.
NO, REALLY, THOUGH, THAT CAT WASN'T HERE BEF--WAIT. W-WHAT...?
JOSIE... AND THE...
YOU GUUUUYS!
CATS ARE SO GOOD.
CATS! CATS! CATS!
GREAT NAME, GO ME!
WOULD YOU LIKE TO MEET ONE OF OUR MOST GENEROUS DONORS?
HE'S A MOST RENOWNED AND TALENTED MUSIC PRODUCER...

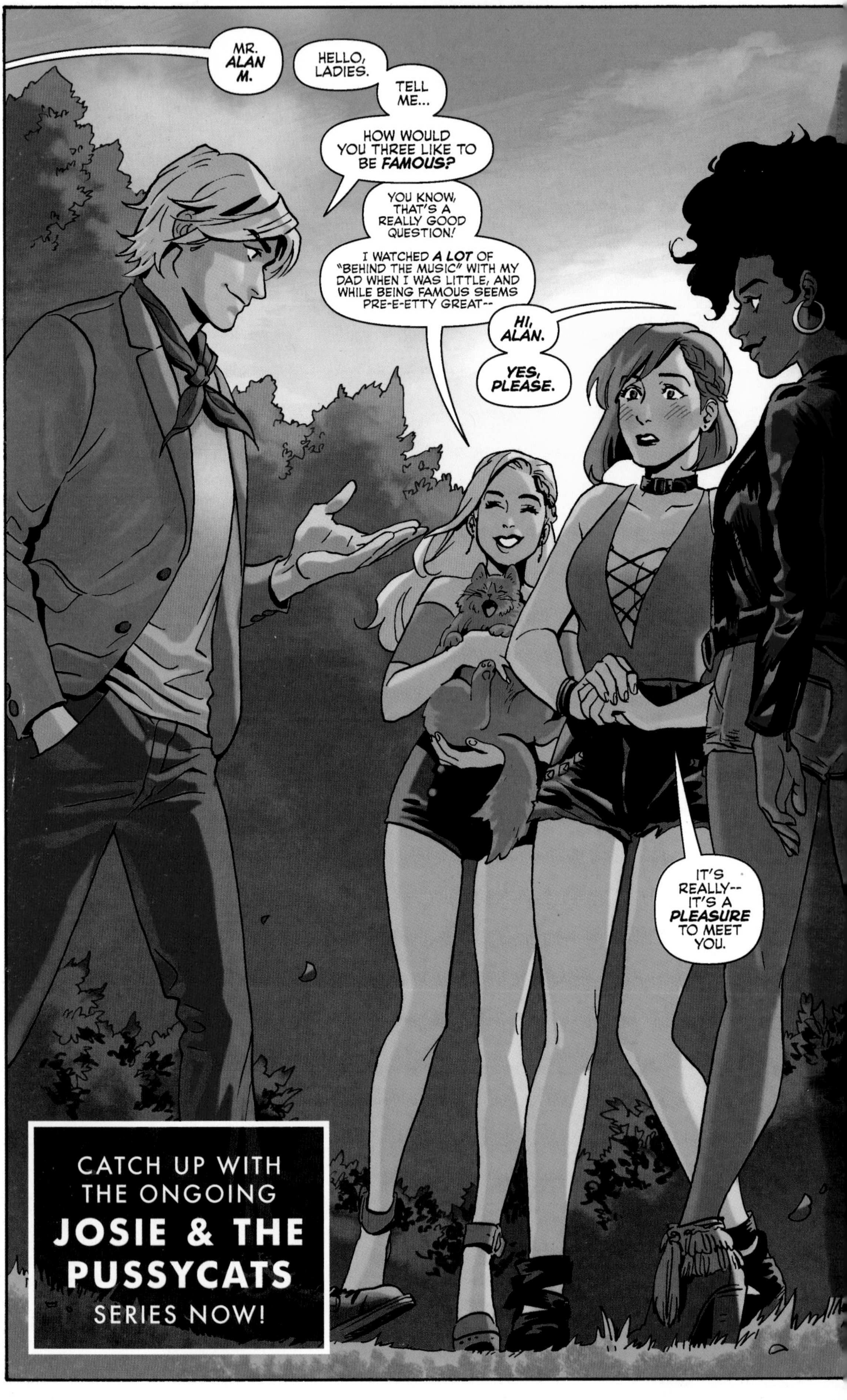
MR. ALAN M.
HELLO, LADIES.
TELL ME...
HOW WOULD YOU THREE LIKE TO BE FAMOUS?
YOU KNOW, THAT'S A REALLY GOOD QUESTION!
I WATCHED A LOT OF "BEHIND THE MUSIC" WITH MY DAD WHEN I WAS LITTLE, AND WHILE BEING FAMOUS SEEMS PRE-E-ETTY GREAT--
HI, ALAN.
YES, PLEASE.
IT'S REALLY-- IT'S A PLEASURE TO MEET YOU.
CATCH UP WITH THE ONGOING JOSIE & THE PUSSYCATS SERIES NOW!